Encyclopedia of Furniture Making

Encyclopedia
of Furniture Making

ERNEST JOYCE

STERLING
PUBLISHING CO., INC.   NEW YORK

The first and last lesson of the useful arts is, that Nature tyrannizes over our works. They must be conformed to her law, or they will be ground to powder by her omnipresent activity. Nothing droll, nothing whimsical will endure. Nature is ever interfering with Art. You cannot build your house or pagoda as you will, but as you must. There is a quick bound to your caprice.

Emerson—*Essay on Art*, 1841

Published in 1979 by
Sterling Publishing Co., Inc.
Two Park Avenue
New York, N.Y. 10016.

Library of Congress Cataloging in Publication Data

Joyce, Ernest.
Encyclopedia of furniture making.

Bibliography: p. 490
Includes index.
1. Furniture making. I. Title.
TS880.J68   1976   684.1   76-48087
ISBN 0-8069-8302-7
(previously ISBN 0-87749-068-6)

Contents

Acknowledgment

The author would like to express his appreciation and thanks to all those designers and manufacturers named throughout this book who have supplied photographs or information, and particularly to Miss Thelma M. Nye of Messrs B. T. Batsford Limited for her generous help and great patience at every stage.

Preface

Any textbook concerned with the techniques of furniture-making must deal primarily with the basic handcrafts for it is upon this groundwork that machine production is built, and in fact all the machine can ever do is to translate the essential hand operations into rotary movements of the cutting tool. In effect, therefore, mechanised production is no more than a speeding up of hand production, simplifying wherever possible but not radically interfering with methods which have taken over 4000 years to perfect, for wood is a natural material and imposes its own strict limitations. Where other forms of material are concerned techniques can of course differ, and no doubt in the future both plastics and metal will usurp much of the importance of wood, but it is hardly likely that it will be altogether supplanted, at least in the foreseeable future, for quite apart from aesthetic values it is still the cheapest medium; it can be worked with the simplest hand tools and is always easily repairable. To those pundits, therefore, who may claim that the teaching of hand skills is no longer relevant in this day and age it can be pointed out that anyone who has only been shown how to force a piece of wood against a mechanised saw will have learnt very little, but if he has had to saw that piece of wood by hand he will be more likely to know that much more about it, he will have greater respect for it and will understand in greater depth the problems that will have to be faced in its manipulation.

Additional to this need for all machine operators to know their material and how best it can be shaped are questions of quality, not only in the artefact, but also of the artificer himself. Actuating a lever all day long is soul destroying, and modern civilisation must eventually deal with the inherent problems the machine imposes. Handwork allows a man to express his own individuality; it is creative, it is definitely therapeutic. The ideal of more handwork, more individual fulfilment, less automation of both man and machine may be economically impracticable, but it should not be dismissed out of hand for sooner or later we shall be forced to come to terms with the leisure automation will increasingly thrust upon us. Handwork, whether it be sawing a piece of wood or shaping a lump of clay, is one answer, and no apologia is needed.

11

Introduction

Scope of the work

Terms in daily use often stretch their meanings and the expression 'handmade' can no longer be accepted as signifying only that work which is produced exclusively by hand-methods without recourse to the machine. Instead, it must now be taken as more descriptive of the approach than the means adopted, and a fair interpretation would include pure hand methods and those other methods which enlist the help of the machine without allowing it to dictate in any way. The inherent danger of mass production is that costly and complex machinery is always greedy for output in order to justify its existence, and it will tend to impose limitations on the designer and actively influence his work. In the so-called 'handwork' no such limitation is permissible and man continues to be the master, using the machine as an extension of his hands only and not as an independent entity liable at any time to question his decisions. It is with this 'handwork' and with this 'machine-assisted work' that the book is chiefly concerned and not with the mechanics of quantity production which belong more properly to the theory of wood machining, a subject which calls for a high degree of engineering skill. Having made the point the term 'handmade' is retained failing a more comprehensive description.

The general term 'cabinet-maker' is also outdated, for so-called 'cabinet-work' is no longer confined to straight carcase furniture, with chair-making and other special activities as separate trades. Moreover, the Furniture Industry increasingly uses plastics, plastic laminates, metal sections, and many other new materials, all of which the cabinet-maker should know about, and he should be prepared to undertake any work within the general context 'Furniture', with the possible exception of deep upholstery and hand and spray polishing, both of which require other aptitudes and training. The tendency, therefore, is to replace the term 'cabinet-maker' with the more comprehensive 'furniture-maker', but custom dies hard and both terms must be regarded as synonymous.

It remains to define what precisely is meant by furniture as distinct from joiners' work. The traditional sharp division between the two types of craftsmen has to some extent disappeared and is now more a matter of approach than anything, for each follows the same principles of construction and both have the same basic skills. Joiners' work which is normally considered to be part of the fabric of a building is usually strong, sturdy and not so intimately concerned with appearance, whereas the cabinet-maker's approach is towards compactness, lightness and delicacy of treatment. In self-contained, free-standing furniture there is no doubt as to the more suitable type of craftsman, but a good deal of fixed church-work, panelled work and particularly built-in fitments could be done equally well by either and it is difficult to draw sharp demarcations. In substance, however, the book is concerned with furniture only, which includes chair-work and those types of built-in fitments which are designed to replace free-standing furniture. It excludes such things as shop fitting, museum- and ship-work, etc., as specialist trades outside its province.

The order of the book follows a natural sequence. Firstly, Tools, Equipment, Workshop Organisation, Workshop Drawing, etc.; secondly, Materials; thirdly, the Technical Processes involved in their manipulation; fourthly, the Problems of Construction; fifthly, the End-product; and sixthly, Miscellaneous Information. The actual cabinet-work illustrated and described has been chosen to depict general constructional principles or special applications, and not necessarily current styles in furniture which unfortunately change too rapidly to be captured in a technical work which has taken some years of careful preparation. On the other hand some traditional design-work and some old methods of construction have been included, not merely from academic interest but because they are still valid and as likely to be revived as the tambour front and the Elizabethan draw-leaf-table principle which have been lifted from obscurity to become the most popular idioms today.

Craft societies

Various societies exist in the United Kingdom for the promulgation and encouragement of individual creativeness in the applied arts (craftwork). One of the chief amongst these is the *Art Workers' Guild*, formed in 1884, which has its own premises at 6 Queen Square, London W.C.1, with a flourishing membership of architects, painters, sculptors, designers and craftworkers. Entry is by merit and submission of representative examples of work done, but the Guild does not stage public exhibitions and confines its activities to fortnightly lectures, demonstrations and background encouragement of the crafts. Actual exhibiting societies selling direct to the public include the *Society of Designer Craftsmen*, originally formed as the Arts and Crafts Exhibition Society in 1888 with a committee which included William Morris, and the *Red Rose Guild of Designer Craftsmen* formed in Manchester in 1921. Both these societies were at one time widely known, but the high cost of city premises has brought the inevitable financial difficulties, and membership of each has tended to fall away so that future prospects are somewhat uncertain; nevertheless they continue to hold annual or biennial exhibitions of members' work, and generally speaking the standards of handcraftsmanship have been preserved, with entry again based on excellence of work submitted for candidature. Other smaller provincial societies with the same general aims are the *Guild of Gloucester Craftsmen, Guild of Lakeland Craftsmen, Devon Guild of Craftsmen, Society of Craftsmen, Worcester Guild of Craftsmen* and other local associations. Particulars of all these craft societies can be obtained from the *Rural Industries Bureau*, 35 Camp Road, Wimbledon, London S.W.19, which receives an annual Government grant for the active encouragement of country crafts, and has always done invaluable work in helping and advising craftsmen who wish to establish their own rural workshops or extend their markets. The Bureau's local organisers work closely with rural Councils of Social Service throughout the country, and local libraries can be consulted for further information.

The chief selling medium for the maker of handmade furniture concerned with integrity in materials and workmanship was undoubtedly the original *Craft Centre of Great Britain* formed in 1948 under the active leadership of the late John Farleigh, an artist of repute keenly interested in the crafts and author of several books on the subject. The Centre accepted its members through five constituent societies each with rigid rules of selection, and enjoyed both an annual Government grant and relief from Purchase Tax on certain classes of craftwork including furniture. However, support for the Centre was never sufficient to ensure financial independence: both Government grant and Purchase tax relief were arbitrarily withdrawn, whilst internal friction resulted in the splitting of the Centre into two groups, the existing Craft Centre of Great Britain with a showroom at 43 Earlham Street, Covent Garden, London W.C.2, and the Crafts Council of Great Britain with offices at 25 Hill Street, London W.1. Both are now struggling to recapture public interest and to regain lost ground and are worthy of every support, but adequate financial backing is hard to find. Past mistakes were active suspicion of industrial-work in which the designer is divorced from the actual maker, with over-reliance on pure craftsmanship alone, and some elements of preciousness were therefore inevitable, although the aims were always sincere. With the lessons well learnt the societies have now widened their appeal to embrace industrial work, for the true designer-craftsman, i.e. one who believes that the designer himself must either make or be responsible for the making of the artefact if true quality is to be achieved, is rare indeed, and good craftsmen with some notable exceptions are not necessarily good designers. Given the right kind of publicity there seems no reason why both ventures should not now succeed, always providing the work produced is modern in conception, for there is a latent and steadily growing demand for work of the highest quality, well designed and scrupulously made.

Craft-training in Great Britain

Training of professional furniture-designers with State-aided grants as in other forms of higher education is amply provided for, and certain selected colleges of art offer a three-year Diploma course in Design, with the option of further post-graduate courses for selected candidates. Particulars of these courses can be obtained from the

Department of Education and Science, Curzon Street, London W.1, and Local Education Offices will give details of the facilities offered.

Training of all apprentices and learners in the industry is covered by the Industrial Training Act of 1964. The training is in two sectors; 'In Company' training concerned only with the basic needs of the particular factory concerned, and day release or block release 'Out Company' training at centres of higher education to fit the apprentice for a career in any factory within the industry as a whole. This advanced general training follows the Revised Syllabus (Parts 1 and 2) of the City and Guilds of London Institute and covers wood machining, furniture-making, wood technology and wood finishing, metal, plastics and upholstery, with the requisite theory, history and design appreciation. Non-professional (amateur) workers are well catered for in evening classes held in local technical colleges, colleges of art or adult training centres, and no one need go short of basic instruction, although it must be frankly admitted that training to high levels of craftsmanship is hard to find. However, the really keen aspirant should not be discouraged, for many highly skilled cabinet-makers have been either wholly or partially self-taught, and no amount of academic training can implant skills or even fully develop latent skills—the real training is always a voyage of self-discovery.

Future prospects

The field of prophecy is dangerous terrain and one can only suggest possibilities. Ever-increased mechanisation of the industry seems inevitable; new materials and new methods of construction will continue to be developed with greater emphasis on plastics, metal, reinforced card-board and man-made woods (chipboard, etc.); but one has the feeling—although it may only be wishful thinking—that wood itself will continue to hold pride of place if only because it is completely individual, a natural and inexhaustible fund of pure pattern never repeated from one tree to another. The chief disability of plastics and other man-made materials is their endless repetition and the individual will always hanker after some variety. There are increasing signs also of public rebellion against the shoddiness of

much production-work, and a healthy omen is the growing number of small groups of designers and craftsmen either banding together or working independently to produce work which is clean, honest, intelligent and individual. As regards design itself, beyond an increasing use of space-saving built-in fitments and a possible extension of expendable furniture, it is impossible to forecast its probable destination. It will no doubt continue to spark in all directions, anonymous and inclined to gimmickry. Whether any form of national style is now possible in the sense that Chippendale for all his use of outside influences was essentially English, and Empire furniture essentially French, is highly debatable, for all design-work tends to become more and more internationally minded and therefore more impersonal, but one must always allow for the individual need to seek some element of permanence. The reverence for the antique is partly dictated by purely mercenary considerations, but also by the wish to hold on to some fixed element in a veritable sea of change.

Metrication (metric system)

The changeover from the imperial to the metric system of weights and measures (Système International (SI)) is scheduled to take place within the period 1969–71 with a terminal date of not later than 1975 for most sectors, although it is realised that it may be many years before existing stocks of feet/inch materials are exhausted. The changeover is complicated by the fact that many countries have yet to ratify the recommendations of the Conférence Générale des Poids et Mesures (1960); that industry as a whole is a network of separate sectors, primary producers, mani-pulators (tool-makers, etc.) and manufacturers; that there are very many existing standards and each separate sector has its own built-in customs and usage. All these have to be reconciled if the scheme is to be truly universal and intelligible to the customer at large. Thus it is not merely a question of arbitrarily converting existing standards to metric units on a strictly mathematical basis but of rethinking the entire range of mensuration in the light of present-day needs and conditions, simplifying wherever possible and eliminating unnecessary variety.

Whilst the engineering industry, as the key

industry upon which most other sectors depend, has established its programme and set the pattern for others to follow, other sectors are still engaged in deciding upon their course of action. Thus engineers will use metres and one sub multiple (millimetres) only, and working to as many as three decimal places of a millimetre, but this is hardly practicable for the timber industry and allied trades in which the tolerances are much less narrow. Strict mathematical conversion of inch fractions yields decimal places of a millimetre which are unworkable or unacceptable under normal workshop conditions, for woodworking is not a precision trade in the engineering sense and 1 mm (approximately $\frac{1}{25}$ in.) with the occasional use of 0·5 mm (approximately $\frac{1}{37}$ in.) are sufficient for most requirements. Therefore, all metric conversions must be approximated, i.e. rounded off to the nearest whole or one half millimetre (0·5) until such time as a code of practice has been established and a logical progression of millimetre measurements chosen for general use which will replace the existing progressive inch fractions. In the meantime the metric conversions given for all imperial weights and measures quoted in the succeeding pages are approximations only to the nearest workable value according to the use, and it has been assumed that as the degree of accuracy called for in furniture design is not particularly high, design measurements in general can be quoted in centimetres throughout, whereas practical detailing (timber dimensions, jointing, etc.) needs millimetre dimensioning. Individual workers can of course alter and amend the approximations according to their needs, and page 488 gives conversion tables and other data.

Part 1 Tools and equipment
1 Hand-tools (1)

Note Introduction of the metric system of mensuration will eventually necessitate changing the sizes of all standard tools now conforming to inch measurements. As this is likely to be a lengthy process, and as the conventional sizes to be adopted have not yet been established, all the tools mentioned in this and subsequent chapters are inch patterns with the approximate metric equivalents given in parenthesis.

The basic tools of woodwork and the elementary processes of sawing, chiselling and smoothing wood are widely known, and detailed repetition is hardly necessary. What is of concern here is the specialised application of these basic techniques to the fabrication of timber components, usually of small dimension, which will eventually become pieces of furniture. Therefore, although the tools employed and the methods of manipulating them are in principle the same as

for any woodworking trade, the furniture-maker must always endeavour to work to precision limits, and this differing approach is best exemplified in the wedged through tenon of the carpenter and joiner, in which any slight slackness in the fit of the tenon itself is immediately taken up by the wedges hammered home. But the furniture-maker cannot show his tenons—although he may sometimes use the through tenon for its decorative possibilities—therefore he cannot wedge them from the outside and they must truly fit. So although he may use the same kind of saw, chisel, plane, etc., as any other woodworker, the saw will tend to have finer teeth, the chisel will be of the lighter, bevelled edged variety, the smoothing-plane will be the standard tool but it will be keener and more finely set. In the main, therefore, his tools will be orthodox but more numerous; they must be the very best of their respective kinds and he must be scrupulous in maintaining them.

1 Handsaws: rip and crosscut

Saws and sawing

A standard kit for hand work would automatically include *rip-*, *crosscut-* and *panel-* (small crosscut-) *saws*, *tenon-* and *dovetail-saws*, with *bow-*, *scroll-* and *pad-saws*, etc. for circular cutting. Where machinery is available the rip and big crosscut might not appear necessary, but there will always be the occasion when it is easier to take the saw to the wood rather than the wood to the machine, therefore to some extent they are indispensable. Whilst the rip-saw (1:1) has upright teeth (1:2) filed square to the blade (1:3) —the arrows give the filing direction—and cuts with a chisel action (1:4), all other saws are of the crosscut type (1:5) for cutting across the grain, the teeth are raked (1:6) and with the exception of the fine dovetail-saw are filed to a bevel of about 65° (1:7) so that the set of the teeth scores two parallel lines across the wood and the waste or 'kerf' between crumbles away in dust (1:8). The 'set' or alternative bending outwards of each tooth which practically every saw must have if it is to clear itself must never be more than is required to give fractional clearance to the blade as it passes through the wood: whilst in the case of the larger saws (rip-, large crosscut- and panel-saw) the blade itself should have the full thickness along the teeth but the back should be taper ground, i.e. 'swaged', about 4 gauges thinner from handle to point for heavy saws, and correspondingly less for lighter saws. The blade also should be tensioned by hammering the centre of the blade to expand it, and the test of a handsaw of good-quality tempered steel and correctly tensioned by the maker is that it should neither sag nor exhibit any tendency to floppiness when held by the handle in a horizontal position. The teeth also should be of even height and shape, filed to the correct bevel, with each individual tooth set to about half its depth only, so that the kerf made in the wood is never more than about 1½ times the thickness of the blade.

A convenient size for rip- and big crosscut-saws for cabinet-work is 26 in. (660 mm) long not including handle, with 4½ points (teeth) to the inch (25 mm) for the former and 7 or 8 points for the latter. The smaller crosscut- or panel-saw, one of the most useful of saws if in good condition, should be about 22 in. (558 mm) long with 10 points to the inch (25 mm). Tenon-saws (2:1) and dovetail-saws (2:2) which are not taper ground, have their blades stiffened with a rib or back of steel or brass (apart from appearance it hardly matters which), and convenient sizes would be 12 in. (304 mm) long with 12 to 14 points for the tenon, and 8 in. (203 mm) long with 18 to 22 points (the finer the better) for the dovetail. Both these saws have a more pronounced rake to their teeth (2:4), but the dovetail teeth are so fine it is difficult to file a correct bevel, and the teeth are usually left square across their faces as in the rip. An open or pistol-grip handle is preferable for the dovetail if it can be obtained (2:2) but most manufacturers seem to regard it as just another tenon-saw, which of course it is and is not. It cuts so finely there is always the temptation to use it indiscriminately, but it should be kept exclusively for dovetails and fine mitres. An even finer saw is the *bead-saw*, sometimes known as the 'joiner's fancy' or 'gent's' saw, with bradawl-type handle (2:3), a blade from 4 in. (101 mm) to 8 in. (203 mm) long and with 32 points to the inch (25 mm). As it is a little difficult to file the teeth evenly it is sometimes discarded when too blunt to cut, for it is relatively inexpensive.

2 Handsaws: miscellaneous

1

3

2

4

Sharpening saws

Skilled craftsmen sharpen their own saws, using a pistol-grip saw set to bend the points, and a suitable three-cornered tapered saw-file which is gripped with both hands. For the rip-saw the file is held level as a chisel edge is necessary to the points; but for crosscut-saws the near or back hand should bear slightly downwards to form a point to the teeth. In all cases alternative teeth are filed from one side, the saw reversed and the remaining teeth filed, making sure that the 'gullet' or space between each tooth is kept constant and only sufficient metal is taken off to destroy the 'shine' which is the evidence of a blunt tooth. If the worker does not feel confident of setting and filing his saws correctly—and fair practice is needed—then they should be sent to a saw-doctor via any ironmonger who deals in tools.

Saw-chops

Saw-chops composed of two wood jaws held by a bolt and wing-nut and gripped in a bench-vice are used for holding saws during sharpening. Figure 3:1 shows saw-chops for handsaws and (3:2) for circular saws. Figure 3:3 shows a more

3 Saw-chops

convenient type for handsaws of all sizes, requiring no bolt. The stand is made up of two pieces of 2 in. (50 mm) by 4 in. (100 mm) deal, 3 ft 7 in. high (1092 mm), with 1 in. (25 mm) by 2 in. (50 mm) deal cross-braces 18 in. (457 mm) long nailed across either side. Taper notches are cut in the uprights and the loose chops are also taper housed to hold them in position and to grip the saw firmly as they are tapped down. All three types are usually made by the craftsman himself.

Contour cutting

A flexible blade is necessary for contour cutting, and for fairly wide sweeps the clumsy but efficient wooden *bow-* or *turning-saw* (2:5) is suitable. The detachable blade is tensioned by a length of twisted blind-cord or a wire stretcher. For smaller curves the 6 in. (152 mm) metal frame *scroll-* or *coping-saw* (2:9) is useful, and both bow- and scroll-saw can be used for interior openings as the handles fully rotate, thus the blades can be detached, threaded through a pre-bored hole with the teeth pointing away from the handle, and turned to the correct angle for the cut. For openings further in than the throat of the saw will allow other means must be adopted, either by drilling a series of holes and chopping out with chisel and gouge, or if the sweep is fairly easy cutting with a 12 in. (304 mm) *keyhole-* or *pad-saw* (2:10) which is in effect a very narrow cross-cut-blade held by retaining screws in a slotted bradawl-type handle. Larger variants are the *compass-saw* with fixed handsaw-type open handle (2:7) or a nest of saws, *table, compass* and *keyhole*, with detachable handle (2:8). For very fine cutting in thin material the *hobbyist's fret-saw* (2:6) with a throat of 20 in. (508 mm) and a range of wood- and metal-piercing saws is invaluable. It can be used to cut with a forward movement with the teeth pointing upwards as with the bow-saw, or downwards against a cutting-table with the teeth pointing towards the handle.

Controlling the saw

Rip- and crosscut-saws should be gripped as illustrated (4), with the angle of cut low to start with and raising the saw to about 45° as the cut proceeds. At the commencement of the cut the 'heel' or handle end of the saw should be placed square to the wood, and with the thumb of the left hand resting lightly against the blade to steady it (102). After the cut has been established with one or more upward strokes the thumb should be withdrawn and the full downward strokes commenced with moderate pressure only until the back edge of the plank has been reached, the left hand should then be brought over the front of the saw to grip the unsupported timber which will otherwise splinter off. Some professional workers end with one powerful downward stroke which severs the remaining fibres without splintering, but it must complete the cut in one sweep and requires a little judgment. Tenon- and dovetail-saws are similarly held, with the left thumb supporting the blade on the marked line and in a truly upright position, but if the dovetail-saw has an open handle (115) then the forefinger can lie along the top of the saw, enabling it to be pointed very accurately pistol fashion. Some workers knock the set off the fine dovetail-saw by running a file lightly along the side of the teeth, which gives a finer cut, but the teeth must be in good condition.

4 Holding saw

Care of saws

Saws should never be allowed to rust, for microscopic pitting of the steel will prevent the formation of really sharp facets to the teeth. They should be lightly oiled from time to time, particularly the bow- and compass-saws, etc., which are not often used. The best lubricant for use during sawing is a few strokes of a candle end along the blade. If the rip- and crosscut-saws are buckled they can only be restored by a skilled saw-doctor, but slight buckling of a backed tenon- or dovetail-saw can sometimes be overcome by gently tapping the back down first at one end and then the other, thus driving the blade further into the back.

Edge tools

Chisels

It is hardly necessary to have complete sets of mortise-, firmer- and bevelled edged chisels for furniture-making, as the bevelled-edged will do everything necessary. Nor are complete sets of any one type essential, for there will always be three or four favourites to which the hand automatically turns. A first selection could be $\frac{1}{8}$ in. (3 mm), $\frac{1}{4}$ in. (6 mm), $\frac{3}{8}$ in. (9 mm), $\frac{1}{2}$ in. (12·5 mm) and $\frac{3}{4}$ in. (19 mm) *bevelled edge* (5:1A) with the addition of a $\frac{1}{16}$ in. (1:5 mm) *firmer* type (5:1B) and perhaps a $\frac{1}{2}$ in. (12·5 mm) *mortise-chisel* (5:1C), with the later addition of a long *paring-chisel* (5:4B), and a *butt-* or *sash-pocket* chisel (5:4C) for fitting work away from the workshop.

Various types of chisel handle are shown in 5:3. Figure 5:3A shows the universally popular *box* or *ash* carving handle; 5:3B the traditional round *ash*; 5:3C the oval splitproof plastic handle, either in polypropylene or the transparent cellulose acetate butyrate which is tougher but more expensive, and 5:3D the typical steel-hooped mortise handle. It is, of course, false economy to buy cheap sets of chisels, for the keenness of the edge depends entirely on the grade of steel which varies from maker to maker, and a really good chisel should last a lifetime. A recent development is the introduction of high-speed tipped firmer and bevelled edge chisels manufactured by Ward and Payne Ltd of Sheffield, which the writer has tried and found excellent. They are considerably more expensive, but are capable of a fine and long-lasting edge which can be ground on the high-speed grinder without drawing the temper.

5 Chisels and gouges

Gouges

Two types are used, *firmer pattern* (5:5A) with cutting bevel ground on the outside of the curve and yielding a sloping cut, as the bevel tends to drive the tool out of the wood; and *scribing pattern* (5:5B) with inside ground bevel for upright cuts. The old-type scribing-gouge had a slightly different shoulder shape, but both firmer- and scribing-gouges are now forged to the same pattern; whilst it is now usual to class them as 'outcannelled' (outside ground) for firmers, and 'incannelled' (inside ground) for scribers—the old names will, however, probably persist.

The various curves or sweeps have also been standardised and the normal gouges are now made to one work circle only. Figure 5:6 shows the widths available. Additional curves are only possible in the long outcannelled paring-gouges used by pattern-makers, and in the standard carving-gouges which are still made in great variety.

Grinding and honing angles

Most manufacturers grind to a bevel of about $22\frac{1}{2}°$ to $25°$ and advocate a secondary honing or sharpening bevel of about $30°$, but this is more applicable to stout joiners' tools, and one long bevel (5:2A) is preferable for bevelled edge chisels with about $30°$ for firmer-chisels and $35°$ for heavy mortising chisels. The long continuous bevel may be more troublesome to preserve in honing and the actual cutting edge may not last as long as a stout secondary bevel—and in fact will tend to crumble if used for heavy chopping —but it will always be sharper and will cut more sweetly, moreover the bevel will rarely want regrinding. For those who tend to round their bevels over when honing on the oilstone (and the knack of working with the elbow and not the wrist takes time to acquire) a honing-gauge mounted on a ball or roller and set at the correct cutting angle is a useful accessory. It is more difficult to keep this long bevel in sharpening gouges, although one should always attempt to do so. Carvers' gouges, which are always outcannelled, are sometimes sharpened with an additional inside bevel, but this is not applicable to cabinet-gouges which should be kept flat on the non-bevelled inside face.

The bevel of any cutting edge does of course exercise a wedge-like action, driving the tool into the wood on its flat unbevelled side, whilst an easy slope to the bevel offers less resistance and gives a cleaner cut. Figure 6 gives the cutting actions. In 6A the single bevel lifts the chip without much tendency for the chisel to be driven

6   Cutting actions: chisels

into the wood, but where the bevel is steep as in 6B the greater resistance offered will either drive the chisel into the wood or split the chip ahead of the cut. In 6C with bevel under, the tendency is to lift the chisel in the direction of the arrow, whilst in downward chopping at 6D the bevel tends to drive the cutting edge away from the true direction of the cut, and in order to maintain a square shoulder it is first necessary to chop away a recess as at 6E. Figure 6F shows the effect of reversing the chisel, which again does not give a square shoulder. In cutting end grain (6G) there is no problem as the chip is too brittle to offer any resistance, whilst if a heavy chip is required along the grain it is better to reverse the chisel as at 6H. All cutting along the grain should always be downhill or with the grain as at 6I, otherwise there is a tendency for the tool to dig in and lift the fibres. The skilled worker soon learns to 'read' the grain whether he is using a hand-tool or a machine, and it rapidly becomes instinctive. Shearing or slicing cuts where the forward movement of the cutting edge follows a diagonal path offer less resistance as the cut is spread over a greater area and the slope of the cut, governed by the combined grinding and honing angles, is reduced.

Hinge-slotting chisel

A continental chisel not available in this country until recently is the *fischbandeisen* (pin-hinge chisel) or *einlasseisen* (slotting-tool) which is used for cutting very narrow, deep slots for some types of hinge. There are several forms of these chisels which are obtainable in widths from $\frac{3}{4}$ in. (19 mm) to $1\frac{3}{4}$ in. (44 mm) and about $\frac{3}{32}$ in. (2·5 mm) thick. The chisel is used in the same way as a mortise-chisel, moving it along the slot to clear the waste, and 7 shows the most useful pattern.

Planes

One of the most useful of all planes is the 22 in. (558 mm) *try-plane* No. 07 (8A) with $2\frac{3}{8}$ in. (60 mm) cutter. Shorter planes in this category are known as '*fore*' for general levelling, and longer planes '*jointers*' for shooting square edges, etc., but the middle size will do everything necessary. *Jack-planes* can either be 14 in.

8A   Try-plane (jointer)

(355 mm) or 15 in. (380 mm) long with 2 in. (50 mm) or 2⅜ in. (60 mm) cutter (Nos. 05 or 05½)—the name itself is probably a corruption of 'jackass' or 'Jack of all Trades 'and fit for anything; it is, therefore, reserved for the rougher work although it is as much a precision tool as any other. It is often recommended that the jack-plane iron should be ground to a slight arc, but whilst this makes heavy cuts easier it destroys the plane's general usefulness and the cutting edge should be ground truly square, although the corners can be nicked or rounded over if preferred. Smoothing-planes for final surfacing follow the same general pattern and can either be 8 in. (203 mm) long with 1¾ in. (44 mm) cutter (No. 03), 9 in. (228 mm) with 2 in. (50 mm) cutter (No. 04) or 10 in. (254 mm) with 2⅜ in. (60 mm) cutter (No. 04½); the middle size is probably the most useful. Detachable cutting edges for the irons have lately been reintroduced after many years, but it is doubtful if they offer any real advantage. All the sizes and numbers quoted above refer to metal planes throughout, with screw-adjustable cutter, lateral lever-actuated depth movement for the cutter and adjustable mouth (the latter movement is rarely used as much as it should be, for a finely set iron and fine mouth are invaluable for surfacing hard or difficult timbers). The merit of all these metal planes over their wooden counterparts is their ease of adjustment, but wooden jack- and smoothing-planes are still obtainable and their stouter cutting irons can be an advantage, whilst there is probably less friction as between wood and wood and metal and wood. Marples Ltd take advantage of this by supplying a pre-fabricated beech plane which embodies the easy adjustments of the metal variety. Again, metal planes are obtainable with corrugated soles which, it is claimed, cut down friction and tend to hold the lubricant applied to the sole. This lubricant should never be oil or soft grease, but a few strokes of a hard candle end along the sole will make an astonishing difference.

A smaller version of the smoothing-plane not available in wooden form which can be held in one hand is the metal *block-plane* (8B), and the 6 in. (152 mm) plane with 1⅝ in. (41 mm) cutter, adjustable mouth and cutter depth, etc., as with the larger bench-planes, is probably the most suitable. The cheaper versions are not fully

8B Block-plane

8C Bench rabbet-plane

8D Improved rabbet-plane

adjustable and the cutter position must be set by trial and error otherwise there is little difference. For working large rebates (rabbets)* in which a heavy section is to be taken out, a special *bench rabbet-plane* (8C) is obtainable, and for general light rabbeting, etc., the *improved rabbet-plane* (8D) which, if fitted with sliding fence, depth-stop and spur for scoring across the grain ahead of the cutter to prevent tearing out, becomes the *rebate-* and *fillister-plane*, although the term 'fillister' is tending to die out. Trueing up the sides of rebates and cleaning up the shoulders of

* *Rabbet:* probably a carpenter's corruption of rebate (to deduct from, to diminish). *Fillister* also means a groove or rebate.

8E   Improved shoulder rabbet-plane

8F   Multi-plane

8A–F *by courtesy of C. J. Hampton Limited*

9   'Old Woman's Tooth' router

tenons, etc., can be done with the *shoulder rabbet-plane* (8E) with machined parallel sides and through cutter. This plane is worked with both hands, whilst the smaller, single-handed version known as the *bullnose rabbet-plane* usually has a detachable nose, distance-pieces and variable mouth for fine or coarse work. If the nose is detached it becomes a *chisel-plane*, allowing the cutting-iron to work up to the end of a stopped rebate. Both these planes should have screw adjustment to the cutting-iron which should be ground truly square to the machined body of the plane, as there is no lateral adjustment. For cutting grooves within the body of the work, i.e. away from the edge, either with or across the grain, some form of adjustable grooving-plane is necessary. This should have a sliding fence, depth-stop for determining the finished depth of the groove, spurs for cross grain and a range of cutters for different widths of groove. In its simplest form it can be bought as a *plough-plane* with three cutters, as a *standard plough* with eight cutters, and as a *combination-* or *multi-plane* which will undertake rabbeting, ploughing (grooving), tongueing and grooving, beading, etc., and if fitted with special bases and cutters, rounding and hollowing. Figure 8F shows the Record multi-plane No. 405 which is supplied with 23 standard cutters and a range of special-purpose bases and cutters.

The standard plough or multi-plane is usually supplied with two sets of arms permitting grooves to be worked up to 5 in. (127 mm) from the edge of the timber, but for greater distances or where the groove or trench is curved on plan then a *router-plane* is necessary (10A). This has an upright cranked cutter rather like a jackboot which cuts with a chisel action, bevel uppermost, and flat to the wood; the cutter is clamped to a cutter-post and fed down by a knurled screw as the work proceeds until the correct depth is attained. As the square-edged cutter will tend to tear up cross grain a spear-headed smoothing-cutter is provided which cuts with a slicing action, whilst for narrow surfaces the wide throat can be closed with an adjustable shoe. This is a two-handed tool, but a smaller single-handed version (10B) with closed throat and single cutter is useful for fine work. Failing a metal router and also for the odd occasion a suitable chisel wedged into a block of wood on the principle of the 'Old

Woman's Tooth' (9) can be used, but the metal router with its easy adjustability will pay for its keep.

A useful plane for trueing up the shoulders of rebates, grooves, etc., is the metal *side-rebate* or *edge-trimming plane* (10C) whose upright sole allows it to be used in narrow spaces. It has two crossed irons allowing right- or left-hand working, detachable nose and reversible depth-stop. Here again the cutting-irons must be very carefully ground at the required angle to give equal projection of the cutting edge.

Shaped edges which are convex can be worked with a smoothing- or block-plane provided the sweep is not too acute, but for quick curves and concave edges a metal *compass-plane* (10D) is obtainable whose flexible spring steel face can be adjusted to any arc. This is an expensive tool proportionate to the amount of use which could be found for it, and given a true eye most curved edges can be worked equally well—but rather more slowly—with *spokeshaves* which have either a flat face for convex work (10E) or a round face for concave work. The screw-adjustable type illustrated is easier to handle than the cheaper version in which the cutter is secured with a thumb-screw and which must be set by hand. A *chamfer* version with two adjustable fences set at a true angle of 45° was manufactured until recently and is probably still available. For

10C Side-rebate plane

10D Compass-plane

10A Router-plane

10E Spokeshave (flat face)

10A–E *by courtesy of C. J. Hampton Limited*

difficult woods there is much to be said for the wooden spokeshave illustrated, in which the iron (11A) is flat to the wood, cutting bevel uppermost, and the writer has always preferred this type, although it is probably only a matter of individual preference. For rough and rapid shaping the *carpenter's drawknife* (11B) will get rid of a great deal of timber in the shortest possible time, but it must be razor sharp. In the hands of an expert it can be made to work to precision limits. It can be used bevel down for either light cutting or convex shapes, or bevel up for heavy cutting or concave shapes.

In all spokeshaving operations a slight shearing or diagonal direction to the cut will minimise any tendency to clatter or form ridges which may be difficult to eradicate.

11   Spokeshave and drawknife

Moulding-planes

Some types are still available although they have been almost entirely superseded by the spindle-moulder and high-speed router; moreover the traditional flutes, reeds, ovolo and ogee mouldings are rarely used in contemporary work. When such work was done by hand exclusively it was usual for the cabinet-maker to have a half set of *rounding-planes* (12:1A) for working hollows, etc., and perhaps a few *hollow-planes* for working rounds (12:2) together with several *beading-*, *ovolo-* and *ogee moulding-planes*, some of which

he would make for himself out of short ends of red park beech always set aside for tool-making. A typical ovolo-plane is shown in 12:3 and whilst the continental pattern worked upright the English pattern worked at an angle which was always marked on the end of the plane.

These planes are always worth acquiring whenever possible—the writer bought a full half set (eighteen) of rounding-planes and some dozens of moulding-planes for sixpence each in a junk-shop just before the Second World War—for although the machine might be regarded as indispensable there will always be the time when an odd length only of a particular moulding is required. Given the necessary tool it will be much quicker to work the length by hand rather than spend an hour or more grinding a special cutter and setting up a machine. Figure 332 shows the fluted drawer front of a cocktail cabinet worked entirely with a round moulding-plane.

12   Moulding-planes

26

Scratch stock

Failing a suitable moulding-plane small mouldings were often worked with this simple tool illustrated below, moreover it is still extremely useful for cutting narrow grooves for inlays, strings, bandings, etc. It is simply made, either from a solid block (or two pieces of suitable hardwood screwed together) with a saw cut through the arm to take a piece of old saw- or scraper-blade ground and filed to the shape required (13B), and held in the correct position by a pinch-grip with suitably placed screws (13A). The cutter can be filed square edged and burred over as for a scraper, in which case the scratch stock is worked backwards and forwards with a rocking movement, or it can be bevel ground and burred over as for a scraper-plane iron.

13 Scratch stock

Miscellaneous planes

Several other types of plane have occasional uses, some of which can be bought, others will have to be made. Figure 14:1 illustrates the *cooper's stoup-plane* with sole rounded in both length and width, and with the iron curved as shown; it is useful for dishing fairly large surfaces, stool seats, etc. It can be converted from a standard wooden *smooth-* or *coffin-plane*. Another good tool is the *Jarvis spokeshave-plane* (14:2) used by wheelwrights for rounding spokes, with metal spokeshave-type flat iron ground to a hollow, and knock-in wooden wedge. Figure 14:3 shows the wooden *scrub-*, *rougher-* or *Bismark*-plane which is still manufactured, and is invaluable for knocking off the rough preparatory to either hand- or machine-surfacing. Also available from the same makers (Marples Ltd of

14 Miscellaneous planes

Sheffield) is the traditional wooden *skew rebate-plane* with single iron set at an angle to give a shearing cut. Figure 14:4 shows the standard *toothing-plane* (see *Veneering*, Chapter 22) in which a series of corrugations in the iron scores the surface of the wood. It is used for keying the groundwork preparatory to veneering with hide glue, and for levelling bumpy veneers, etc. Mention must also be made of the incomparable *Norris planes*, smooth-, jack- and *low-angled mitre-* or *piano-finishers' plane*. They are no longer manufactured, but second-hand planes in good condition command high prices and the writer counts them amongst his most prized possessions, not for any sentimental reason but because they happen to do their job extremely well. For the final surfacing of really difficult timbers, ebony, East Indian satinwood, etc., they are excellent, and no doubt the secret lies in the extra stout iron of first-class steel and the heavy and robust body which always seems to hug the wood. Before quantity production became the rule and not the exception the old craftsmen always treasured their extra long and heavy wood *jointing-planes*, and several of the smaller bench-planes they made for themselves from rough gunmetal castings; nor is there any reason why the enthusiast with some slight engineering skill should not do the same. Single and double plane-irons in all sizes are still freely available and can be ground to fit. Beech and rosewood are excellent for plane-making; the wood should not be oiled as is sometime advocated, but coated with shellac varnish to seal the pores.

Cutting angles

All bench-planes for general levelling, i.e. jointer-, try-, fore-, jack- and smooth-planes have double irons (15:1) composed of the cutting iron proper and the cap-iron whose function it is to stiffen the cutting edge and break up the shaving as it is raised so that, robbed of its stiffness, it does not tend to run ahead of the cut in a series of small splits in the surface of the timber. The closer this cap-iron is to the cutting edge the sooner the shaving is bent over and broken, therefore fine cuts or difficult timbers require a close-set cap-iron and a narrow mouth which, in the case of metal bench-planes, is easily adjustable. Practical experience will give the best

15 Cutting angles: planes

setting of the cap-iron, which may vary from a hair's breadth for the final surfacing of difficult timbers to $\frac{1}{16}$ in. (1·5 mm) for the first rough levelling. This use of the cap-iron means that the grinding bevel of the cutting iron must be underneath, therefore the cutting angle is dependent on the pitch or angle of the iron in the plane, irrespective of the grinding angle. Usually a compromise angle of 45° is used for bench-planes, for raising the angle gives more of a scraping action and lowering it more of a slicing cut.

In the case of metal shoulder rabbet- and block-planes which are only used for trimming and final levelling, often on end grain, the mouth must be kept as small as possible and the iron supported right up to the cutting edge to prevent clattering. As there is no room for a cap-iron the iron is reversed bevel uppermost, which in turn raises the cutting angle, therefore the pitch is lowered, giving an effective angle of about 50° which is about right for a scraping cut on end grain. Moulding-planes also cannot be fitted with a cap-iron even though the bevel is underneath and to prevent any tearing out of the grain the angle is raised to about 55°. Toothing-planes which merely score the surface of the wood are set at an angle a little short of upright. The remarks regarding the advisability of preserving one long bevel to cutting edges advocated for chisels equally apply to plane-irons. Figure 15 illustrates the various pitches: 15:1 for bench-planes fitted with cap-irons whose function it is to support the cutting edge and break up the chip as it rises, 15:2 shoulder rabbet- and block-planes with bevel uppermost, 15:3 moulding-planes and 15:4 the toothing-plane. All these pitches are empirical, i.e. the result of long experience and not scientific enquiry. Whereas a good deal of research has been done into cutting angles for machine-cutters, it is a little surprising that manufacturers of hand-tools have not experimented with variable pitch planes, in which the cutting angle can be altered for difficult timbers, interlocked grain, etc.

Miscellaneous cutting tools

One of the most useful of hand-tools is the steel *cabinet-scraper*, which is merely a blank of steel about 12 gauge in thickness, $2\frac{1}{2}$ in. (63 mm) wide and from 4 in. (101 mm) to 6 in. (152 mm) long (the 5 in. (127 mm) size is most popular). The long edges must be filed flat and truly square with a mill-saw or similar file, the side burrs taken off on the oilstone and the edges honed to a mirror finish. These edges are then burred over with a ticketter (burnisher), which is nothing more than a short length of silver steel suitably hardened, and the scraper is either held upright at the edge of the bench or laid flat as shown below. A few heavy strokes of the burnisher (some workers lick the steel to give it an extra bite) at an angle of about 85° should be sufficient to raise an effective cutting burr (16:1, 2) which can be restored several times without refiling simply by wiping the burr back on the flat faces and then re-forming at a slightly lower angle. The scraper is held in both hands, thumbs in the centre with sufficient pressure to bend the steel in a slight arc, and pushed forward at an angle of about 120° to the body; the angle can be reversed and drawn towards the body if preferred.

Properly sharpened and held correctly the scraper should be capable of taking long shavings of tissue thinness from even the most refractory of timbers, and it is therefore invaluable for the last fine finishing, especially of veneered work. However, in scraping out torn grain or other imperfection on surfaces which will be gloss polished great care must be taken not to localise the strokes, but to spread them over a fairly wide area, otherwise hollows will be created which will eventually show rather like a bumpy road under a car's headlights. A sound rule to follow is one stroke over the bad patch, one ahead, one behind and one each on either side. For scraping difficult surfaces, especially when they are impregnated with resin glue, the floor-finisher's trick of dampening the surface with water can be adopted, whilst for curved work and simple mouldings the standard scraper-blade can be ground and filed to conform to any sweep.

A good scraper in first-class condition can become hot enough to blister the thumbs and some workers pad the thumb-tips with surgical tape. Others prefer the scraper-plane (17) in which a steel blank is set at an angle of about 10° from the vertical in a suitable handled holder, with the blade bevel-ground like a plane-iron, and the bevel burred over at an angle of about 15° from the grinding bevel as shown in 17A. A thumb-screw in the centre bows the iron so that it cuts in the centre as in the hand-scraper, and the plane is pushed away from the body with the cutter leaning forwards.

17 Scraper-plane

17A Scraper-plane iron

16 Sharpening steel scraper

2 Hand-tools (2)

Marking, measuring and testing tools

Traditionally the furniture-maker has relied upon the standard 2 ft (609 mm) fourfold rule, the joiner on the 3 ft (914 mm) pattern, both marked in eighths and sixteenths of an inch, and obtainable as standard or blindman's, the latter with extra bold figurings, but with the introduction of the metric system the lengths of the rules will no doubt be changed to more convenient units. For long lengths the standard draughtsman's boxwood rule or the engineer's long one-piece rule are preferable to flexible steel tapes which should not be used for highly critical work on the bench. Finely divided semiflexible engineers' steel rules are very useful, also the stout square-end type not finely divided which can be used as either rule or short straight-edge, for if the edge of the rule is rubbed over the wood it will immediately highlight ridges and raised spots which are not discernible to the naked eye with a black metal shine. A useful accessory is the Stanley combination try-mitre-square and depth-gauge incorporating a sliding-rule (19:1), whilst the vernier caliper gauge (19:2) is invaluable for measuring exact thicknesses. These can be obtained as engineer's precision pattern, or as a more robust pattern specially designed for woodworking factories, but for ordinary bench-work the cheapest pattern procurable is sufficient and could be obtained for a few pence before the Second World War. All rules should be used with the markings actually touching the work as illustrated in 18.

Straight-edges are essential in any workshop and should be plentiful (19:11); they are usually made out of $\frac{1}{2}$ in. (12·5 mm) by $2\frac{1}{2}$ in. (63·5 mm) mild Honduras mahogany, pitchpine or straight-grained yellow pine, waxed or varnished, and in a range of lengths up to 6 ft (1524 mm); whilst at least one metal straight-edge 4 ft (1·21 m) long or more should be provided for cutting veneers, etc. It can be the cheaper mount-cutter's pattern rather than the more expensive draughtsman's or engineer's precision-ground straight-edge. Also necessary are *winding-sticks* (19:4) in matched pairs, usually about 2 ft (609 mm) long by 2 in. (50 mm) wide by $\frac{1}{2}$ in. (12·5 mm) thick of good mahogany or similar timber planed up truly parallel, the edges bevelled as shown and small sighting insets of white wood (19:4A) inlaid into the rear stick. Stub dowels and sockets are also provided so that the sticks can be kept together and hung from a nail, as any deviation from the straight, or uneven shrinkage across the width of either, will result in false readings. If these sticks are placed at either end of a planed-up board and sighted through from a few feet away the whitewood insets will immediately confirm any slight tilt, disclosing that the board is 'in winding', i.e., both edges may be straight but the diagonal is curved, giving a twist or wind to the timber. *Squaring-rods* (19:12) of about 1 in. (25 mm) by $\frac{5}{16}$ in. (8 mm) straight-grained timber in various lengths and blocked and pointed at one end are used for checking the squareness of carcase openings, etc., for it is never safe to rely upon the try-square alone over a large area (see *Carcase Constructions*, Chapter 27).

Gauges

Beech *marking-gauges* (19:3) are cheap enough and several should be provided, thus saving time in multiple setting out. The brass-plated variety offer no real advantage, but boxwood thumbscrews are preferable if they can be obtained as the plastic screws tend to snap off if dropped. In

18 Measuring with rule

circular work the flat-faced gauge will give a false reading, and stubs of dowel-rod rounded over (19:5A) to give a two-point bearing are necessary, whilst for concave edges one face of the gauge can be rounded (19:5B), and for pencil-use a hole can be bored in the end of the stem (104). Marking-gauges are primarily intended for scoring with or on the end grain; if used across the grain they will either scratch or tear unless the pins are needle sharp, and a *cutting-gauge* (19:6) is more suitable. This has a small knife in lieu of a steel pin, secured by a brass wedge shown alongside (19:6A); the knife is pointed and bevelled on one side and used with the bevel

facing the fence, pulling the fence tight against the work and preventing any tendency for the knife to ride with the grain. *Mortise-gauges* (19:9) are in effect double marking-gauges with two pins, one of which is adjusted for distance by a threaded rod passing through the stem. These gauges are usually made of rosewood which is a somewhat unnecessary refinement, for the brass movement is rarely good enough to last a lifetime, and the points of the pins wear out.

All these gauges are held in one hand hard against the edge of the timber, the fence inclined away from the body and pushed forwards so that the pin is always trailing; the movement can

20 Marking, measuring and testing tools (2)

then be reversed to impart a rocking movement to the gauge. (It is for the individual worker to find his own particular method of handling as with all other types of hand-tools.)

The long *panel-gauge* (19:10) is used for pencil gauging panels to width; a wooden wedge secures the fence which is rebated so that it does not tip under its own weight. The stick should not be less than about 20 in. (508 mm) long to take in the extreme width of an average-size carcase. Figures 20:7 illustrates the T-gauge or *grasshopper-gauge* with extra long fence for riding over projecting mouldings as shown.

Squares, bevels, etc.

Joiners' try-squares can be either all-metal, metal blade secured in a rosewood stock (19:7) or L-shaped metal blade running through the stock; it hardly matters which so long as the square is accurate and robust enough to stand inadvertent dropping. It is useful to have three sizes, say, 4 in. (101 mm), 8 in. (203 mm) and 12 in. (304 mm); whilst for highly critical work a 6 in. (152 mm) precision-ground engineer's square (19:8) costs very little more than the equivalent joiner's square. A useful adjunct is the *bright Mason's square* or *carpenter's standard roofing-square* with legs 24 in. (609 mm) and 18 in. (457 mm) long for squaring greater widths, whilst some craftsmen make up their own large try-square (20:8) with 11 in. (279 mm) by 2½ in. (63 mm) by ¾ in. (19 mm) stock and 20 in. (508 mm) by 3 in. (76 mm) by ¼ in. (6 mm) blade out of good mahogany, rosewood or ebony. A small inset stop (20:8A) is provided to support the heavy stock on the work. For setting out angles, dovetails, etc. the *joiner's adjustable level* is used. The slotted screw adjustment shown (20:1) is preferable to the brass lever locking-nut which often has a multi-start thread, and if displaced and threaded in the wrong position will foul the work. Figure 20:4 shows a wooden template for marking out dovetails, cut out of a hardwood block about 2½ in. (63 mm) by 2 in. (50 mm) by 1¾ in. (44 mm) overall thickness, with the sides planed up to the required rake, in this case 1 in 6 (see *Dovetailing Joints*, Chapter 19). Other tools in this general section include *marking-knives* with hardwood handles (20:2A), and *striking-knives* with awl ends (20:2B) for

scribing. If the knife has a single cutting bevel only it can be used as an accurate trimming-knife. The *Stanley trimming-knife* is a useful all-purpose knife with a wide range of blades, including a scoring-knife for the clean cutting of decorative laminated plastics (formica, etc.). Good knives can also be made from old hack-saw blades with the teeth ground off as shown in 20:3A, also an excellent dovetail-marker (20:3B) which is more positive than the tip of the dovetail-saw customarily used. The *carpenter's wing-compass* with locking-screw is shown in 20:6, as ordinary compasses and dividers tend to catch in the grain and disturb the setting; whilst instead of the draughtsman's beam-compass, *trammel-points* (20:5) are used which slide along a suitable wooden lath. One head has a steel point and the other a socket for a pencil end.

Sawing and planing appliances

Reversible *bench-hooks* (21:1) are used to support small sectioned timber whilst it is being sawn or cut, and at the same time protecting the bench-top from incidental damage. They can be either bought or simply made out of hardwood about 10 in. (254 mm) by 6 in. (152 mm) by 1 in. (25 mm) with 1¼ in. (32 mm) square cleats screwed on both ends as shown (the position can be reversed for left-handed workers). Straight *shooting-boards* (21:2) for the accurate squaring

21 Bench-hook and shooting-board

of ends can also be purchased or again made by the worker; preferably out of good dry beech, although softwood will do equally well provided it is well seasoned and free from knots. The bed can be in two pieces with grain direction reversed, screwed together to form a rebated bed whilst the headpiece should be taper housed and screwed but not glued. A shallow groove is usually provided between the two beds ostensibly for loose dust, etc., and the headpiece or stop can be extended out as shown by the dotted lines to support wide timber. In making up these boards great care should be taken to ensure that they truly square in every detail, otherwise the whole object is defeated. An average size for normal work, i.e. squaring ends and shooting the edges of small pieces of timber with the try-plane, would be 2 ft (609 mm) long, 9 in. (228 mm) wide overall of which about 3 in.

(76 mm) is reserved for the side of the plane, with the stop out of 1¼ in. (32 mm) square timber. Larger boards up to 4 ft (1·21 m) long are also useful for trimming veneers, etc., and can be simply made from two pieces of dry deal boarding, with the top board kept back to provide a shoulder for the stop to butt against, and the whole screwed together so that it can be knocked apart and lined up afresh whenever necessary, for all boards do require periodic checking.

Mitre tools

Figure 22:1 shows the fixed *mitre-square* for setting out true mitres, (22:2) the combined *square* and *mitre-template*, (22:3) a brass *mitre-template* for stuck mouldings, and (22:4) a wooden version cut out of a 5 in. (127 mm) by 1½ in. (38 mm)

22 Mitre tools

square block of close-grained hardwood. Uses for these tools are described under the appropriate chapters on *Framed and Mitred Work*, etc. A *mitre sawing-box* is shown in 22:5 which requires no description; it can be bought or very simply made. For the most accurate sawing of squares and mitres the *Ulmia mitre-saw* is recommended which can be set at any angle by a quick-release finger-grip. Figure 138 illustrates this saw in use, also the *mitre-trimmer* extensively used by picture-framers but an invaluable tool also in any workshop. Figure 22:6 shows a *mitre shooting-board* for flat stuff, approximately the same size as the straight shooting-board, for use where the mitre cut is across the width as in picture-frames, flat mouldings, etc. This board cannot be used for mitres in the thickness, and 22:7 shows the *mitre shooting-block* with wood or metal screw which will accommodate small box sides, plinth and heavy cornice mouldings, etc. The screw actuates a sliding chop (22:7A), with a fixed chop (22:7B). The sliding chop is retained in position by a crosspiece screwed to the prongs of the chop under the frame, and tight enough to ensure an easy but positive slide. Both chops should be either heavily waxed or covered with a renewable surface material, stiff card, etc., to take the wear of the plane-iron, and if the back faces of the chops are truly square the block can be used for squaring ends. The traditional *donkey's-ear shooting-board* for mitreing in the thickness is illustrated in 22:8A, and an alternative form in 22:8B.

Holding devices

Various devices are used to hold the timber or support the tool, and the test of a good craftsman is his ability to improvise. Figure 23:1 shows the *rounding-cradle* for supporting square-sectioned stuff whilst it is being rounded; and 23:3 a planing-board with different-size grooves for holding thin laths, etc. Figure 23:2 shows the *bench-holdfast*, which is merely inserted in a hole bored in the bench-top and will remain in any position once the screw-pad is tightened on the work; whilst long edges which have to be worked with a rabbet- or moulding-plane can be lifted clear of the bench by gripping them in a T-bar sash-cramp G-cramped to the bench-top. Failing an end vice to the bench (see *Workshop equip-*

23 Holding devices

ment, page 57) there can be no possible objection to nailing battens to the bench to grip long lengths, wide panels, etc., whilst they are being planed up, always provided only panel-pins or lath-nails are used, and they are carefully withdrawn immediately after. The over-fastidious craftsman might object to this, but the important thing is the piece of work on the bench, not the bench itself.

Drills and drilling

For drilling holes both the *joiner's ratchet-bit* or *arm-brace* with ball-bearing head (24:1) and the *hand-drill* (24:2) are used. The ratchet-brace is designed for slow, powerful cutting, usually with wing-bits having a square taper shank. The alligator jaws will also accept standard twist-drills with parallel shanks up to $\frac{3}{8}$ in. (9·5 mm) diameter, although they are inclined to slip under load if the jaws are at all worn.

This brace can be obtained in a range of

sweeps, i.e. the circle through which the arm turns, from 8 in. (203 mm) to 14 in. (355 mm), with the larger sweeps yielding the greater power; whilst for confined spaces the *electrician's ratchet-brace* with 5 in. (127 mm) sweep is invaluable. The standard hand-drill (24:2) is designed for the rapid boring of small-diameter holes, and has a three-jaw chuck accepting $\frac{1}{4}$ in. (6 mm) or $\frac{5}{16}$ in. (8 mm) parallel shank bits and drills. For larger shank sizes up to $\frac{1}{2}$ in. (12:5 mm) diameter the engineer's pattern two-speed drill with breast-pad for extra power is necessary. These hand-drills will not accept taper shank bits. Very fine needle-bits and the smallest twist-drills require a much lighter drill, with collet-type or similar chuck, and the traditional *archimedean* or *push-drill* (24:3) is used.

24 Boring and drilling tools

Types of bit
Bits are probably the most abused of all wood-working tools, for too often the wrong type is chosen, or the bit is incorrectly or over sharpened. The general run of bits are supplied with either square taper shanks (25:1) for use in the arm-brace, or parallel round shanks (25:14) for hand-drills. A few types are also available with parallel shanks turned down to $\frac{1}{4}$ in. (6 mm) diameter (25:13) for use in the standard drill-gun, and with *Morse taper* shanks for lathe heads or specialised drilling-machines. In the main, parallel shank-bits are classed as machine-bits with a constant shank diameter of $\frac{1}{2}$ in. (12·5 mm), but the universally used *Russell Jenning's auger-* and *dowel-bits* are also supplied with $\frac{1}{4}$ in. (6 mm) and $\frac{3}{8}$ in. (9·5 mm) diameter shanks. Types of bit are as follows.

Jenning's pattern auger-bit (25:1)
The best smooth boring bit for general cabinet-work. Also available as the standard 5 in. (127 mm) dowel-bit.

Solid centre auger-bit (25:2)
Extra strong general-purpose bit with greater chip clearance.

Single-spur solid centre-bits (25:3)
For deep boring, also difficult or stringy timbers.

Scotch square-nose auger-bit (25:4)
Designed for boring hard and rough timbers.

Solid nose auger-bit (25:5)
Unbreakable nose for tough, difficult drilling and boring at an angle.

Expansion-bit (25:6)
Primarily intended for softwoods, although it can be used in medium hardwoods provided care is taken and large-diameter holes are not attempted. Available in two sizes, each with an additional cutter (25:7) to give a range of diameters from $\frac{1}{2}$ in. (12·5 mm) to $1\frac{1}{2}$ in. (38 mm) and from $\frac{7}{8}$ in. (22 mm) to 3 in. (76 mm).

Shell-bit (25:8)
For clean boring of short, small-diameter holes.

Old-type centre-bit (25:9)
Always a good bit for shallow holes, and still used as a machine-bit for large diameters. The

brad-point enables holes to be bored from either side of the timber, thus preventing splintering out on the underside.

Improved pattern centre-bit (25:10)
A fast, clean-cutting bit for shallow holes.

Forstner bit (25:11)
Unequalled for boring any arc of a circle, and unaffected by knots or the run of the grain. As it is guided by its circular rim it gives a flat-bottomed hole, useful in some work.

Dowel-sharpener (25:12)
Useful for chamfering the ends of dowel-pegs for easy entry.

Flat-bit (25:13)
A revolutionary and inexpensive bit which relies on speed for its cutting ability, therefore its use is confined to drill-guns and drilling machines.

Improved twist-drill (25:14)
A wood-cutting version of the standard metal-boring twist-drill.

Snail-horn countersink (25:15)
Countersink for timber, with taper shank for hand-braces.

Rose-head countersink (25:16)
General-purpose countersink for wood and non-ferrous metals, available with both taper and parallel shanks, and in 90° and 120° included angles.

Machine bit (25:17)
With brad-point in lieu of screw lead to the nose, as the latter will snatch at the wood if driven at speed, with risk of serious injury in hand-held timber. Brad-points are not self-driving and require feed pressure, therefore they are advisable for all high-speed drilling, unless the work can be very securely clamped down.

Twist-drills
The standard jobber's twist-drill primarily intended for metal boring is also used extensively by the woodworking trades for small-diameter holes, although it will never cut as cleanly as a correctly sharpened wood bit. Moreover, it has neither screw lead nor brad-point, and is always

more difficult to position accurately. On the other hand it retains its direction, and is not deflected by knots or the run of the grain. The cheaper carbon steel varieties are good enough for wood provided they are not allowed to burn. Twist-drills are not suitable for use in the ratchet-brace, as they require a higher speed than it can achieve for clean cutting.

William Ridgway and Sons Ltd, who take a justifiable pride in the excellence of their products, give the following instructions for the use and upkeep of wood-boring bits:

1 A good bit should draw itself easily into the timber, cutting a clean hole without undue pressure on the brace.
2 A bit should never be used to bore a hole at one operation deeper than the length of its twist or flute. Where deeper holes are required the bit should be repeatedly withdrawn and the chips cleared as they rise.
3 Generally speaking bits are sharpened more often than necessary, and the life of the bit considerably shortened by incorrect filing.

Sharpening bits

Basic rules as laid down by Ridgway are: (1) always sharpen from the inside or underneath, never outside or on top; (2) maintain original shape and angles; (3) use suitable smooth-file, never grind and always file lightly, removing as little metal as possible and preserving the balance of the bit so that each side does the same amount of work. The illustrations on page **39** give the procedure, and are copied from Ridgway's booklets. In 26:1, A is the side wing, **B** the cutters, C the spurs and D the throat. The sequence of sharpening is as follows:

Sharpening the side wings (26:2). Rest the bit in the bench with the screw lead down. File with the file working through the throat of the bit. Never file the side wings on the outside or the clearance will be spoilt (the appropriate **file** section is shown alongside each drawing).
Sharpening the spurs (26:3). Hold the bit **nose** uppermost with its twist firmly against the edge of the bench. File the inside of the spurs. Never file the outside as this reduces the clearance, causing binding and clogging of the bit.
Sharpening the cutters (26:4). Hold the bit **as in**

1

2

3

4

(26:2) and file the cutting edges on the under-side only, i.e., with the file working through the throat of the bit. The cutters must be at the same level so that they cut chips of equal thickness.

Another wood-boring tool which is always abused is the common *bradawl*. It should be carefully sharpened with a fine file and finished on the oilstone, and is used for boring fine holes for nails or the threads of screws and not the clearance hole for the actual shank of the screw which should be made with a shell-bit or twist-drill. The birdcage-pattern bradawl with square shank bores with a reamer-like action, and can be used on the thinnest wood without splitting. Reamers for use in the arm-brace can also be obtained, and are used for widening existing holes.

Striking and driving tools

Figure 27:1 shows the *ash handled Warrington* or *joiner's pattern hammer* with cross pein for starting nails, etc., 27:2 the heavy *claw-hammer* with split claw for drawing nails, and 27:3 the light *pattern-maker's pin-* or *telephone-hammer*; whilst the *upholsterer's hammer* which can also be obtained in magnetic form, is shown in 27:4. An average weight for the joiner's hammer would be either 10 or 12 oz (340 g) head, and 4 oz (113 g) head for the pin-hammer. The *carpenter's mallet* is shown in 27:5, and a useful size would be with head out of a 5 in. (127 mm) by $3\frac{1}{2}$ in. (89 mm) by $2\frac{1}{2}$ in. (63 mm) thick beech block, and $1\frac{3}{8}$ in. (35 mm) by $\frac{3}{4}$ in. (19 mm) handle 13 in. (330 mm) long overall. The handle is not glued but fractionally tapered as shown so that the head cannot fly off. Figure 27:6 shows the *carver's mallet*, useful for light chopping, and turned out of a 4 in. (101 mm) square beech block 7 in. (178 mm) long, leaving 3 in. (76 mm) for the mallet head and about 4 in. (102 mm) for the $\frac{7}{8}$ in. (22 mm) diameter handle. Alternatively, the handle can be turned separately, taken through the head and glued and wedged.

The standard *cabinet-screwdriver* is shown in 27:7 and this is usually the best pattern for general work; and a useful *dumpy-screwdriver* with loose toggle-bar for working in confined spaces in 27:8. Nail sets are shown in 27:9, type (A) for punching in larger nails, and the *pin-punch* (B) for small veneer-pins. Type (C) shows the *centre-punch*, useful for marking centres when using twist-drills, etc. The square-headed types of nail set give a greater striking surface, and are not so inclined to boss over with repeated use.

Hammer faces should always be kept clean and polished on a waste scrap of abrasive paper, otherwise they tend to bend the nails over, whilst the downward stroke should be directed with a slight pushing action away from the body. Screwdrivers should be cross ground to fit the screw-slot and not merely bevelled at the tip.

Grinding and honing stones, files, rasps, etc.

Most edge tools are now dry ground on high-speed grinders instead of the much slower cutting water-lubricated grindstone. The latter is always the better method as there is never any danger of withdrawing the temper of the cutting edge, nevertheless the high-speed grinder will give good results if care be taken. The wheels for these grinders, which can be hand or power driven, are either carborundum (silicon carbide) or Aloxite (crystallised fused alumina), and there is little to choose between them except that carborundum is harder and Aloxite tougher.* They are available in a variety of shapes and sizes from 1 in. (25 mm) diameter by $\frac{1}{4}$ in. (6 mm) thickness upwards, and in a range of grits, 6 to 10 very coarse, 12 to 24 coarse, 30 to 60 medium, 70 to 220 fine and 240 to 700 very fine. They are also letter graded which denotes the strength of the bond and not the hardness of the grit which does not vary, from A soft to Z hard, with the main grades F to T. A fair average for the carbon steel used in wood-cutting tools would be about 60 grit F grade; always remembering that the softer the grit the cooler the cut,

* Generally speaking and grit for grit carborundum stones cut faster and wear more rapidly than the denser, tougher Aloxite stones, therefore carborundum is normally used where the stone is applied to the tool, and Aloxite where the tool is applied to the stone.

27   Striking and driving tools

therefore hard steels require soft wheels and soft steels hard wheels, whilst narrow-faced wheels cut cooler as do slow-running wheels, for less steel is taken off at each revolution and therefore less heat generated. Glazed wheels generate heat rapidly, and all wheels should be regularly dressed with a proper wheel dresser. To prevent burning of the tool edge, which not only draws the temper but also causes minute cracks in the bevel, the steel should be frequently quenched in cold water, with the side feed across the face of the wheel as rapid as possible so that only a fractional amount is removed at each pass. Providing all these precautions are taken there is little danger, but careless grinding can soon ruin a good tool, and a blued edge must be avoided at all costs. The above remarks do not apply to high-speed tipped edges.

For the whetting or honing of ground edges (and all edge tools are supplied ground but not honed) a variety of stones are necessary. They can be either India, carborundum, or the slower cutting Washita, which is an inferior form of Arkansas. The old familiar Turkey and Charnley Forest stones are no longer available, whilst true Arkansas are very scarce and expensive. Both India and carborundum grits are artificial, therefore their quality is consistent, but Washita is a natural stone and can vary considerably, with an occasional piece almost too hard to cut: the best, however, will give an excellent edge. All these stones are usually bought in the standard size of 8 in. (203 mm) by 2 in. (50 mm) by 1 in. (25 mm) for sharpening chisels, plane-irons, etc., and should be mounted in a wooden box with a lid as illustrated below, or otherwise covered when not in use.

28　Oilstone box

A nail driven into the base of the box and pinched off to leave about $\frac{1}{16}$ in. (1·5 mm) protruding will prevent the box slipping on the sharpening-table. For general use three oilstone grits are available, coarse, medium and fine; the coarse for the rapid restoration of grinding bevels and the medium and fine for general honing, but for occasional use only double-sided combination stones with coarse and fine grits are obtainable.

For small cutting-tools, gouges, moulding-plane irons, etc., round-edge slip-stones tapering in their thickness are used; also a graduated gouge-stone shown in 29 which will fit an endless variety of sweeps. All abrasive stones must be lubricated to prevent over-heating of the steel, and to float away the accumulated sludge, but on no account should linseed or any other drying oil be used, as they will rapidly oxidise and gum up the stone. Any light machine-oil will serve, or a mixture of 1 part heavy lubricating-oil and 4 parts paraffin well shaken together will both lubricate and clear the pores of the stone. Some stones are sold oil sealed; if not they must be soaked until absorption ceases. Worn stones—and stones for chisels and plane-irons must be perfectly flat—can be resurfaced with carborundum powder and paraffin for artificial stones, sprinkling the mixture on a flat hardwood block and rubbing the stone over it with a circular movement. Natural stones must be rubbed down on a piece of York grindstone or paving-stone, using silver sand and water only.

29　Gouge-stone

Strops

An effective strop for fine cutting edges can be made out of an odd piece of cowhide, unmounted for carving tools so that it can be bent to shape, or glued to a wood base rough (undressed) side uppermost for chisels and plane-irons. The leather is dressed with oil and sprinkled with fine carborundum powder. The old school of craftsman always used the palm of his hand as a very effective strop, but the practice is not to be recommended as it coats the palm with dirty oil which is bound to transfer itself to the wood surface. A basic necessity for the furniture-maker is to keep his hands clean and free from grease, otherwise he will spend half his time cleaning off dirty thumb-prints.

Rasps, files, etc.

Cabinet-rasps are very coarse files but with single pocket-shaped teeth (30:A), instead of the diagonal serrations raised by the stabbing tool in file-making; they are used before the file for the preliminary rapid abrasion of the wood in shaped work. The usual sections are half round (horse-rasps are flat), with one flat side and relatively thin edges, but their use has largely been supplanted by the range of familiar *Surform* tools—flat, half-round and round file, etc.—in which the chisel-type teeth are raised and perforated in a length of spring steel tensioned in file-shaped or planer-type holders. The perforations allow the sawdust to escape without clogging the work, and the cutting action is therefore very rapid, requiring care in handling otherwise the form of the work is soon lost. Files are either single cut (30:B) or double cut (30:C), the former generally used for the softer materials, although steel cutting edges are usually filed with the single cut, which gives more of a true cutting rather than scratching action. They are also made in a range of cuts, rough or coarse, middle, common or bastard, second, smooth, dead smooth and double dead smooth. Probably the best type for wood is the bastard double cut, which cuts with a rasping action, and a compound movement should be used, combining a forward push with a slight rocking action which will level the inequalities left by other tools. Files for saw-sharpening are the

mill saw-file for circular saws, with rounded edges for forming the gullets, and three-corner saw-files for handsaws. Band-saws require a special band-saw taper-file with more pronounced round to the edges, otherwise the acute gullet formed by the sharper edge of the ordinary taper saw-file is very liable to start small cracks in the band-saw. Needle-files are very useful for sharpening small tools, bits, etc., and the dead smooth file for coaxing a fine finish to intricate wood edges which the scraper or sanding block cannot reach.

All files should be treated with respect and not thrown into a box with other tools. Wood-working files can be cleaned with wire file card, or if the teeth are heavily choked with resinous sawdust, gently heated sufficient only to scorch the dust, which can then be brushed out of the serrations. Files used for soft brass or aluminium alloy should be rubbed over with french chalk which helps to prevent clogging. It is not generally realised that a softish brass can blunt the teeth of a file quicker than hard steel, and render it useless for other work. Worn-out mill saw- and flat-files need not be thrown away, for the steel is usually very high quality with high carbon content and carefully hardened. Excellent tools, including chisels and scrapers for lathe turning, can be made from them by careful grinding.

Miscellaneous tools

Illustrated below is the box and tap for cutting wood screws. Such screws are best made from box or hornbeam, although beech can be used if the threads are coarse enough. The screw itself is turned up to the required diameter, 1 in. (25 mm), ¾ in. (19 mm) etc., the end chamfered for entry, and the box or die turned round it in the usual manner to cut the threads. The hole for the tap is then bored to the exact diameter of the circle always marked on the side of the box, and the taper tap fed in.

30 Files

31 Wood screw box and tap

Sanding rubbers

These are blocks of resilient cork or felt-faced wood of convenient size to fit the hand, and usually about 4½ in. (114 mm) by 2½ in. (63 mm) by 1 in. (25 mm) thick to take a quarter sheet of standard 11 in. (280 mm) by 9 in. (228 mm) abrasive paper for straight-line sanding. Shaped blocks to fit hollows, rounds and moulded sections are made up out of softwood as required, and the use of such blocks is always to be preferred, for so-called 'touch sanding' tends to follow depressions and round over edges. For large surfaces a weighted block to take a whole sheet of abrasive paper is invaluable, as small blocks tend to linger over rough patches and create slight undulations which may not be apparent in the white, but which will show up badly under a high gloss polish.

Veneering-hammer

The illustration below shows the simply made veneering-hammer with brass tongue (steel rusts badly with hide glue). An average size for the head will be about 4 in. (101 mm) by 4 in. (101 mm) by $\frac{7}{8}$ in. (22 mm) with a $\frac{3}{4}$ in. (19 mm dowel-rod taken through and wedged. If there is much hand-veneering to be done smaller hammers are useful for inlays, cross-bandings, etc.

32   Veneering-hammer

Glue-pots

The familiar cast-iron double glue-pot with water-jacket and tinned container for use on gas-ring or Primus stove has been largely superseded by the electric glue-pot, either water-jacketed or waterless, and thermostatically controlled to give a constant temperature of around 54 °C (130 °F) which is the safe maximum for hide glue. The advantages of the electric pot are obvious.

Woodworking-vices

The standard 9 in. (228 mm) quick-release woodworking vice with American pattern front dog on the outer jaw is illustrated in figure 42. The front dog is used for holding work against a batten fixed to the bench-top.

Plug-cutters

Cross-grain pellets or plugs for filling screw-holes can be cut with the Stanley plug-cutters illustrated in 33, and available in three sizes for Nos. 6, 8 and 10 screws. These are virtually hollow drills cutting a circular path, of which the core or waste forms the required pellet. Larger sizes cutting standard $\frac{3}{8}$ in. (9·5 mm) and $\frac{1}{2}$ in. (12·5 mm) diameter plugs can be obtained for use in the drill-press or drilling machine.

33   Stanley plug-cutter

Timber-scribe

This is a folding knife with hooked blade as shown below, giving a gouge-like cut and sometimes called a 'raze-knife'. Used for marking the superficial footage on the ends of timber planks, and for scoring the weathered face of the timber to determine grain and colour.

34   Timber-scribe

Cramps and cramping devices

Figure 35A illustrates the usual pattern *G-cramp* with swivel shoe which adapts itself to the contour of the wood, 35B the *Record spin-grip* G-cramp which can be adjusted with one hand

35A Light pattern G-cramp

35B Spin-grip G-cramp

35C Deep-throat G-cramp

35D Light pattern sash-cramp

35E Heavy pattern T-bar sash-cramp

only, and is an excellent improvement on the older type which required two hands to locate and tighten it, and 35C the *Record* deep-throat G-cramp. Light bar *sash-cramps* and lengthening bars are shown in 35D, and the heavy pattern *T-bar* in 35E, whilst 35F is the *Deacon patent tail-slide*, which again is a considerable improvement over the old-type loose shoe and pin. The light bar-cramps with either $\frac{1}{4}$ in. (6 mm) or $\frac{5}{16}$ in. (8 mm) bar section are usually considered to be sufficient for normal cabinet-work, and the heavy T-bar for joiner's work, although lengths over 5 ft (1·5 m) are always T-bar section. In choosing the right cramp for the type of assembly a compromise must be effected between weight and stiffness. Light pattern cramps are inclined to pull the bars hollow if the strain is great, whilst heavy cramps may exert too great a pressure, or with their own weight pull a delicate carcase or framing in winding. All cramping must, therefore, be done on a firm and level base, and the completed assembly carefully checked from every angle to ensure that there is no distortion of any kind.

35F Deacon patent tail slide

35A–F *by courtesy of C. J. Hampton Limited*

Special cramps

Band-cramps are used in shaped work and have a flexible steel band which conforms to the contours. Figure 36:1 shows a simple version. Figure 36:3 is the corner cramping device for mitred frames, etc., simply made out of four hardwood blocks (36:3A) threaded on a length of blind-cord and tightened with a stick; the cramping pressure is positive and considerable. Folding-wedges are shown in 36:4 and an improved version of the old wooden hand-screw in 36:2. The old type has beech chops and hornbeam screws, but the new version has metal screws through pivoted centres, and localised pressure can be applied with the tips of the chops as far inward as the chops will reach according to the size of the cramp. This type of cramp is particularly useful for laying blisters in veneered work, and for all gluing operations away from the edge which the standard G-cramp will not reach. It is axiomatic that no workshop ever has enough cramps of the right kind at any given time, therefore the provision of cramping devices should be as generous as possible. Down-ward pressures can also be obtained with old scale weights up to 56 lb (25·4 kg), sometimes procurable at scrap prices from local dealers' yards; whilst a fletton brick is reasonably flat, square and weighs about 5 lb (2·26 kg), thus a fair pressure can be built up with a small pile of bricks.

In all cramping operations the working surface must be protected by padding the cramp jaws with blocks of thin wood, folded newspaper or pieces of felt or rubber, for even a lightly applied G-cramp can leave an indentation in the wood surface which may be difficult to eradicate. Pressures should also be spread with stout blocks or bearers, particularly in carcase and framed-up work. Metal cramps should be frequently overhauled, the hard glue cleaned off and sash-bars lightly oiled, for there is nothing quite so desperate as a tail slide which refuses to move in the midst of a critical assembly. If resin glues and acid hardeners are used, metal cramps should be isolated from direct contact with the wood surface by scraps of paper, otherwise spilt glue may interact with the steel and deeply stain the wood.

36   Cramping devices: special cramps

3 Portable electric tools and accessories

There is an extensive range of power-tools available which can be used on or at the bench; and whilst they can never supplant the fixed sawbench, planer, spindle-moulder, etc., which are essential basic machines in any trade-shop, nevertheless they are extremely useful adjuncts and can lighten the work considerably, giving also a measure of precision which might not be attainable with pure hand methods. For those purists who insist that handmade furniture must be made exclusively by hand, it is only necessary to point out that a good machine will rip up a piece of wood, plane a surface, drill a vertical hole and cut a dovetail housing or a mortise more accurately and very much more quickly than the hand alone can do. Shoddy workmanship is rarely the work of inefficient machines, but more of the operator's inability to handle them correctly.

All power-driven machines can be grouped within three broad classifications: fixed-type floor-mounted machines for heavy and continuous production work; bench-mounted machines of similar function for lighter or intermittent work which are not strictly portable, although their position can be changed at will; portable power-tools with their own integral motors which can be lifted by one pair of hands and taken to the work; accessories for attachment to an independent power-supply such as the standard drill-gun. Before deciding on which type of machine- or power-tool to instal it is necessary to determine the extent to which it will be used, and whether that amount of use will justify the first cost (including the cost of installation), always bearing in mind that no machine must ever be taxed to its ultimate limit, and there must always be a safe reserve of both power and strength. A fair illustration of these points would be the spindle-moulding machine. As a floor-mounted heavy duty machine it will perform an amazing variety of wood-cutting operations, moulding, shaping, grooving, rebating, dovetailing, etc., continuously and at high speed. As a bench model costing only a fraction of the heavier machine it will lose very little of its versatility, but it will not permit heavy or continuous work without serious overloading, and the final finish will not be so good. As a fully portable high-speed router following the same basic principles most of the versatility will be retained, but the actual cut will be lighter still, and a fair degree of

37A   9-in. heavy duty portable saw

37B   High-speed router

manual skill will be required to control it. As a **range** of accessories for attachment to the **standard** drill-gun a little of the versatility is **retained**, but only for the lightest work. It follows, therefore, that for the handyman at home the drill-gun accessories will probably be sufficient; for the furniture-maker working in a small way the portable high-speed router will be more suitable; for the small trade shop the bench spindle-moulder is large enough, with the portable router as a worthwhile addition; but for the production-shop the heavy duty machine, plus a fixed-type floor-mounted high-speed router, will be essential.

As mentioned before this book is not concerned with heavy production-machines, or even with bench models which follow the same general pattern, but only with fully portable tools and accessories which are in essence hand guided, and can, therefore, be regarded as hand-tools, i.e. extensions of the hand. However, before listing the various types available it should be pointed out that, (1) any portable power-tool complete in itself with its own integral motor is structurally more sound and more efficient in performance than any accessory for attachment to, or to be coupled with, another tool or machine; (2) so-called 'Home-maker' kits which include a basic stand with interchangeable attachments for turning, sawing, drilling, sanding, etc., whilst often admirable in their ingenuity, are more suitable for model-makers, and have little serious approach in furniture-making; (3) the cost of the time spent in coupling up an accessory to another machine or power source every time it is needed may, in the end, far outweigh the greater initial cost of the single-purpose integral-motored machine.

Portable power-tools

These are usually of the integral-motor type in which the motor itself is built in as part of the structure, as distinct from independent belt-driven motors attached to the machine. Various types or categories are available, viz. *light duty*, often described as 'home duty' but intended for intermittent use within the limits of the fractional horsepower (kW) available; *general duty* for tradesmen's use, and robust enough for intermittent but reasonably heavy work; *heavy duty*, with consistent power necessary for production work; and in some cases *super duty*, to give 'fit and forget' service over long periods.

Circular saws (37A)

Sometimes known as 'saw cats' or 'builders' saws', and available in both general and heavy duty models, with a range of saw diameters from 6½ in. (165 mm) to 10 in. (254 mm)—the smallest size will cut slightly over 2 in. (50 mm) thicknesses, and up to 3½ in. (89 mm) for the largest. As a rule all these saws are well balanced, fully adjustable for depth and any angle of cut up to 45°, with automatic retractable lower guard and fixed upper guard, splitting- or riving-knife and ripping fence. In spite of their somewhat fearsome aspect they are safe in use, as the blade is

37c Jigsaw

37D Dustless belt sander

at all times covered and overloading merely stalls the motor. A range of saw-blades is available; combination-saws for ripping and cross-cutting; crosscut for fast, smooth crosscutting and therefore more suitable for plywood than the coarser cut combination-blade; planer-blades which give a very smooth cut and can be relied upon not to rag out the cross grain of ply or crumble chipboard; flooring-blades designed for cutting through occasional nails but very suitable for resin-bonded chipboards etc., which quickly dull the edge of average saws; and a range of soft-metal cutting saws. Heavy gauge sheet-steel pedestal saw-tables or bench-stands can be obtained for these saws, but they can never have the accuracy of the orthodox sawbench, and should, therefore, be regarded as a compromise solution only. Probably the chief uses for these saws in the Furniture Industry are the cross-cutting of random plank and ripping up large sheets of plywood which cannot be handled on the normal sawbench. The rate of cut of these saws at the normal peripheral speed of 10,000 ft. (3048 m) per min. (revolutions per minute multiplied by circumference of saw in feet (0·3048 m)), is about ten times that of handsaws in comparable materials.

Portable planes and woodworkers

These are enclosed motorised jack-planes with rotating cutter blocks fitted with either two or three knives according to the type. They are in essence builders' tools with little application in furniture, as the width of cut is only 4 in. (101 m).

High-speed routers (37B)

These have power-driven vertical spindles on which the appropriate cutters are mounted and fed down to the work; whilst some models have an adjustable side swing movement enabling the width of cut to be increased or extended without moving the router-fence or changing the cutters. Usually these tools rely on speed rather than power output, therefore the depth of cut obtainable at any one setting is fairly small, but the degree of finish is quite high. Many models are available from fractional up to $2\frac{1}{2}$ hp (1·864 kW) with cutting speeds up to 27,000 rpm for the

light-weight models, and a range of cutters for straight-line and circular grooving, moulding, veining, dovetail housing, rebating, slot cutting, edge trimming, etc. The router itself with double handles can be moved freely in any lateral direction, but a range of guides for straight and circular cuts, trammel-points for circles and bases for working against templates give the tool wide versatility. It can also be mounted horizontally, or turned over to act as a fixed spindle-moulder; whilst various dovetail guides and templates will allow box-locking, carcase- and drawer dovetailing up to 25 in. (635 mm) in width. Particular care should be exercised in choosing one of these machines and the nature of the work for which it will be used fairly assessed, for whilst the light-weight models have $\frac{1}{4}$ hp (0·186 kW) motors and a net weight of about $3\frac{1}{4}$ lb (1·475 kg) only, the heaviest models weigh up to 26 lb (11·793 kg), all of which has to be lifted and guided on to the work by one pair of hands. There is of course no kick or side thrust with a good machine, but even so the heavy models do require a certain amount of effort to guide them through heavy cuts and often the light-weight model is a more practical proposition. Properly chosen, in good working order and with a range of cutters, it is, however, an outstandingly versatile machine in the hands of a capable operator. The cutters themselves can be bought to fixed specifications, but some makers quote for 'specials'. Usually both high-speed and tungsten-carbide cutters are obtainable, the latter much more expensive but lasting very much longer in materials bonded with, or composed of, synthetic resin in any form. It is often more satisfactory to send the cutters back to the suppliers for regrinding otherwise the critical profile may be lost, but some makers supply a bit- and cutter-sharpener which uses the machine itself to grind its own cutters. Typical operations performed by these machines are illustrated in 38 and all manufacturers issue fully descriptive literature covering the entire scope.

Veneer-trimmer

A smaller version of the router expressly designed for the rapid trimming of veneered tops, with provision for flush or bevel trimming of acute, obtuse or right-angled laminated edges.

A veneer-trimming attachment is also available for use with some types of standard router.

Jigsaws (37c)

Sometimes known as 'sabre saws' which is more correct as the term 'jigsaw' could also be taken to mean power-driven fretsaws in which the blade is secured at either end. Available in home, general and super duty, some with vertical stroke, others with a cycloid action which keeps the teeth clear of sawdust. The no-load speed is usually around 3000 strokes per minute, with a stroke depth of from $\frac{1}{2}$ in. (12·5 mm) to 1 in. (25 mm) and a cutting depth of up to $2\frac{3}{8}$ in. (60 mm) in softwoods and 1 in. (25 mm) in hardwoods and resin-bonded ply. Various types of blade can be obtained with fine, medium and coarse teeth for sheet metal, fibreglass, plastics, wood, plywoods and chipboards, etc., also knife-blades for leather, latex foam and fibrous materials. As a woodworking-saw it is extremely useful for external or internal straight-line or contour cutting, and for ripping large sheets of ply and chipboard. The rate of cut is fairly slow, but the saw can be operated with one hand only, is easy to guide and can be used for bevel cuts up to 45°.

Electric sanders

The perfect sander hardly exists and the ideal would probably be some form capable of 'random orbit'. At the present time the following types are used: (a) flexible disc sander grinders;

(b) dustless belt sanders; (c) orbital and oscillating pad finishing sanders. Type (a) is of little interest to furniture-makers and is, therefore, not considered, whilst type (b) is the best compromise between disc- and pad sander for the rapid removal of stock, but requires greater care in working, whilst the heavier models tend to overload the fractional horsepower motor with their own weight alone.

Dustless belt sanders (37d)

Available in belt widths of from $2\frac{1}{2}$ in. (63·5 mm) to 4 in. (101 mm), with belt speeds from 1000 to 1700 ft per min. (304 m to 518 m) over a pad size or effective sanding area of about 6 in. (152 mm) long by the full width of the belt— the 3 in. (76 mm) model is the best compromise between weight and power. The vacuum unit incorporated usually sucks about 80 per cent of the fine dust into the detachable bag, therefore the cutting action is not impeded by the loose dust and is considerably faster in consequence. For the rapid removal of stock in wood, metal or plastics these machines can be extremely useful but care should be taken with veneered surfaces as they are inclined to dub over at the ends and cut through the veneer unless waste pieces of material are positioned at each end to prevent the belt dipping. Most models are designed to cut against the belt rotation for easier control, and the direction of the cut should be at a slight angle as shown in 39:1B, rather than with the grain (39·1A). The tool works under its own weight and no bearing down to increase the rate of cut should be attempted.

37E   Heavy duty finishing pad sander

37F $\frac{5}{16}$ in. two-speed drill gun

37A–F *by courtesy of Black and Decker Limited*

V-grooving bit

Beading-bit (two flutes)

Rounding-over bits (two flutes)

Straight bit (single flute)

Straight bits (two flutes)

Veining-bit (single flutes)

Dovetail-bits

Core-box bits (two flutes)

Cove-bit (two flutes)

Chamfering-bit (two flutes)

Rabbetting-bit (one length)

Hinge-mortising and gaining bit

Straight-face cutters

Concave cutter

Convex cutter

Corner bead-cutter

Pad finishing sanders (37E)

Two types are available. Reciprocating (straight-line), in which the pad moves with a backward and forward stroke to give true straight-line sanding with the grain (39:2D): Orbital, in which the pad is rotated in a series of small orbits of about $\frac{1}{8}$ in. (3 mm) to $\frac{3}{16}$ in. (5 mm) diameter (39:2E). There is also an oscillating (swivel) type (39:2C) in which the movement describes an arc only and not an orbit, but these have been superseded by the orbital action type except for drill-gun accessories.

In theory at least the reciprocating type should prove more effective, but in practice there is probably little to choose between it and the orbital type, for with the speed of the cut (4000 to 5000 orbits per min.) there is virtually no scratching across the grain, and in fact a diagonal movement across the grain (39:1B) helps to level out inequalities in the surface. Practically the only drawback with these pad sanders are slight swirl-marks caused by loose grains from the abrasive paper, but if the surface is kept well dusted in advance of the cut they should cause no trouble. The point to remember is that applied pressure does not increase the rate of cut to any appreciable extent, and in fact heavy bearing down may result in the machine itself orbiting rather than the grit.

Various types are obtainable, differing mainly in weight and ruggedness, for the pad size is usually standardised to take a half sheet of 11 in. (280 mm) by 9 in. (228 mm) abrasive paper. The general pattern is a felt-faced or foam-rubber pad permanently attached to the body with an easy lock and release for the abrasive paper, but models are available in which the pad is removable for wet and dry sanding and for contour sanding with thick foam pads. Dust-extractors are fitted to some models, and at least one type has an optional adjustment for either straight-line or orbital sanding built into the machine which offers some advantage, for moulded sections cannot be sanded with the orbital action, but cork counter-profiles can be fixed to reciprocating pads.

All machine sanders require garnet or aluminous oxide papers (see *Abrasives*, chapter 13), and the grit used is generally some grades coarser than for equivalent work by hand methods, owing to the speed of the cut. An 80 grit aluminous oxide paper for instance, will give a sufficiently fine finish on open-grained timber, whereas hand-sanding might require 120 grit for a comparable scratch-free surface.

Drill-guns (37F)

Possibly no single tool is more abused than the standard drill-gun, and it is always surprising that it can accommodate such rough treatment. A multiplicity of types is available, from the $\frac{1}{4}$ in. (6 mm) chuck capacity home model with a chuck no-load speed of 2600 rpm to the $1\frac{1}{4}$ in. (32 mm) capacity heavy duty drill running at 275 rpm. Drills over $\frac{3}{8}$ in. (9·5 mm) chuck capacity are usually two-handed as they have low speed and maximum torque for penetrating the toughest materials, but the usual pattern for woodworking is the pistol-grip gun with a capacity of $\frac{1}{4}$ in. (6 mm), $\frac{5}{16}$ in. (8 mm) or $\frac{3}{8}$ in. (9·5 mm), the $\frac{3}{8}$ in. preferably with two speeds as the normal no-load speed of about 1000 rpm is on the slow side for wood. Capacities up to $\frac{3}{8}$ in. (9·5 mm) are obtainable in home, general and heavy duty guns, and for use with accessories either the general or heavy duty type should be chosen although the light-weight models will perform an amazing number of operations provided they are not sustained and the feed-rate is gentle. The heavier drills are, of course, more robust, usually double insulated, and some have automatic cut-outs to provide against overload. Drilling capacities are usually stated to be up to $\frac{1}{4}$ in. (6 mm) in steel and $\frac{1}{2}$ in. (12·5 mm) in hardwood for the $\frac{1}{4}$ in. (6 mm)

39   Portable sanders: direction of cut

light-weight gun, and up to $\frac{3}{8}$ in. (9·5 mm) and 1 in. (25 mm) respectively for the $\frac{3}{8}$ in. (9·5 mm) model, but much depends on the type of gun and the nature of the hardwood. Stub twist-drills, jobbers' twist-drills and woodworking twist-drills up to $\frac{1}{2}$ in. (12·5 mm), flatbit-drills up to $1\frac{1}{4}$ in. (32 mm), and Jenning's pattern dowel- and auger-bits up to $\frac{3}{4}$ in. (19 mm) are all available with shanks turned down to $\frac{1}{4}$ in. (6 mm) diameter for drill-guns. Great care should be taken when using 'auger-bits with screw-points (see page 38) as the snatch at high speed is very considerable, and can be positively dangerous unless the wood is securely anchored down. Speed reduction units are available, also right-angled speed-changers which will either double or halve the stated speed of the gun,

whilst a positive clutch screwdriving unit will drive up to No. 12 screws providing the gun speed does not exceed 1000 rpm.

Accessories for drill-guns

Numerous accessories are obtainable for sawing, rebating, jigsawing, sanding, polishing, etc., but these are in the main hobbyists' tools. Two accessories are, however, very useful and call for mention.

Vertical drill-stand (40A)

Vertical pillar drill-stands with spring-loaded instant-return feed and fixed table are usually available for all models of drill-guns. With the gun clamped in position the stand becomes an effective vertical table-drill or drill-press for vertical drilling of wood and metal. It lacks the versatility of the orthodox drill-press but will perform most of the main functions of the heavier tool.

40A   Pillar-stand for drill-gun

40B $\frac{1}{2}$ in. capacity five-speed table drill

Dovetailing attachment (135)

Without doubt the most useful of all accessories for use with the ¼ in. (6 mm) or greater capacity gun. Accurate and tight-fitting machine lap dovetails can be cut at ¾ in. (19 mm) pitch in hardwood up to 9 in. (228 mm) in width in any combination of thicknesses from ⅜ in. (9·5 mm) to 1 in. (25 mm). Multi-pitch attachments are also available providing for additional pitches which enable the spacing of the dovetails to fit within any width of timber without clipping off the end pin. No marking out is necessary and both drawer front and side are cut at one operation. The attachment is complete with the necessary guides, templates, dovetail-cutters and roller-bearing arbor for connection to the gun chuck. A dovetail-housing joint accessory which will cut housings in timbers up to 9 in. (228 mm) wide is also marketed, but takes rather long to set up accurately and is of more interest to those who lack experience in cutting this particular joint. (See also *Dovetailing joints*, Chapter 19).

Bench-grinder and drill-press

Strictly speaking these are not portable tools as they should be fixed to a bench or stand. The bench-grinder (40c) is virtually indispensable for the rapid grinding of cutting edges, moulding blanks, etc., and the various abrasive wheels are listed on page 40.

The table-drill or drill-press (40B) equipped with ½ hp (0·373 kW) motor has a range of pulley speeds for wood and metal, graduated feed, locking handle to the feed and swivelling table which can also be tilted for angle drilling. Its ½ in. (12·5 mm) capacity chuck will accommodate all types of machine bits and drills, and it can be used not only for all vertical drilling operations to any preset depth, but also for veining, shallow grooving, light hollow-chisel mortising, bobbin sanding and polishing, etc.

40c   8 in. high-speed bench-grinder

General note

It must always be remembered that wood-working machines with their constantly varying loads as the cutters strike the hard and soft grain of timber are gluttons for power, and that portable tools usually rely more on speed than power output or torque for their performance, therefore they should never be expected to undertake the heavier tasks which should rightly be given to the large horsepower fixed machines. Manufacturers give full and precise instructions and some issue their own handbooks on the techniques to be employed. They are also concerned to make their portable tools as safe as possible in use, but it is the rough usage to which the tools are often subjected which constitutes the danger, and no amount of foresight on the manufacturers' part can prevent a careless worker standing on wet concrete and trailing bare wires everywhere from electrocuting himself. Given correct treatment, with the wiring periodically checked, properly earthed, and the motor itself never taxed beyond its stated capacity the average portable tool, and in particular the drill-gun, will give good service over many years, and have become essentials in every workshop.

40A *and* c
by courtesy of Black and Decker Limited 40B *by courtesy of Startrite Machine Tool Co. Limited*

4 Workshops and workshop equipment

The perfect workshop hardly exists; it will always outgrow itself, or changing fashions will create other demands in working space or equipment. Ideal working conditions regardless of expense could doubtless be formulated; but in all professional work the overriding necessity is to keep the capital outlay within the framework of the turnover to be expected, and every penny spent on premises, equipment or materials must earn its keep if the business is to be successful.

Production-workshop

Mass-produced, i.e. quantity-production, furniture is more the result of business expertise and engineering skill than the application of fine craftsmanship, although furniture is and probably always will be a craft-based industry whilst it continues to use a natural and viable material. The modern factory employs porters, kilners, setters-out, machinists, machine- and hand-sanderers (more highly skilled jobs than they might appear to be), assemblers, finishers, polishers, upholsterers and inspectors, etc., and in the narrow sense expert cabinet-makers might have no place at all in the organisation. However, most large concerns keep a nucleus of skilled craftsmen for prototype-work, whilst all learners and apprentices do, or should receive, Day Release training in either wood machining or the basic hand-skills. In effect, therefore, a modern furniture factory which is efficient, well organised, and anxious to maintain a standard of quality is the basic handshop vastly extended, systemised and mechanised in which the skilled fingers which once held chisels, wielded planes and coaxed satin surfaces from wood have now learnt to use machines for precisely similar functions.

Hand-workshops — planning and equipment

Only general observations are possible for there are so many factors to be considered, number of personnel, type, variety and standard of work which is to be produced, the amount of fixed machinery which is to be employed. In factory production the work-flow can be systematically planned from the kiln-drying units to the polishing-shop through a system of intercommunicating units. In the small handshop which caters for 'specials', 'one off' or contract furniture, with an occasional prototype for a large concern, short runs of smaller items, coffee-tables, etc., and a certain amount of bread-and-butter repair-work, most if not all of these activities must be carried on under one roof and compromises are inevitable.

Siting of the workshop is not of paramount importance, for the handshop is not necessarily dependent on easy road and rail access or a convenient pool of near-by labour, and there have been good shops on mountain-slopes and over mill-streams. More immediate considerations are a three-phase electricity supply, good natural lighting, a dry shop and pleasant surroundings, for the psychological effect is considerable with skilled craftsmen working to high standards. Concrete, asbestos and galvanised iron for the structure should be avoided wherever possible for they all condense heavily in changeable weather, which is bad for work and tools alike. The ideal would be either cavity brick or a timber-clad structure lined with insulation board, and a tiled, slated or boarded and felted roof. Windows should be adequate to give a general flooding, for lighting from one side only can create dark shadows and dangerous twilight areas. North lighting may be cool, clean and factual, but is psychologically unhappy over long periods, whilst south lighting is good but must be screened in summer otherwise hot sunshine through glass can play havoc with unprotected wood surfaces. Artificial lighting should be plentiful*; but whilst fluorescent

* Workshop lighting. Suggested illumination levels are: rough sawing and bench-work, 15 lumens per sq. ft (929 cm²); medium machine- and bench-work, veneering, etc., 20 lumens per sq. ft (929 cm²); fine bench- and machine-work, sanding and finishing, etc., 30 lumens per sq. ft (929 cm²). Colour matching/north-light fluorescent

lighting is excellent for general flooding it creates little if any shadow and it is then difficult to judge both depth and surface texture, therefore drop pendants over each bench are essential if there is much working after nightfall. In particular all fixed machinery should be lit from every angle with no harsh shadows; but the quality of the lighting must be such that all moving parts are seen to be moving. Power-points should be numerous also, and here again pendent leads over each bench will keep the working surfaces free from trailing cables.

If heavy machinery is included in the workshop some form of concrete raft is necessary, with the working areas round each machine heavily dressed with coarse carborundum powder in the surface screeding; but the rest of the working area is better capped with wood if possible, for bare concrete surfaces are cold, dusty, hard and tiring to work on, and inimical to dropped tools. Wooden floors should not be waxed or polished in any way for they soon become slippery, and this is the chief objection against composition floors. Heating should be sufficient to conform to the minimum requirements of the Factory Act (15 °C), (60 °F), and there is much to be said for the old-fashioned round coke-burning stove which radiates its heat in all directions and can also be used for burning all the rubbish. It does not constitute any additional fire risk providing it is placed on a raised concrete platform, that the ashes are not allowed to accumulate, and the floors are kept free from shavings. The aim should be to maintain an even temperature not too hot and certainly not overdry, and localised electric fan-heaters which can be swivelled in any direction are not the happiest solution, for if forgotten they can soon ruin unprotected work. For heating the old water-jacketed glue-pot a gas-ring is better than an electric boiling-ring, whilst a water service with glazed sink is essential for modern adhesives.

---

tubes are suitable for veneer matching, staining and polishing, etc., whilst the final inspection of furniture where surface perfection is looked for should be done in a light source large in size and low in brightness. The ideal is inspection on a revolving platform against a brightly illuminated screen.

Regulations

Planning permission must be obtained for all hand-workshops unless previous ownership has established the use. New authorisations are rarely given except in areas specifically set aside for industrial use, but there could be no possible objection to a householder equipping an existing room or building as a workshop entirely for his own enjoyment. Once he employs other people, however, then his workshop becomes a factory within the meaning of the Act; the district Factory Inspector must be notified and the regulations regarding personnel, safety and hygiene conformed with. The local bye-laws must also be consulted, particularly those controlling the use of spray-booths for inflammable materials (cellulose, etc.). For the owner's own protection he should make doubly sure that he is amply covered by insurance for Fire, Theft, Consequential Loss, Employers' Liability, Contingent (Third Party) Risks, Work in Custody, Goods in Transit, etc., etc. If his turnover is over £500 per annum then he must register with the Customs and Excise and pay Purchase Tax at the rate currently in force. The ruling does not mean that the first £500 of his expected turnover is free of tax (*that amount which with the appropriate amount of tax added shall equal or exceed £500 per annum*). Once he goes over he pays on everything, and the relief is only designed to help small craftsmen who do not regularly exceed that figure.

The list of things to be done and which cannot be done in this modern society is formidable, and country workshops are fortunate in that the admirable Rural Industries Bureau of Wimbledon, Surrey will help, guide and advise on all matters relating to the craft, from the acquisition of a small workshop to the final cost accounting of the finished product. The facilities are gratis and paid for out of a Government grant, but are, unfortunately, not available to town workshops. However, the booklets issued by the Bureau are available to anyone.

Workshop equipment

Fittings, fixtures, loose tools, etc.

Good benches are indispensable for handwork; the joiner's softwood bench usually knocked up from 3 in. (76 mm) by 9 in. (228 mm) deals is not suitable. Cabinet-benches should be of hardwood, preferably beech, rock steady and perfectly level, for the eye will always attempt to compensate for any slope, thus vertical cuts are likely to be out of square if the bench-top is sloping. A quick-action woodworker's vice (42) should be fitted and an end vice also; and 43 gives the constructional details of a standard bench with 2½ in. (63·5 mm) beech top and underframing, which should not be less than 6 ft (1·828 m) long. Benches of this type are obtainable from Parry and Sons Ltd of Old Street, London. Assembly-benches need only be softwood and require no vices but here again they should be robust, steady and truly level. Separate benches for gluing up, especially for the hand-coating of glue on veneers, etc., are probably a luxury but well worth the extra space if it can be provided, for resin glues set glass hard and have an unholy knack of badly scarring wrought surfaces if allowed to harden on working-tops. Oilstones and bench-grinder also deserve a special bench or table, preferably with metal-lined top, and placed in the most convenient position with equal access for every maker. This saves litter on work-benches and helps to keep the surfaces clean.

A long slot for hand-tools is provided at the back of the standard bench (43:1), but wall-mounted racks over the bench are more convenient and leave the bench-top free for wide work. At least two sawing-horses (44) are needed for supporting planks whilst crosscutting, also two low stools of similar construction 12 in. (304 mm) high and with 9 in. (228 mm) wide tops as stands for carcases in the making, and a low platform-trolley on stout castors is invaluable for moving furniture or heavy planks of timber. Cramping devices should be conveniently racked for immediate use, with G-cramps hung in graded sizes on pegs or long nails, and sash-cramps either from wall-pegs or in a special rack (41). Other items necessary will be dust-sheets for the protection of finished work; softening blankets for bench-tops to protect delicate surfaces (ex-army blankets are excellent); a good pair of household or greengrocer's scales with some additional small weights for resin glues; dusting-brushes or a portable electric blower which is also invaluable for cleaning machines; photographic rubber rollers for spreading glue; a few metal-workers' tools including an engineer's vice; innumerable small containers, tins, jars, etc., for mixing small quantities of glue; old newspapers or cellophane sheets for press-work; soft rag . . . the list is well-nigh endless, but three months actual working will provide the answers.

Storage

This can be a nightmare if unorganised and should be methodically planned. Timber in bulk can be stored in open sheds protected from the weather; but plywoods, blockboards, etc., and timber for immediate requirements should be kept in a warm store or conditioning-room adjacent to the workshop. Veneers are best kept in cool, not overdry conditions or they become brittle; but they desperately need floor space and

41 Cramp-rack

42 Woodworker's vice with end dog
By courtesy of C. J. Hampton Limited

2 SECTION TOP

1

B

A

5
METAL
STOP

6 METAL
VICE A

FIXED

MOVING

3

1
FEET   0   1   2

2, 3, 4
FEET   0   CMs   1

1   0 5   15   25   35   45

2, 3, 4   0   5   10   15   20   25

4

SECTION
END VICE B

UNDER PLAN END VICE B

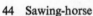
44 Sawing-horse

covering cloths, for constant turning over or exposure to strong sunlight will speedily ruin them. The problem will always be short ends of valuable timber, but a balance must be struck between the intrinsic value of the wood and the cost per man-hour of unearthing a particular piece from underneath a pile of junk, therefore it will pay in the end to be fairly ruthless. Dowel-rod should be kept high up in the main shop where the warm air circulates. It is always debatable whether cupboards or open shelving are best for storing the innumerable small tools and effects which are soon collected in a busy workshop. Brasswork and ironmongery, particularly screws and nails, etc., should have their own closed containers or screw-cabinet, but for the rest, open shelves collect dust especially if machines are used in the workshop, whilst cupboards take up valuable space and tend to hide their contents. The owner must therefore decide for himself which is more suitable, but he will never have enough shelving.

Machines

Certain basic machines are indispensable to every workshop even where handwork pre-dominates. These are in order of priorities (a) sawbench, (b) jointer or surface-planer, (c) thicknesser (panel-planer) which can be combined with (b) as a surface-planer and thicknesser, (d) bandsaw, (e) spindle-moulder or portable router, (f) lathe, (g) drill-press, (h) hollow-chisel mortiser, (i) dowel-borer, (j) radial arm-saw. If much veneer-work is done then either a screw-operated or vacuum-bag veneer-press will need a high priority, whilst production shops would place the dovetailing-machine and belt sander high on the list. Where it is intended to instal only the most basic machines then obviously the sawbench, planer and band-saw will take pride of place.

Circular sawbench (45A)

As a rough approximation it is usual to take one-third of the diameter of a circular saw as its effective cut, therefore a 15 in. (381 mm) saw giving a cut of about 5 in. (127 mm) would be about the minimum for general work. However, many large concerns do not use timber thicker than 1½ in. (38 mm) building up for larger dimensions, and this greatly simplifies their stocks, whilst large-diameter saws are no longer necessary and most of the work is done on the 12 in. (304 mm) sliding-table panel-saw (45B) which is an excellent compromise if large boards of ply and chipboard are used to any great extent. Additionally it is never advisable to fit small saws for ripping out stringings and bandings, etc. to large-diameter sawbenches, but they could be used in the smaller benches. Whatever sawbench is chosen it should be robust, adequately guarded, with rise and fall spindle and tilting fence, and with a minimum 3 hp (2·237 kW) motor for 12 in. (304 mm) or 15 in. (381 mm) benches.

45A   20 in. sawbench

45B   12 in. sliding-table panel-saw

Planer (45c)

A skilled machinist can accurately thickness a panel on an overhand-planer (jointer) but it requires some practice. Large concerns would have both types, i.e. overhand planer and combined over-planer and thicknesser (45D), but in small workshops the latter will do everything necessary. It should be as large as the budget will allow, preferably not less than 16 in. (406 mm) (overhand) by 9 in. (228 mm) (thicknessing), and the overhand-tables are essential for taking out the wind on one surface of the timber or the thicknessing rollers will merely flatten the wind before the cut is engaged, and the board will revert to its former shape. The effectiveness of the machine is, therefore, dependent on the width of the overhand and not the depth of the thicknesser, which is made large enough to take builders' 3 in. (76 mm) by 9 in. (228 mm) deals.

45c   16 in. hand-feed planer

45D   Surface-planer and thicknesser

Band-saw (45E)

The effectiveness of this machine is governed by the throat depth, i.e. distance from saw to body framework, and a 20 in. (508 mm) band-saw will cut a width of 19½ in. (495 mm) and a depth or thickness of 13 in. (330 mm). The smaller machines (12 in. (304 mm) throat, etc.) have small-diameter saw-pulleys imposing greater strain on the band-saws, therefore here again it should be as large as possible. All machines have (or should have) tilting table and ripping fence, and the larger models semi-automatic tensioning to the saw-blade, including a warning signal for slack saws, foot-brake, cleaning brushes to the saw-pulleys, and positive adjustment to the ripping fence. If the machine is large enough it can be considered as a dual-purpose substitute for the circular sawbench.

Combination woodworker (45F)

This is more of a builder's or small joiner's machine, but where working space is heavily restricted, or where the amount of use will hardly justify installing individual machines there is much to be said for a combination woodworker in which a sawbench, radial arm-saw, combined planer and thicknesser and boring head are incorporated in one body, thus reducing the total cost by up to 30 per cent. Obvious disadvantages are the restricted working-tables and the time lost setting up for the individual operations.

Various other production machines are illustrated in 47, i.e. *hollow-chisel mortiser*; *Maka swing-chisel mortiser* which can be used as a

45E   Band-saw

45F   Combination woodworker

45A–E *by courtesy of Wadkin Limited*, 45F *by courtesy of Dominion Co. Limited*

MORTISER

6'0"
1·82 m

X

SAWBENCH

6'0"
1·82 m

X

PLANER

6'0"
1·82 m

X

CROSSCUT
SAW

18'0"
5·48 m

X = OPERATOR

fixed or portable mortising-machine and deep-slotter; single-type spindle-moulder; 6 in. (152 mm) under and over belt sander; high-speed router. (The illustration on page 63 shows a typical example of the type of work done on the high-speed router). A home-made dowel-borer is shown in 48. This was assembled out of engineering scrap with a $\frac{1}{2}$ hp (0·373 kW) motor, screw-actuated rise and fall, and dovetail slide horizontal movement for the working-table taken from an old milling-machine bought in the local scrap-yard. A $\frac{1}{4}$ in. (6 mm) sliding rod under the table provided an effective distance-stop, and the $\frac{1}{2}$ in. (12·5 mm) capacity Jacobs chuck was mounted direct on to the motor spindle. With the table set at the right height and pushed forward by the pre-set distance against the revolving bit it gave very accurate borings, and such machines, either independent or as accessories coupled to other machines, are invaluable for accurate dowel-work. Minimum safe working distances between machines are shown in 46; and where space is limited the 'in' or 'out' feed distance can often be increased by placing the machine in line with a doorway, or fitting sliding hatches to the adjacent wall.

47A Hollow-chisel mortiser

47C Maka swing-chisel mortiser

47D Single-spindle moulder

47B 6 in. under and over belt sander

47E   High-speed router

48   Dowel-boring machine

47A, B, D–F *by courtesy of Wadkin Limited,* 47C *by courtesy of Maka*

Safety precautions

Special regulations lay down the legal require-ments in respect of guards and appliances which must be fitted to and used in connection with woodworking machines (SR & O 1922 No. 1996 and SR & O 1945 No. 227). Forms Nos. 227 and 279, issued by the Ministry of Labour and obtainable from any H.M. Stationery Office, give information on the various safety pre-cautions, and although they are only enforceable where outside labour is employed, nevertheless any craftsman on his own should for his own safety acquaint himself with the requirements. Additionally, as handshops inevitably attract visitors warning notices should be prominently displayed on the following lines:

VISITORS

Keep well away from the machinist and from all moving parts of the machine.

Never distract the attention of the machinist whilst he is working.

Do not startle him or address any remark to him whilst the machine is running.

47F   Square turning on legs with high-speed router

5 Workshop organisation

Costing and estimating

Costing is the pricing of completed work taking into account not only all the direct expenses, materials, wages and insurances, fuel and power, machining costs, workshop expenses, etc., but also a fair proportion of the indirect expenses or Establishment charges, salaries, office expenses, rent, rates, depreciation, interest on capital, etc., expressed as a percentage addition to the workshop cost. Estimating is the intelligent anticipation of what the total cost is likely to be, and as such must have a basis of actual costing experience. In other words good estimating is the product of sound judgment and careful appraisal of the amount of labour involved in the proposed work, in the light of past experience of other comparable work.

In costing and estimating for quantity production the work can be broken down into a sequence of bulk operations, and accurately priced by cost accountants and experts in work-study. Where large runs are contemplated, or where a totally new design is to be introduced, a finished prototype will be made by skilled craftsmen, knocked down into its component parts, further simplified or systematised for repetition machining, and then costed either with trial-runs of the individual components or recorded costing of other similar operations. This measure of accuracy, often carried to decimal points of pence per item, is not attainable in hand-production for most of the work will be continually breaking fresh ground, therefore the estimator must rely on his own good judgment, building up as he goes his own personal file of cross-reference. There are, however, certain guiding principles which, whilst they will not solve his equations for him, will at least suggest a method.

Costing for handwork

The cost of any piece of woodwork will consist of several factors, each of which must be independently valued. Some, if not all, of these costs are always present in any analysis or build-up, and should be itemised as follows:

Materials

Timber, plywoods, veneers, etc.: actual net bulk purchase or replacement cost, whichever is higher, including haulage, stacking, weathering, etc., to which must be added the appropriate wastage factors.

Brasswork, ironmongery, etc.: cost of screws, nails, brasswork, special fittings, etc. at purchase price or replacement value.

Sundry materials: all other miscellaneous materials, including glue, glasspaper, polishing materials, etc., directly chargeable to the work. As it is sometimes difficult to assess the amounts of such items as glue, sanding and polishing materials, etc. consumed in any one job, the total cost over the year is sometimes expressed as a percentage addition, but the system is likely to be unfair to some classes of work, and it is better to itemise wherever possible.

Labour

The total cost of labour in man-hours at the rates paid, plus overtime rates where applicable, and apprentices' hours at the appropriate percentage rate plus allowance for Day Release training, plus National Health Insurance, Graduated Pensions, Selective Employment Tax, Holidays with Pay, Redundancy Pay, etc. Here again these may be added to the hourly rate, or as percentage additions to the wage total. Strictly speaking, either method is not really accurate, for most of the charges remain the same whether a man works 40 or 60 hours a week; but the percentage addition is the simplest method.

Machine costs

The cost per running hour of each machine arrived at in accordance with the following typical example:

Sawbench

Initial cost	£200

Estimated life 20 years, depreciation per year	£10
Interest at 6 per cent per annum	£12
Annual value	£22
Annual cost of maintenance and repairs	£15
Annual electric power consumed	£20
Annual saw replacements, sharpening, etc.	£20
Annual cost	£77

(The figures quoted are purely hypothetical for illustration purposes only.)

Assuming that the average use of the sawbench is 20 hours a week for 50 weeks in the year, then the hourly rate will be £77÷20×50=1/6·48 pence (7·7 new pence) per hour, exclusive of the machinist's wages. If the use is only 10 hours per week then the hourly rate will be doubled, or, if more, reduced accordingly. Where, however the machine or machines are only used intermittently and by several craftsmen instead of one particular machinist, which is more often than not the usual practice in handshops, then it may be difficult or impossible to keep accurate records, and the only method which can be adopted is to value the machines as above, and to include the total costs of all machines, not including craftsmen's wages, in workshop overheads. The latter method was used by the writer in his own handshops, and worked reasonably well over a number of years.

Subcontractors

Where fixed sums for specialist subcontractors have to be included in an estimate, i.e. P.C. (Prime Cost) sums where the exact cost is known, or Provisional sums to cover the probable cost, it is usual to add a 5 per cent charge for handling.

Carriage of goods

If the proprietor maintains his own transport for the conveyance of finished furniture the cost per running mile must be arrived at and added accordingly; or if transport is to be hired on each occasion then the estimated cost can be added

before or after Establishment charges have been included in the final estimate.

Percentage additions

To the cost of labour, materials and machine costs, etc. must be added a fair proportion of the workshop overheads and the Establishment charges. Workshop overheads will be all the expenses (indirect expenses) incurred by the workshop which cannot be debited *in toto* to one particular job, i.e. foreman's time in general supervision, heating, lighting, maintenance and repairs, carriage of goods 'in' and sundry materials, etc., but not including rent, rates, insurances or interest on capital. Establishment charges will be salaries, rent, rates, insurances, office expenses, car expenses, depreciation, audit fees, interest on capital, profit, etc., etc. Both workshop overheads and Establishment charges will be expressed as percentage additions to the direct cost of the work.

Where the business has been in existence for some time accurate assessment of all indirect expenses can be made, but commencing businesses will have to estimate for them until sufficient data has been accumulated. A typical costing where many of the factors are still unknown could be as follows:

Estimated total yearly wages paid say £1000		
Estimated Insurances, HWP, Pensions, etc. say 10 per cent	£100	
		£1100
Estimated workshop overheads at 40 per cent on £1100	£440	
		£1540
Estimated materials consumed at cost	£500	
15 per cent profit	£75	
		£2115
Estimated Establishment charges at 20 per cent	£423	
Estimated total turnover		£2538

From the above example it will be seen that out of the total estimated turnover £515 would be available for all the indirect expenses of the workshop, and an additional £423 to provide for all expenses incurred in running the business, including the owner's own remuneration and profit over and above the wages he would pay himself if he also worked at the bench with his craftsmen. Working masters who do not employ labour often price their work at the standard craftsman's rate per hour plus 50 per cent, plus the bare cost of the materials used, but they will usually find that they are either grossly underpaying themselves or rapidly drifting into bankruptcy.

Estimating labour in handwork

Where no previous records are available the proprietor must assess his own capabilities and those of his employees. Unfortunately Builders' Price books for Joinery, in which the labour content of all normal woodworking items are listed in detail, do not apply; but the method of detailing, *viz.* 2 in. (50 mm) two-panelled door 2 ft 6 in. (762 mm) by 6 ft 6 in. (1·981 mm) moulded one side and square: labour cutting out and planing $1\frac{1}{2}$ hr, grooving $\frac{1}{2}$ hr, moulding $\frac{1}{2}$ hr, mortising and tenoning and framing-up $3\frac{1}{2}$ hr, total 6 hr (machining would be listed separately) is sound enough if it can be followed, but more than likely to grossly underestimate the labour content in comparable furniture-work. Common joinery items (and the price books are based on 'run of the mill' joinery) are usually in softwood of fairly large dimensions, with no careful selection of materials and no elaborate detailing. In furniture, hardwoods require from 10 per cent to 20 per cent more time to work, more time to cut the smaller joints, more time to finish off; and a cabinet-door only a quarter of the size of a standard softwood door might take twice as long to make. The only practical method, therefore, is to see the work as a whole and attempt an assessment of the hours required to make it in terms of one man's labour; then to itemise the various operations, i.e. making working drawings, setting out, preparation of jigs and templates, getting out stuff (plenty of time should be allowed for this as it entails careful selection), sawing out and planing up for carcase, jointing carcase, getting out drawer stuff, framing drawers, fitting drawers (again allow plenty of time), etc., etc., timing each operation individually and thus arriving at an alternative total. With a little experience and given the normal perspicacity

the two totals should not be far apart and the average reasonably accurate. Points to watch will be (1) a general tendency to underestimate for small work, particularly where there is fine detailing, (2) failure to allow for the extra labour involved in lifting, handling and helping to set up large and heavy work, which may necessitate the help of several craftsmen as the work progresses, (3) failure to allow for mistakes in setting out, or defects in material which develop in the making. One thing is reasonably certain, the average newcomer will usually underestimate the amount of labour involved, for it is a perfectly natural failing to overestimate one's own speed and accuracy. In the first few months of working, therefore, the time allowance should be generous, for again the newcomer will be frightened of allowing too much, and will often quote at uneconomic prices in his anxiety to secure the work.

Setting out

Full-size drawings or rods are necessary for setting out the work, showing the exact dimensions and constructional methods to be employed. Normally, design-drawings do not show the constructional methods unless they are of an unorthodox nature; and it is generally assumed that the furniture will be made in accordance with established custom; therefore the setter-out must decide the kinds of joint which will ensure adequate strength and rigidity in the construction, within the framework of the price factor and the designer's clear intention. In other words he must be a sympathetic interpreter, but at the same time completely practical in his approach.

Working drawings can be on paper, on sheets of plywood or on rods. The rods were almost invariably used in joiners' shops, and the lines were broken to condense the overall dimensions into a narrow pine rod about 9 in. (228 mm) wide and $\frac{1}{2}$ in. (12·5 mm) thick. The method is useful for tall fitments, large bookcases, fitted wardrobes, panelling, etc., but a full-size drawing which is ummistakably clear is always simpler in the end. Front elevation, side sectional elevation and plan can be superimposed on one drawing if necessary, outlining the side view in blue pencil and the plan in red; but here again it is better to keep them apart if the furniture-piece is at all complex. Figure 331 shows a fairly typical example of a full-size working drawing (reduced in scale for reproduction purposes only) of the cocktail cabinet described in Chapter 37. Figure 331:1 shows the front elevation, 331:2 the side elevation, 331:4A and B the plan halved on the centre-line to show the lower framing and the upper carcase with shaped interior shelf. Working details of the carcase construction, leg framing and lower shelf are shown in 331:6, door construction in 331:5, and drawer details in 331:7. Alternative methods of carcase construction and applied lippings are illustrated in 331:3, but in actual practice only one method need be shown.

In preparing working drawings the scaled dimensions of the original design-drawing must be followed and no allowance made for fair facing, etc. Thus a section shown as 3 in. (76 mm) thick must be taken as 3 in. (76 mm) thick finished section; whereas in joinery practice it is taken for granted that a specified dimension will conform to the standard sawn sizes for softwoods, or if shown as, say, 3 in. (76 mm) by 2 in. (50 mm) will in reality be ex sawn 3 in. (76 mm) by 2 in. (50 mm) or approximately $2\frac{3}{4}$ in. (70 mm) by $1\frac{3}{4}$ in. (44 mm) net finished thickness, unless expressly stated to the contrary.

Jigs

Jigs are work-holders or guides for shaping; thus the bench-hook is a simple form of jig to support small sections of timber during cutting. They are widely used in machine-work, particularly in spindle moulding and routering, and the reader is referred to machine-handbooks for

details. The term 'jigsaw' is an abbreviation of 'jigger' saw and has no connection.

Templates

Templates or patterns will be required for curved and shaped details, mouldings, etc. These can be cut from thick card, ·06 in. (1·5 mm) ply or zinc sheet according to the amount of use; whilst the outlines can be traced with carbon paper, by rubbing the back of the drawing with a soft lead pencil and then tracing through, or by pricking through with a needle. The templates must be dead accurate and carefully sanded or filed to the correct outline, with the position of any abutting member, i.e. rail to leg, pencilled in. A simple card template for a shaped leg is illustrated in 50, and careful setting out will save valuable timber as shown.

Measured work

Where new work has to be fitted to existing work or built to arbitrary dimensions, as for instance, built-in cupboards or panelling, on-site measurements must be taken. Assuming that an interior has to be measured (49:1) individual details should not be measured separately, but a running total should be preserved. Where corners or angles occur then templates should be made up from slat-wood (49:2), screwed together and carefully numbered; they can then be unscrewed, bundled and reassembled in the workshop. Curves or irregular shapes can be scribed by fitting a waste piece of ply, etc. up against the curve and scribing with a pair of wing-compasses, small block or the workshop rule, or a piece of stiff brown paper can be slit

49 Site measurements and templates

PLAN

1

2

3

as shown in 49:3, the paper pushed against the curve and the strips bent back as in the dotted line. The approximate outline is then transferred to a piece of ply and corrected as necessary. For small details the Maco brass template shown in 219, Chapter 30 is invaluable. Cupboards which have to fit existing openings must either have scribing fillets planted on or extra wide stiles or marginal moulds which are scribed and cut to the opening on the site. It is never wise to assume that plastered walls will be straight, corners square or floors level, for they rarely are.

Copying details

Impressions of carvings, mouldings, etc. are taken with artist's modelling-wax, hot paraffin-wax or dental quality plaster of Paris obtainable at most chemists. Plaster will give the cleanest impression providing there is no undercutting and the original is heavily waxed to facilitate release. From this first impression a mould can be struck, again with plaster of Paris, which can be used as a pattern for metal casting. More permanent moulds can be formed with resin-impregnated glass fibre (see also Chapter 14, page 160) and for small work with intricate detail Araldite epoxy cement with or without reinforcement. CIBA (ARL) Ltd, Duxford, Cambridge will give the necessary technical information. Details of flat relief carvings, frets, etc. can be obtained by laying a sheet of paper on the carving and rubbing over with heelball or soft-lead pencil. Inlays and marquetry-work can also

50 Setting out with card template

be rubbed in this way, for there is usually sufficient proudness or recession of the individual pieces to give a reasonable impression which can be sketched in more firmly.

Cutting lists

Cutting lists are prepared from the full-size drawings and rods and precisely enumerate all the individual pieces of timber required. They can be dead nett or finished dimension, allowing only for jointing, or including the standard allowances for cutting, etc., viz. $\frac{1}{2}$ in. (12·5 mm) on each length and $\frac{3}{16}$ in. (5 mm) ($\frac{3}{32}$ in. (2·5 mm) per wrot face) in the width (thicknesses are always actual). The finished-dimension list is probably less confusing, whilst each piece can be easily identified on the drawing. Where tenons, dovetails or housings, etc. occur it is easier to measure right across the carcase or framework, not just the shoulder length of the bridging-piece plus the length of the tenons, etc. A specimen cutting list for the cocktail cabinet illustrated in 331 and 331A is shown below. The dimensions are net throughout with allowances for jointing. Requisitions for brasswork and ironmongery can be made on the same list or on a separate schedule.

Timber calculations

In calculating the timber content of a cutting list for costing purposes the appropriate wastage factors must be added. Whereas softwood in scantling dimensions may only need from 5 per cent to 10 per cent addition, square-edge hardwoods will require 15 per cent to 20 per cent, and most waney edge boards and planks 60 per cent, with the exception of certain wasteful timbers, English walnut, rosewood in the log, etc., where the true waste factor may be as high as 200 per cent. Plywoods, blockboards, etc. bought carefully to suit the dimensions needed may only require 10 per cent, but an average 20 per cent is safer, whilst most veneers will need at least 50 per cent. Where there is any doubt it is always better to debit the whole planks, sheets or leaves to the job and credit back the useable surplus, not including rippings and offcuts.

Cutting list

Job No ......
Cocktail Cabinet—English Walnut
Customer.................................

Order No. ....
Date ....

Mark	Description	No.	Length		Width		Thick		Wood	Notes
			in.	mm	in.	mm	in.	mm		
	Carcase									
A	Top	1	30	762	17 13/16	452	3/4	19	Solid	
B	Base	1	29 5/8	752·5	17 13/16	452	3/4	19	Solid	
C	Sides	2	26 13/16	681	17 13/16	452	3/4	19	Solid	
D	Fixed shelf	1	28 7/8	733·5	17 3/4	452	5/8	16		Not lipped
E	Back	1	26 5/8	676	29 5/8	752·5	1/4	6	Ply	Rebated
F	Adjustable shelf	1	28 1/2	724	6	152	1/2	12·5	Ply	
G	Shaped shelf	1	28 1/2	724	16 1/2	419	1/2	12·5	Solid	
H	Front lippings		10 ft	3048	3/4	19	3/16	5	Solid	No tongues
	Doors									
I	Stiles	4	20 7/8	530	1 11/16	43	3/4	19	Solid	
J	Rails	4	14 1/4	362	1 11/16	43	3/4	19	Solid	
K	Panels	2	17 7/8	454	11 1/4	286	5/8	16	Solid	
	Drawer									
L	Front	1	28 1/2	724	4	102	7/8	22	Solid	
M	Sides	2	17	432	4	102	1/2	12·5	Oak	
N	Back	1	28 1/2	724	3 1/4	82·5	1/2	12·5	Oak	
O	Bottom	1	27 7/8	708	17	432	1/4	6	Ply	Limba
	Stand									
P	Legs	4	21 1/2	546	1 7/8	48	1 7/8	48	Solid	Tapered to 1 in (25 mm)
Q	Long rails	2	29 1/4	743	2	51	7/8	22	Solid	Tenoned
R	Side rails	2	17	432	2	51	7/8	22	Solid	Tenoned
S	Shelf rails	2	17 3/8	441	1 1/4	32	3/4	19	Solid	Tenoned
T	Shelf	1	29	737	12 1/2	317·5	3/8	9·5	Ply	Veneered
U	Shelf lippings	2	28 1/2	724	5/8	16	1/2	12·5	Solid	
V	Shelf veneers	2	29	737	12 1/2	317·5	—	0·7	Walnut	

Brasswork
4 Brass handles; 2 pairs 2 in. (50 mm) brass butts and screws; 8 Shelf pegs brass; 36 Sockets for pegs; Screws for ply back

Note. Metric conversions are approximate only.

6 Workshop geometry and drawing

Some knowledge of elementary geometric drawing is necessary for the preparation of workshop drawings or 'full sizings', which are in effect accurately drawn full-size outlines of the object to be made, prepared from the smaller scale drawings of the designer. No elaborate equipment is necessary, nor need the setter-out be a skilled draughtsman, but he should understand the principles involved.

Equipment

Drawings can be made on narrow rods (see 'Setting Out', Chapter 5), on plywood sheets, or on a drawing-board which can be a piece of good-quality ply or laminboard with an outer facing of close-grained timber, planed up truly square on all four edges. A 30 in. (762 mm) T-square is necessary which the craftsman can make for himself (51:1), using $\frac{1}{8}$ in. (3 mm) finish straight-grained mahogany for the blade, which should taper from about 4 in. (101 mm) at the heel to 2 in. (50 mm) at the tip, and a 12 in. (304 mm) by 2 in. (50 mm) by $\frac{1}{2}$ in. (25 mm) stock secured to the blade with short brass screws and a small dab of glue in the centre only. The stock is usually lipped with a darker timber, ebony or close-grained rosewood, bevelled off as shown at 51:1A and B, and the blade is similarly treated, with the lip tongued. A hole is bored at the tip for the square to be hung under its own weight, and the wood is sealed and polished with shellac varnish or cellulose. Set-squares are also required, both 60° and 45° and up to 12 in.

(304 mm) in length (the key-jointed mahogany square lipped with ebony (51:2) is excellent for workshop use), also a long wooden straight-edge, adjustable set-square or protractor, scale rules, dividers, pencil-compass and a beam-compass or set of trammel-points for large sweeps. Pencils should be HB, H and 4H of good quality, sharpened to a long point with about $\frac{1}{4}$ in. (6 mm) of lead exposed. Paper when used need only be the cheaper detail paper obtainable in widths up to 5 ft (1:5 mm), or rolls of good-quality paperhanger's lining paper which can be taped together to form larger sheets. Drawing-pins are now rarely used, and the paper can be taped to the board with draughting or cellulose tape.

Drawings

Drawings should be lightly done at first, using a medium hard pencil and boldly outlining when correct, whilst a 4H pencil should be used for critical measurements. Moulded sections should be heavily outlined to show the correct profile, and all end-grain sections cross-hatched for easy identification. Curved lines should be drawn first and straight lines carried into them, whilst tracing through to another sheet or to the bare wood can be done with carbon paper or rubbing the back of the drawing with a very soft pencil and then tracing through from the face. Both plans and elevations can be superimposed on one sheet, outlining them in different coloured crayons, but to avoid confusion it is better to keep them well apart wherever possible.

51   Drawing instruments: T-square and set-square

Scales

Design-drawings are made to a fixed scale or representative fraction, with special features, mouldings, free-hand curves in which the radius is not constant, etc., drawn full size. Inch scales can be $\frac{1}{12}$ (1 in. representing each actual foot in length), $\frac{1}{6}$, $\frac{1}{3}$, etc., or more usually $\frac{1}{8}$ ($1\frac{1}{2}$ in. to each foot), $\frac{1}{4}$ (3 in. to each foot) and $\frac{1}{2}$ (6 in. to each foot). The latter set are more easily translatable in the workshop for each $\frac{1}{8}$ in. on the full-size workshop rule is then equivalent to 1 in. on the $\frac{1}{8}$ scale drawing, with $\frac{1}{4}$ in. or $\frac{1}{2}$ in. equivalent to 1 in. on the larger scales. Metric scales are usually $\frac{1}{1}$ m (full size), $\frac{1}{2}$ m (1 m $=2$ m or 1 cm$=2$ cm, etc.), $\frac{2}{5}$ m $\frac{1}{5}$, m, $\frac{1}{10}$ m, $\frac{1}{20}$ m, etc. The larger scales are divided into centimetres and millimetres and the smaller into centimetres only, except in engineers' precision steel rules which can show very fine millimetre divisions. If other scales have to be constructed then it is necessary to know how to divide a given line into any number of equal parts and 52:1 shows the procedure where AB is the given line, AC another line drawn at any convenient angle and marked off with the workshop rule or dividers into the exact number of parts required: if B and C are then joined and parallel lines drawn from the upper marks with two set-squares (52:2) then AB will be similarly divided. Any scale, therefore, can be constructed on this principle, and assuming that a $\frac{1}{8}$th scale is required then the base-line AB (52:1) is drawn exactly $1\frac{1}{2}$ in. long to represent 1 ft of actual measurement, with AC divided into 12 equal parts; and metric scales constructed in the same manner with AC divided into tenths. In some scales showing very fine divisions only the first whole unit is subdivided and marked 0 as in 52:5, and the scale is then read from right to left. Finer scales can be constructed on the diagonal principle to mark any number of divisions, but they must be very accurately drawn and 52:6 shows the method of construction where each base-line division is $\frac{1}{8}$ in. and each upright division $\frac{1}{8}$ of $\frac{1}{8}$ equalling $\frac{1}{64}$. To read the scale add the number of base divisions to the number of vertical divisions; thus in the illustration 5 base divisions at $\frac{1}{8}$th$+5$ vertical divisions at $\frac{1}{64}=\frac{45}{64}$. Metric scales showing divisions up to 100ths can be similarly constructed.

Proportional division

Lines can be divided proportional to each other in the manner described above and 52:3 gives the details where AC is to be divided in the same proportion as AB. The method is also useful in dividing a given line into any number of equal parts (as in setting out dovetails) where AB (52:4) which is assumed to be $5\frac{1}{2}$ units (inches or millimetres) long has to be divided into 4 equal parts. AB is first drawn the correct length and AC any convenient length easily divisible by four. Parallel lines from AC will then equally divide AB.

Where a line has to be divided into two equal parts, i.e. bisected, then 52:7 shows the method in which arcs with equal radii are struck from A and B to intersect at C and D, and a vertical line drawn through CD will then bisect AB. This method can also be used for striking a perpendicular to a given line, and 52:8 shows the method in which a semicircle is described from point A on BC, and using the same radius throughout describing arcs D and E from B and C and intersecting arcs from D and E to F; a line drawn from F to A will then be truly perpendicular. If compasses are not available then perpendiculars can be drawn using the theorem attributed to Pythagoras (scale of equal parts) in which the square on the hypotenuse of a right-angled triangle is equal to the sum of the squares on the other two sides. Thus in 52:9 if AB is drawn 3 units long, then measurements of 4 units from B and 5 units from A (or any multiples of all three measurements) will only coincide at point C on a line which is at true right angles to A.

Angles

Angles are formed by the convergence of two straight lines, or more precisely by the rotation of a straight line about a fixed point, and the method of bisecting them is shown in 53:1 where an arc is struck from centre A and further equal arcs from B and C. From the point at which these two arcs intersect a line drawn to A will bisect the angle. This method can be used to strike all the commonly used angles, e.g. a right angle of 90° can be bisected to produce a true mitre of 45° and again bisected to produce a half-mitre of $22\frac{1}{2}°$. Angles of 60° can be struck by

52 Division of lines, scales, etc.

describing an arc BC from A (53:2) and a similar arc AC from B. If lines are drawn from C to A and B then the figure thus formed will be an equilateral triangle with all sides and all angles equal. As the sum of the angles contained in a triangle must equal 180°, then each angle will be 60°, and bisecting them further, angles of 30°.

Triangles

Triangles are shown in 53:3. Right-angled triangles (53:3A) have two sides at right angles to each other, the third side is known as the "hypotenuse' and the angles so formed by this line equal in sum to one right angle, i.e. 45° each. Equilateral triangles (53:3B) have three equal sides and therefore three equal angles of 60°. Isoceles triangles (53:3C) have two equal sides and two equal angles, and scalene triangles —acute scalene (53:3D) and obtuse scalene (53:3E)—have three unequal sides and therefore three unequal angles.

Parallelograms

Parallelograms are quadrilaterals with opposite sides equal and parallel to each other, therefore the opposite angles are equal, the diagonals bisect the figures into similar triangles and also bisect each other. They are simple to construct as shown, where 53:4 is a square, 53:5 a rectangle, 53:6 a rhombus and 53:7 a rhomboid.

Polygons

Regular polygons—a pentagon has five sides (54:1A) a hexagon six sides (54:1B), a heptagon seven sides (54:1C), an octagon eight sides (54:1D), etc.—have more than four sides, the sides are equal and the angles also equal. All the corners must, therefore, lie on the circumference of the circumscribing circle, and given the circle it is only necessary to divide the circumference into equal parts representing the number of sides required. Alternatively, any regular polygon can be drawn on a given base-line AB (54:2) by erecting a perpendicular BC equal in length to AB and joining C to A. AB is then bisected at Y and a perpendicular XY of indefinite length erected which bisects the diagonal AC to yield the centre of a square raised on AB. If a quadrant (quarter-circle) is now drawn with centre B and radius AB, then where it cuts the perpendicular XY will lie point 6 which is the centre of a circle circumscribing a hexagon, whilst midway between points 4 and 6 the point 5 will give the centre of a pentagon, and similarly placed points 7, 8, 9 and 10, etc. the centres of other polygons. Other methods of drawing regular polygons are also shown. In 54:3 a hexagon on the given side AB is simply drawn with a 60° set square forming six equiliteral triangles, whilst 54:4 illustrates the construction of an octagon within a given square ABCD. The diagonals of the square are first drawn, then with radius equal to half a diagonal arcs are drawn from centres A, B, C, D giving points of intersection which when joined become the sides of the octagon. Figure 54:5 shows the construction of a regular polygon within a given circle. The circle is first drawn with diameter AB, and a semicircle of any convenient radius with centre A. If this semicircle is divided into, as many parts as the required polygon is to have sides—in this case a heptagon —then radials extended from A through these points will cut the circumference and give points of connection for the base-lines of the required figure.

Circles

The various terms used in connection with circles are illustrated in figure 55. *Arc*, any part of a circumference; *chord*, any straight line shorter than the diameter terminated by the circumfer-

ence at both ends: *diameter*, a chord which passes through the centre of a circle; *radius*, a straight line drawn from the centre of a circle to the circumference and therefore half the diameter; *normal*, a straight line drawn from any point on the circumference radial to the centre; *tangent*, a straight line touching the circumference at any one point at right angles to a normal at that point (55:1). *Quadrant*, sector which is a quarter of a circle; *semicircle*, a segment which is a half of a circle; *minor segment*, part of a circle contained between a chord and its arc and less than a semicircle; *major segment*, part of a circle greater than a semicircle; *minor sector*, part of a circle contained within two radii and less than a semicircle; *major sector*, part of a circle greater than a semicircle (55:2). Additionally 55:3 shows *concentric circles* having the same common centre but different radii, and 55:4 *eccentric circles* each of which has a different centre.

The circumference of a circle is approximately $3\cdot1416$ or $3\frac{1}{7}$ times the diameter, usually expressed by the Greek letter π (pi). Thus the circumference is $\pi \times d$ (diameter), whilst the area is πr^2 (radius). In practice. the development or length of the circumference can easily be found by dividing it into any number of equal parts which are then plotted as straight lines and measured off, but the method is not strictly accurate as the plotted units are in reality chords of the circle. Alternatively, dividing the diameter into seven equal parts and adding one part to three times the length of the diameter will give a reasonable approximation.

Methods of describing circles to pass through given points, between converging lines, tangential to each other or inscribed within two equal arcs are used in the full sizing of *fan* (Gothic) *tracery* and are illustrated in 56 and 60. Figure 55:5 shows the construction of a circle about the fixed points A, B, C, where AB and BC are each bisected and the intersection of the perpendiculars at O will give the centre of the required circle. Where a circle has to be inscribed within a triangle (55:6), as the circle will be tangential at points B and C which are equidistant from A, a perpendicular erected on B will provide one radius, and the bisection of the angle at A another, whilst the point at which they intersect at O will thus be the centre of the

1 A B C D

5 6 7 8

2

X

10
9
8
7
6
5
4

C

A Y B

3

60° 60°
60° 60°
60° 60°
60°

A B

4

D C

45° 45°

A B

5

B

1

5

3 4 5

2 6

1 7

A

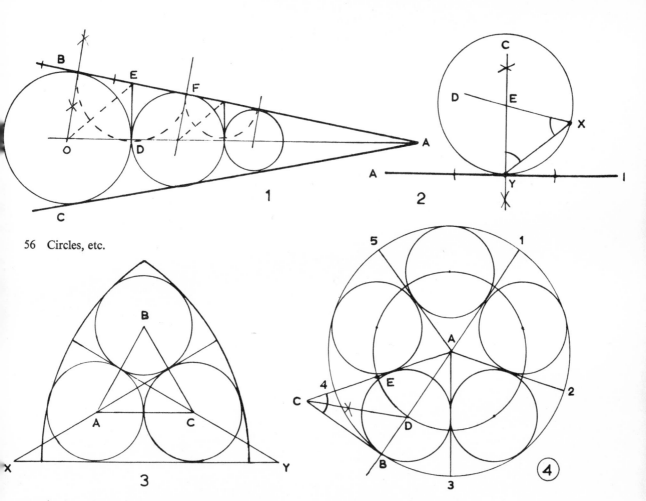

56 Circles, etc.

required circle. If a series of circles have to be inscribed tangential to two converging lines (56:1) then the angle BAC is first bisected and the first circle drawn as already described, after which the angle BOD is bisected and from centres E with radius EB an arc is described to cut AB at F. A line drawn from F parallel to BO will give the centre of the next circle, and centres for succeeding circles are found in like manner. If a circle has to pass through a given point X (56:2) and touch a line AB at a given point Y, then erect CY perpendicular to AB. Join XY and construct the angle DXY equal to the angle CYX. At the point of intersection of DX with CY the point E will now form the centre of the required circle as EX and EY have equal angles and are, therefore, also equal.

Where three equal tangential circles have to be inscribed within two equal arcs as in a trefoil to a pointed arch (56:3), an equilateral triangle ABC is first drawn, and three circles with radii equal to half the length of the sides are described with centres A, B, C. A horizontal line is then drawn tangential to the base circles and where the bisectors of the angles BAC, BCA intersect this line will lie the points X, Y which are the centres of the arcs. A method of inscribing any number of equal circles within a given circle is shown in 56:4. First divide the circumference of the given circle into the same number of equal parts as the number of circles required, and join each division to the centre. One of the sectors so formed is then bisected at AB and a tangent is drawn passing through B and extended (developed) to meet the sector division AC. If the angle ACB is then bisected and extended to meet AB at D it will give the centre of the first circle with radius DB. A circle is now drawn from centre A with radius AD, and the centres of the remaining circles found by stepping off distance DE from the intersection of the inner circle with the radius of each sector.

77

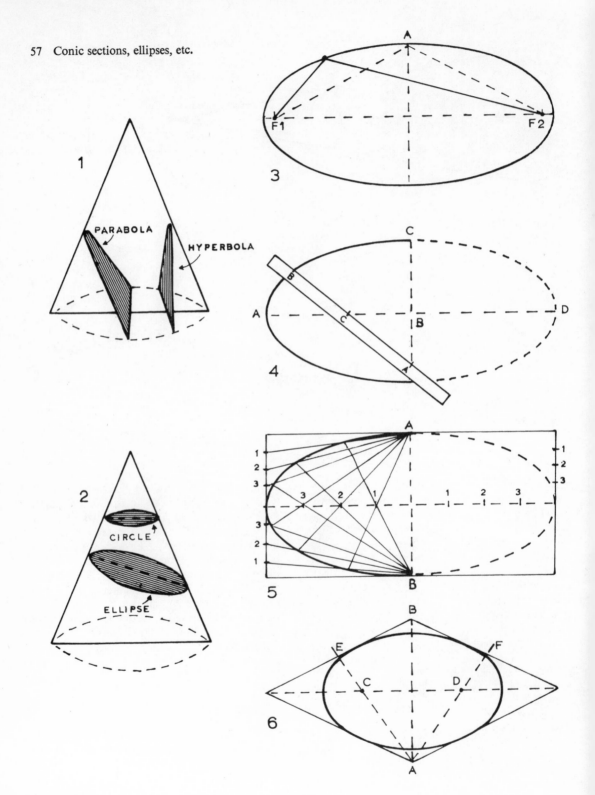

Conic sections

A *cone* is a pyramid with a circular base (57:1), and a vertical cut through the axis will yield a section which is a *triangle*, parallel to the axis a *hyperbola*, and parallel to one of the sides a *parabola*. If the cut is parallel with the base then the section will be a *circle* (57:2), and inclined to the base an *ellipse*. Of these conic sections the ellipse is of considerable importance in the setting out of oval-shaped work, gate-leg tables, etc., and although it can be drawn by hand it is more satisfactory to construct it geometrically.

Ellipses

Several methods are available of which the *foci* method (57:3) is the most common. The major axis which is to be the larger diameter of the ellipse is drawn first, and the minor axis at right angles to it. Focal points (foci) are then found by taking half the length of the major axis, and from point A on the minor axis striking an arc to cut the major axis at the foci F1 and F2. If pins are inserted at A, F1 and F2 and a length of string stretched taut round them, with pin A removed and replaced by a pencil the curve can be traced by keeping the pencil taut against the string. Another familiar method (57:4) uses a trammel composed of a thin lath or strip of stout paper. The major and minor axes are drawn as before, the trammel is then marked with half the length of the major axis AB and half the minor axis BC, and if the point C is kept on the former and the point A on the latter then the point B will trace out the ellipse.

Ellipses can also be constructed by the rectangle method (57:5), in which both major and minor axes are divided into the same number of equal parts, and lines drawn through each division will yield points through which the ellipse can be drawn. Where, however, a geometric ellipse gives too elongated a shape, an approximate ellipse of four arcs corresponding to the isometric projection of a circle can be used as shown in 57:6. First construct a rhombus whose sides are equal to the dimater of the circle which is to be the basis of the ellipse. Draw in the diagonals and from point A bisect two sides of the rhombus at E, F. With radius CE and centres C and D describe the smaller arcs, and with centres A and B the larger arcs.

Developments

Compound shapes cannot be measured accurately from a two-dimensional drawing of elevation and plan, and require development, i.e. the parts opened out and flattened on one plane. Figure 58:1, 2 illustrates a typical hopper with all sides splayed, from which it will be seen that the elevational outline is correct, but the given width of both sides and ends do not allow for the actual splay or leaning outwards towards the observer which cannot be shown. To develop these true measurements first draw the plan ABCD (58:3), extend as shown by the dotted lines, draw AB, BC, CD and DA parallel to the plan at a distance equal to X and Y in 58:1, 2 and complete.

58 Developments

4

Surfaces of double curvature

Surfaces of double curvature (domes, etc.) cannot be developed with complete accuracy, nevertheless the method illustrated in 58:4 is sufficiently accurate for most practical purposes. Assuming that a hemisphere has to be developed to provide the exact shapes of the constructional ribs and of the covering veneers, first draw the elevation and divide horizontally into any number of zones A, B, C, D, E, F, etc. The outer circumference of the dome is then drawn on plan, and the zones in elevation projected downwards to the corresponding circles on the plan B, C, D, E, and F. The circle on plan is then

divided into any number of equal parts 1, 2, 3, 4, 5, etc., and the radii drawn in. To develop any one zone in the elevation, for instance the zone contained within the horizontal lines C and D shaded on the drawing, draw a straight line CD through C and D from point O to meet the central axis R extended, and with centre R and radii RD and RC describe arcs. These arcs are then plotted off to correspond with the division of the appropriate circles D and C on plan and numbered similarly (the drawing shows part of the development only and 12 divisions will be required to plot the exact circumferential length of the zone).

To plot the shapes of the individual gores or lunes draw verticals from the points of intersection of each individual circle on plan with any two adjacent radii and, where these verticals intersect the horizontal limits of each zone, will lie points through which smooth curves will define the gore. The true approximate shape of the gore can be developed by bisecting one sector on plan 2–3, plotting off the distances from A to F in elevation along the bisecting line 2–3, and with radii equal to the corresponding circles on plan describing arcs through the plotted points. If parallel lines (radiates) to the bisecting line are then produced from the appropriate arcs of the sector to contact the arcs already drawn in the development, the intersections will provide points through which smooth curves can be drawn to yield the outline of the gore. As already mentioned the development can only be approximate because the distances measured off to provide the arcs A, B, C, D, E, F in the development are in reality chords of the true arcs of each zone, therefore, in cutting veneers for gores, an allowance must be made for trimming in position.

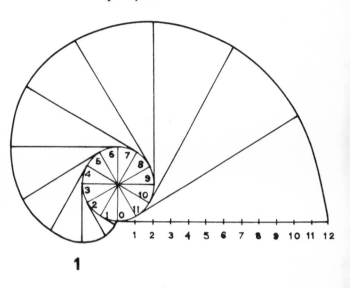

1

Geometric decoration

Volutes and spirals

Classic architecture made considerable use of volutes and spirals as decorative elements. The former conforms to the convolution or twist of the spiral shell of certain molluscs (snails, etc.), and 59A:1 gives the method of construction in which a circle is first drawn and divided into any number of equal parts, in this case 1 to 12. A tangent is then drawn at o equal in length to the circumference of the circle and similarly divided. If further tangents are drawn at each point of the circumference progressively increasing in length according to the number of divisions on the first tangent, i.e. from point 1 one part, point 2 two parts, etc. they will yield points for the free-hand drawing of the curve.

Spirals are shown in 59A:2, 3. In (2) the containing circle is divided into any number of equal sectors (eight are shown). One radius (radius vector) is then divided into the same number of equal parts, and concentric circles described through each division. The spiral is then unwound from point o at the centre of the circle, gaining one division as it travels through each sector. If necessary the number of divisions in the radius vector can be doubled, i.e. 16, and the curve will then travel twice round the containing circle to form a double spiral; whilst the spiral need not start from the centre of the circle but from any point on the radius sector provided the divisions 0, 1, 2, 3, 4, 5, etc., are marked off from the commencement of the spiral and not from the centre of the containing circle.

Spirals of constant pitch built up of quadrants are constructed as shown in 59A:3. A square 1234 is first drawn and a perpendicular x erected equal in height to eight times the side of the square. The arcs are then drawn from centre 1 with radius one part (one side of the square), centre 2, two parts, centre 3, three parts, centre 4, four parts, centre 1, five parts, etc.

2

3

Entasis

Tapered shafts or columns with straight sides give the optical illusion of curving inwards, therefore Classic architecture gave a slight outward dwelling to counteract the tendency, and to convey an impression of the weight-bearing function of the column. Various methods are used of which 59B gives one of the simplest and most satisfactory, for the curve must be subtle or the effect becomes exaggerated. The height of the column AB is first drawn, also the top EF and bottom diameters CD. Semicircles with centres A and radii AC and BE are then drawn, and perpendiculars erected from the smaller semicircle to cut the larger semicircle at 3. The arc C3 is then divided and from points 1, 2 perpendiculars are erected to cut corresponding divisions in the height of the column, yielding points through which the curve CE can be drawn.

Arches

Various forms of arch are shown in 60:1 together with the geometric construction. The points from which the curve of the arch springs is known as the *springing-line*, the exterior curve the *extrados* and the interior curve the *intrados*.

Tracery

Gothic tracery used as infilling or 'foliation' in window arches, etc., and still called for in traditional church-work, is based on geometric principle, and 60:2 gives various examples with their constructions. Where there is a demand for this type of work local church examples should be examined.

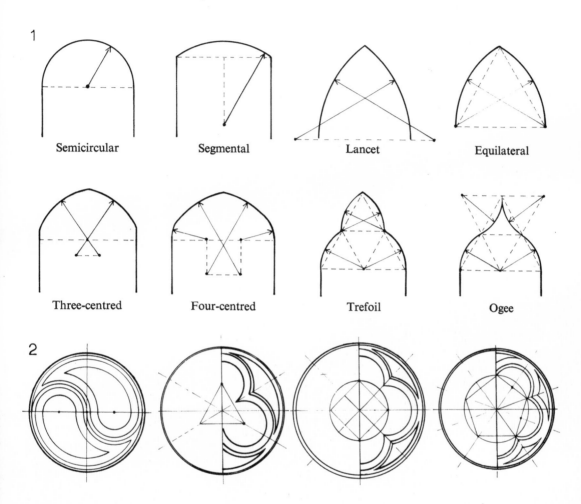

1

Semicircular Segmental Lancet Equilateral

Three-centred Four-centred Trefoil Ogee

2

Repeat patterns

Practically all decorative patterns, whether carved, moulded, inlaid or applied have a geometric basis, and are in essence composed of curved or straight lines repeated in regular sequence. Even representations of fruit, flowers, shells, etc. are stylised to fit within circles, squares and diamonds, etc., and the acanthus-leaf pattern inlaid in brass in a Regency chair-back illustrated in Chapter 44 is firmly based on limiting circles. Once the principle has been established it is relatively simple to break down the pattern into its component parts, and thus establish the structure on which it is built up.

Proportional reduction and enlargement

The principles of reduction and enlargement are based on the properties of a triangle in which there is a progressive diminution from base-line to apex (the proportionate division of lines described on page 71 is founded on this principle). Any line, therefore, drawn parallel to the base of a triangle (61:1) will form another triangle either smaller or larger, of similar angles and therefore of similar shape. If a series of lines are drawn from points on the base of a triangle (61:2A) to the apex they will cut any other parallel line (61:2B) in exactly the same proportion. The

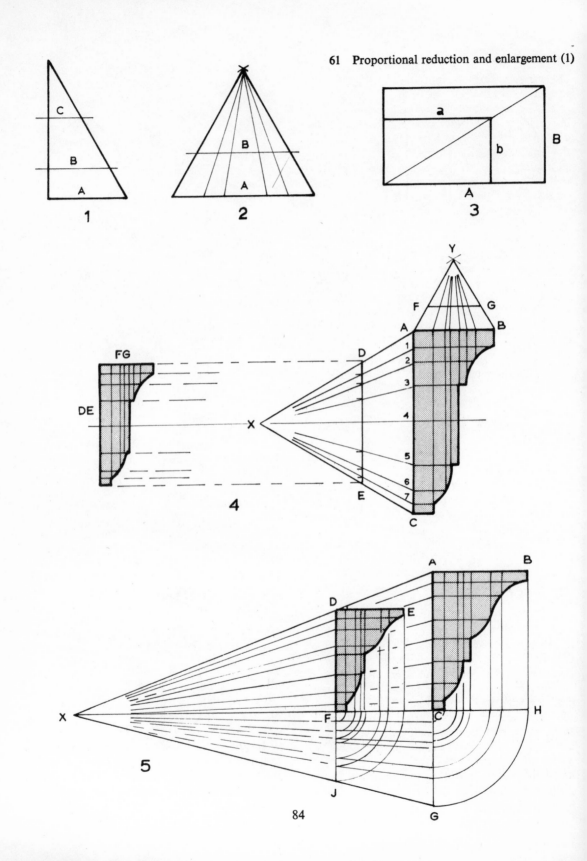

triangle can be of any shape, but in practice either equilateral or right-angled triangles are normally used.

Where the figure to be reduced (or enlarged) is a rectangle it is only necessary to draw the diagonal (61:3) to create two triangles in which the smaller rectangle (ab) is in strict proportion to the larger (AB). If a given moulding has to be reduced in section, for example to two-thirds its original size, then the procedure is shown in 61:4. The full-size section CAB is first drawn, and at a convenient distance the required height of the reduced section DE. A triangle AXC is then drawn on base-line AC to enclose DE. If DE is placed centrally as shown then the triangle will be equal sided, but if DE is placed on a horizontal line drawn from C it will be a right-angled triangle. Salients points of the moulding 1, 2, 3, 4, etc. are then drawn from the profile outline to the bed AC, and from there diminished to X, cutting DE in exactly the same proportion. The thickness of the reduced moulding section FG is then enclosed in a similar triangle erected on AB and additional salient points produced and diminished to Y, yielding points on FG which can be stepped off on the reduced section DE, FG. Alternatively, the reduced thickness can be plotted as shown in 61:5, where salient points in the thickness are drawn to the base-line CH and from centre C swung round to AC extended to G, and from there diminished to X, cutting DF extended to J. From DJ with centre F they are swung back to plot the reduced thickness of the required section FDE. In all cases the procedure can be reversed for the enlargement of any given section, and if the moulding section FDE (61:5) is to be enlarged to CAB then FDE is drawn first and the enlarged section developed from it.

The application of these methods to turned-work (balusters, table legs, etc.) is identical, and it is only necessary to draw an axis or centre-line and treat one half of the turning as a flat-bedded moulding as described above. If reeded or fluted columns in tapered legs or pilasters have to be reduced then the simpler method shown in 62:1 can be used. The thickness of the reduced section EF can be determined by describing an arc from centre C with radius BC in the section ABCD, and describing a further arc with centre F and radius taken from F to the plotted point to yield the proportionate thickness FG. If the moulding arcs are compass drawn and must also be proportionately reduced in depth (62:2), then draw in the centre-line EF for the radius centres of the arcs, and with centre D and radius DE describe an arc to DC, and from there diminish to G to give the required arc to H, which in turn will yield the compass line HJ.

Where a moulding has to be reduced in width but not in thickness, then it can be done by drawing the normal section BAC (62:3) and the reduced width AD at any angle from A. Salient lines are drawn parallel to AB as shown and swung from centre A to CA extended to D, whilst salient lines in the thickness which is not to be reduced are drawn horizontally. It should be pointed out that in all the foregoing examples the greater the number of salient points the more accurate will be the plotting of the required curves in the altered profile.

Intersection of mouldings

Raking moulds

Where two mouldings of unequal width intersect on one plane then the junction is a bevelled mitre as distinct from a true mitre of 45° (see *Mitre practice*, Chapter 20); but where two mouldings of equal width intersect then the mitre lines on each must be the same length, therefore the angles must be equal, or as commonly stated, the mitre must halve the overall angle. Figure 62:4 shows the correct mitre line of two pieces of equal width meeting at an angle, and the dotted lines the effect of unequal angled cuts, where the cut (A) is longer than the cut in the opposite member. This halving of the overall angle is not possible in raking moulds in cornices, pediments, etc. as the side or return mould must have a right-angled cut, and the raking or face mould an inclined cut vertical to the side of the carcase or door framing, as shown in the dotted line at A (62:4).

It is necessary, therefore, to alter the section of either the side mould or the raking mould so that they correspond, and 62:5 shows the method. As the raking mould is normally to a fixed section this is drawn in first and the profile added as A. Lines are then drawn through salient points parallel with the slope, and from the points of intersection other lines at right angles

to the slope. From point x draw a true horizontal xz equal in length to xy which is the thickness of the face mould, and on the centre x describe arcs as shown, dropping verticals from xz to meet the lines drawn parallel to the rake. The points of intersection will then enable the profile of the return mould to be drawn in B. To ascertain the profile of the top return mould (c) it is only necessary to transfer xy with its plotted points to the horizontal plane and drop verticals to give points of intersection as with B. If the raking mould is curved (62:6), the arbitrary lines through the salient points of the profile A must be drawn at right angles to the bed of the mould, and should not follow the axis of the sweep.

Curved mouldings

The junction of a curved and straight moulding, or of two curved mouldings of dissimilar sweep or direction is not in a straight line, therefore either the profile of one must be altered or the mitre line itself must be curved. Obviously, the latter method is always simpler and the drawing below shows the procedure. Arbitrary lines are drawn either from the salient points of the profile A below or if the moulding is composed of one large member only, at any convenient spacings, and the curve is then drawn through the points of intersection.

63   Curved moulding mitre-line

A

Projections

Orthographic (orthogonal) projection

The standard method of representing a three-dimensional object in two-dimensional form, i.e.

as a scale drawing on one plane, is by orthographic projection in which related views give the various aspects, viz.:

Plan Representation of the object on the horizontal plane, i.e. looking down.

Front and side elevations Representation of the object on the vertical plane, i.e. level with the eyes.

Section The object cut through either on the horizontal or the vertical plane to show details which would not be visible in simple outlines of plan and elevation. Vertical sections are usually included in a side elevation projected from the front elevation, and horizontal sections included in the plan, although if the object is complex several such sectional drawings may be necessary.

All these drawings are to a convenient scale, but full or half-size details are necessary for free-hand curves where a compass radius cannot be stated, or where the particular detail calls for amplification.

First-angle projection

Where a horizontal plane intersects a vertical plane (VP) dihedral angles are formed, of which both the first and third angles are used in orthographic projection. Where the first dihedral angle is used (64:1) the object is placed between the observer and the vertical plane (64:2), thus the front elevation is seen first (the arrow points the direction), the side elevation is projected from it by folding back the side vertical plane on the vertical trace (VT), and placing it alongside the front elevation. The horizontal plane is then folded down on the horizontal trace (HT) xy, known as the xy line, and therefore appears below the front elevation. Figure 65 shows a scale drawing using the first dihedral angle.

Third-angle projection

This method is popular abroad and increasingly so in this country, although it hardly matters which method is adopted provided the drawing is quite clear as to what it is intended to represent. In third angle projection the object is placed behind the vertical plane (64:3), the plan is seen first, the front elevation below it, and the side elevation projected alongside the front elevation.

64 Projections (1)

HP Horizontal plane
VP Vertical plane
XY Horizontal trace (XY line)
VT Vertical trace

FRONT ELEVATION
SIDE ELEVATION
V.P.
H.P.
PLAN

2

H.P.
V.P.

3

Scale drawings

As already mentioned scale drawings prepared by the designer are not concerned with visual aspects (perspectives, etc.), but with the accurate outline representation of the object to be made, drawn to a representative fraction of the full

size. They can be projected from either the first dihedral angle (first angle drawings) or the third dihedral angle (third angle drawings), and 65:1 gives a typical layout using the first angle and drawn to a scale of $\frac{1}{8}$ ($1\frac{1}{2}$ in. to the foot) or to metric scale. The details given show (65:1B) the front elevation of a simple wooden plinth with a circular recess on the face for an inlaid metal plaque; (65:1A) the plan of the plinth showing a stepped housing for a statuette; and 65:1C a vertical side section on the centre-line XY (65:1A). Full-size details of the stepped housing and the circular recess are shown in 65:1D and 65:1E and no further information should be necessary. Where the drawings are of complex objects, however, it may be necessary to add a three-dimensional project for clarification.

Oblique projection

The elevation of the object is drawn to scale and parallel to the observer as in orthographic projection, but receding lines, i.e. the sides of the plinth not visible in 65:1, are drawn at a convenient angle 30°, 45°, or 60° according to the set-square available. Figure 65:2 shows the plinth side drawn at an angle of 45°. If the receding lines are short the angle should be fairly large; if they are long the angle should be acute, otherwise an exaggerated effect is produced. Figure 65:3 gives the effect achieved by drawing the side to half the scale of the front which gives a more pleasing appearance, but a warning notice should be included in the drawing if this method is adopted. Circles and parts of circles can be drawn with the compass in oblique projection, and the method is invaluable for showing details of constructional jointing, etc.

Isometric projection

This method gives a closer approximation to the visual appearance (65:4). For normal work the sides are inclined at an angle of 30° using the 30° set-square, but the angles can be varied within wide limits, using for instance, 20° for the front elevation, and 40° or 50° for the side elevation—actual experience alone is the only true guide to the most satisfactory angle of representation for any particular view. Isometric scales proportionate to the true scale were formerly used, but

B

C   (X-Y)

A

X
Y

SCALE = 1/8 & F/S

(METRIC 1/10 & F/S)

1

REBATE

D

RECESS

E

FIG 2   45°   OBLIQUE

FIG 3   45°   OBLIQUE

ISOMETRIC
FIG 4   AXONOMETRIC
                                FIG 5

30°   30°

60°   30°

FIG 6

FIG 7

the practice has now been abandoned, and the drawings are made to the true scale.

The method of drawing curves or irregular shapes is shown in 65:6 and 65:7. A plan of the curve is first drawn and included in a square. Ordinates* are then drawn in 65:6, and the square with its ordinates is then drawn in isometric projection 65:7, and the critical distances for the curve plotted off. In the example given the circle becomes an ellipse.

Axonometric projection

This is a variation of isometric projection, sometimes known as 'bird's-eye' perspective, as it gives more of a downward view (65:5). The true plan is first drawn to scale at angles of 45° and

* *Ordinate*: half the chord of a conic section in relation to the diameter which bisects it.

45° or 30° and 60° to the horizontal, and the verticals projected from it. This projection is chiefly used for interiors, and it is interesting to note that the base of the socket housing in the plinth only becomes visible with this method.

Perspective projection

Perspective drawings are used to illustrate the appearance of the object so that it is completely understandable to a third person. Actual measurements are not taken from such drawings, as they are only concerned with the mechanics of vision in which receding lines appear to converge and diminish. Various methods are used, many of which are highly technical and require special study, but 66 shows a simple compromise which should be sufficient for most practical purposes. Figure 66:2 shows the elevation of a simple chest of drawers, and in 66:1 the plan ABCD

66 Perspective projection

90

is drawn to scale at an angle to the horizon (eye-line) dependent on the viewpoint required (in this case 45°). The station point (SP) is placed to represent the eye of the beholder, and only trial and error can give the most satisfactory position. Whilst the angle or cone of vision represented by lines drawn from the extremities DB of the plan ABCD to the station point (SP) should be between 40° and 60° for a normal aspect (the normal camera lens takes in about 55°), a narrower angle, even though it increases the distortion, helps to contain the vanishing points within the drawing, as a little experiment will show. Lines are now drawn to form a right angle at SP and cut the horizon at VP1 and VP2, which are the vanishing points to which all receding lines converge. A base- or ground-line is drawn approximately 5 ft (150 cm) scale measurement below the eye-line or horizon, whilst a perpendicular dropped from A to H will provide a height-line on which all significant measurements can be transferred from the elevation (66:2). Lines are then drawn from all the salient points on the plan ABCD to the station point SP, and from where they cut the horizon verticals are then dropped as shown. If from the line AH (66:1) the various heights are connected to VP1 and VP2 the completed drawing will then be automatically developed.

As the object of such a perspective drawing is to convey the visual appearance only, and not to serve as an accurate scaled representation from which critical measurements can be taken, small details should be drawn free-hand rather than rigidly adhering to mechanical projection with its inevitable distortion. Curves are also better drawn as free-hand ellipses after plotting the general position.

Part 2 Materials
7 Timber (hardwoods)

Sound jointing techniques upon which the stiffness, rigidity, appearance and general usefulness of furniture depend must take into account the natural movement of timber, and its propensity to shrink, swell and warp under fluctuating atmospheric conditions. It is, therefore, vitally important that the woodworker should understand exactly what kind of structural material it is which ceaselessly moves in sympathy with its surroundings, and what precautions he can usefully adopt to minimise that movement. Surface protection with paint, polish or even metal coatings may conceivably delay the natural process but can never wholly arrest it; and it is not generally realised that whilst **age itself** may exercise a certain restraining influence, no matter how old the timber may be, the innate tendencies will continue to persist throughout its effective life.

Timber growth and structure

All trees are exogens, increasing their woody fibre by the annual addition of a new layer (annual ring) under the bark, and forming a typical cone-like structure of yearly increments (67:2). As producers of structural material they are conveniently grouped within two main classifications—*coniferae* or cone-bearing, needle-leafed trees usually evergreen, yielding the typical softwoods of commerce; and *dicotyledonerae* or broad-leafed trees, usually deciduous, yielding hardwoods. (A third classification includes palms and bamboos which are strictly speaking giant grasses.) There are the inevitable exceptions of course, for the very soft poplars and willows are broad-leafed and therefore classed as hardwoods, whilst the harder, needle-leafed larch remains a softwood even though it is deciduous, and yews and hollies are true hardwoods though they are evergreen. However, the classifications are near enough for all practical purposes.

Every tree has a complete circulatory system in which water and dissolved mineral salts collected by the roots and commonly known as 'sap', is drawn upwards in the growing season through innumerable pipes or hollow vessels by the rapid evaporation from the surfaces of the leaves. In turn, the action of sunlight on the chlorophyll or green colouring matter in the leaves converts the rising sap through a complex process of photosynthesis into the essential food sugars and starches which travel down the bast or inner skin underlying the bark, and are conveyed into the heart of the tree at every point by an elaborate system of radial medullary rays (67:3) clearly visible in the so-called 'flash' or flower of quartered oak and chestnut. There is also a respiratory system whereby the leaves inspire oxygen and carbon dioxide during the day, which is again suffused throughout the living structure of the tree, whilst the waste products of combustion, chiefly carbon dioxide, are transpired at night. All this constant passage of essential water, food and oxygen throughout every part of the tree necessitates a complex honeycomb structure of pipes or vessels, soft pithy cells and structural wood fibre, which even when fully dried retains sufficient elasticity to behave as a typical sponge, capable of absorbing or giving up moisture in a ceaseless effort to maintain itself in a constant state of equilibrium with its surroundings.

The actual structure of the tree is illustrated in 67:1, 3 and the sectional drawings show the details. The function of the bark is to protect the tree from injury and shield the precious bast layer which is the sole conveyor of food. Immediately under the bast is the cambium or growth layer, one cell thick and therefore only visible as a coat of slime. This layer creates new bast on one side and sapwood on the other, whilst the sapwood in turn ages and creates fresh heartwood. The function of the sapwood is to convey the water to the leaves, whilst the heartwood acts as a

SECOND LENGTH

BOUGH WOOD

CROTCH

TENSION WOOD

COMPRESSION WOOD

4

2

A

A

GROWTH

BURR

BARK

CAMBIUM

BAST

SAPWOOD

PITH

HEARTWOOD

MEDULLARY RAYS

SPRING WOOD

SUMMER WOOD

3

ANNUAL GROWTH RINGS

1

BUTT LENGTH

BUTTRESS

stiffening rib to the tree. At the exact centre of the annual rings, but not necessarily at the centre of the tree, lies the pith which is merely the decayed remnants of the original shoot or wand.

The growth in the cambium layer is very rapid during the spring when the constant evaporation from the leaf surfaces and the continual unfolding of fresh leaves exercises the strongest pull on the rising sap, therefore ensuring an abundant supply of food; not so rapid in summer when the first impetus has been lost; and altogether ceasing in winter when the tree remains dormant. Both rapid spring and slower summer growth combine together to create one annual ring whose number determines the exact age of the tree; whilst the heartwood itself is sapwood which, deprived of essential food and oxygen, has been literally choked to death by the ever-encircling rings of sapwood. Once the tree has started to make heartwood the amount of sap-wood remains constant throughout the life of the tree, and for each new growth ring added one matures and dies. Before it dies, however, all food is withdrawn from its cells, the fibres harden forming stiffer, denser heartwood, whilst the typical darker coloration evident in most—but not all—timbers is the result of subtle chemical changes in the nature of the wood. The point to be stressed is that these chemical changes must take place within the living tree; and no amount of after-treatment will darken sapwood, harden its fibres or drive out the sugars and starches locked in its cells which form the essential food-stuffs of all destructive wood-boring pests. This latter is the chief reason why sapwood should never be used in furniture, although apart from that there is little if any difference in the struct-ural strength. Sapwood will, however, always be wetter, for the pores of heartwood are blocked with gum-like bladders (*tylosis*) which prevent the free movement of water, therefore they contain more air and froth.

Figure 68 shows a hollow pine tree caught in a forest fire several years ago. Although much of the heartwood and nearly all the highly resinous sapwood has been consumed, there is still suffi-cient bast and cambium layer to support a full head of leaves. Figure 69 shows a slice cut from a laburnum tree (laburnum oyster) illustrating very clearly the sharp division between heart-wood and sapwood which need not necessarily follow the annual rings. The spacing of the rings, the alternation between rapid and slow growth in succeeding years, the greater freedom of growth on one side due possibly to climatic conditions, prevalent winds, etc., or overshadowing or poor soil on the narrow side, is clearly visible, also the medullary rays radiating inward from every point on the bast to the centre pith. These rays are always the weakest link as the split plainly shows, for they deflect the longitudinal fibres and thus form the natural cleavage-lines along which most timbers will readily split.

Felling and conversion

Hardwoods rarely if ever grow in vast tracts of a single species, and are usually intermingled in groups of many varieties, although in this country stands of beech do occur on chalk uplands. The usual procedure is to 'cruise' the forest, determining the approximate total foot cubeage (cubic metres) of each individual species, and the buyer will then undertake to extract all the standing hardwood over a given diameter regardless of quality or species. In tropical forests covering vast distances, and with perhaps an average of only 18 or so timber trees to the acre (0·4047 hectares), this may take several years, and the ultimate profit will depend not so much on the amount of prime (firsts and seconds) timber extracted, but on finding a market for the vastly greater percentage of low-grade or unfamiliar timber. Thus many unknown varieties are continually appearing on world markets, and are always worth considering providing tests are made of their performance, for they will always be cheap until they become better known. A striking example of this is utile, which was almost rubbish price when first introduced, but is now so much in demand for cheaper furniture that it costs almost as much as an average African mahogany. Exceptionally valuable timbers stand-ing alone or in isolated groups are usually bargained for separately; each tree is measured and the price per foot cube of usable timber in each butt negotiated. This is more often than not the practice in Great Britain, where worthwhile virgin stands of valuable hardwood have practi-cally ceased to exist, and the buyer has to rely on isolated pastorage or hedgerow timber.

It is customary to fell standing timber in

69 Laburnum oyster

autumn and winter in this country, although there is no real objection to summer felling, for a growing tree can transpire up to 50 galls (227 l) of water a day through its leaves in hot weather, thus depleting the moisture content of the trunk. However, summer felling does increase the risk of too rapid drying and consequent severe checking and splitting of the logs, therefore winter schedules are usually adopted. Tropical timbers are felled at any time dependent on the prevailing conditions, for they have no fixed period of growth (and therefore no pronounced annual rings); whilst certain heavy timbers, notably teak, greenheart, etc. are girdled or ring-barked at the base of the trunk about two years before felling, thus cutting off the supply of food and sap. As the tree continues to transpire through

its leaves the overall weight is drastically reduced, enabling it to be hauled or floated.

If a tree is a large one and the timber above the first main break (67:1) is usable, then the whole trunk is felled and taken to the saw-mill, otherwise the second length above the break (branch or fork) is split for cordwood, and only the butt or main trunk is extracted. Except in tropical rain forest trees, where lack of light and overcrowded conditions encourage very straight, clear cylindrical boles often up to 180 ft (55 m) high in emergent trees, second length timber is usually inferior in quality, with large knots, twisted grain and a much smaller percentage of heartwood. Such timber is, therefore, only suitable for building construction work, although an occasional second length will yield good-quality narrow plank. Boughwood is not used, for not only is the proportion of heartwood very small but the pith is off centre (67:4), with the annual rings in tension at the top and in compression underneath, therefore shrinkage is considerable. Occasional prime walnut, mahogany and ash trees, etc. yield at the convergence of the two sets of annual rings (67:1) the exceptionally beautiful crotch, curl and feather figuring, whilst good burrs when they occur (67:1) are cut off and sold to the veneer-merchants. The stumps or root bases of some walnuts, notably the American black walnut, can also yield the very bold stump figuring, and these trees are uprooted bodily and not felled. It is a little sad for the handmaker that all the best of timber, prime oaks of 40 in. (1 m) quarter girth and up, fine walnuts, clean sycamores, and in fact all exceptional trees, are immediately bought for veneer cutting at

prices far higher than they would reach for conversion into solid board and plank, but he cannot have it both ways.

Home-grown hardwood logs are not debarked at the saw-mill, for although the bark does encourage insect pests it helps to protect the trunk from over-rapid drying. Imported timbers are, however, always debarked, and most are also desapped to prevent the depredations of the ambrosia beetle (pinhole borer), and to cut down the weight, for the logs are sold with the customary allowance for bark and wane, and there is little point in incurring heavy transport costs for useless dunnage. Where extraction costs are high with long distances to be covered, and where there are ample forest reserves to cover the capital costs, local saw-mills are usually erected to convert the logs into square edge timber. Teak and other valuable hardwoods are invariably

70   De-sapped agba logs at Sheffield Park Sawmills, Sussex

exported square edge; whilst most of the common timbers can be obtained in round logs trimmed of sap (70 shows the incredible precision of native adze work) or in square edge timber, the latter usually only 'shipping dry', with a moisture content below the danger level for fungoid attack (25 per cent), but otherwise unseasoned.

Saw-milling

Conversion of the round log into thick plank is usually confined to the autumn and winter months in this country, but thin boards can be cut throughout the year provided they can be adequately protected from hot sun. Prior to conversion the logs are crosscut to length, odd kinks adzed or sawn off, and debarked if the bark is loose or gritty or if hidden nails are suspected (a constant hazard in hedgerow timber).

Treatment of the butt, the side or angle from which it is to be cut, whether it is to be cut 'through and through' to provide waney edge boards, or 'billet' fashion for quartered stuff, is at the discretion of the head sawyer, for inexperienced conversion can destroy much of the value of a prime butt. The actual 'breaking down' of the log is done either by large circular saws which are still used for certain refractory timbers, or more usually by vertical band mills in which only $\frac{3}{32}$ in. (2·4 mm) is lost in sawdust for each cut, as against $\frac{1}{4}$ in. (6·3 mm) for the heavy circular rip-saws. Logs are also cut with the horizontal band mill, which is slower but gives a more even cut, as the weight of the plank is downwards and not against the side of the saw. The most accurate of all is obtained with the old-fashioned horizontal reciprocating or 'German' saw, in which a fixed blade moves backwards and forwards with a piston action, but the cut is much too slow for modern requirements. The primitive method of pit-sawing by hand, in which the log is placed over an open pit with one man on top of the trunk and another underneath to pull the long pit-saw downwards, is still used in native districts where labour is cheap and power facilities not available. The expression 'top-sawyer' originated from this method of sawing, for the man on top guided the saw, whilst his helper below did most of the hard work in cramped and difficult conditions.

Figure 71 shows the methods of conversion.

In 71:1 the log is cut 'through and through' to yield waney edge boards. This tangential cut perpendicular to the radius is known as *flat cut*, *plain cut* or *slash sawn*, and shows the annual rings in a series of contour markings (71:4). In 71:2 the log is 'billet' sawn (timber-merchants' terms vary and each has his own method), in which a centre-cut through the heart of the log yields two billets which are then sawn 'through and through'. This method is sometimes known as *bastard wainscot* or *wainscot billet*, and is usually adopted where there is a pronounced star shake in the centre of the log (in which case a 'pith' or 'crown' plank about 2 in. (50 mm) thick is first taken out) or where there is the probability that wide boards across the log will go heavily in rounding (see 'Shrinkage of timbers', page 109). The modern method of quartering timber, ie. radial cuts following the natural lines of cleavage, is shown in 71:3, where the heart is first 'boxed out' and flat cutting as shown then yields a fair preponderance of truly quartered or rift-sawn boards. This latter method has almost entirely superseded the old method of true radial cutting (71:6) which is both wasteful and laborious. It will be seen from the drawings that both logs (1) and (2) yield a small proportion of true quartered boards. The difference in behaviour between tangential-cut (through and through), and radial-cut (quartered) timber, is described under 'Shrinkage of timber', page 110.

Where the cut includes the natural shape of the log without preliminary squaring or trimming then the plank or board is known as *waney edge* (71:8), and square edge timber (71:8A) is obtained by trimming off on either side. If the plank is wide enough the offcuts are used to provide (71:8B) *short narrows*, and (71:8C) *long narrows*, both of which are sound timber, but correspondingly cheaper. It is obvious that square edge timber will be more expensive than waney edge timber owing to the extra sawing, waste, etc., but the economy in the latter is largely illusory. Imported sawn hardwoods are usually square edge to save shipping space, but some producers export in the form of 'boules' or complete logs cut through and through, whilst a fair proportion of African timbers are exported in the round. Very valuable timbers, ebonies, kingwood, blackwood, lignum vitae, etc., which

72 Natives felling trees at Sapele, West Africa *By courtesy of United Africa Company*

73 Cross-cutting butt at Sheffield Park Sawmills, Sussex

74 Debarking butt at Sheffield Park Sawmills, Sussex

75 Cutting log on band-mill *By courtesy of Turner and Kennedy Limited*

are of small dimension, and larger trunks of rosewood and satinwood, etc., are exported in log form only and sold by weight.

Marking and measuring timber (British measure)

Freshly sawn home-grown timber is marked with the foot superage 'board measure', i.e. square foot superficial measure, on the butt end of each plank prior to stacking. The marks are incised with a timber-scribe (raze-knife) using Roman numerals throughout. Figure 76 gives the details where every crossed line counts as 10, whilst 5 (V) can be added to any existing 10 as shown.

In all cases the measurement is expressed in square feet over the superficial measure irrespective of thickness, and must be multiplied by the thickness in inches to arrive at the true cubic content. Thus a plank 4 in. thick marked as XV will contain 15 sq. ft multiplied by 4, or 60 ft board measure 1 in. thick, and if then divided by 12 will yield the 'foot cube' content written as cube 5, ft 0, in. 0. This system of measurement is used because a single log may be converted into boards and planks of different thicknesses, and it is simpler to quote a standard price throughout. If the price quoted for, say, prime English quartered oak is 60s per cube, then as there are 12 running feet of board 12 in. wide by 1 in. thick in a cube, the cost will be 5s per ft super board measure 1 in. thick. If the plank is 2 in. thick then the board measure is doubled (24 ft) instead of quoting 10s per ft super 2 in. thick.

76 Measurement marks in timber

In measuring waney edge plank* lengths are taken to the nearest 3 in., except in very valuable timbers which may be measured to the nearest inch. An average of three widths across the face about 1 ft from each end and across the middle is then taken, and if the planks are undercut, i.e. with the edges heavily waned or rounded as they follow round the circumference of the log, then the widths are either taken across the face and across the underneath, and the average struck to give the true width through the middle of the thickness, or across the narrow face only, but out to one protruding edge of the underneath.

The content of any piece of timber can be calculated with the aid of the following formula:

Length in feet × width in feet × thickness in inches to yield the foot superage as inch, and if divided by 12 the foot cubage. Thus the calculation for a piece of timber 4 ft 6 in. long by 18 in. wide by $1\frac{1}{2}$ in. thick will be as follows:

$$4\frac{1}{2}\text{ ft} \times 1\frac{1}{2}\text{ ft} \times 1\frac{1}{2}\text{ in.} = \frac{9}{2} \times \frac{3}{2} \times \frac{3}{2} = 10\frac{1}{8}\text{ ft super.}$$

This would be written as cube 0, ft 10, in. $1\frac{1}{2}$.

Marking and measuring timber (metric measure)

Continental exporters cut to inch dimensions for the British market and are content to do so for so long as the demand exists. However, the general adoption of metric weights and measures will necessitate a complete overhaul of existing practices, and it has yet to be decided what conventional units will be adopted. At present bulk quantities of timber in continental countries are often measured in cubic metres (stères) but as a cubic metre contains 35·3150 cu. ft some smaller unit may eventually be adopted. In the meantime the procedures already mentioned are the same. Thus the calculation given above would read in metric quantities:

$1·3716\text{ m} \times 0·4572\text{ m} \times 0·0381\text{ m} = 0·023\ 892\text{ m}^3$

* The average of three widths over the face usually favours the buyer, and a measuring device incorporating sensitive fingers has been developed which will give extremely accurate readings. A similar device has been used for many years in the leather trade for measuring hides.

8 Timber seasoning, movement, etc.

The growing tree which is full of sap can contain anything from 50 per cent free water (up to 200 per cent in certain swamp-grown softwoods). A single cubic foot (0·02832 m³) of green oak can, for instance, contain up to 14 qt (16 l) of water which must be reduced to at least 2 qt (2·27 l) before the timber is fit for use. The object of seasoning is, therefore, to accelerate the evaporation of this surplus moisture, rendering the timber lighter, harder, stronger, less susceptible to discoloration and mould attack, and much less liable to shrinkage and distortion.

The water in the tree is contained in the actual fibres which are saturated (bound moisture), and in the open pores or vessels which are filled with a mixture of water and froth (free moisture), and immediately the tree is felled the vessels will start to drain (the process can be somewhat accelerated by upending the butt in the growing position). This process of natural bleeding is very slow in whole logs, but can be speeded up by converting the log into plank form, when the water-level will fall steadily until a fibre saturation point is reached (usually 30 per cent moisture content) in which the vessels are empty but the fibres remain saturated. From then on the water loss will be at a slower rate until the timber has reached an equipoise with the surrounding atmosphere. The amount of moisture thus left in the wood is termed the 'equilibrium moisture content' according to the 'relative humidity' of the prevailing atmosphere, and before describing methods of seasoning it is necessary to define these terms.

Relative humidity

Even in the driest of weather the atmosphere will always contain a certain amount of invisible water vapour which can vary considerably from hour to hour, and which is generally, but not necessarily, higher in winter than in summer. The actual degree of moisture vapour present at any one time (relative humidity) is measured with a wet and dry hygrometer, and is expressed as the percentage of moisture in the air at a given temperature, compared with the maximum amount (saturation point) the air would hold at the same temperature without actual precipitation. In this island country, surrounded by water on every side, the humidity rate is relatively high, with approximately 70 per cent humidity as fairly typical of a fine spring day, moreover it can fluctuate rapidly. Fortunately, wood is a slow conductor, therefore rapid fluctuations either side of the seasonal average can usually be ignored.

Equilibrium moisture content

As wood is an organic and hydroscopic material susceptible to moisture changes it will always endeavour to reach a state of equipoise with the surrounding atmosphere, giving up or taking in water like a sponge until the balance is achieved. The term 'equilibrium moisture content' is therefore an evaluation of the prevailing atmospheric humidity in terms of the corresponding actual water content the wood has achieved in that humidity, and expressed as a percentage of the dry weight of wood substance (see 'Measurement of moisture in timber', page 108). The important point to remember is that no matter how old the timber happens to be it will always respond in precisely the same way, and that as its environment changes so will its moisture content move in sympathy. As an approximate guide (for timber species differ slightly in their reactions), any wood stored under cover but exposed to the open air in this country will attain an equilibrium moisture content within the range of 15 per cent in dry summer weather to 22 per cent in average winter conditions.

Methods of seasoning

The whole object of seasoning is to bring the moisture content of the wood down to acceptable levels, according to the use to which it will be put, as speedily but as gently as possible. The drying out of the actual fibres after the pores are emptied is accomplished by surface evaporation and consequent capillary attraction from the moist interior of the wood, and if the evaporation rate is too fast then partial vacuums will be created in the wood substance and the cell walls will collapse, causing widespread splitting and distortion. If, however, the drying-rate is controlled, then the water loss will be replaced by air and the natural strength and elasticity of the wood will always strive to accommodate the strains imposed. In the literal sense, therefore, 'seasoning' means controlled drying, and any timber which has been satisfactorily dried down to an acceptable level is usually regarded as seasoned timber, but there is no doubt that additional storage time over the prescribed minimum does bring certain advantages not measurable in any scientific way. In effect it will have matured like wine, it will be no drier but the moisture will be more evenly distributed, and it will be kinder, more mellow, and more mature, and therefore not so liable to distort. These advantages may be fractional but they do exist, and the old craftsmen who matured their oak for 14 years under the shade of apple trees, and surrounded by breast high nettles, did so not through any mystique but for definite practical reasons.

Two methods of seasoning are currently practised (1) *air drying*, (2) *kiln drying*.* Generally speaking air-drying is slower and cheaper, kiln drying simpler but more expensive. However, as air drying can never reduce the moisture content to much below 15 per cent kiln drying is always necessary for lower levels, but as certain timbers do not respond satisfactorily to kilning in the green state preliminary air drying is advisable. Any lingering prejudice against kiln drying—and it still exists—has no basis in actual fact, for both methods are complementary.

Air drying

Ideally, hardwoods should be converted and piled for drying in winter as humidity rates are

---

* Methods of drying timber by chemical treatment or by radio-frequency heating have not yet reached the economic stage.

high and initial drying relatively slow; but in practice most merchants cut and pile thick timber in autumn, winter and very early spring, and thinner boards throughout the year, stacking the boards fairly close so that the drying-rate is not too rapid. On no account should green timber be close piled without air spaces between each plank, as this will inevitably invite mould and fungi attack (the same applies to seasoned timber unless it can be adequately protected from the rain). The normal procedure therefore, is to sweep the sawdust from each plank as it is cut (77), and stack as soon as possible on firm, level foundations in such a way that an uninterrupted flow of air is maintained over every surface. The stack itself should be built up on brick or concrete piers or creosoted timber sleepers, with wood bearers across the piers not less than 9 in. (23 cm) above ground level, and the planks or boards piled exactly over each other and separated by stickers of neutral wood – fir, poplar, horse-chestnut, etc.—placed from 18 in. (45 cm) to 24 in. (60 cm) apart according to the thickness (71:7A). These stickers can be 1 in. square section (25 mm) for thick planks piled in winter and $\frac{3}{4}$ in. (19 mm) by $\frac{1}{2}$ in. (12·5 mm) for thinner boards and summer piling, the $\frac{3}{4}$ in. (19 mm) dimension laid flat so that the stickers do not roll over as the boards are positioned. The line of the stickers must correspond with the position of the lower bearers, and they must be exactly over each other throughout the height of the stack, with the ends of the planks or boards well supported and not overhanging each other in random lengths, for the function of the sticker is not only to permit the free passage of air throughout the stack but also to restrain as much as possible any tendency to warping. When completed the top of the stack should be weighted down with odd timber slabbing, and well protected from heavy rain and hot sun by a suitable lean-to roof with a generous overhang all round. Rain driving into the sides of the stack is not harmful always provided the timber has a chance to dry out, therefore the stack should be kept as narrow as possible and never over 6 ft (1·82 m) wide, but shielding from very hot sun, particularly at the ends, is advisable in the early stages. Some form of degrade (splitting, checking, etc.) must be expected on the ends where the moisture is drawn from the cut pores fairly rapidly, but this can be kept within reason-

77 Brushing sawdust from log prior to next cut

78 Converted logs in stick at Sheffield Park Sawmills, Sussex

79 Furniture squares in stick at Sheffield Park Sawmills, Sussex

able limits by masking the ends with special paint, hoop-iron bands or wooden cleats nailed on. The first method is undoubtedly the best, using an end coating paint made up to the formula devised by the Forest Products Research Laboratory, viz. 8 parts quicklime, 100 parts resin, and 57·5 parts spirits, to which has been added 25 parts barytes and 25 parts asbestine. It cannot be obtained in any proprietary brand but is usually made up to special order, and has been used by the writer for many years with excellent results. Unfortunately, merchants cannot afford these extra precautions for the common run of timber, but some square edge timbers imported from tropical countries are end coated in this manner.

As a general rule most hardwood timbers in this country are air dried out of doors and can remain there indefinitely, although at a later stage the better logs are usually moved into open-sided storage-sheds where they can be fully protected from the rain. Beech and sycamore should, however, be taken under cover after six months, whilst walnut and plane are vulnerable to fungoid attack if dried in the open. Much depends on the locality of the mill and whether it is exposed or sheltered, therefore customs differ from one merchant to another.

Drying times

The usual time allowed for the air drying of timber to the normal equilibrium moisture content of from 15 to 22 per cent according to the season is one year in stick for every inch in thickness, but given favourable conditions 1 in. (25 mm) hardwoods piled in autumn will in all probability be down to 20 per cent by the following summer, and 2 in. (50 mm) planks to the same moisture content a few months later.* Further drying to 15 per cent is only possible in very dry weather, and in exceptional heat-waves 12 per cent might be reached, but under normal conditions the moisture content will swing backwards and forwards within the higher range, and any further drying time will make no difference beyond distributing the remaining moisture more evenly, and helping to equalise the built-in strains. For lower moisture contents other methods must, therefore, be adopted.

Kiln drying

The use of hot air in drying timber requires specialised knowledge, and is beyond the scope of this work, therefore the process is described in

* Softwoods will dry to about 20 per cent moisture content in three months.

broad outline only. For further information the booklets issued by the Timber Research and Development Association should be consulted.

The principles are simple enough, but require expert handling at every stage. In essence, timber is stacked as for air drying in enclosed compartments or buildings through which hot air is passed, either by natural draught (natural-draught kilns), or by power-driven fans (forced-draught kilns). As the heated air would induce very rapid moisture evaporation from the wood surfaces, with consequent severe shrinkage and distortion, live steam is injected into the compartment, so that the rate of evaporation is always maintained at a safe level. Constant control is necessary, as the degree of heat and level of humidification must be adjusted so that there is a progressive fall in the relative humidity, until the timber has reached the requisite moisture content. As timbers differ widely in their reactions, specific schedules have been laid down for practically all the timbers in common use; but other factors, i.e. timber quality, intended use, thickness, method of conversion (quartered or plain sawn, etc.), permissible degrade (defects), must also be taken into account, so that much depends on the skill and judgment of the operator.

The advantages of kiln drying are obvious, for green timber can be satisfactorily dried down to any given moisture content in a matter of weeks only, moreover much lower values are possible than with air drying. Whilst it is true that any tendency to warp or buckle is increased in kilning, this can be mitigated by keeping the initial temperature low and thus extending the drying time, or by air drying the timber down to 20 per cent and then kilning, and this latter method is probably ideal. As a rough guide, green hardwoods can be kiln dried to a moisture content of 10 per cent in from three to twelve weeks, according to the species and the schedules adopted; and air-dried hardwoods with 20 per cent moisture content down to the same value in 1 to 4 weeks. It must not be forgotten, however, that immediately the timber leaves the kiln it will commence to take up moisture again (moisture pick-up), and will gradually revert to the normal equilibrium content of 15 to 22 per cent. It should, therefore, be placed in a warm store, or otherwise close piled and sheeted with tarpaulins until used.

Permissible moisture contents

Timber which has been stored in the open even under the most favourable conditions is hardly dry enough for use in heated interiors. Whilst little shrinkage takes place in wood seasoned from green to fibre saturation point (30 per cent), from then on the shrinkage is appreciable with maximum movement within the range 20 per cent down to 10 per cent. The maximum moisture content of timber in use should, therefore, not exceed the amounts shown below if excessive shrinkage is to be avoided.

22 to 15 per cent	Usual limits of moisture content in thoroughly air-dried timber.
20 per cent	Dry rot safety line.
16 per cent	Outdoor furniture.
15 per cent	Joiners' work in new buildings. Normal church-work in intermittently heated interiors.
12 to 14 per cent	Bedroom furniture with only occasional heating.
11 to 13 per cent	Living-room furniture with normal heating, including reasonable central heating.
9 to 11 per cent	Furniture in flats, offices and public buildings, etc. with continuous high degree of central heating.
8 per cent	Radiator shelves and casings, etc.

The upper values in each case are usually safe enough, dependent on the timber species, as there is always some air movement from open doors, windows, etc.

It should not be assumed that because a workshop happens to be continuously heated throughout the winter months wood stored in it will automatically dry down to the lower levels. It might conceivably fall to 6 per cent in exceptional circumstances, but owing to the continual movement, opening of doors, etc. it is more likely to be within the range 10 per cent to 12 per cent and even 14 per cent, and it is the average value which counts, for timber moves slowly and is virtually unaffected by day to day changes. Therefore, some method of conditioning the timber before use may have to be adopted; but whilst the old adage that it should be stored for at least six weeks in the room in which the completed furniture is to stand is very sensible, it is hardly practicable. However, it is possible to create a small warm store, or even a very simple kiln, built of insulating materials and with a gentle source of heat, for even electric-light bulbs in a closed compartment will give sufficient for small sections, but care must be taken not to overdry and at too rapid a rate. On occasions the writer has even pressed a heated linen-cupboard into service, but a close watch should be kept for splitting and distortion, with the wood sections cut slightly oversize for after-levelling. Additionally, it is always wise to protect the completed furniture at the first possible opportunity, for oil-paint (3 coats) will give 50 per cent protection, french polish and cellulose (2 coats) 30 per cent, and wax-polish 3 per cent against moisture absorption over a period of one month, with much higher values over seven days.

Measurement of moisture in timber

The most accurate method of measuring the moisture content of timber is the oven method, in which thin slithers of the wood to be tested are accurately weighed, heated in an oven or drying-chamber, repeatedly reweighed until it has been established beyond question that all the

moisture has been driven off, and the moisture loss then calculated in accordance with the formula—net weight minus dry weight over dry weight and multiplied by 100, to yield the percentage moisture content. Thus, if the timber sample weighed initially 5 gm, and after reweighing only 4 gm, then the calculation would be:

$$\frac{5 \text{ gm} - 4 \text{ gm}}{4 \text{ gm}} \times 100 = 25 \text{ per cent moisture content}$$

Care must be taken not to scorch the wood, and the weighing must be done on an accurate chemical balance, whilst knots and other defects should not be included in the sample.

A simple oven using one or more 40 watt electric-light bulbs as described by the Forest Products Research Laboratory is illustrated in 80.

Whilst the results obtained by the oven method are extremely reliable they are more applicable to scientific research, and for field-work the electric moisture-meter will give instantaneous readings accurate enough for most practical purposes. These meters work on the principle that as wood itself is a bad conductor of electricity, any moisture present will facilitate the passage of an electrical current passing between two electrodes spaced apart and inserted into the wood, and the measure of resistance to the passage of the current can be expressed in terms of moisture present as a percentage of the total bulk. One such meter uses a transistorised sensing-plate to record the effect of the material being tested in a high-frequency electrostatic field; but most common forms of meter employ contact, clamp or drive-in pin electrodes attached to cable leads, with the meter actuated either direct from the mains, or with standard dry-cell high- and low-tension batteries.

The range of measurement varies according to the type of meter, with a normal coverage of from 6 to 30 per cent, and a margin of error of from 1 to 2 per cent. It should be borne in mind, however, that the presence of mineral salts in the wood may affect the readings, whilst some timbers give large errors, especially in the upper moisture range; but most manufacturers give a table of adjustments covering many of the commonly used timbers.

In taking any measurement, whether by oven method or moisture-meter, the readings should

80 Drying-oven for testing moisture content

COPPER GAUZE

ASBESTOS

16 SWG

not be taken from the end of the plank, but from the thickness of a cut section at least 9 in. (228 mm) in from the end and immediately the cut has been made, otherwise surface evaporation may falsify the test (82). If an approximate moisture content only is required, then the electrodes should be pushed into the surface at several points throughout the length of the plank not less than $\frac{3}{16}$ in. (4·5 mm) deep, and the average struck.

Shrinkage of timber

A full understanding of the reasons for the shrinkage of timber, the probable extent of the movement and the direction it is likely to take (wood is not an homogeneous solid and the movement is not equal in all directions) is essential if furniture is to be soundly constructed, for it is impossible to lock wood fibre permanently against its natural inclinations, and its strength is such that it will eventually overcome every effort to confine it. Furthermore, the increasing use of artificial heating means drier atmospheres and greatly increased shrinkage values, and this

82   Measuring moisture content in timber

equally applies no matter how old the wood is, for even antique furniture will rapidly disintegrate in over-heated surroundings. It should be pointed out, however, that heat alone is not inimical to wood; it is the degree of dryness occasioned by the heat which is the deciding factor.

81   Effect of strong sunlight on freshly sawn timber

The probable extent and direction of the shrinkage is best understood by visualising the tree as a compact cylinder composed of innumerable smaller cylinders or annual growth rings fitted tightly within each other. As the tree dries out so the shrinkage will take place in every direction except in the length, the circumference of the outer cylinder will grow shorter and the cylinders within will each grow progressively smaller and more tightly packed (83:1, 2). This circumferential shrinkage along the length of the annual rings is always greater than the shrinkage between the rings, and whilst a precise ratio is not possible (for the figures depend upon the density of the timber species and the oil and resin content of the fibres), it is generally assumed that the amount of shrinkage between the rings will only be a little over half that along the length of the rings.

The effect of these shrinkage values is illustrated in 83:3, 4. In 83:3 the greater amount of shrinkage in a tangentially cut plank will be across the width as shown by the heavy arrows, with about half that amount between the rings as indicated by the smaller arrows; whereas in radial or quarter cut timber the main shrinkage will be in the thickness, which is relatively unimportant (the amount shown in the drawings is exaggerated for illustration purposes). Thus, the radial or quarter cut plank (83:4, 5A) is always more stable, for not only is there less shrinkage across the width, but the pull is fairly equal from one annual ring to another, therefore there is no tendency towards distortion; whereas in (83:5B) the annual rings in the tangentially cut plank are of different lengths, and the pull on the underside away from the heart will be much greater than on the side nearer the heart. A tangentially cut plank will, therefore, pull in rounding as it dries as shown by the arrows, whilst circular sections (83:6) will go oval and square sections (83:7) diamond shaped. Where the grain direction is irregular as in (83:8), then the plank may twist in several directions across the width, whilst a further complication in tangential timber is that in conversion from the log the saw cut is parallel to the long axis of the tree (67:2A) and, therefore, diagonal to the growth rings. It must be accepted, therefore, that timber is always somewhat unpredictable in its behaviour, and only very generalised rules are possible.

Shrinkage factors

Shrinkage factors along the length can usually be ignored for they are only fractional, but both tangential and radial shrinkages can be considerable, according to the particular species. Unfortunately, the greatest degree of shrinkage takes place between the critical moisture contents of air-dry timber (20 per cent) and fully conditioned timber (9 to 10 per cent). For example, English oak, which is usually classed as a medium stable timber, will shrink approximately $\frac{5}{16}$ in. (8 mm) for every 12 in. (304 mm) of width across the face of a tangentially cut board and $\frac{3}{16}$ in. (4·5 mm) for a radially cut board, if dried down from 20 to 12 per cent moisture content; whilst beech, which has a large shrinkage value, will shrink $\frac{3}{8}$ in. (9·5 mm) and $\frac{7}{32}$ in. (5·5 mm) respectively. There is, however, no conformity between species, and English elm will exhibit less tangential and more radial shrinkage.

Dimensional changes for some of the more commonly used timbers are given below. As the moisture content of timber at any given humidity-rate varies with the species, the values are based on conditioning from an outdoor humidity-rate of 90 per cent down to an environmental humidity of 60 per cent.

Approximate comparative movement of timbers

Timber	Moisture content range 90%–60% humidity %	Tangential shrinkage		Radial shrinkage		Class
		in. per ft	mm per m	in. per ft	mm per m	
Afzelia	14–9·5	$\frac{1}{8}$	10·4	$\frac{1}{16}$	5·2	Very small
Abura	18–12·5	$\frac{13}{64}$	16·9	$\frac{1}{8}$	10·4	Small
Afromosia	15–11	$\frac{5}{32}$	13·0	$\frac{5}{64}$	6·5	Small
Agba	17–12	$\frac{7}{32}$	18·2	$\frac{3}{32}$	7·8	Small
Beech	20–12	$\frac{3}{8}$	31·2	$\frac{13}{64}$	16·9	Large
Chestnut	17·5–12·5	$\frac{5}{32}$	13·0	$\frac{5}{64}$	6·5	Small
Elm	20·5–12	$\frac{9}{32}$	23·4	$\frac{3}{16}$	15·6	Medium
Idigbo	15–11	$\frac{1}{8}$	10·4	$\frac{1}{16}$	5·2	Very small
African mahogany	20–13·5	$\frac{5}{32}$	13·0	$\frac{7}{64}$	9·1	Small
C. Amer. mahogany	19–12·5	$\frac{5}{32}$	13·0	$\frac{1}{8}$	10·4	Small
Muninga	13–10	$\frac{5}{64}$	6·5	$\frac{1}{16}$	5·2	Very small
English oak	20–12	$\frac{5}{16}$	26·0	$\frac{3}{16}$	15·6	Medium
Yellow pine	17–11	$\frac{3}{16}$	15·6	$\frac{7}{64}$	9·1	Small
Ramin	20–12	$\frac{3}{8}$	31·2	$\frac{3}{16}$	15·6	Large
Sitka spruce	19–12·5	$\frac{5}{32}$	13·0	$\frac{7}{64}$	9·1	Small
Teak	15–10	$\frac{5}{32}$	13·0	$\frac{3}{32}$	7·8	Small
Utile	22–14	$\frac{3}{16}$	15·6	$\frac{11}{64}$	14·3	Small

Distortion, i.e. warping, winding, etc., is not dependent on shrinkage values, but generally speaking timbers whose tangential and radial shrinkages are near to each other (utile, etc.) distort very little.

9 Timber characteristics and defects

Grain, texture and figure

Whilst the general term *grain* is normally used to cover many different characteristics of timber, viz. straight grain, coarse grain, curly grain, raised grain, etc., etc., strictly speaking it should only denote the direction or arrangement of the wood fibres in relation to the longitudinal axis of the tree or of the converted plank, with the term *texture* as descriptive of the relative size and arrangement of the constituent cells, and *figure* denoting the ornamental markings brought about by structural characteristics.

Grain

Where the wood fibres follow or are parallel to the long axis of the tree or plank then the term *straight grain* is used. Any slight deviation from the parallel is known as *oblique* or *diagonal* grain, and pronounced deviation *cross grain*. If the arrangement of the fibres twists about the long axis then the twist is known as *spiral* or *torse*; whilst regular waves or ripples create *wavy* grain, and irregular curves *curly* grain. The term *interlocked grain* refers to a condition in which, for some unknown reason, the direction of the fibres regularly changes or reverses in successive growth layers, and is often known as *ribbon* or *stripy* grain (sapele, etc.). All these grain arrangements occur naturally in the tree, although diagonal grain can be caused by faulty conversion, and spiral grain cut through and through in the normal way will show as simple diagonal grain on the face. Additionally, the term 'grain' is used in connection with methods of conversion, etc.; thus a straight cut across the face of the plank will show *end grain*, whilst cuts parallel to the long axis (ripping cuts) produce *long-grain* timber, and oblique cuts *short-grain* timber. Quarter-sawn timber is sometimes known as *edge-grain* timber, and slash or flat sawn (through and through) as *flat sawn* timber. The terms *rough grain*, *raised grain*, *smooth grain*, etc., are not descriptive of the innate characteristics of the wood, but only of the finished surface.

Texture

Texture is concerned with the relative size and arrangement of the cells. Thus a wood with large open pores usually referred to as *coarse grain* is more correctly *coarse textured*; with small pores set close together which can be brought to a good finish as *fine* or *close textured*; with uniform pores showing little difference between springwood and summerwood *even textured*, with the reverse for *uneven textured*. Oak, ash and elm are coarse-textured (coarse-grained) woods, because there is an alternation of large open pores of the springwood with the densely packed fibres of the summerwood.

Figure

Structural characteristics, medullary rays, pronounced or irregular growth rings, variations in colour or texture, knots and abnormalities all produce the ornamental markings or 'figure' on the surface of the wood, and are of great importance to the furniture-maker. All these are innate, i.e. natural characteristics, and can be further developed or exaggerated by the methods of conversion adopted. For example, radial cuts in true quartered oak and chestnut follow the path of the medullary rays, and show the typical 'flash' or 'silver grain' to best advantage. These rays are also visible in quarter-cut beech, whilst sycamore will sometimes produce a magnificent flame figure, and plane a rich lacy pattern (lacewood). Again, quarter-sawing of some timbers produces very straight regular grain patterns, instead of the usual contour markings of flat-sawn timber where the saw cuts through the annual growth rings. If there are concentric bands of colour encircling the tree as in Rio rosewood, Macassar ebony and other exotics then quartering will produce boldly marked vertical stripings, and plain sawn wood large irregular blazes of predominant colour. Timbers with a marked contrast between springwood and summerwood often show the annual growth rings very conspicuously if plain cut, and even more so if rotary cut into veneers, of which typical examples are the resinous softwoods, Douglas fir (Columbian pine), yellow pine, pitch-pine, etc., and the ring-porous hardwoods, ash, oak, elm, etc. Bold demarcations between sap and heartwood yield the prized laburnum oysters, the strong pattern of royal walnut, and the delicate feathering of some walnut crotches.

Some of the most beautiful figurations are obtained from irregular grain structure. Wavy and curly grain can yield quilted and swirl figure, and the very beautiful dapple and mottle in which alternate light and dark bands cross the grain direction instead of running with it. This transverse movement can occur in many woods, and has always been highly prized in sycamore for the backs of violins. A variation of the stripy figure is 'roe', in which local irregularities break up the stripe, whilst similar irregularities or dimples in the cambium layer produce the blister grain of Douglas fir, and smaller inward-growing dimples one type of burr as in burr maple. Sometimes the crotch or fork of the tree produces the self-descriptive and highly prized fan, feather, swirl and curl figuring; whilst the buttress or root base of some trees, notably walnuts, the very bold-patterned stump figure.

Some abnormalities produce striking figure, notably burr formations caused either by fungal irritation of the cambium layer, severe pollarding or lopping, or in the case of elm, natural growth irregularities. Burrs can also be caused by large numbers of small twigs which fail to develop, and yield the familiar bird's eye in maple, etc. Examples of some of these figure markings are shown in 84, but it would be impossible to include all the known varieties, for practically every species of tree is capable of yielding outstanding effects in grain, texture and colour, and there are many recorded instances of exceptional logs fetching four-figure sums for conversion into veneers.

Timber coloration

The natural colouring agents in timber are water soluble, and will tend to leach out if repeatedly soaked or exposed to weathering for long periods. Typical colour examples are logwood which yields a commercial water-soluble fierce red dye, and fustic a khaki-yellow. Generally speaking, timber is lighter in colour when freshly sawn and gradually darkens as the wood surfaces oxidise, but as the colours are not permanent they may ultimately fade. The sapwood of timber is usually lighter than the heartwood, and this serves as the usual method of identification; but some species exhibit little if any difference, notably ash, sycamore, beech, holly, silver fir, etc.

84   Grain and figure in timber   English oak

Bird's eye maple

The precise description of colour in any timber specimen is virtually impossible, as so many factors apply. No two trees are ever alike, and at best a timber can only be described as having general characteristics modified or accentuated by growth conditions, exposure to air, heat, sunlight, etc. In general, most woods, with the exception of jet-black ebonies and blackwood, and pure white holly, have a yellowish cast which can never be bleached out completely. It is this predominant yellow in conjunction with reds and blacks which give the innumerable shades of brown. Greens do exist, but are usually the result of abnormalities, whilst clear greys are the result of weathering or treatment by chemical means.

Timbers which change colour under normal indoor conditions with only occasional exposure to direct sunlight, include the following:

Timbers which fade rosewood, walnut, mansonia, teak, agba, gaboon, etc.

Timbers which yellow African mahogany, sapele, walnut (most species), agba, gaboon, maple, plane, sycamore, oak, etc.

Timbers which redden cherry, yew, beech, kingwood, purpleheart, padouk, etc.

The lists are by no means complete, and individual specimens may not necessarily behave in the manner indicated, whilst all polishes tend to darken timber in time, and oil and wax pronouncedly so.

Timber odour

Most timbers have trace odours, some very pronounced, due to the presence of essential oils which often decide the use of the wood. Notable examples are cedrela or cigar-box cedar, camphorwood, etc. Some timbers are also known by their particular scent or odour, as sandalwood, rosewood, jamwood, sneezewood, stinkwood, etc. Teak, Australian walnut and certain African timbers have a highly objectionable smell when freshly worked; but most scents and odours, with the notable exception of camphor and cedar which are used as moth deterrents, rapidly fade on exposure to the air, due to the surface evaporation or drying out of the essential oils.

Durability of timber

Hardness is no criteria of durability even though most, but not all, durable timbers are essentially hard and dark in colour, due to the higher content of wood substance and the presence of antiseptic tannins and resins. A notable exception is western red cedar, which is not a true cedar but a very light softwood so impregnated with phenolic-type resins that it is almost impervious to decay.

The question of durability hardly arises in indoor domestic furniture, for all timbers are sufficiently durable under controlled conditions.

Australian silky oak

Quilted maple

Where, however, continuous moist conditions occur in the presence of free oxygen then the timber is immediately subject to decay in various forms. Beech or elm for instance will last for centuries, either as furniture or totally immersed in water or deeply buried in the earth; but if either is laid on wet soil, or only shallowly buried in the upper layers which contain free oxygen, it will speedily rot.

Timbers for all work exposed to weathering must, therefore, be chosen carefully for natural durability and resistance to decay. Unfortunately, it cannot be assumed that because a timber is highly resinous it is therefore extremely durable, although it will be more durable than timbers with a low resin content. Timbers of proved durability include oak, chestnut, yew, teak and greenheart; whilst if the work is to be painted or otherwise protected then obviously timbers of only average durability can be used. Some timbers are, however, inclined to repel paint, whilst others will not absorb sufficient preservative except under pressure, therefore reference should be made to the standard textbooks on timber preservation.

Fire resistance of wood

Although wood might appear to be one of the most inflammable of materials, some species, notably crabwood, jarrah, iroko, padouk and teak are very resistant, and all timbers of large dimension char outwardly, cutting off the supply of oxygen necessary to support combustion. However, built-in fitments and fixtures in exhibition-work, public buildings, etc. are sometimes required to be fireproofed, or composed of fire-retardant materials. Plywoods and chipboards in fire-retardant quality can be obtained to special order; or the completed fitment can be coated with special paints or clear varnishes; or treated with various chemical preparations, the most widely used of which is ammonium phosphate. Alternatively, plywood panels or partitions can be interleaved with plasterboard or soft asbestos to give a 'one hour' standard resistance.

It is, or should be, the responsibility of the buyer or his agent to specify precisely the degree of resistance required, and the materials or treatment to be used; but the terms 'fireproof' or 'fire-resistant' should not be accepted without qualification, otherwise they may be liable to serious misconstruction. It is usually more correct to claim that a combustible material suitably treated is 'fire-retardant' only.

Defects in timber

Every tree is a prey to defects from the moment

Satinwood

African mahogany

it emerges as a seedling to the last stages of seasoning, and these defects can be innate (inherent vice), such as the characteristic natural shrinkage of timber; acquired defects occasioned by seasonal checks, insect and fungal attack, etc.; and artificial defects caused by incorrect conversion and seasoning. As, however, any one defect may arise from several causes it is more convenient to classify them as *natural* or *artificial*.

Natural defects
Knots

These are in effect the basal stumps of incipient or cast-off branches in the living tree. Where the tree itself naturally prunes its branches owing to lack of light caused by overcrowding, or where such branches are artificially pruned in controlled forestry and cleanly sawn, then the cambium layers will heal over the wound and the knot is then live or embedded (85:1A). Where, however, a mature branch is broken off, leaving a long ragged stump, then the cambium layer cannot heal the wound and the stump dies, forming a deal or loose knot, often rot effected (85:2A).

All knots whether live or dead affect the mechanical strength of the timber, owing to the abrupt change in the direction of the fibres, and constitute blemishes which detract from the value. They are, therefore, graded as follows:

Pin knots Small knots $\frac{1}{2}$ in. (12·5 mm) or under, often caused by the shedding of early branches. Usually allowable in prime timber.
Spike or splay knots (85:3). Knots sliced through their length during conversion, and commonly known as 'slash' knots. They are difficult to plane up, especially in softwood timber, whilst large specimens are not permissible in hardwood timber unless allowed for in the measurement.
Encased knots Dead knots which are still sound and difficult to dislodge, and often ringed with resin in softwood timber.
Branched knots Two or three knots springing from a common centre.

Knots are classified as small, medium and large, the latter usually $1\frac{1}{2}$ in. (38 mm) in diameter and over; but gradings are not precise and vary according to the country of origin.

Shakes

Both the medullary ray and springwood cells of ring-porous hardwoods are weaker than the remainder, and built-in tensions are created which tend to level out, either in the growing tree under certain adverse conditions or in the felled log during seasoning. Thus extensive splitting may occur in the weakest links, i.e. radially along the medullary rays, and tangentially at the junction of springwood and summerwood. Various forms of shake are common, as follows:

Radial shakes The log splits from the pith or heart radially along the medullary rays, usually indicating that the tree has passed its prime. Conversion losses can be minimised by placing the cuts either side of the shake, always provided the growth of the tree does not twist upon its axis, in which case the shakes become spiral, rendering the log useless for long lengths. Where only one shake is present it is known as a 'simple heart shake', whilst two shakes in line compose a 'double heart shake' (85·4), and several a 'star shake' (85:5).
Frost shakes (85:7) project inwardly from a definite frost rib on the cambium and are, as their name implies, the result of severe weather.
Tangential shakes The soft springwood of the log splits away from the harder summerwood, either during seasoning or through shearing stresses in the growing tree caused by old age, excessive bending under strong winds, intense heat, etc. A frequent cause in oak is the depradations of the tortrix viridána moth, whose caterpillars strip the young leaves in early summer, with the result that growth is checked and the wood rings fail to cohere. Where such shakes run along part of the annual ring only, then they are known as 'cup shakes' (85:6A); but where the log is completely encircled then they become 'ring shakes' (83:6B). Usually such shakes seriously detract from the value of the timber. English walnuts are particularly prone to cup and ring shakes, as the trees are rarely felled until they are long past maturity.
Cross shakes (*thunder shakes*) These failures are caused by compression and not by splitting or shearing, whilst the actual rupture is across the grain and not with it as with all other shakes. The probable cause is not thunder as the name suggests, but either felling shatter (the sudden

CUP　　　BOW　　　SPRING　　　WARP

impact as the felled log hits either hard ground or another fallen log), or mechanical strain in the living tree. Chiefly confined to the softer varieties of tropical hardwoods, and appearing either as a definite fracture or an overriding of the fibres, showing only as a faint raised line across the width of the plank (85:8), they destroy the usefulness of the timber which will snap like a carrot under strain. This particular type of shake often occurs with a soft condition in the heartwood, known as 'brittle heart', 'carrot heart', etc., and agba is particularly liable to this defect. End splitting and sun checking (page 119) are usually regarded as artificial defects due to errors in seasoning, but a marked propensity to split and check may be inherent in some timber species and such defects may be part natural and part artificial.

Pitch veins, pitch pockets, etc.

Sometimes known as resin pockets, they can appear either as thin veins or shallow cavities filled with resin. Usually caused by damage to the cambium layer in resinous woods, they may remain hidden and thus constitute a serious defect in structural timbers.

Pith flecks

Repeated damage to the cambium layer by small insects is often healed over with bark, and may show as small dots or patches of brown cork deeply buried in some timbers, notably birch, alder and sycamore. They have no effect other than that of unsightliness.

Rind galls, etc.

Patches of ingrowing bark, probably caused by exterior damage to the growing tree. Other natural defects include 'callus', or tissue formed over a wound in a tree resulting in unnatural growth incorporated in the normal wood growth; 'canker', caused by fungoid disease; and 'cat face', a partially healed fire scar.

Internal sapwood

Normally, the sapwood dies ring by ring, forming heartwood, but on occasions patches of

sapwood survive within the heartwood, and show as lighter patches sometimes seen in Rio rosewood. It is not known how the condition arises. Sapwood also can be prematurely killed by frost or other agents, whilst the cambium is repaired and continues to grow, forming new sapwood over the dead patches which appear in later years as a dark ring. The wood usually separates and breaks away along the ring during conversion.

Burrs

These are not usually classed as defects as they may enhance the value of the timber considerably; they are, however, true defects. They can be caused either by fungal or insect attack irritating the cambian layers, and resulting in large rapid growths, usually at the base of the tree, or by numbers of small twigs which fail to develop owing to insufficient nourishment, forming a dense mass. The knobs in severely lopped or pollarded trees, and the witch's broom in birch trees, are typical examples.

Artificial defects

All timbers shrink on drying, some pronouncedly so, thus creating internal strains and stresses. Normally, the natural elasticity of a healthy wood structure will distribute these stresses evenly, but if the structure is unequal or lacking in elasticity (innate defect), and if incorrect seasoning imposes too great a strain, then various forms of distortion, splitting, etc. will occur. The weighting down of timbers during seasoning helps to reduce distortion.

Cupping or rounding (85:13)

The plank hollows across the width, forming a rounding on the underface, often due to incorrect piling.

Bowing (85:14)

The plank is curved like a bow throughout its length. A succession of short bows is usually caused by sagging between too widely spaced stickers or by stickers which are not placed exactly over each other.

Springing (85:15)

Sometimes known as 'edge bend', the wood remains flat but bends edgewise on its own plane.

Twisting (85:16)

The plank twists on its longitudinal axis with the result that the long edges are straight, but the diagonals are curved. Usually known as 'in winding'.

Warping, casting

Synonymous terms for distortion in one or more directions. (See Twisting.)

End splitting (85:9)

The butt end of the plank splits open, usually caused by too rapid drying, but some species will always split.

Sun checking (85:10)

The wood surface is covered with small splits along the grain caused by too rapid drying in hot sun. Not serious unless the splits penetrate deeply.

Flaking

The surface of the wood lifts in innumerable small flakes or layers which spring under the cutting action, preventing a smooth surface. Sometimes due to structural weakness, but can also be caused by incorrect seasoning.

Diagonal grain

The grain runs obliquely to the longitudinal axis, usually due to incorrect sawing, but some timbers exhibit marked deviations in grain direction which cannot be avoided. Although the condition may make surfacing more difficult it is not important, except in structural members where the impact strength loss is high, and in bending where a grain slope of 1 in 25 may mean a bending strength loss of 4 per cent, and a 1 in 5 slope a loss of 45 per cent.

Case hardening (85:11)

If the wood is kiln dried too quickly then the surfaces dry out at a rate quicker than the rate of movement of moisture by capillary attraction from the centre of the plank, with the result that the dry outer layers are in tension, and the moist interior in compression. Cuts which close ahead of the saw are often due to case hardening. Provided the actual wood fibres are not ruptured the condition can be cured by steaming and redrying.

Honeycombing (85:12)

If the kilning of case-hardened timber is continued to dryness then the natural shrinkage movement of the moist interior as it dries will be locked in by the rigid outer skin, resulting in severe internal stresses and subsequent checking or disruption of the wood fibres, not visible from the outside. There is no cure for the condition, which severely depreciates the value of the timber.

Collapse

The too rapid kiln drying of green timber can result in a flattening of the wood cells, caused by vacuums created by the withdrawal of water to below fibre saturation point at a rate faster than it can be replaced by either air or live steam. This condition is known as 'collapse' and is characterised by extensive shrinking and warping, particularly in the springwood, giving a washboard effect. It can also be caused by too slow drying at too high a temperature, or too high a humidity-rate, and can sometimes be remedied by steaming and rekilning.

Stains in timber

These can be caused by harmless fungi as distinct from wood-rotting fungi, soil conditions, frost factors, etc., chemical contamination, and natural oxidisation or weathering.

Mould- and sap-staining fungi, etc.

Certain harmless moulds feed on the carbohydrates in the wood cells and can produce grey, grey-blue, pink, white and black stains. Usually this type of staining is confined to the surfaces of the wood, and can, therefore, be eradicated by brushing or sanding down; but several types, of which the best known is *Ceratostomella pini*, attack the sapwood, producing the characteristic blueing of badly seasoned softwoods. This discoloration cannot be satisfactorily bleached out, and is due almost entirely to an optical effect, similar to the apparent blueness of watered milk. All these fungi have little if any mechanical effect on the timber, as the hyphae or mould threads constrict considerably where they pierce the cell walls, whereas wood-destroying fungi bore large apertures, and consume the cellulose.

Some fungi actually increase the value of the timber, as in the case of the beef-steak fungus (*Fistulina hepatica*) which can sometimes be seen growing on old, standing oak trees, the early stages of which produce a rich golden brown; and the much rarer *Chlorosplnieium* sp. which stains oak a vivid green. Both have some mechanical effect on the timber, but not enough to impair its usefulness in decorative-work. All species of fungi require a certain minimum moisture content, usually well over 20 per cent, therefore dry, seasoned timber is not affected.

Mineral stains

Certain soil conditions can cause pronounced staining, usually in brown or greyish streaks, as for example black-hearted ash, brown-hearted beech, and the reddish-brown mineral streak in the heartwood of Parana pine. As these are natural pigment-stains they do not affect the mechanical properties of the timber. They cannot be satisfactorily bleached out. Some timbers show actual deposits of white and grey crystalline mineral salts in the grain, and at times actual calcium stones which penetrate some distance into the wood. The difficult working properties of some exotic timbers is often due to the dulling action of these mineral salts on cutting edges.

Chemical stains

Practically all timbers contain sufficient colour-forming compounds to produce staining when brought into contact with acidic or alkaline chemicals, and in this respect behave much like litmus paper, producing reds, pinks and browns with acid reactions (french polish, urea glues, etc.), and blues and greens with alkaline reactions (soap, detergents, etc.). Additionally, most timbers contain appreciable amounts of tannic acid which if wetted will react in greater or lesser degree with iron in any form, producing the characteristic blue-black staining of iron nails in exterior oak-work. Other timbers besides oak showing strong reactions are afromosia, camphorwood, Douglas fir and sweet chestnut; whilst African mahogany, coigue, idigbo, gedunohor, sapele and utile react slightly to produce slight staining. Timber for scrubbed table-tops, draining-boards, etc. should be as neutral as possible. Teak, maple, sycamore, oak and deal are usually unaffected by soap and water, but agba, ayan, idigbo and afzelia are known to be unsuitable. Where there is any doubt a thorough test should be made beforehand.

Natural oxidisation, weathering, etc.

Freshly converted green timber will oxidise rapidly if the wood surfaces remain wet for any length of time, due to the formation of chemical compounds which act on the colour-forming properties of the wood, producing brown or grey staining. This chemical effect is most marked in light-coloured woods, such as sycamore, which must be surface dried immediately it is converted if the overall whiteness is to be preserved. Moreover, sticker marks can penetrate quite deeply, particularly where there is chemical action between the actual sticker and the wood surface, and for this reason stickers should always be neutral woods, deal, horse-chestnut or poplar which have been thoroughly dried.

Additional to seasoning discolorations is the effect of weather and sunlight on wood which can either bleach or darken surfaces very appreciably. Cherry, for instance, will darken considerably if exposed to strong sunlight for a few hours, so also will mahogany, whilst freshly sawn dry teak will rapidly oxidise from light green to dark brown. On the other hand, direct sunlight will bleach dark rosewood to a medium walnut colour, and walnut itself will lighten considerably, whilst kingwood will rapidly fade from deep purple to dark red-brown. The general rule would appear to be that dark woods lighten and light woods darken, but it is hardly safe to assume that the rule follows automatically, and tests should always be made. Some synthetic lacquers contain ultra-violet light barriers which to some extent inhibit the bleaching action of strong sunlight, but only certain woods are protected and the results are never altogether permanent.

Stain identification

Positive identification of any particular type of stain can be difficult, but as a rule fungal and mineral stains are of variable intensity, fading slightly at the edges and following the grain. Stains with a hard edge which do not follow the grain are usually chemical in origin, whilst overall discoloration is probably due to weathering or incorrect seasoning.

Bleaching stains

Iron stains can be satisfactorily bleached out with either a saturated solution of oxalic acid in water or methylated spirit, hydrogen peroxide, some household bleaches, ink-eradicators, etc., and light chemical staining from other sources may also respond to several applications. The bleaching out of fungal stains, mineral discolorations and natural oxidisation is never really feasible, although proprietary two-solution bleaches can assist in masking the discoloration by rendering the surfaces of the wood more opaque. Bleaching of entire surfaces often—and to the writer's way of thinking, horribly—perpetrated on oak and pine, owe much to the lavish use of white grain fillers which choke the wood surface. The action of most bleaches is, of course, the release of free oxygen as the active bleaching agent.

Timber diseases and pests

Wood which is deeply buried in the ground or completely submerged in water does not decay, as witness the highly prized black bog oak which has been buried for centuries under layers of wet peat, and the use of timber baulks for underwater piles and breakwaters. However, where there is free oxygen, living fungi will attack the wood, provided there is moisture present; and although most of these fungi are relatively harmless, causing little more than local staining, two main types of rot actively feed upon the wood substance and eventually destroy it.

White rots

These are usually outdoor types, commonly known as 'wet rots' (rotting logs, fence posts, etc.). They consume both the cellulose and lignin content of the wood, leaving only a white, pithy or slimy residue.

Brown rots

These are mainly of the indoor type, but can also occur out of doors. They attack the cellulose content only, leaving the lignin content intact, and are commonly known as 'dry rots', with the wood residue usually brown, spongy, dry and deeply cracked with and across the grain, giving a characteristic charred appearance.

Dote

This is an outdoor type of brown rot known commercially as 'dote' or 'punk'. Living trees are affected, also felled logs full of sap and awaiting conversion, the infection spreading through the heartwood and finally emerging as a bracket-shaped fruit-body on the bark. Incipient dote is easily recognisable (88), as the wood is peppered with round or oval greyish-white spots which do not appear to affect the mechanical strength to any great extent, but in later stages the wood becomes brown, dry, with spongy white streaks. The fungus cannot exist in the dry state, therefore sound unaffected timber need not be treated. As some harmless fungi cause similar brown staining, doteiness can be tested for by lifting a small splinter of the wood surface with a knife; if dote is present the splinter will break easily with a brash fracture. Fruit woods, pear, apple, cherry, plum, etc., are particularly susceptible to this form of rot (87:1).

True dry rot *(Lacrymans merulius)*

This is an indoor type, and of all the wood-destroying fungi the most serious as it will attack dry seasoned timber if the conditions are suitable. Initially, the infection needs damp, badly ventilated surroundings, but once the fungus has taken hold it will carry its own water in thick thread-like hyphae which can penetrate thick brickwork in search of fresh material which it rapidly consumes, leaving the characteristic deeply cleft, cube-like charring, often hardly noticeable under painted surfaces except as local sinkages. In dark conditions the fungus may appear as a white woolly growth, or a smooth fan-shaped grey skin with ragged edges exuding moisture droplets, but if light is present then the typical fruit-bodies will appear. Those who have seen a fully formed fruit-body, sometimes many feet across, with its leprous-grey skin suffused with livid patches of white, yellow and lilac-blue, and peppered with rust-red spores are hardly likely to forget the experience.

Treatment for dry rot must be drastic: all infected woodwork cut away and burnt, infected brickwork and non-timber materials scorched with a blowlamp, and treated with an efficient antiseptic. Sound timber in the vicinity should be thoroughly brushed over with either a water soluble preservative such as commercial sodium fluoride (4 per cent), zinc chlorate (5 per cent), applied hot if possible; or one of the proprietary solvent-type preservatives recommended for the purpose. Care should be taken with all these chemicals in confined spaces, for although they are not intrinsically dangerous to handle they must necessarily be highly toxic if they are to be effective.

Several other dry rots, notably the cellar fungus *(Coniophora cerebella)*, attack house woodwork, but require continuous moisture, therefore they present no hazard to dry timber.

Insect pests

Most important of these are the lyctus, death-watch and furniture beetles; and of secondary importance in that they attack only unseasoned, sickly or softwood timber, the pinhole borers, longhorn beetles and giant wood-wasp. All these pests are winged and capable of flight in search of suitable breeding-places and in every case it is the larvae or worm which actually attacks the wood.

Pinhole borers (ambrosia beetles)

These are confined to tropical countries and attack the sapwood and heartwood of freshly felled logs waiting for extraction. Wood attacked by pinhole borers can be recognised immediately by the very small neat exit holes, usually stained with fungus, and the straight tunnels empty of dust running both with and across the grain. Usually, structural damage is slight, and timber which has been attacked can safely be used in this country, although obviously there must be prejudice against it owing to the apparent similarity with the ravages of the true furniture beetle.

Lyctus (powder-post) beetle (86:B)

Several species exist and are common to timber-yards where they attack the sapwood of hard-woods with large pores, notably oak, ash, elm and coarse-grained walnuts. Close-grained woods and softwoods are usually immune, as the large eggs are not laid in cracks or crevices but in the actual pores of the wood which must be wide enough to receive them. The attack usually dies out as the wood becomes seasoned and the available starch is exhausted, but in the meantime the entire sapwood can be reduced to a flour-like dust. The mature beetle is dun coloured, with a narrow body about $\frac{3}{16}$ in. (4·7 mm) long, slightly larger than the furniture beetle, and with a more pronounced head.

Common furniture beetle *(Anobium punctatum)* (86:A)

Commonly known as *woodworm*, this is the most serious pest, and as a generalisation it may be stated that there are few if any domestic dwellings in the southern half of this country whose roof rafters, floors or general woodwork, including furniture, do not show some evidence of infestation. A few flight holes on the surface of polished timber may not appear serious, but the wood below may be so tunnelled as to reach the point of total collapse, therefore a constant watch should be kept on every item of woodwork.

The mature beetle is oblong shaped, from $\frac{1}{5}$ in. (5 mm) to $\frac{1}{10}$ in. (2·5 mm) long and dusty dark brown in colour, with wing-cases covered with lines of small punctures (hence the specific name). It commonly breeds in the dead branches of living trees, fencing-posts, etc., to enter the house by any open window during the dry season summer. After the female beetle has mated about 20 eggs are laid in any suitable crack or crevice, and in particular the exit or flight holes of previous larvae, and the curved white grub, which is equipped with strong biting jaws, hatches in about six weeks to commence its tunnelling by consuming the wood and excreting small pellets of granular dust. When it has reached maturity, which can be anything from one to two years according to the starch content of the wood, the grub which is now about $\frac{1}{4}$ in. (6·3 mm) long moves to close under the surface, where it pupates and tunnels its way upwards to emerge finally as an adult beetle at any time from late May to August. It can then fly off to mate and renew the cycle.

Whilst the sapwood of any timber is particularly liable to infestation (and it is for this reason that sapwood should never be used in furniture), the heartwood of certain sweet timbers, notably birch, beech, alder and some soft walnuts, are also attacked, whilst any timber affected by dampness or incipient decay is also prone. Alder, in particular, speedily becomes

86 Wood-boring beetles

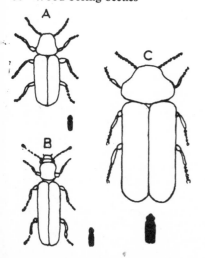

riddled with furniture beetle, hence the wise-acres claim that it is better to have a plank or two of alder lying about the timber-yard to attract any migrant beetles—a highly invidious contention, for the alder then becomes a first-class breeding-ground. Polished and painted surfaces do, of course, accord protection against the egg-laying female beetle, but invariably there is some hidden crack or crevice or an old flight hole which invites attack, therefore carcase backs and the underframing of furniture should be periodically examined for freshly expelled fine dust. Birch or alder plywoods glued with animal or vegetable glues are particularly susceptible, but resin-glued ply is normally resistant.

Death-watch beetle *(Xestobium rufovillosum)* (86:c)

This is a larger cousin of the furniture beetle, about $\frac{1}{4}$ in. (6·3 mm) to $\frac{1}{3}$ in. (8·5 mm) long and without the characteristic punctures on the wing-cases. The mature beetle raps the wood with its head during the mating season in early summer, producing the familiar ticking sound which is magnified by the wood and can travel considerable distances—hence the specific name of 'death-watch' beetle.

The life-cycle closely resembles that of the furniture beetle, but can extend over anything from one and a half to several years, dependent on the condition of the timber; whilst after pupation the mature beetle does not emerge immediately, but usually waits until the following spring. The seasoned heartwood of most timbers can be attacked, but infestation is usually confined to old oak in which some subtle change, probably induced by damp conditions, has rendered the wood more digestible, hence its incidence in old buildings, church roofing etc. where the stoutest structural timbers can be reduced to mere shells. Infestation is rare in furniture, and is immediately recognisable by the large exit holes and characteristic bun-shaped pellets of wood-dust.

House longhorn beetle *(Hylotrupes)*

This pest is extremely destructive on the continent of Europe, but virtually confined to certain pine-forest regions of Surrey in England. Soft-wood only is attacked, and infestation is usually limited to roof or attic. The mature beetle is from $\frac{1}{4}$ in. (6·3 mm) to $\frac{3}{4}$ in. (19 mm) in length, varying in colour from brown to iridescent green, with characteristic long curved feelers, whilst the oval exit holes can be very large and up to $\frac{3}{8}$ in. (9·5 mm) in size. Any attack by this beetle should be reported immediately to the Forest Products Research Laboratory, Princes Risborough, Buckinghamshire, as it is essential to keep track of its movements.

Certain other types of longhorn beetle infest the sapwood of both hard wood and softwoods. They do not as a rule attack seasoned timber, and are, therefore, confined to forest and timber-yard.

Giant wood-wasp

These only attack the living tree, and are, therefore, the foresters' concern. An occasional mature wasp of somewhat terrifying aspect, much bigger than a hornet and with a long egg-laying probe which could be mistaken for a sting, can sometimes be seen haunting the wood-pile in late summer, but can safely be disregarded.

Methods of treatment for insect pests

No treatment is required for Pinhole Borer as the tunnels are always empty, but infestation by furniture and death-watch beetle should be taken in hand immediately, the entire surface cleaned with a powerful vacuum-cleaner to clear the flight holes of dust, and a proprietary wood-worm killer of the solvent type, usually a metallic or chlorinated naphthalene, liberally brushed or swabbed over the surface. Each flight hole should also be injected with the fluid, using the cheap polystyrene squeeze bottles with nozzle stoppers available, so that the hidden tunnelling can carry the fluid into the body of the wood. The entire treatment should be repeated in the following spring just before the beetles emerge (for the insecticide will not necessarily reach all the hidden grubs which will continue to pupate), after which a yearly check should be made for any signs of fresh dust, and measures taken accordingly. Most proprietary woodworm des-troyers do not stain the wood permanently or interfere with the existing polish, and should be applied as liberally as possible, for they are quite safe to handle. However, spraying in confined spaces should not be done unless efficient face masks are worn; and in any case liberal brushing is always preferable to spraying, as the oily fluid tends to bridge over existing flight holes, thus failing to penetrate.

Notes on buying timber

Buyers of waney edge timber in small quantities direct from the saw-mill or timber-merchant must expect to pay considerably more per foot cube than buyers of complete logs of say 50 cube of any one variety, moreover they cannot assume the right to pick and choose individual planks, but must be prepared to accept them 'as they rise' from the pile. However, most co-operative merchants will allow selection, particularly to known customers, although they must necessarily charge higher prices. Imported square edge timber is stacked according to thickness; the planks may be from different logs but the quality is usually fairly consistent throughout the pile, therefore it is reasonably safe to buy 'as they rise' and only paying extra for small quantities. Wide boards cut 'through and through' are usually obtainable in home-grown and some African timbers, but as they are cut from the centre of the tree, pith defects and pronounced rounding must be expected. Quartered timber can sometimes be obtained in fairly wide boards, particularly in English oak, but are obviously more expensive. Wide boards in teak, Honduras mahogany and other valuable timbers are un-fortunately now almost unobtainable owing to past over-exploitation; any such extra wide or long boards and planks command considerably higher prices. A fair average specification for teak and Honduras mahogany is now about 8 in. (200 mm) wide and 8 ft (2·4 m) long, but African timbers have not yet been over-exploited, and greater widths and lengths are commonly available. In ordering teak it is more economical to give the timber-merchant exact descriptions of the minimum widths, thicknesses and lengths required so that he can pick the nearest. Assuming that planks 8 in. (200 mm) wide and 7 ft (2·1 m) long will suffice, then he may be able

87   Defects in timber

1   Dote in cherry

2   Shakes and knots in English walnut

3   Rind gall in cherry

to supply widths of 8¼ in. (210 mm) and lengths of 7 ft 3 in. (2·2 m), thus saving valuable timber. Thicknesses are usually very full indeed, but only charged for at the nominal grading.

Seasoned timber

The terms *dry*, *bone dry*, *well seasoned* are relatively meaningless without supporting evidence, for any timber which has been sticked one year for every inch (25 mm) of thickness may be counted as air dry or seasoned, as distinct from green. The moisture content will, of course, depend on the season of the year, and not on the number of years in stick; it should not exceed 20 or 22 per cent in exceptional circumstances in this country, unless it is water wet with drifting rain or snow. Whilst further drying over the prescribed minimum will not make any difference to the moisture content (for all timber will always remain in equilibrium with the surrounding atmosphere), nevertheless additional years in stick help to equalise out the built-in strains and stresses; and whilst a 1 in. (25 mm) board of English oak which has been seasoned for five years might show little intrinsic difference from one which has been dried for one year only, nevertheless it will be more mature and tend to be milder mannered and more stable.

Timber-merchants converting their own logs keep exact records, and will always give the number of years in stick, whilst if they have bought the logs from other merchants the pedigree is usually available. Retail merchants who do not convert their own can rarely give the seasoning time, marketing the timber as 'seasoned' only. This also applies to all square edge imported timber, which may only be 'shipping dry' (approximately 25 per cent moisture content) when received from the importer. However, reputable merchants can be trusted to advise the buyer to the best of their ability.

A typical log entry for a prime selected English wainscot oak butt cut by a reputable saw-mill could read as follows:

No.	Log size	Cutting
4190	16 ft 0 in. (4·87 m) by 27 in. (0·685 mm)	21 at 1¼ in. (31·7 mm) boards
Cube 81 (2·29366 st)	*Sticking* Nov. 1962	*Comments* Very good

Choosing timber

The inch (25 mm) dimension of the log size is, of course, the quarter girth and not the circumference, and such a log would yield a few boards quarter cut and the remainder plain cut.

There is no consistency of quality in timber, and every merchant can only offer the best of what is available in the particular species at any particular time, therefore first-hand inspection of the stock is always essential. Again, only active experience can give the knowledge of what constitutes good quality in any particular species. As an example the writer would probably accept large rotten cores in rosewood logs, large knots in prime quality English walnut, very small pin knots in prime English oak, but no defects whatsoever in Honduras and African (grand bassam) mahoganies, sapelewood or Burmah teak.

In choosing timber the planks or boards should be turned over and abnormal defects rejected or allowed for in the measurement. Top boards which are badly cast or showing considerable sap should not be included. Thicknesses up to 1 in. (25 mm) should be reasonably free from splits except at the extreme ends, and if there are knots or shaky patches they should be ringed with chalk and allowed for in the final measurement. A certain degree of splitting in thicker planks must be expected, but is only permissible if usable timber is left on either side. Some degree of rounding in wide boards is inevitable (but not in quartered stuff), but here again a centre-cut should yield reasonably flat surfaces on either side. Again, slight bowing in the length is allowable, but pronounced kinking, casting or cupping is not, although much depends on the nature of the timber, and a richly figured log might exhibit very considerable distortion. Heart and star shakes in the pith or crown plank are almost inevitable in logs from mature trees, but pronounced cup or ring shakes should be rejected out of hand as they have a habit of following up the tree for considerable distances, and may thus render the planks useless for all normal purposes. Seasoning defects should be looked for, particularly deep sticker-marks, extensive discoloration, sun checking, etc., although dry English oak may show large tarry patches which do not penetrate below the surface. If a mild working timber is required then the annual rings should be examined; they should be evenly spaced and as regular as possible and from 8 to 16 rings per in. (25 mm). Generally speaking, the wider the rings in hardwoods the stronger the timber, but the reverse applies to softwoods. Figure 88 shows examples of beautifully grown yellow pine with tight, evenly spaced rings beside a comparable example of mild English oak. As the true colour of the wood and the extent of the sap is usually masked by dirt or weathering most merchants will allow scoring the butt end with a raze-knife, although they would object to its use across the face, therefore it is better to carry a small block-plane for testing. Thicknesses should be rather more but never less than the nominal size quoted, and a sharp eye should be kept for badly sawn or taper-cut planks which occasionally pass unnoticed. Imported square edge tim er does not

as a rule exhibit the same defects as waney edge timber, as these have been rejected during conversion, moreover the plank and boards are usually graded before shipment. Points to look for are bowing in the length and inferior gradings slipped into the pile, otherwise the timber can be accepted as it rises, choosing the most suitable widths and lengths. As the length of seasoning time is unknown the moisture content should be tested before use, and it is always better to buy square edge timber well in advance of requirement. Kiln-dried timber will be more expensive than air-dried timber unless the latter has been in stick for several years. It is not wise to assume that kiln-dried timber will contain any less moisture as this depends entirely on how long it has been in store since kilning. On the whole, however, good kiln-dried timber no matter where it has been stored will tend to be less liable to subsequent distortion as the initial drying will have been carefully controlled.

88 Examples of well-grown timber showing evenly spaced rings

English oak

Yellow pine

10 Prefabricated timbers

Prefabricated timbers can be grouped within three broad classifications: (*a*) those composed of layers of wood cemented together in simulation of solid timber, viz. plywood, laminboard, blockboard, battenboard, densified laminated, board, etc., and classed together under the general heading of plywoods; (*b*) those composed of wood chips bonded together with synthetic resin glue and pressed or extruded into rigid sheets, i.e. particle-boards (commonly known as 'chipboards'); (*c*) those composed of longitudinal wood fibres mascerated in water with or without a small percentage addition of synthetic resin glue, and pressed at high temperatures into thin sheets of varying densities according to the degree of heat and pressure applied, viz. hardboards, fibre-boards, etc. The furniture-maker is not concerned with the last category to any great extent, although hardboard printed with wood grains is used in panelling, etc., and may be further developed, but plywoods and chipboards are used in ever-increasing quantities, and such use in all probability already exceeds that of timber in solid plank and board.

Relative advantages and disadvantages of plywood as opposed to solid timber are as follows:

Advantages of solid timber

1 First cost is often less than of plywoods, etc., in equivalent thicknesses, except for the rarer hardwoods.

2 Solid timber can be jointed with ease, shaped, moulded, carved, and bent to small radii.

3 Badly fitting joints and members out of alignment can be flushed off level after assembly.

4 Edges do not have to be protected or disguised in any way.

5 Solid timber has a natural elasticity without fatigue, thus screws and nails are securely gripped and will not work loose under normal loading. It will withstand rough treatment and can always be resurfaced. It has an effective life of many centuries.

6 It responds to careful finishing and has a depth of surface not obtainable with thinly veneered or composite surfaces.

Disadvantages of solid timber

1 As timber is a non-homogeneous material with its greatest strength in a direction along the grain and its greatest weakness across the grain, it is very liable to cleave or split. Moreover, unseasoned timber shrinks, warps and distorts considerably in drying, and will continue to do so throughout its effective life, dependent on the surrounding atmospheric conditions.

2 Waste factors are always higher than with prefabricated timbers available in large sheets of uniform thicknesses, therefore savings in first cost may be illusory.

3 Boards and planks must be trimmed, flatted and planed to thickness before use.

4 Quality is always variable in spite of careful grading, whilst as a rule less varieties are commercially available in solid form than in veneers. Heavily figured timbers (burrs, curls, etc.) usually have little strength or rigidity, and cannot be used in any thickness.

Advantages of plywoods

1 Plywoods and laminboards, etc. have no natural line of cleavage and cannot be split across the length or width, as the grain direction of each alternate layer is opposed to the direction of the force. General stiffness and rigidity is also much greater, and a strip of plywood is stiffer than a strip of steel of equal weight, therefore thicknesses as opposed to solid timber can be reduced by as much as 25 per cent. Particle-boards do not have the same high strength/-weight ratio and are relatively weak in all directions, nevertheless they have much the same dimensional stability, and sufficient strength and stiffness for most purposes.

2 All prefabricated timbers are available in large sheets, sanded smooth to uniform standard thicknesses, thus no preparation is necessary and much initial labour is saved.

3 Large sheets are always more economical in cutting, and waste factors are much lower, whilst quality is consistent from sheet to sheet.

4 Construction is balanced, therefore movement is negligible under normal conditions, thus they are ideal for large or flush surfaces. Plywood in particular possesses a natural resilience which enables it to be bent to reasonably small radii of curvature without damage.

5 The utilisation of common timbers in plentiful supply which can be face veneered with decorative hardwoods conserves stocks of the more valuable timbers, which otherwise might be insufficient to meet the demands of modern production.

Disadvantages of plywoods

1 Good locking joints are more difficult to make in plywoods and particle-boards (though relatively easy in laminboards and blockboard), therefore different techniques must be adopted which in turn influence and sometimes dictate to design practice.

2 Surfaces are usually plain rotary-cut veneers out of common timbers with exaggerated grain effects not suitable for face surfaces, therefore it is necessary to veneer with decorative hardwoods.

3 Face nailing and screwing is satisfactory, but edges of plywood and particle-board tend to laminate or crumble and have little real holding power. Laminboards and blockboards do not suffer from this defect, dependent on the type and position of the core.

4 Edges of all prefabricated timbers must be lipped or masked to hide the individual plies or core strips, etc. which have a tendency to creep fractionally if left exposed.

5 Proud surfaces cannot be flushed off after assembly, and jointing up must be positive. Surfaces are also more easily damaged and more difficult to repair.

Generally speaking—and one cannot arbitrate over the matter—prefabricated timbers are used for flush carcases, doors, panelling, etc. because of their small movement and freedom from distortion; and solid timbers for thick sections such as rails, bearers, lippings, underframings, etc., or where the individual members are shaped, rounded or carved; but in most other respects there is complete freedom of choice within the limitations listed above. There are, of course, still some lingering prejudices against the use of plywoods but they have no foundation whatsoever, and even the particle-boards are beginning to emerge, not as cheap substitutes, but as logical extensions or adaptations of timber in solid form.

Plywood (three ply, multiply, etc.)

The technique of gluing together thin sheets of wood in a balanced construction with each layer crossed at right angles (89:1) so that the wood grains are locked in position, effectively preventing all shrinkages across the width, dates from the seventeenth century, but it was only in 1896 that plywood was commercially produced for cheap tea-chests. Since then ceaseless development has produced a bonded sheet which is completely free from lamination, and which is generally available in thicknesses of from $\frac{1}{32}$ in. (0·8 mm) to 1 in. (25 mm), in a range of qualities for every purpose.

The original tea-chest ply was composed of three layers, a central core and two balancing veneers (89:1), hence the familiar term 'three-ply' which is still used for three-layer construction. Plywoods with more than three layers are usually classed as multiply (89:3), although the term 'five-ply' (89:2) is sometimes used for five-layer construction. Obviously, the layers or veneers of which the ply is composed must be relatively thin or the strength of the timber and its tendency to shrink and distort will be greater than the strength of the bonding adhesive; therefore for stout plywood additional layers must be used, one on either side for each increase in thickness, so that the total number will always be odd for a balanced construction, as distinct from an unbalanced assembly of an even number of veneers which will have a greater tendency to pull or distort. In practice, the central core can be relatively thick ($\frac{1}{8}$ in. (3 mm) or $\frac{1}{6}$ in. (4 mm)), and of lower density timber to reduce the overall weight; but wherever possible the combination of veneer thickness and timber species should be chosen to give the finished sheet equal stiffness both parallel and perpendicular to the grain of the face veneers; and for this reason each pair of balancing veneers, including the face and backing veneers, is usually of the same thickness and of the same or comparable species. The number of glue-lines also affects the overall stiffness, and the thinner the veneers, with the consequent increase in the number of glue-lines, the greater the rigidity of the finished sheet will be.

Plywood manufacture

Not all timber is suitable for plywood manufacture, and certain well-defined species are normally used, in general, timber from trees with clean, cylindrical boles which peel easily with little waste, yielding a smooth tear-free surface, good gluing properties and a minimum of natural defects. Certain species can be peeled straight from the log ponds, but most timbers, including nearly all hardwoods, require preliminary softening by steaming or boiling in

large vats. After peeling (90) the continuous thin sheet of veneer is trimmed, cut into convenient lengths and dried in heated ovens to a specific moisture content dependent on the type of adhesive used, and generally within the range 5 to 14 per cent. It is essential that all the veneers in any one sheet of ply should be of the same moisture content, otherwise internal stresses will develop as the sheet equalises itself.*

During the preliminary trimming of the veneers prior to oven drying all large defects are cut out, but after drying the sheets are carefully graded, splits caused by drying taped, and small knots and defects punched out and plugged with pieces of the same veneer. Narrow strips of sound

* Cheap wet-cemented plywoods are totally unsuitable for furniture owing to the surface checking which occurs as the veneers dry out.

89 Prefabricated timbers

A 48″ by 72″ 120 by 180 cm

B 72″ by 48″ 180 by 120 cm

90 Peeling log in plywood manufacture *By courtesy of United Africa Company*

91 Peeled veneer for plywood *By courtesy of United Africa Company*

92 Gluing veneers in plywood manufacture   *By courtesy of United Africa Company*

veneer from the trimmers are guillotined and edge jointed on an automatic tapeless splicer to form larger core sheets, whilst the face veneers can be either whole sheets straight from the trimmers and showing the characteristic whorl grain of rotary peeling, or made up of carefully matched strips of even colour showing a minimum of defects, according to the grading of the sheet. The composite layers, either three, five, seven, nine, eleven, etc. in number, dependent on the thickness of the required ply, are then roller glued, sandwiched together under pressure, trimmed to exact size and scraped or sanded smooth to a uniform thickness. The final moisture content of the finished sheet should not exceed 12 per cent.

Grading and classification of plywood

Clear distinction must be drawn between the grading of ply, which is concerned only with the quality of the face veneers, and the classification into groups or types, which is concerned with the nature of the bonding adhesive and the durability of the actual timber used. Hitherto plywoods were loosely grouped into *interior* and *exterior* qualities, but these terms are fairly meaningless. Admittedly, furniture-makers do not require weather-resistant plywoods, but they must be confident that the plies are well bonded and will not laminate, and that they will withstand bacterial and fungoid attack, therefore the type of bonding media used is of importance. It is, for instance, hardly sufficient to describe a plywood as *well-glued* or *resin-bonded*, for the former term may include weak vegetable glues, whilst the latter may be so extended with fillers compounded of cereal flours, etc. that the implicit moisture-resistant properties are lost.

Plywood grades

Grading rules differ according to the country of origin, and the following list is therefore a general indication only.

Foreign plywoods

A   Face and back veneers practically free from all defects.

A/B Face veneers practically free from all defects. Reverse veneers with only a few small knots or discolorations.

A/BB Face as A but reverse side permitting jointed veneers, large knots, plugs, etc.
B Both sides as reverse of A/B.
B/BB Face as reverse of A/B. Reverse side as reverse of A/BB.
BB Both sides as reverse of B/BB.
WG Guaranteed well glued only. All broken knots plugged.
X Knots, knot-holes, cracks and all other defects permitted.

British-made plywoods

Grade 1 *Veneer* Jointed veneers equal in width and well matched permitted, but not end jointing. Free from all knots other than dormant buds, and all defects which would be objectionable in plywood used in its natural state.

Grade 2 *Veneer* Veneers jointed but not matched. Sound knots permitted, also slight discolorations and plugs or wood inlays. Warranted bonded with an adhesive appropriate to the type of plywood, and suitable for painting or veneering.

Grade 3 *Veneer* Including all defects excluded from Grades 1 and 2, including rough cutting, overlaps, gaps, splits not impairing the serviceability or use of the plywood in positions not normally visible.

Marine Quality High-quality product usually of makoré or similar highly durable wood throughout, bonded with phenolic resin glue to WBP specification.

Additionally the United Africa Company grade their Cresta plywoods under Gold, Silver and Blue labels. Construction is the same throughout, and the grading refers to the face appearance only. The bonding is phenolic resin to WBP specification, and every sheet is impregnated against insect attack (lyctus, furniture beetle, termites, etc.), which does not affect the gluing or polishing properties.

In practice it is not wise to go below B/BB, BB or grade 2 for veneering, whilst Douglas fir ply is altogether unsuitable owing to the upraised grain, therefore grading rules for this particular kind of ply have not been included. It can be assumed that unless specifically stated all plywoods are dry cemented, i.e. the veneers dried before gluing, and that except for the very lowest grades not suitable for furniture both the face and reverse are sanded flat for immediate use.

Types of plywood

The original plywoods were bonded with animal glues, and the use of casein, cassava (tapioca starch), silicate of soda, blood albumen and soya-bean flour followed on; but it was not until 1930 that the first true waterproof phenol formaldehyde adhesive was used, creating the distinction between 'exterior' and 'interior' quality ply. This broad classification still persists, but it is hardly accurate enough for modern requirements, and in this country at least standards have now been laid down which define the type of adhesive and the requisite minimum performance to be expected. Not all producing countries give the information, but most of the primary producers of better quality plywoods use resin glue in some form or other, with Russia, Poland, the United States and some other small producers also using blood albumen, casein, soya bean and extended resin glues. There can be no objection to this providing the limitations of each type of adhesive are realised, and the use to which the ply is to be put arranged accordingly. The qualities of the various adhesives are as follows:

Interior quality plywoods

Blood albumen glues give moderately strong bonds with high but not prolonged resistance to boiling water if hot pressed. They are, however, liable to attack by micro-organisms in damp conditions.

Casein glues yield strong bonds if kept dry, but have only a short life under moderately severe conditions of exposure, and are also subject to micro-organism attack.

Soya-bean flour glue is similar in many respects to casein glue.

Exterior quality plywoods

Urea formaldehyde (UF) glues give high-bonding strength and resistance to prolonged soaking in water at normal temperatures, but will break down under continuous exposure to extreme conditions. They are immune to micro-organism attack, and have high resistance to acids and alkalies, and conform to British Standard Moisture-resistant (MR) glues.

Melamine formaldehyde (MF) glues compare favourably with phenol formaldehyde, and are often combined with UF glues to give increased resistance to boiling water. They are superior in both chemical and physical properties to UF glues, but more expensive and the dry strength is no greater. They conform to British Standard Boil-resistant (BR) glues.

Phenol Formaldehyde (PF) glues give high strength under all conditions of exposure, with maximum durability and resistance to micro-organism attack. They are also very resistant to common solvents, fire-retardant chemicals and most acids. They conform to British Standard Weather and Boil proof (WBP)* glues.

Resorcinol Formaldehyde (RF) glues equal, if not exceed, the performance of PF glues, but are more expensive and are principally used as special purpose adhesives or as fortifiers of other synthetic resin glues. They conform to standard WBP glues.

It must be borne in mind that the practice of extending synthetic resin glues with fillers of cereal flours, etc. to cheapen production costs may, if carried to excess, so weaken the glue that it no longer conforms to the minimum requirements for moisture- or water-resistant adhesives, whilst the bond strength may also be seriously impaired. Therefore, the general term 'resin bonded' without the qualification of 'MR' (Moisture resistant), 'BR', or 'WBP' may be quite meaningless. The Japanese practice of grading their plywoods for export into four adhesive types, and each type into four qualities of face veneer, has therefore much to commend it.

Properties of plywood, etc.

The strength/weight ratios of plywoods compared with other materials are as follows:

$\frac{3}{16}$ in. (5 mm) Douglas fir ply	1·00
$\frac{3}{16}$ in. (5 mm) gaboon	0·95
$\frac{3}{16}$ in. (5 mm) sapele	0·90

* WBP. Must withstand 72 hours boiling in water without failure of the glue-lines.

Structural aluminium alloy	0·88
Structural high-tensile steel	0·62
Structural mild steel	0·39

Stability

As timber is a hygroscopic material, shrinking and swelling under varying temperature/humidity conditions, plywood, which is composed entirely of timber, must also shrink and swell, but the total movement is very small owing to the strength of the glue-lines which lock the fibres in all directions. For instance, the Forest Products Research Laboratory has established in test on 22 different timber species of $\frac{3}{16}$ in. (5 mm) thick three-ply that the mean swelling is only 0·18 per cent along the grain, and 0·27 per cent across the grain when subjected to a humidity range of 30 to 90 per cent, equivalent to raising the moisture content from 7 to 20 per cent. For all practical purposes in furniture the movement can be disregarded, although it will show on the edges of untreated ply as a fractional creep of long-grain veneers. The thicker the ply the less the movement is and the greater the measure of stability, whilst synthetic resin glues give greater measures of stability over other glues. An additional advantage is that plywood has no line of cleavage and, therefore, will not split under adverse atmospheric conditions. This absence of lines of cleavage also affects the impact strength of plywood which is greater than that of solid wood subjected to a similar loading, and in all practical applications thicknesses over solid timber can be reduced, with a $\frac{3}{4}$ in. (19 mm) thickness of ply roughly equivalent to a 1 in. (25 mm) thickness of solid timber.

Bending properties

Although plywood is normally used as a flat material its natural resilience enables it to be bent to reasonably small radii of curvature without fracturing. The safe minimum of curvature will depend on the overall thickness, the individual thickness of the veneers, the species of timber employed and to a lesser extent the nature of the adhesive, whilst three-layer plywoods composed of equal veneers will bend more easily than plywoods composed of thick cores and thin outer veneers (91). Therefore, it is always better to make up thick curved panels out of several thin plys rather than one thick ply, as the following table shows:

Radius of curvature

Thickness	Along grain	Across grain
$\frac{1}{4}$ in. (6·3 mm)	2 ft 0 in. (0·609 m)	1 ft 3 in. (0·381 m)
$\frac{3}{8}$ in. (9·5 mm)	4 ft 6 in. (1·371 m)	3 ft 0 in. (0·914 m)
$\frac{1}{2}$ in. (12·7 mm)	8 ft 0 in. (2·438 m)	6 ft 0 in. (1·828 m)
$\frac{5}{8}$ in. (15·8 mm)	10 ft 0 in. (3·048 m)	8 ft 0 in. (2·438 m)
$\frac{3}{4}$ in. (19·0 mm)	12 ft 0 in. (3·657 m)	10 ft 0 in. (3·048 m)

The above figures were prepared by the Forest Products Research Laboratory in connection with the use of Douglas fir plywood, but offer a reliable guide as to the bending movements of most other hardwoods bent dry at ordinary room temperatures. Synthetic resin bonded plywoods can also be soaked or steamed, and will then bend to smaller radii dependent upon the timber species. As will be seen from the table above the bending movement is greater across the grain than along the grain, therefore cross-grained panels should be chosen (see below). Plywood can also be scarf jointed provided the same type of adhesive be used, and the inclination of the joint is not less than 1 in 10 for boards under $\frac{1}{2}$ in. (12·5 mm) thick and 1 in 8 for over $\frac{1}{2}$ in (12·5 mm).

Plywood dimensions

In all usual sizes the length of the face grains is given first, irrespective of the length of the sheet. Thus a plywood sheet quoted as 48 in. (122 cm) by 72 in. (183 cm) will be 72 in. (183 cm) in actual length and 48 in. (122 cm) wide across the sheet and parallel to the direction of the face grain (89:8A). Such a sheet is cross grained as distinct from long grained (89:8B), as the face grain of the former runs counter to the length of the sheet, and it is important to remember this when choosing sheet sizes for subsequent face-veneering which must be at right angles to the face grain of the sheet. Thus two wardrobe ends each 6 ft (183 cm) by 18 in. (46 cm) which are to be face veneered must be cut from a sheet 36 in. (92 cm) by 72 in. (183 cm), and not from one quoted as 72 in. (183 cm) by 36 in. (92 cm) in which the face grain runs the length of the sheet. Thicknesses in plywood commonly available with their nearest inch equivalents are as follows:

mm	in.	mm	in.
0·8	$\frac{1}{32}$	8	$\frac{5}{16}$
1·2 }	$\frac{1}{16}$	9	$\frac{3}{8}$
1·5 }		12 }	$\frac{1}{2}$
2	$\frac{3}{32}$	12·5 }	
3	$\frac{1}{8}$	15	$\frac{5}{8}$
4	$\frac{5}{32}$	18	$\frac{3}{4}$
5	$\frac{3}{16}$	22	$\frac{7}{8}$
6	$\frac{1}{4}$	25	1

Plywoods can normally be obtained in any of the following timber species: agba (tola branca), alder, basswood (Japanese lime), European and Japanese beech, European birch, Chilean pine, Douglas fir (Columbian or Oregon pine), elm, gaboon (okoumé), lauan, limba (afara), African mahogany, makoré, red meranti, obeche, Parana pine, European pine, poplar, sapele, sen, red and white seraya, red and white sterculia, tamo (Japanese ash), utile and yang. Most suppliers will, however, only stock the most popular, i.e. gaboon, lauan, birch, alder, Douglas fir, and limba, etc. Of these gaboon, birch and limba are excellent for veneering, but gaboon is inclined to woolliness in face-work, and birch is difficult to stain evenly. On the other hand, limba is medium textured, moderately hard and stiff, and its natural light gold-brown colour can be stained in simulation of oak, walnut and mahogany, therefore it is a good all-round choice. In all cases the timber species quoted refer to the face veneers only, and not to the cores which may be of low-density woods.

Blockboards, laminboards, etc.

In these the principle of construction is a series of wood core strips glued together side by side to form a slab, which is sandwiched between outer layers of veneer or thin ply whose grains are crossed at right angles to the length of the core strips. In blockboard (89:4) the core strips should not exceed 1 in. (25 mm) in width, although they can be of any thickness dependent on the thickness of the completed board, and in theory at least the grain direction of the strips should run counter to each other, although in practice a random selection is adopted. The outer or face veneers can be a single thickness of from $\frac{3}{32}$ in. (2 mm) to $\frac{9}{64}$ in. (3½ mm), or two veneers glued together with grains parallel to make up a $\frac{3}{32}$ in. (2 mm) thickness, or where the length of the sheet exceeds the width a five-ply construction of core strips, $\frac{3}{32}$ in. (2 mm) veneer either side at right angles to the core, and outer veneers of about $\frac{1}{16}$ in. (1·5 mm) parallel to the core. Laminboard (89:5) adopts the same construction, but the core strips must not exceed $\frac{9}{32}$ in. (7 mm) wide, and some varieties, notably Finnish birch, utilise core strips made up from plywood trimmings. Laminboard is heavier and stiffer than blockboard owing to the greater number of glue-lines, and the use of gaboon or spruce for core strips rather than low-density softwoods; the cost, therefore, is greater, and use is limited to high-class work for which it is eminently suited as it does not exhibit the bumpiness or ripple, i.e. core-strip sinkage, sometimes found in cheaper grades of blockboard. Battenboard (89:6) is a variation in which the core strips can be up to 3 in. (76 mm) wide, unglued and saw kerfed either side to allow for shrinkage, but it has little if any application in furniture. Both blockboard and laminboard can be obtained in sizes up to 60 in. (152 cm) by 120 in. (305 cm) and occasionally 144 in. (366 cm) in Finnish birch, and up to 60 in. (152 cm) by 201 in. (510 cm) in gaboon, beech, etc., both measured in the same way as plywood, with the length of the face grain first quoted. Sheet thicknesses range from $\frac{1}{2}$ in. (13 mm) to $1\frac{3}{4}$ in. (44 mm) and $1\frac{7}{8}$ in. (47 mm) in flush door sizes only.

Blockboards and laminboards are usually obtainable in beech, birch, limba, gaboon and agba glued to MR and BP specifications. They are not normally marketed in 'exterior' quality, although WBP specification can be obtained. Their chief merits lie in the larger sizes available, their increased rigidity (they cannot be bent to any appreciable radii unless deeply saw kerfed) and the ease with which they can be jointed by the usual methods. They are thus eminently suitable for general carcase-work, table-tops, flush doors, etc.

Densified laminated wood, etc.

This is composed of thin veneers, usually beech, impregnated with phenolic resin glue before assembly, or alternated with resin-impregnated papers, and sandwiched under pressure of 6000 lb per sq. in. (421·842 kgf/cm²) at 82 °C (180 °F) followed by curing at 149 °C (300 °F); the pressure and temperatures are highly critical.

The resultant product has high mechanical and dielectric properties. Plywoods can also be obtained already veneered with metal sheeting, plastic veneers and laminates for use on table-tops and wall cladding, and also as composite boards with cores of insulating materials, cork, asbestos fibre, foam rubber, etc. There seems little doubt that these composite boards could find a use in furniture if a suitable cheap light-weight and semi-rigid filler could be found, but at present their use is confined to heat and sound insulation in wall cladding, etc.

Particle-boards (chipboards) (89:7)

These are composed of wood chips carefully graded, mixed with synthetic resin glue and either pressed or extruded into rigid, self-supporting sheets of uniform thickness which are sanded down to close tolerances. Flax-sheaves are sometimes used instead of wood chips (flax-boards) and have virtually the same properties, although they tend to be lighter in weight and not so strong for any given density. Considerable research has gone into the development of both types of board, and wood-chip boards are marketed in several forms, flooring grade for general purpose in the Building Industry, low-density boards for door cores, partitioning, etc., standard all-purpose boards for built-in fitments, panelling, etc., and special furniture-boards (Weyroc 38) for carcase components. The last-mentioned boards are of graded density construction, with the finest chips near to the face, giving a high-density smooth, close-textured surface eminently suitable for veneering, as there is little tendency for the individual wood chips to show (grin) through under high polishes. They are invariably pressed, as distinct from extruded boards in which the wood chips lie at right angles to the board surfaces, resulting in poor bending strength and lower stability.

Particle-boards are heavier than most other wood materials (33 to 40 lb per cu. ft or 528·609 to 640·739 kg per cu. m according to the density) as the glue content is relatively high, moreover they have no long fibres, thus they have little bending strength and tend to crumble at the edges if roughly treated. Always provided that these boards are not treated merely as substitutes for solid timber and forced to conform to long-established constructional methods, but regarded as valid materials in their own right, well worthy of new methods and applications, there is no doubt whatever that their use will continue to expand, and indeed become the standard material for furniture-making. With their obvious advantages this is almost inevitable, for not only do they make use of what is virtually waste material (forest thinnings, bough wood, etc.) but the very fact that they are man-made materials means that there is always scope for research and development in the production of lighter, stronger, stiffer and cheaper boards.

Working properties

Particle-boards are very stable with little dimensional change (shrinking, warping, etc.), and even the absence of long fibres can be turned to advantage, for as there is no end grain boards can be glued and butt joined together at any angle without supporting constructional joints. Working properties are as for other prefabricated timbers and present no problems; they can be cut, planed, spindled, routered and bored with all normal tools, provided the cutting edges are kept sharp and feed speeds a little slower than for solid timber. For quantity production, tungsten-carbide cutting edges are recommended, as the high glue content is heavy on normal steels. Planing to thickness is not advised, as cross planing is inevitable and bound to create rough patches, but the boards are obtainable in a variety of thicknesses to close tolerances, and where surfaces have to be reduced it is better to sand them down. They are not intended for exterior use as the edges are susceptible to moisture penetration, although some manufacturers now incorporate a proportion of wax emulsion in the glue which gives a certain measure of protection. Screw- and nail-holding properties are not as good as long-grain materials, but sufficient for all but the heaviest loadings.

Uses for particle-boards are the same as for blockboards and laminboards, viz. carcases, flush doors, shelving, panelling, partition-work, etc. A point in their favour is that they have no hidden defects (see 'Defects in plywoods, etc.', page 138) and they are thus eminently suitable for large veneered table-tops polished to a high gloss, and as a groundwork for plastic laminates. They can be satisfactorily veneered provided synthetic resin glues are used, and the best-quality boards no longer require counter-veneering to hold back any tendency for the wood chips to grin through the face veneers. If the tops are well supported there is also no necessity to counter veneer on the reverse side to equalise the pull of the face veneers as the pick up of moisture from the glue is very slight. Thicknesses of standard boards range from $\frac{3}{8}$ in. (9 mm) to $1\frac{3}{8}$ in. (36 mm), and furniture-boards from $\frac{1}{2}$ in. (12 mm) to $\frac{7}{8}$ in. (21 mm), and boards can be obtained already veneered with a wide range of timbers.

Bending moduli

As particle-boards have little if any natural elasticity owing to the absence of long fibres it is useful to know the modulus of rupture (maximum bending strength) for shelf loadings, etc. Airscrew-Weyroc Ltd of Weybridge, Surrey issue a data sheet in graph form, from which the safe spans for uniformly distributed loads on both end-supported and fixed shelving can be calculated. It can be assumed that fairly typical loadings would be in the neighbourhood of 15 lb per sq. ft (73·23 kgf/m²) for clothes, 35 lb (170·89 kg) for records and 60 lb (292·95 kg) for groceries, books, etc.

Fibre-boards, etc.

Fibre building boards are sheet materials made by a felting process from wood or other fibres as in paper-making, and are usually designated as 'fibre insulating boards', softboards or hardboards according to the density. The former have no application in furniture, but hardboards are composed of pure wood fibre with or without the addition of a small percentage addition of synthetic resin glue, and bonded together under considerable steam heat and pressure in hydraulic multi-platen presses to form a high-density homogeneous sheet, with limited applications in drawer bottoms, carcase backs, painted door panels, etc. in the cheapest work. Considerable development has also taken place in the printing of wood grains on hardboard, and there is also interest in moulded hardboard sections, although the weight factor is a disability.

Hints on working prefabricated timbers

Generally speaking plywoods, blockboards and laminboards should require no preliminary treatment, as they are invariably scraped or sanded on both surfaces to exact dimensions, but certain timber species, notably gaboon, often exhibit badly plucked grain which should be filled with a glue-absorbent filler (plastic wood, brummer, etc.). Particle-boards and hardboards should have the glazed skin broken through with light sanding to enable the glue to take. Cheap foreign plywoods, machine-sanded with flint-papers should be very carefully examined, sanded afresh and thoroughly dusted, for there have been several cases of embedded flint-dust setting up a chemical reaction with synthetic finishes. Cutting of some plywoods presents difficulties, and certain varieties, notably birch tend to rag out under the saw. The remedy is either to use finer teeth to the saw, clamp a waste piece firmly under the ply to receive the rag of the saw, or to score the cutting-line deeply with a knife in advance of the cut—a preliminary trial will always show what propensity there is to splinter out. In machine-sawing, if the surface breaks out on top, increase the projection of the saw; or if underneath then decrease the projection, and if possible keep the board tight to the saw-table with spring arms, etc.

Defects in plywoods, etc.

Certain defects regularly occur during or after manufacture, and should be diligently searched for otherwise they may give endless trouble. Figure 93 give the most common defects. Ripples or bumpiness (93:1) caused by swelling of the core strips in laminated construction can be detected with a knife-edge straight-edge, or passing the palm of the hand over the surface (closing the eyes increases the sensibility). Planing off the bumps is not always satisfactory, as the cores may shrink back in drier conditions, forming undulating hollows, therefore it is better to reject bumpy boards for face-work and use them only for unseen interiors. Figure 93:2 shows hidden blisters which can only be detected by tapping the surface with the finger-nail for any hollow sound; they must be glued back or subsequent veneering is bound to lift them. Overlapping veneers are shown in 93:3, and will eventually show as a long spine under a high polish. Long splits in the face (93:4) are easily

93   Defects in plywoods, etc.

rectified, but hidden gaps in the core (93:5) are often difficult to detect and may only declare themselves at later stages. Here again laboriously tapping with the finger-nail is the only answer, whilst all freshly cut ends should be critically examined. Figure 93:6 shows a method adopted in some constructions, in which the core strips are grooved across to take a string binder during assembly, and such boards should not be used in face-work. All these defects may not necessarily detract from the structural strength, but will certainly mar the surface quality if not rectified.

Badly cast boards, particularly in the thicker grades, should be rejected out of hand, for it is never wise to assume that holding frameworks will pull them straight or subsequent veneering correct them. More often than not the whole carcase will be pulled in winding. All prefabricated timbers are dried to a moisture content of around 9 per cent during manufacture. They pick up moisture slowly but also give it up as slowly, therefore they should be stored flat on level foundations and in dry conditions.

94 Veneered chipboard of inferior quality showing high percentage of large chips and bark in centre layer

11 Veneers

The term 'veneer' is unfortunate as it can mean to 'gloss over' or 'to cover up', but the practice of veneering dates from before the time of the Pharaohs, and is not, as some people still mistakenly imagine, a cheap method of glossing over poor workmanship and materials. Cogent reasons for the practice are fourfold: (*a*) a more balanced construction is achieved, free from the inevitable splitting, checking, warping and distortion of solid timber; (*b*) the availability of rare and highly decorative timbers is vastly extended by using them in sheet form; (*c*) decorative effects, duplication of identical grain configurations to form matched panels and patterns, are possible which would be extremely difficult with timber in solid form; (*d*) certain rare and costly burrs, curls and abnormal grain effects have very little structural strength, and would split, buckle or distort if used in any appreciable thickness. The only disadvantages of veneered work, i.e. chipping and lifting of edges, fragility of top surfaces, etc., and lack of sparkle in the wood itself due to excessive glue penetration, have now been largely eliminated with the use of resin glues which form permanent bonds that do not—or should not—penetrate to the wood surface; and synthetic lacquers which provide extremely hard protective coverings which are proof against most risks in normal use.

Manufacture of wood veneers

Before the introduction of power-driven circular saws all veneers were sawn by hand, usually $\frac{1}{8}$ in. (3 mm) and over in thickness, with deep saw kerfing which had to be planed off before laying or the ribbing would ultimately show through the polish. At the turn of the century specially large circular saws up to 18 feet (5·48 m) in diameter with very fine saw teeth and little set were introduced which could cut veneers from $\frac{1}{32}$ in. (0·8 mm) to $\frac{1}{16}$ in. (1·5 mm) in thickness, or about 12 sheets to the inch (25 mm). In all cases about half the wood substance was lost in sawdust, and with the exception of certain difficult woods, notably the kingwoods, ebonies and some satin-woods, which must still be cut with the saw, all veneers are now sliced with the knife and waste is eliminated. It should be pointed out, however, that saw-cut veneers are always better quality, for the slicing action of the knife across the grain does to some extent tear or distress the wood fibres.

Two methods of knife slicing are currently practised: (1) rotary cutting or peeling; (2) flat slicing. A third method of semi-rotary slicing is now only used in special cases.

Rotary peeling

Most timbers can be cut by this method, but apart from certain special effects (bird's-eye maple, etc.) its use is confined to the production of core veneers for plywood and laminated work, etc., using the more common hardwoods of large dimension, clean cylindrical boles and free cutting grain structure which allows of easy peeling. Suitable logs are first cross cut to length, debarked, adzed to shape and after prolonged immersion in boiling water, mounted on a giant lathe whilst still hot and peeled with a fixed knife which is fed forwards with each revolution. The lathe is run slowly at first until the bole is a true cylinder and there is little if any torque, then the speed is greatly increased and the bole unwinds as a continuous ribbon of veneer the full length of the log, after which it is cut into sheets by pre-set guillotines and force dried in mechanical driers (90:1). Veneers can be cleanly cut by this method from $\frac{1}{80}$ in. (0·3 mm) to $\frac{3}{8}$ in. (9·5 mm) in thickness, but the grain effect follows round the annual rings, giving an exaggerated onion-slice effect, moreover in some species the fibres tend to crack under the knife (all veneers are sliced across the grain), and microscopic examination will disclose innumerable slight tears or cracks. For this reason all veneers should be laid at right angles to the grain direction of the groundwork, otherwise the fibres are not locked in position and unseen cracks will tend to open. The true advantages of rotary slicing are cheapness of production, and the extremely large dimensions possible, but apart from these flat slicing is always the better method.

Flat cutting or slicing

Originally carefully selected flitches of timber suitable for veneers were dogged down to a horizontal bed within the machine, and a heavy knife mounted on a stout carriage slid backwards and forwards over the table to give a shearing cut. In more modern machines, however, the bed is vertical, moving upwards and downwards, again with a diagonal shearing action, against a fixed knife usually $\frac{1}{2}$ in. (12·5 mm) thick, 7 in. (178 mm) wide and capable of cutting a 17 ft (5·18 m) length with every stroke. The knife is fed forwards by the thickness of the veneer being cut for each downward stroke of the bed, and is capable of very fine adjustment and accurate cutting of veneers from $\frac{1}{250}$ in. (0·1 mm) to $\frac{1}{4}$ in. (6 mm) or more in thickness.

Flat slicing of veneers gives a smoother, finer cut than rotary peeling, even so there is always a tendency for the fibres to be plucked or torn as in hand-planing across the grain. The best and most decorative results are obtained from true quartered flitches, where the direction of the cut is at right angles to the annual rings, whereas if the cut transverses the full width of the log it will go with the rings for half the width and against them for the other half. The effect can often be seen in sliced gaboon constructional veneers, where one half of the width of the sheet is cleanly cut and the other half woolly and uneven.

The cutting of all veneers is highly specialised, for the logs must be steamed correctly, at exactly the right temperature for cutting (wet heat softens wood), and dogged down at the right angle, with the thickness and speed of cut determined by long experience only, and an instinctive appreciation of how the wood is likely to behave. Face veneers, as distinct from constructional veneers, are usually cut either 0·88 mm, 0·83 mm, or 0·71 mm thick (28, 30 or 35 to the inch), the last familiarly known as 'seven mil' (0·71 mm), with the thicker veneers a better compromise against excessive glue penetration and torn grain. Continental veneer-cutters often cut 40, 50 or even 60 sheets to the inch (25 mm) with little regard for plucked grain and tissue-thin patches.

Such veneers are much cheaper, but should not be used in good work.

Reference has already been made to 'Semi-rotary' cutting, in which suitably shaped flitches are mounted off centre in the lathe so that the cut is half-slice, half-rotary peeling action. This cutting method is sometimes employed for special grain effects, notably in Rio rosewood, etc., but has been largely abandoned owing to the enormous torque created by the off-centre flitch, and consequent heavy wear on the lathe.

Types of veneer

Whilst rotary peeling is usually reserved by plywood manufacture, constructional veneers for laminated work are normally sliced in 1, 1·5, 2·5, 3 and 4 mm thicknesses from beech, obeche, gaboon, limba and similar timbers. Backing quality veneers used as balancers on the underside of groundworks (see *Veneering, marquetry and inlays*, Chapter 22) are usually peeled or sliced to $\frac{1}{32}$ in. (0·7 mm) or thinner out of sapele, straight-grain mahogany, makore (cherry mahogany), etc. Both constructional and backing veneers are normally sold in bulk quantities, but can be obtained in small amounts from retail factors if specially ordered. They are considerably cheaper than the usual run of face veneers, and one suspects that backing veneers are often used for face-work in cheap furniture. There can be no objection to this for the veneers are cleanly cut from prime logs and are usually lacking only in decorative effect, although occasional bundles will be the equivalent of a good African mahogany or sapelewood face veneer. Saw-cut veneers are now virtually unobtainable except as odd lots, but kingwood is still saw-cut, and a tour of the East End factors in London will probably unearth bundles of old saw-cut walnut curls and Cuban mahogany, although the cost per square foot will be scarcity value. Face or decorative veneers are usually sold by the cutters in part or complete logs, composed of several bundles according to the number of flitches the log has yielded. This 'buying as they rise' and taking the good with the bad—for practically all trees have some defect or other—is obviously much cheaper than choosing selected bundles from any one stock, and most veneer-cutters in a large way of business will not permit 'breaking the log'. It is only fair to say, however, that the writer has always been most generously treated by such firms as William Mallinson Ltd and John Wright (Veneers) Ltd who have always allowed him to choose the best bundle from exceptional logs for special furniture. For the small user there are many retail factors who buy in bulk and sell a few leaves at a time, although the price asked must necessarily be several times that of a bulk purchase.

In choosing veneers it is always a wise precaution to examine each bundle very thoroughly, for beautiful veneers are international currency, they may pass through several hands and are easily damaged. Reputable firms do not hide defective or damaged leaves in the middle of the bundle as a matter of policy, but transposition can occur. Curls, burrs and feathers, etc. are numbered and should be in strict order as cut, for although there may be no apparent difference between adjacent sheets, the small variations build up, and the difference between the first and last sheet of, say, a 30-leaf bundle can be very considerable. Such bundles are rarely if ever split, and must be bought as a whole. Highly decorative veneers should never be ordered from one sample leaf only. To cite only one example— a single Rio rosewood log may yield bundles ranging from a very plain light tan to rich inky black figuring, therefore inspection of the whole stock is essential.

Veneer varieties

It would be impossible to list all the varieties available at any one time, for every timber species is capable of yielding veneers, and every tree in the species an individual with different grain structure, coloration and abnormalities. Add to this different methods of cutting, rotary peeling, semi-rotary peeling, quartered slicing, crown cut (tangential cut), etc., and the permutations are endless. There are, for example, over 300 different species of oak commercially available, the mahoganies form a vast family, whilst walnuts include English, French, Italian, Ancona (Italian), Circassian, Caucasian (Persian), Australian and American. Names also change according to the locality or at the whim of the timber-exploiter, with common agba elevated to tola branca, white tola, etc., to give only one example. Add to this abnormal grain effects, roe, bird's eye, blister, dapple, mottle, quilted, stripy, swirled, burr, crotch, stump, pollard, fiddleback, curl, fan, feather and flame, and the endless variety ensures that wood as a means of decoration is irreplaceable so long as people remain individuals and hanker after individual things. A full description of the matching, jointing, preparation and laying of all types of veneer is given in Chapter 22.

Man-made veneers

Reference should be made to a comparatively recent development which for lack of a better term can only be described as 'man-made veneers'. The process, first developed by John Wright (Veneers) Ltd and known as *Fineline* veneers, and later also by Aaronson Ltd under the trade-name *Arofleur*, is prefabricated in the sense that stacks of different-coloured veneers are glued up into a solid block, and then sliced across the artificial grain thus created by the separate layers to yield a regular and repeatable pattern. A crown-cut pattern is also introduced by Aaronson Ltd into the middle of the sheet. Some of the veneers so produced, which are, of course, free from all defects and therefore much more economical in use, are rather too brash and regular, but the best have a quiet dignity and a subtle colour modulation which lends itself to simple contemporary designs of good shape and proportionment. In normal veneers the waste factor is high, and a minimum of 50 per cent is generally allowed, but with these fabricated veneers dimensions are fairly constant, and do not vary throughout the stock. Prices compare very favourably with normal straight-cut veneers, taking into account the low waste factor.

12 Adhesives

All matter is composed of countless separate molecules which exert their own powerful electro-magnetic forces, and thus adhere together by mutual attraction. In theory, therefore, any two smooth surfaces should also adhere, and in fact will do so providing the surfaces are in reality perfectly smooth. However, these inter-molecular forces have only a very short range, and any roughness of the surfaces will prevent the molecules adhering except at local high spots. Where the surfaces are rough—and a steel plate polished to mirror smoothness will still be extremely rough by molecular standards—a bonding agent is necessary whose own molecules will flow out over the rough surfaces, and render them smooth enough to adhere together. Simple liquids such as water, which exerts considerable forces of attraction (one ton per square inch), are in effect powerful adhesives, but they have low viscosity and high volatility and are, therefore, totally unsuitable. Any good adhesive, therefore, must be not only highly mobile and free flowing, but it must be non-volatile, with adequate tensile strength, and with little if any propensity to shrink back as it solidifies; moreover, certain additional characteristics are necessary according to the type of material for which it is to be used. Wood, for instance, will

95 Wall fresco, Egyptian tomb (Pharaoh Rekhamen)

143

require cheapness, ease of preparation, a measure of flexibility to accommodate residual strains and stresses, resistance to fungoid and insect attack, water-resistance, acceleration of the set by heat, and absence of staining.

History of glues

The first glues used were in all probability natural exudations from resinous tree-trunks, tar, bitumen, possibly animal blood and crude forms of casein glue. So-called animal glues, i.e. hide or Scotch glue,* fish glues, etc. were known to the Egyptians nearly 4000 years ago, and 95 shows a wall fresco in the tomb of the Pharaoh Rekhamen which depicts carpenters boiling glue over a charcoal fire, spreading glue with a spatula, and sawing and adzing wood. The glue was made much as it is today by boiling animal skins and bones, etc., but the strained jelly had no keeping qualities, and craftsmen were always forced to make their own glue as and when required until long-storage cake glues were commercially exploited at the beginning of the nineteenth century. Later developments perfected liquid glues by lowering the gel point with acetic acid and improving the storage life in semi-liquid form with suitable preservatives (formaldehyde, etc.), and considerable quantities of this type of glue (Croid, etc.) are still used in industry. The greatest development has been in modern plastic glues which were first used in the 1930s, and once the commonly held belief that good adhesion relied entirely on the mechanical interlocking of porous surfaces with little dowels of glue forced into those surfaces was disproved, then enormous impetus was given to the whole field of research into the principles of adhesion.

Types of glue

The perfect glue hardly exists except under laboratory conditions, and most professional

* The terms 'adhesive' and 'glue' have the same meaning and are virtually interchangeable, although traditional practice prefers the term 'glue' when used for bonding paper and wood, and 'adhesive' for bonding all other materials. Animal glues made from hoof, horn and hide are commonly known as 'hide' or 'Scotch' (United Kingdom only) to distinguish them from casein glue which is also animal in origin.

users, recognising the limitations of any one kind of adhesive, match the glue to the work. Generally speaking all adhesives fall within three main categories: (1) *animal* glues prepared from bones, hides, fish offal, blood, milk, etc.; (2) *vegetable* glues prepared from dextrine, rye and soya-bean flours, rubber latex, etc.; (3) *mineral* glues prepared from synthetic resins, coal-tar, crude-oil derivatives, etc. This is a good enough division, although chemists would prefer to divide them into (1) temperature-change glues; (2) solvent-release glues; (3) chemical-change glues, but as this can be confusing to the layman the first-mentioned categories are normally used in everyday parlance.

Animal glues

The universal type is *Hide* prepared by boiling bones, hides, etc. in water, and obtainable in hard cake form which must be broken up in an old piece of sacking and steeped for 12 hours before heating; in pearl, grain and bead forms requiring only a short steeping time; and in liquid glues (*Croid, Adams*, etc.) in which the addition of formaldehyde keeps the glue sweet in storage, and acetic acid lowers the gel point. Casein glues prepared from milk curds are excellent all-purpose glues requiring the addition of cold water only, but stain woods rich in tannic acid although so-called non-staining types are available. They are no longer used to any great extent in the United Kingdom, but are still a favourite type in other countries, notably the United States. Fish glues prepared from fish offal and skins (*Seccotine*, etc.) are extremely useful for small repair-work, but lack sufficient strength for structural work. Animal-blood glues are water resistant if hot pressed and are used in cheap foreign plywoods. All these glues set by chilling or absorption or evaporation of the water content.

Vegetable glues

Dextrine (British Gum) and rye-flour glues have no application in assembly-work, and are only used for table-lining, etc. Cassava-starch and soya-bean glues are used for interior quality plywoods, whilst rubber glues are used in leather-work and upholstery, and also for laying decorative laminated plastics.

Synthetic resin (plastic) glues

Whilst a great deal of furniture is still glued with animal adhesives, synthetic resin glues are extensively used in practically every manufacturing industry, and offer unparalleled advantages in certain classes of work where ease of working, rapid setting, great strength, permanence and water-resistance properties are called for. A considerable advantage for small craftsmen is their tolerance of low temperatures, for they can be satisfactorily worked in relatively cold conditions (10°C), whereas animal glues require heated conditions for satisfactory results. Conversely, all synthetic resin glues are thermo-setting, and respond to heat which greatly accelerates the setting-rate.

The type of synthetic resin glue most commonly used in furniture-making is *urea formaldehyde* (UF), which has adequate strength, durability and water-resistance for all types of indoor-work, will set at normal room temperatures, and is relatively inexpensive. *Phenol formaldehyde* (PF) is used where great strength, durability and water resistance is necessary, but heat is required for the set and the glue-line is dark coloured, therefore it is confined to heavy constructional work, plywood manufacture including 'exterior' quality ply. *Resorcinol formaldehyde* (RF) has outstanding durability under the severest conditions, therefore it is used mainly for exterior work. Here again a dark glue-line is formed which is sometimes used for its decorative possibilities (archery bow laminations). *Melamine formaldehyde* (MF) is more expensive, and is usually employed as a fortifier of other glues and for the top coating of decorative laminated plastics (formica, etc.). *Polyvinyl acetate emulsion* (PVA) is ready mixed, requires no accelerator and is extensively used for sticking or strengthening a variety of substances, but it lacks the great strength of straight synthetics, and tends to creep from thick joints under humid conditions.* *Epoxy resin* glues require no volatile

* Many so-called PVA adhesives are no longer composed of polyvinyl acetate and a better term is, therefore, *emulsion glue*. They are thermoplastic, with high-tensile

solvent, and are, therefore, capable of bonding non-porous materials, metals, glass, china, etc. A comparison of the various types is listed on page 149.

Preparation, working properties, etc.

Hide (Scotch) glues

Hide- or Scotch-type glues in cake, pearl and bead forms require preliminary steeping in water and heating in water-jacketed pots to not more than 54°C. Greater temperatures or constant reheating destroys much of the adhesive strength, and the heated glue should always be a dark honey colour, sweet smelling and liquid enough so that a slight rattle is heard as it runs from the brush. Components must be slightly warmed and pressure applied before the glue gels, for the chilled gel itself has no adhesive properties. Liquid hide glues only require slight warming in the tin in cold weather and give more latitude. All types are freely soluble in water and are not, therefore, resistant, but they can be reconstituted and, therefore, there is no waste. Their great advantages in some classes of work are their flexibility, and the strong tack or suck they give, so that freshly glued surfaces can be rubbed together and will grip without cramping pressure. Glued components should be left for 12 hours under normal workshop conditions, and longer if the workshop is cold or the components under strain. Cramps should be tightened up after the first 15 minutes, as absorption by the wood or squeezing from the joint edges may have reduced the pressure. If the cramps must be removed as soon as possible a test-piece coated with glue should be laid alongside, and only when the glue-film cannot easily be indented with the thumb-nail should the pressure be released. The old craftsmen used a minimum of glue, but it is

strength but little inherent strength in thick films and with little if any penetration, therefore they should not be used in tropical climates, for gap-filling work or for dowelling. They are, however, useful for close-contact work with moderate pressure, and as they do not become brittle with age they can be used for laying plastic laminates. Bearing in mind their limitations they are in all probability the most popular type of glue for the small user.

better to glue both surfaces thinly, and wipe off the squeezed-out surplus with clean rags soaked in warm water.

Hide glues can be used equally well for assembly-work and veneering, and will tolerate thicknesses of $\frac{1}{16}$ in. (1·58 mm) in the glue-line. They are invaluable for antique repair-work.

Synthetic resin glues

Preparation of synthetic resin glues is more exact and the makers' instructions must be closely followed. Two types are used: (1) gap-filling assembly glues for general constructional work permitting glue thicknesses of up to 0·05 in. (1·27 mm); (2) veneering glues which have little if any gap-filling properties, and require intimate contact between the surfaces. Some veneering glues (*Aerolite KL*, etc.) can have gap-filling properties imparted to them with suitable powder hardeners, and are thus dual-purpose glues. Additionally, synthetic resin glues are divided into (*a*) separate application glues; (*b*) mixed application glues. With the exception of polyvinyl acetate glues all synthetic resins require an acid accelerator or catalyst hardener, and set by chemical action plus evaporation or absorption of the solvent, thus they cannot be reconstituted. They have no natural tack, and require sufficient cramping pressure to bring both surfaces into intimate contact.

Separate application resin glues

All plastic (synthetic resin) glues are formed by the reaction at elevated temperatures of the components (phenol or urea, etc. with formaldehyde, for PF or UF glues). This reaction or polymerisation provides resins for moulded and extruded plastic-ware, etc., but if carefully controlled and arrested adhesives are compounded which can be supplied either as fine-grained powders or water-based thick syrups. However, the reaction cannot be halted completely, therefore all resin glues have a limited working life only, which should always be stated on the container. To promote the ultra-rapid setting of these glues a suitable hardener, often known as an 'accelerator' or 'catalyst', is added, which sets the glue into an intensely hard, infusible solid, and at the same time imparts

water-resistant properties. Beyond that, and in the nature of all true catalysts, this hardener has no other function than promotion of the reaction, therefore the simplest method of using resin glues is to coat one surface with the syrup and the other with the hardener. In this way there is no mixing to be done, no waste, and the minimum amount of hardener is used, for all solvents used to liquify the glue so that it can be spread on the wood surfaces, and all liquid hardeners added, must disperse either by evaporation or absorption, and if present in excessive quantities will become trapped within the body of the glue during the rapid chemical set, and may eventually set up crazing or fracturing. Single application UF glues with spirit hardener of the type *Aerolite* 300 (CIBA (ARL) Ltd), and obtainable either in powder form for long storage life or as a ready-for-use syrup (effective life three to four months), are amongst the strongest in this class, and will accommodate glue-line thicknesses of up to 0·05 in. (1·27 mm) in assembly-work without fracturing. This type of glue cannot be used for veneering work as the application of either hardener or syrup to the veneers will immediately curl them, nor must the hardener be premixed with the syrup, as the setting is much too rapid.

Mixed application glues

With these (*Aerolite KL*, etc.) both glue and liquid or powder hardener are carefully weighed or measured in the correct proportions, and mixed together before application. They are thus ideal veneering glues whose setting time can be greatly accelerated by the application of heat. Glues are also available in which a suitable powder hardener is incorporated with the powder glue (*Cascamite One Shot*, etc.), and mixing with water releases the acidifying action of the hardener and initiates the set. These glues are principally gap-filling assembly glues, but are also quite satisfactory for veneered work, although they are not so responsive to heat as straight veneering glues. They require no elaborate weighing or measuring out, are easy to mix, and are sufficiently strong and moisture resistant for most purposes. The storage life in closed containers is the same as for most other powder resin glues, i.e. one year or more.

Miscellaneous synthetic glues

Epoxy resin glues and hardeners (*Araldite*, etc.) are in the form of stiff creams which are intimately mixed together prior to use, thus there is very little initial solvent present, and no volatile matter is evolved during the reaction. These glues have wide applications in bonding notoriously difficult surfaces, metal, glass, china, plastics, wood, rubber, etc., and with a suitable filler can be used as a waterproof mastic for bonding plastic working-tops to steel and porcelain sinks, etc. Polyvinyl acetate emulsion glues are white creams which form transparent glue-lines and set by evaporation of the water content. They are ready-mixed general-purpose assembly glues, not water-resistant but with considerable tensile strength and durability, and a curious affinity for brick, cement, glazed tiles, paint, etc. They have a tendency to creep from open joints in humid conditions, and are therefore not suitable for tropical conditions. Cellulose (vegetable) glues with added synthetic resins (quick-setting cements, balsa cement, etc.) have practical uses in the workshop, but not for general assembly-work.

So-called *impact* glues are synthetic or natural rubber latex glues in suitable solvents, and are widely used for laying decorative laminated plastics *in situ* where cramping or pressing facilities are not available; the natural resilience of the rubber gives the necessary amount of flexibility between the inert plastic and the creep or movement of the wood. They are sometimes used for assembly-work and laying small strips or inlays of veneers, but this is not their rightful function, and must be regarded as an expedient only, not suitable for permanent work.

Heat acceleration of glue sets

As already mentioned, synthetic resin glues (not impact glues) are thermosetting, and once set cannot be resoftened by heat. The acceleration of the set by applied heat is very marked, as the following tables show:

Separate application glues

Aerolite 300
OR 306 Powder Glue with

Hardener	50 °F / 10 °C	60 °F / 16 °C	70 °F / 21 °C	80 °F / 27 °C	90 °F / 32 °C
Hardener GBQX	5–6 hr	2½	1¾	1¼	1
Hardener GBMX	—	—	3½ hr	2½	2

GBQX has an assembly time (first contact between glue and hardener) of 5 minutes only, therefore GBMX with an assembly time of 20 minutes is more suitable for hot-weather working.

Mixed application glues

Aerolite KL with Powder Hardener

Minimum clamping time

	60 °F / 16 °C	80 °F / 27 °C	100 °F / 38 °C
	7 hr	1½	¾

Basic setting time*

130 °F / 54·5 °C	150 °F / 66 °C	180 °F / 82 °C	210 °F / 99 °C
6½ min.	2¼	1¼	¼

Preparation of surfaces, etc.

Timber containing a high percentage of moisture cannot be glued satisfactorily with any type of adhesive, although casein is more tolerant than other glues and synthetic resins more critical. A moisture content of 20 per cent is about the limit, and higher values lower the viscosity of the glue to such an extent that starved joints may result, and the excess of moisture may cause the glue to harden as separate particles instead of a continuous film, thus reducing the ultimate strength. For good results, therefore, the wood should be in equilibrium with the average air conditions within the range 8 to 16 per cent, and only up to 20 per cent when that happens to be the normal environmental content.

Contrary to the widely held belief there is little to be gained by sanding or toothing the wood surfaces prior to gluing, and in fact such treatment may positively interfere with the bond. Ideally, the wood should be glued immediately it has been worked, and there will be no appreciable difference in adhesion between planed-up and fine-sawn surfaces provided that blunt cutters have not burnished the wood. Where gluing has to be delayed the surfaces should be only lightly sanded, and then well dusted to dislodge the greasy dust which any unprotected surface will gradually accumulate. Teak and certain other oily and notoriously difficult woods are quite straight-forward with synthetic resin

---

* An additional time allowance according to the thickness of the veneers, etc., must be added to the basic setting time (see makers' instructions). Pot life of the mixed Aerolite KL glue is 15 hr at 10 °C (50 °F), to 1½ hr at 27 °C (80 °F).

and even hide glue, provided the surfaces are glued within a few hours of working, for it is the seepage of natural oils to the surface which prevents the bond. If necessary oily timber can be degreased with any suitable solvent (cellulose thinners, etc.), but never with carbon tetra-chloride which is sometimes advocated, for in conjunction with cigarette smoke it can produce a lethal gas (phosgene). End grain of wood rarely permits an effective bond, therefore sufficient side grain should always be available, but if for any reason end-grain timber must be glued it should be repeatedly sized with well-diluted hide glue (not decorators' powder glue size). Synthetic resins can also be diluted with water or methylated spirit for sizing purposes, and each successive coat should penetrate and harden before another is applied. The usual dilution for size is from 3 to 5 parts water or solvent to 1 part glue, dependent on the viscosity of the latter.

Glues can be coloured to match the wood, using flake-white for light-coloured woods, and gas-black, mineral-earth colours or aniline dyes for ebony, blackwood, etc. Alternatively, Salisbury or rabbit skin glue, often employed in water gilding and gesso-work, can be used for delicately coloured inlays, whilst PVA emulsion gives a translucent glue-line. A method often adopted by the writer in gluing up light-coloured woods, cherry, sycamore, holly, etc., was to rub the edges of the joints with ordinary blackboard chalk before applying the glue, and this worked well with highly absorbent butt-jointed veneers. Hide glue will accept most colouring agents without appreciable loss of strength, but tests should be made with resin glues as the acid/alkali reaction is critical.

Resin glues are not so tolerant of abuse as animal glues, and all weighing and measuring must be in accordance with the manufacturers' instructions. Where the quantities of glue required are small, hand-mixing is sufficient, but mechanical mixers are imperative for large batches, for if the separate ingredients are not evenly dispersed throughout the body of the glue patchy setting and weak glue-lines will result. In particular, scrupulous cleanliness must be preserved for resin glues, as they will not tolerate oil, grease, acid or alkaline impurities, whilst liquid acid hardeners must never be stored in metal containers or spread with wire-bound brushes. Separate sticks or brushes must be kept for syrup and hardener, for even the slightest trace of hardener on a stick carelessly dipped into a can of syrup can spoil the whole batch. Figure 149 shows the use of a photographic rubber roller for spreading glue, which must be done very thoroughly for resin glues do not flow or adhere so easily, moreover cramping pressure must never be excessive or starved joints will result.

Fillers, extenders, etc.

Suitable fillers (rye and walnut-shell flour, etc.) can be incorporated with synthetic resin glues to extend and, therefore, cheapen the glue, and also to cut down excessive penetration through thin veneers. The amount of filling material can be varied within wide limits according to the type of glue, but large percentage additions will lessen the strength and water-resistant properties, and the makers' instructions should be closely followed.

Gluing difficult materials

Brass, metals, etc. Araldite epoxy resin glue in accordance with maker's instructions, hide glue with the addition of a teaspoonful of Venice turpentine per pint of glue, or plaster of Paris (alternatively rub metal with garlic).

Ivory. Coat with celluloid dissolved in ether, or glue with hide or Araldite.

Tortoiseshell. Araldite or UF resin glue, Salisbury glue or freshly made hide glue. Add flake-white or rouge to colour, or lay on gold-foil.

Leather, baize, etc. Casein, Cascamite One shot resin glue, dextrine, thin hide glue, shoemaker's glue, etc., allowing surfaces to tack off slightly before laying, especially with baize.

Laminated plastics. Casein, *Cascamite One Shot*, *Aerolite* 306 with GUS glycerine-based hardener where pressure is available, otherwise proprietary impact glues. For maximum heat and water resistance use *Aerodux Resorcinal* glue (CIBA (ARL) Ltd).

Rubber to wood. Bostik glue; or treat rubber with concentrated sulphuric acid, wash, dry and glue with *Aerodux Resorcinal* glue.

Wood to glass. Araldite where strains are imposed, or *Durofix* tube cement if only for ornamentation (sham glazing bars, etc.).

Many difficult materials (metal, ivory, etc.) can be glued with simple adhesives provided both surfaces are immaculately clean. A test of the molecular attraction between surfaces can be made by scratch brushing two pieces of soft aluminium, placing together immediately and hitting with a large punch. Both surfaces will then adhere and cannot be separated, but if one surface is lightly touched with the finger it will not bond. The method usually adopted by old craftsmen for inlaying ivory, silver, etc. was to hide glue the ground, dry grind the inlay without touching the critical surfaces with the fingers and immediately place in position. Alternatively, the metal inlays were rubbed with fresh garlic, and whilst it was never exactly known why the garlic acted in this manner, it is possible that the garlic oil cleaned the surface and was itself so finely dispersed that it created no fresh obstacle; but no doubt the scientist could give a more valid reason.

Comparison of main types of glue obtainable through retail outlets

	Hide	Casein	UF resin	PVA	Epoxy	Impact
Shelf life	Indefinite	Long	Syrup (3 months) Powder (1 year)	Long	Long	Long
Preparation	Heat mix with water	Cold mix with water	Cold mix with Hardener	None	Cold mix with Hardener	None
Reconstitution (re-use)	Yes	No	No	No	No	No
Pot life	Indefinite	Short	Short	Long	Fairly long	—
Assembly time	Very short	Short	Short to Long	Fairly Short	Fairly long	Short
Tack or suck	Excellent	Little if any	None	Slight	Very slight	Considerable
Pressure required	Hand or Cramp	Cramp	Cramp	Cramp	Hand or Cramp	Hand
Creep	None	None	None	Slight	None	Slight
Strength and durability	Very good	Very good	Excellent	Very good	Excellent	Good
Elasticity	Good	Very slight	Little if any	Slight	None	Considerable
Dulling of tool edges	Moderate	Moderate	Pronounced	Moderate	Pronounced	—
Versatility	Excellent	Good	Good	Good	Excellent	Restricted
Moisture resistance	None	Good	Excellent	Little	Excellent	Fair

Definitions

Cold-setting glues. Glues which set at normal room temperatures either by chilling or evaporation, etc.

Thermosetting glues. Glues which set with, and cannot be softened by, heat.

Assembly glues. Glues capable of supporting thick glue-lines without crazing—gap-filling glues.

Close-contact glues. Glues which will not tolerate thick glue-lines, but require intimate contact throughout.

Shelf life. Storage life in original containers.

Pot life. Effective working life of mixed glue.

Initial gel. First stage in curing of mixed glue. Gel has no strength.

Hardener. Accelerator or catalyst, usually an acid salt dispersed in water or spirit, or formic acid in solution. Function of the solvent is to ensure complete dispersal of acid throughout the glue, and can be coloured for identification.

Crazing. Hair-cracks in solidified glue set up by excessive shrinkage, trapped solvents or inherent weakness in glue structure.

Extenders. Filling material used to extend volume of glue, or to prevent excessive penetration.

Pressing or cramping time. Minimum time glued surfaces should remain under pressure.

Basic setting time. Minimum hot-press time, to which must be added time allowances according to thickness of veneer, etc.

Note. All adhesives take several days to develop their maximum strength.

13 Abrasives

Old-time cabinet-makers used sand-, brick- and stone-dust, shagreen (shark's skin) and other primitive materials for the levelling of wood surfaces, and it always appears incredible how they managed to achieve such wonderful finishes to their furniture. The manufacturer of modern abrasives is now a highly specialised field, and an enormous range of products for the surface finishing of every kind of material is available.

In all wood finishing the function of the abrasive is to wear away the wood fibres by the cutting or rasping action of innumerable sharp crystalline teeth, firmly anchored to a supporting base. The rate or speed of the cut depends not so much on the amount of pressure applied, for excessive pressure tends to defeat its own object, but on the size of the teeth, their relative sharpness, and their ability to keep their cutting edges without disintegrating. A poor abrasive is, therefore, one whose grits or teeth are relatively soft, or whose crystalline structure does not provide the requisite sharp facets, or which rapidly disintergrates either under pressure or by the heat generated by that pressure, or whose cloth or paper base fails to hold the grits securely so that they loosen easily and grind upon each other. The swirl-marks occasionally met with on surfaces finished with a machine-operated oscillating sanding pad are usually caused by these loose grits travelling round in erratic orbits. It follows, therefore, that in an age in which labour costs account for much of the expenses of furniture production, it is always false economy to use the cheapest types of abrasive, for the rate of cut is slow and the sharpness of the individual grits soon wear off, crushing rather than cutting the wood-fibres.

Sanding papers

Grits for sanding are deposited on the backing support either by gravity or in an electrostatic field in order that each individual grain shall be secured in an upright position, giving maximum cutting performace to the teeth, and 96:1 shows the disposition of the grains where (A) is the backing, (B) the basic adhesive coat, usually of hide glue, (C) the second adhesive coat of hide glue or synthetic resin and (D) the abrasive grain. The use of hide glue for the basic coat imparts a certain degree of flexibility to the sanding sheet, whilst the synthetic resin in the second coat anchors the grain in an upright position and does not soften under the heat generated by the cutting action. Generally speaking, grits anchored entirely by hide glues cut softer because the heat softens the glue, permitting the upright grain to lean over slightly, whilst the use of resin glues throughout gives a harder, fiercer cutting action, and will withstand the considerable degree of heat generated; therfore manufacturers use either one or a combination of both, according to the type of abrasive material and the purpose for which it is to be employed. Waterproof papers for wet sanding are anchored exclusively with synthetic resin glues.

The types of abrasive material available for wood finishing are as follows:

Glass

Originally crushed sand was used, hence the familiar name 'sandpaper', but the grit is now powdered glass, preferably from old gin or beer bottles. Slow cutting, relatively soft and soon

96 Abrasives (sanding paper), detail

exhausted glass is mainly used for cutting down old paint-work, although it is also used for wood finishing as it does not scratch. The flour grade 00 is still a favourite with french-polishers.

Flint

A natural abrasive used for hand-sanding and only slightly harder than glass, it has now been largely superseded by faster materials; moreover flint-dust embedded in the grain of sanded surfaces (cheap plywoods, etc.) has been found to cause a chemical reaction with synthetic finishes.

Garnet

Crushed garnet is used almost entirely for sanding wood. It is much harder than glass or flint, cuts quicker, lasts longer, generates very little heat and consequently rarely burns the wood. It remains a favourite material amongst cabinet-makers, as it yields a very smooth finish.

Aluminous oxide (Aloxite)

An impure oxide of aluminium manufactured from bauxite; the purest forms yield sapphires, rubies and Oriental topaz. The toughness and hardness of this material ensure that the individual grains will not disintegrate under the considerable mechanical strains of high sanding pressures, therefore it can be used to cut harder and faster than other materials. The white is the purest form and is usually dyed orange and reserved for wood finishing, with the impure forms of brown and pink for metals, etc. Occasionally these coarse-cutting impure forms are dyed black.

Silica carbide

The hardest and most expensive grit, produced by heating mixtures of coal and quartz in an electric furnace, and commonly known as 'carborundum'. Scarcely less hard than the diamond, its sharp yet even crystalline formation is eminently suitable for wet or dry grinding, and polishing of very hard substances with a compact surface, viz. cellulose, polyester, paint, glass, plastics, stone, non-ferrous metals, etc. It is, however, more brittle than aluminous oxide, and the latter is to be preferred for wood finishing.

Grading of papers (grain or grit sizes)

Hitherto, papers were marked with the **grade** only, and the principle is still employed for glasspapers which range from 'Flour', 00, to 'Strong 2'; but the grading of other papers has now been standardised to the actual mesh size per square inch for grits within the range 800, which is the finest procurable, down to 12, which is the coarsest. To avoid confusion most papers are clearly marked with both grade and grit size, and the following table gives the various equivalents together with the approximate comparable gradings in flint- and glasspaper.

Approximate comparable gradings in flint- and glasspaper

Grit size	Equivalent grade	Flint-paper	Glass-paper
500	12/0	—	—
400	11/0	—	—
360	10/0	—	—
320	9/0	—	—
280	8/0	—	—
240	7/0	—	—
220	6/0	4/0	—
180	5/0	3/0	Flour 00
150	4/0	2/0	0
120	3/0	0	1
100	2/0	$\frac{1}{2}$	$1\frac{1}{2}$
90 ⎫	0 ⎫	1 ⎫	Fine ⎫
80 ⎬	⎬	$1\frac{1}{2}$ ⎬	2 ⎬
60 ⎭	$\frac{1}{2}$	2	Middle 2
50	1	$2\frac{1}{2}$	Strong 2
40	$1\frac{1}{2}$	3	—
36	2	—	—
30	$2\frac{1}{2}$	—	—
24	3	—	—
12	—	—	—

Both aluminous oxide and silica carbide papers are available in all grits up to 800, and garnet-paper up to 500 grit. The equivalent values for flint-papers are fairly correct, but glasspaper values are an approximation only, for it must be borne in mind that the harder the grit the sharper the crystalline facets and the quicker the cut, therefore there is no exact comparison.

Distribution of grits

The actual abrasive grit is distributed on the backing sheet either as scattered grains commonly known as 'open coat' (50 per cent coverage) or close together and known as 'close coat'. In theory close-coat surfaces should give a greater speed of cut as there is greater grit coverage, but in hand sanding open coats will often cut most wood surfaces faster, for they do not hold the wood-dust and clog the grits. Cabinet-papers, i.e. heavy-weight papers with large grits for preliminary rough sanding with or without portable machine-sanders, can be obtained in both closed and open coatings and should be specified at the time of ordering, but finishing papers, i.e. light-weight papers for final surfacing, are open coat only. Resinous softwoods will require open coats at all stages, also polyester and nitro-cellulose lacquers flatted with aluminious oxide and silicon carbide papers. In case of doubt the manufacturer concerned should be consulted as to the most suitable type for any particular purpose, for ultimate quality depends in large degree on the excellence of the final surfacing, and much time, labour and money can be wasted on unsuitable sanding material.

Backings

Backings or supports for grits can be either vulcanised fibre, which is ideal for disc and drum sanders where the loading is particularly severe; 'combination', comprising a heavy-weight paper laminated with an open-weave fabric, and used with floor and drum sanding machines; close-woven pure cotton fabrics in various weights and degrees of flexibility for machine sanding; and tough raw paper of high-tensile strength in a variety of weights for both hand- and machine-sanding. Cloth backs last longer but are considerably more expensive, and paper is usually suitable for most normal purposes, although a very flexible cloth backing specially prepared for hand sanding is better for pronounced contour-work. In principle, orbital pad sanders require a fairly stout paper backing usually known as 'cabinet-papers' (C or D weight), and these are also used for hand or 'touch' sanding with a cork block in preparatory levelling off using a fairly coarse grit; but for final finishing and delicate work a lighter weight (A) is used, commonly known as a 'finishing' paper. Glasspapers, flint-papers and corundum (aluminous oxide) are usually stout C weight papers.

Sizes, etc.

Glass- and flint-papers are only available in the standard sheet of 11 in. (280 mm) by 9 in. (229 mm), which is torn into four equal pieces for use with a suitable cork block; but all other coatings are available in the standard sheet, in strips for orbital pad sanders, and in an immense variety of roll sizes from which discs, belts, sleeves and drum covers are made up to special order. Belts for portable belt sanders can be made up in the workshop if necessary, but the joint should be diagonal across the belt and the overlaps chamfered off to form a scarf joint (96:2), or the double thickness will bump over the rollers. A selection of abrasive papers for general workshop use is listed at the end of this chapter.

Sanding techniques

Machine-sanding operators are usually skilled personnel with a sensitive touch, otherwise edges are easily dubbed over and veneered surfaces cut through to show bald patches of glue which cannot be masked with ordinary stains. Great care must also be taken with hand sanding, which should be regarded as precision work, for the pressure of the hand is inclined to vary with the movement of the stroke, and there is always a temptation to press more heavily over localised defects. At all costs sharp angles and facets must be preserved, or the effect is lost and the work assumes a woolly appearance.

Hand-sanding rubbers are usually made of cork which gives the requisite firmness and resilience, but wood blocks covered with hard felt or rubber are suitable, also wood alone, although it is inclined to wear the paper through more quickly. In all hand or 'touch' sanding the pressure should be fairly light but firm, as too great a thrust on the block loosens the grit and clogs the surface, whilst too rapid a stroke tends to skate over and crush rather than cut through the fibres. In other words, the innumerable small teeth of the grits must be given time to accomplish their task. Ideally, the wood surface should be brushed clean of dust ahead of the block (97), for it is the loose grits grinding on their fellows which destroy the cutting action more than the actual fibres of the wood, whilst the sanding-block should be tapped smartly on the bench from time to time to clear the paper of accumulated dust. A fine wire card is also useful for clearing the paper. In flat work which is to be gloss polished it cannot be too strongly emphasised that the chief difficulty lies in getting rid of the imperceptible bumps and hollows which are never apparent until the mirror finish magnifies them out of all proportion, therefore the blocks should be large and the stroke as long as possible, particularly with scraped surfaces which always tend to bumpiness. Orbital sanders are excellent for this general levelling, as the size of the pad is equivalent to a half sheet of standard paper, and provided the weight of the machine itself is allowed to do the work without bearing down good surfaces are obtained. Belt sanders cut faster but are not so accurate, and great care must be taken with veneered surfaces or they soon rub through. Practically all belt sanders are grossly overloaded in relation to the fractional horse-power available, and no pressure must be applied or bumpy surfaces are inevitable, and motors soon burn out. A useful precaution in sanding out to the edges of flat work is to nail waste pieces of similar thicknesses at either end, so that the sanding block or belt can travel through without dipping. For sanding curved surfaces, mouldings, etc., short lengths of thick dowel-rod

97 Sanding wood surface

or broom-handle, or shaped rubbers made out of softwood to fit the curve, should be used, and the time spend in preparing them will be well repaid in the cleanness of the final finish. This crispness is particularly important in chamfered work and in simple nosings where the curve dies away into a flat surface, for any softening of the edges or waviness of outline is immediately apparent.

Choice of grits

For all preparatory sanding and levelling off an 80 grit stout-backed cabinet-paper is suitable, and coarse-grained woods such as oak or teak rarely require any finer treatment. For close-grained woods the first coarse sanding should be followed up with a 120 grit finishing paper, and finely veneered surfaces with 180 grit which can be used with a circular movement over mitred corners, etc. For the most delicate work and for easing down polishes a 240 grit can be used. The foregoing are, of course, only suggestions based on the practical experience of the writer, and as individual touches differ other workers may prefer coarser or finer papers. For comparable results with orbital sanders the grits can be coarser, i.e. 60 grit for preparatory work, followed up by 100 grit, and 150 grit if necessary.

Some timbers are woolly textured so that the grits tend to crush rather than cut the fibres, and these should be given a very thin wash coat of white french polish or cellulose lacquer (5 parts spirit or thinners to 1 part polish), and allowed to dry hard before the final sanding. The wash coat raises the grain and sets the loose fibres in an upright position so that they can be cut off. In the best work surfaces are always 'flared off' by damping them with water to raise the grain. This flaring off can be done several times if necessary, but wherever water is used it is essential to dust the surfaces very thoroughly with a stiff brush, for if they have been scraped with steel scrapers iron mould stains may appear, which will have to be bleached out with oxalic acid. The time spent on careful sanding will be well repaid in the excellence of the finished furniture.

All abrasive papers should be stored in a dry place (ideally at 21 °C (70 °F) and 45 per cent humidity) and warmed slightly before use if the backing is at all damp.

154

Selection of hand- and machine-sanding papers

	Bond	Paper weight	Grit	Coat	Materials
Waterproof silicon	Resin bonded	A	600–220	Close	Metals,
Carbide Paper	Resin bonded	C	600–150	Close	Primer's
	Resin bonded	D	120– 60	Close	Cellulose
For wet operations using water or other liquid suitable for hand- and machine-sanding					
Silicon carbide	Glue	C	240–100	Close	Metals,
Cabinet-Paper		D	80– 40	Close	Primers
Dry sanding of all metal and lacquered surfaces					Cellulose
Aluminous oxide	Glue	C	240–40	Close	Wood
Cabinet-Paper			240–40	Open	
Preparatory sanding of all types of wood					
Garnet Cabinet-Paper	Glue	C	240–100	Close	
			150–100	Open	Wood
		D	80–36	Close or open	
Preparatory sanding of all types of wood					
Flint-Paper	Glue	C	220–40	Close	Wood, paint
General woodworking					
Glasspaper	Glue	C	00–3	Close	Wood, paint
General use including cleaning down old paint-work, etc.					
Silicon carbide					Polyester
finishing-paper	Glue	A	500–60	Open	Lacquers, metals,
Dry removal of imperfections in polyester and cellulose by hand or orbital sanders					cellulose
Aluminous oxide					
finishing-paper	Glue	A	400–60	Open	Wood
All finishing operations in hard- and softwoods and flattening cellulose with white spirit					
Garnet finishing-paper	Glue	A	320–60	Open	Wood
Finishing of softwoods, etc.					

Miscellaneous abrasive materials

Wet and dry papers

These are waterproof silicon carbide papers glued with synthetic resin adhesives on a rubberised or treated backing paper. The finer grits can be used dry for flatting polyester, cellulose and catalyst finishes, but it is more usual to employ a lubricant, water and a little household soap for a fast cut, or white spirit alone for a smoother, finer cut. The papers should be kept well soaked, and the sludge wiped clean ahead of the block.

Cutting-down pastes, burnishing creams, etc.

Loose carborundum powder should not be used for cutting down lacquered surfaces, as the cutting action will not be evenly distributed and deep scratching may result. Valve-grinding pastes are also unsuitable, and proprietary cutting-down pastes specially compounded for the work should only be used. If too stiff they can be thinned with water or white spirit according to the makers' instructions. Most motor-car polishes incorporate a small proportion of very fine abrasive material, as do metal polishes of the *Bluebell* type, and both can be used for final burnishing to a high gloss, although the special burnishing creams formulated by most makers for their own lacquer are preferable. Neither cutting-down pastes nor burnishing creams should be used on lacquered surfaces in which the grain is not wholly choked with polish, or the grain will show white deposits which may be extremely difficult to eradicate. A satin matt finish on full-gloss lacquered surfaces can be obtained with either water-floated pumice powder or Silex powder, and the process is described in

Wood Finishing Chapter 42. Lightly polished surfaces can be effectively dulled with No. 0000 wire wool, whilst coarser grades are invaluable for cleaning off old polish in conjunction with a suitable paint-stripper. Wire wool can also be used for dulling chromium plating, stainless steel and brasswork, but care is necessary and the strokes should be even as in brush painting.

Recent developments include a stearite-coated silicon carbide finishing-paper (lubrisil) for polishing work, where the stearite soap coating provides its own lubricant after the manner of a sanding sealer lacquer coat; also an improved aluminium oxide cloth belt (Hitest) which provides a cool, fast-cutting abrasive which will withstand the considerable degree of heat generated in the machine sanding of high-tensile metals (nimonic and stainless steels, etc.). Both are manufactured by the English Abrasives Corporation.

Hardness of grits

Relative hardness of the various types of abrasive in comparison with the diamond which is given a MOH value of 10 are as follows:

Commercial name	Formula	Origin	MOH scale
Crocus	Fe_2O_3	Artificial and natural	5·5–6·5
Quartz (flint, agate)	SiO_2	Natural	7·0
Garnet (Almanite)	$Al_2O_3FeO_3\ SiO_2$	Natural	7·0–8·5
Emery	$SiO_2\ FeO\ Al_2O_3$	Natural	7·0–9·0
Aluminium oxide (corundum)	Complex Al_2O_3	Artificial	9·0–9·4
Silicon carbide (carborundum)	SiC	Artificial	9·5–9·6
Diamond (carbonado)	C	Natural	10·0

14 Miscellaneous materials

Plastics

Spectacular advances in the development of plastics and progressive reduction in costs of production have enabled the Furniture Industry to make increasing use of these wonder materials, and there is little doubt that such use will continue to expand. In fact, there are many who will claim that plastics will eventually become the chief material for furniture of all kinds, but wood still provides the cheapest media in form and content; it can be worked with the simplest tools and is easily repairable, therefore snap judgments should be avoided.

In essence, plastics are long chain molecular structures evolved from common elements and compounds, gases, lime, salt, coal, oil, molasses, cotton, wood, etc. by chemical synthesis. Heavyweight molecules or monomers (one unit), usually but not invariably built up of carbon atoms, are linked together in long chains with or without cross-links to become polymers (many units), with the qualities of hardness, toughness, resilience, stretch, mouldability, translucence, dielectric properties, heat, acid and water resistance, etc., etc., according to the type as determined by the molecules and their arrangement. Thus, in theory at least, the research chemist should be able to arrange the linkage of the molecules to give the physical qualities he requires, although obviously methods of achieving that linkage have to be evolved which are possible, practical and economic.

Types of plastics

All plastics are polymeric and all polymers may be regarded as potential plastics. Certain polymers occur naturally, i.e. casein (milk solids), cellulose derivatives (wood, cotton) etc.; all others are produced synthetically and are divided into two types, thermoplastic and thermosetting. In thermoplastic materials the necessary degree of polymerisation having been achieved the long chain molecular structure can then be activated by heat to allow freer movement between the molecules, thus the plastic can be softened and resoftened without deformation provided the degree of heat is kept below the point of actual degrade of the material. In thermosetting plastics the polymerisation has been arrested at a stage which produces relatively short chain molecules. Later application of certain simple chemicals (hardeners or catalysts) or simple heat carries the polymerisation a stage further, producing cross linkages which destroy the mobility of the molecules, and the plastic sets into a hard, infusible resin which cannot then be resoftened. This latter type is usually known as 'resin plastics' (synthetic resin glues, etc.). In the main, thermoplastics are tough, resilient and can be given controlled flexibility either by arranging the molecular structure accordingly or by added chemical plasticisers, whilst the thermosets are either brittle solids which can be extended with other materials (chopped paper, wood flour, etc.) to form moulding powders, or as viscous syrups for use as surfacing materials, impregnating liquids and glues, although here again the addition of plasticisers or softeners will allow a limited degree of flexibility. It should be emphasised that the chemistry of the various types of plastic is very much more subtle than this brief résumé might suggest, and readers are referred to the standard works on the subject for a thorough understanding of the principles involved. A list of the more important plastics with their applications in the Furniture Industry is given below.

Plastics applications

Plastics applications fall into three main categories: cast and moulded structures and components; extrusions and extruded sections; shaped forms and fabrications. The appropriate method of manipulation is determined by the plastic itself and whether it is thermosetting or thermoplastic, and the nature of the required component.

Types of plastics
Common or chemical names
Thermosetting

	Uses
Phenol formaldehyde (PF)	Wood glues, bonding agents, reinforced laminates, mouldings etc.
Urea formaldehyde (UF)	Wood glues, chipboard manufacture, mouldings, etc.
Melamine formaldehyde (MF)	Wood glues, reinforced laminates, mouldings, etc.
Resorcinol formaldehyde (RF)	Wood glues.
Phenol resorcinol formaldehyde (RPF)	Wood glues.
Polyester	Finishes, lacquers, laminates (glass fibre, etc.).
Epoxide (epoxy resin)	Glues (metal, glass, etc.), castings, pottings, etc.

Thermoplastics

Acrylonitrile butadiene styrene (ABS)	Drawers, doors, knobs, legs, etc.
Casein	Wood and paper glues, small moulded components.
Cellulose acetate (CA)	Sheet, film, small moulded components.
Cellulose acetate butyrate (CAB)	High impact mouldings (tool handles).
Cellulose nitrate (CN)	Finishes, lacquers, small moulded components.
Polyvinyl chloride (PVC)	Rigid and flexible sheet. Extrusions and coatings.
Polyvinyl acetate (PVA)	Wood and paper glues. Contact adhesives.
Polyethylene LD (low density) (polythene)	Films, packaging materials
Polyethylene HD (high density)	Structural mouldings
Polypropylene	Sheet, structural mouldings and components, etc.
Polyurethane	Finishes and lacquers, reinforced laminates.
Polyurethane ester (polyester)	Expanded foam seating, etc.
Polyurethane ether (polyether)	Expanded foam seating, etc.
Polystyrene	Sheet, film, expanded foam
Polystyrene HD (high density)	Sheet, structural mouldings, etc.
Polymethyl methacrylate (*Perspex*)	Sheet, structural mouldings and components
Polyacetal	Door handles, hinges, etc.
Polyamide (nylon)	Fibres, sheet, frictionless moulded and shaped components, etc.

Cast and moulded structures and components

Thermosetting plastics

Special casting or compression moulding resins (PF, UF, MF and Epoxy resins, etc.) are used. In the most simple technique a cold cure resin mix (resin syrup and catalyst) is extended with appropriate fillers and colorants and cast in metal, silicone rubber or plaster moulds without heat. In a more sophisticated technique the resinous solution is neutralised with a suitable organic acid, dehydrated under vacuum, and poured into lead moulds which are then oven treated. A third technique using compression moulding is more widely practised in which carefully measured amounts of powder resin or resin pellets are fed into a heated mould and compressed by a heated plunger; the thermo-setting plastic is thus first heat softened so that it flows into the crevices of the mould, and is then heat cured to the finished shape determined by the mould and its matching plunger. As thermo-setting plastics are more brittle than the thermo-plasts all these techniques are usually reserved for heavier sections.

Thermoplastics

All types of thermoplastics lend themselves to injection moulding which is the most popular process for high-speed production of moulded structures and components. In this technique the resin chips or powder are conveyed by screw or ram along a heated barrel container which converts them into a viscous syrup or flowable solid; this is then ejected through a nozzle into a closed split mould and allowed to chill. Shell mouldings, i.e. thin-walled hollow mouldings, can be obtained by spinning the mould, thus forcing the plastic against the sides of the mould. Choice of plastic is dictated by both technical and economic factors. Press-in components which have to be compressed slightly to enter a prebored hole are formed by flexible low-density polythene, etc.; open components, i.e. handles, etc. of stiff plastic use polystyrene or polypropylene, or polymethyl methacrylate for transparent components. Polypropylene is also used for plastic hinges in which the actual hingeing action is effected by a flexing of the material itself and not by an interlocking knuckle action, and polyamide (nylon) where exceptional strength, toughness and self-lubrication (gliders, hinges, lock components, bushes, bearings, etc.) are required.

Extrusions and extruded sections

Continuous lengths of tube, rod, sheet and various profiles are formed by extrusion processes mainly using thermoplastics, although thermosetting plastics have uses in specific cases. The resin powder or chips are conveyed along a heated barrel by means of an archimedean screw action which forces the softened plastic through a nozzle orifice shaped to the required profile. If a mandrel is supported in the centre of the orifice the plastic will be ejected as a hollow tube. Flexible and semi-flexible sections (wire covering, flexible edging strips, etc.) employ PVC or LD polythene, rigid sections HD polythene or polypropylene. Both cellulose acetate and cellulose nitrate are also used, also nylon for strength and toughness, and perspex (polymethyl methacrylate) for transparent sections.

Shaped forms and fabrications

Vacuum forming is the most interesting technique for the furniture-maker as with this process relatively large recessed shapings can be effectively and economically produced with simple apparatus. Integral chair shell structures which are produced by the injection-moulding process require heavy and expensive equipment, but certain plastics which are not sufficiently

free flowing for injection moulding lend themselves to vacuum forming. The principles involved are relatively straightforward. A presoftened sheet of suitable plastic is securely clamped round the perimeter of an open-top box containing the shaped mould or former; a vacuum is then applied to the box to pull the flexible sheet down over the former and held until the sheet has chilled off and fixed the shape. Stiffer plastics may require plunger assistance, and in this system the moulding former is in the shape of a plunger which is forced down into the softened sheet, whilst for deep drawings a vacuum is employed to assist the deformation by helping to pull the sheet down in advance of the descending plunger. On releasing the vacuum the inherent elasticity of the sheet will pull it back against the plunger. Plastics employed in vacuum forming include polymethyl methacrylate (perspex), polyvinyl chloride (PVC), polypropylene, high-impact polystrene and various copolymer sheet materials recently developed. In particular acrylonitrile/butadiene/stryrene (ABS) is one of the newest and best for it can be cut, tool shaped, glued, screwed and nailed. Methods of sheet forming without pressure include powder casting with low- and medium-density polythenes and PVC in which the resin powder is fed against a heated metal mould. Large surfaces can be covered in this way, as the powder softens in contact with the heated metal forming a continuous layer which can be stripped off when cold. Simple bending techniques for one-way curves can also be used as described under *Perspex* page 161.

Metal surfacing with plastics

Several methods are employed: (1) shrinkage techniques in which a thermoplastic tube or sheet is solvent softened so that it can be wrapped round the metal section and then either heated or allowed to dry off; (2) paste coating in which the plastic and plasticiser is applied in a thick coat, heated and allowed to chill off, or the metal section is dipped if a thin coat only is required; (3) powder coating in which the plastic powder is sprayed on to a heated metal surface, or the metal surface can be made to carry a high-voltage electrostatic charge and the powder can be sprayed cold; (4) Cast surfaces in which suitable monomer resins which require no volatile solvent (polyester, di-alkyl phthalate, etc.) are polymerised by the addition of a suitable catalyst in thick coats which do not shrink back during setting.

Polyester resin fibre-glass laminates (GRP)

Rapid moulding techniques for the production of rigid plastic shapes or shells (chair seats, etc.) require specialist knowledge and advanced equipment beyond the resources of the small workshop, but glass-fibre laminates, familiarly known as GRP, offer a simple method of forming rigid structures whose only disadvantage is that one surface, inside or outside according to the type of former used, will be smooth and the other rough. In essence the shaped moulding is composed of laminations of chopped strand glass mat impregnated with polyester resin. The resin must be thrixotropic, i.e. it must be fluid enough for brush coats, but must be capable of building up so that it stays in position and does not creep downhill. Assuming that a simple box shape is to be moulded, then an exact pattern (98:1) must be made of timber or other suitable material, using waterproof bonding agents (Araldite epoxy resin, etc.), with a generous overhang all round so that the rough edges of the rim can be trimmed up afterwards. The sides of the box should be tapered if possible, as this will facilitate withdrawal, and sharp edges and internal corners should be avoided, or the resin mat will tend to bulge over, leaving a void in the structure of the finished mould. The working surfaces of the mould must be filled (resin and talc, Polyfilla, Alabastine, etc.), cut down smooth, lacquered (polyester wax, polyurethane, shellac, etc.), again cut down with 400 grit wet and dry paper, and burnished with cutting-down paste to a high gloss, after which it is given a heavy coat of wax polish and left to harden overnight.

GRP former mould

The *former*-mould from which the finished moulding will be struck is now made up as 98:2. The wax coat is first buffed off the pattern, which is then coated with a polyester emulsion wax

98 Glass-fibre reinforced plastic moulding

release, followed with an application of wax polish buffed to a high gloss, and then a layer of polyvinyl acetate (PVA) release agent applied with a sponge. A gel coat composed of polyester resin, catalyst (setting agent) and a small percentage of colour paste is then brushed on, followed by a second gel coat immediately the first has cured. The second gel coat should be of a contrasting colour, so that adequate warning is given during any subsequent rubbing down, and when this coat has cured a coat of catalysed resin is brushed on, and a layer of chopped strand glass worked into it, adding more resin with a stiff stippling-brush until the mat is 'wet out' or saturated. Two or more additional layers of glass mat and resin are then added, and the whole assembly stippled and rolled with a split roller to consolidate the layers and eliminate all air bubbles. The mould is then put aside to cure for at least 4 hours at normal room temperature, any roughness smoothed out, washed over with warm soapy water, given a thick coat of wax polish and allowed to age for a further 24 hours.

Finished mould

Exactly the same procedure is followed in preparing the finished moulding 98:3. The former-mould is treated with emulsion wax, wax polish and PVA release agent, then a single gel coat followed by the requisite thickness of glass mat (minimum two layers) and resin. After curing the mould is released, washed with soapy water and trimmed to exact size; it should not require any further polishing.

The method described above gives a smooth surface on one side only, marked (A) on the drawings, as the undersides will have been formed by the roller. They can be ground off smooth if necessary but will show the cut ends of the glass fibres and should be painted or otherwise protected.

Perspex

Perspex or acrylic sheet (polymethyl methacrylate) is readily obtainable in clear transparent, pastel shades, full colours, and transfusing and fluorescent colours in thicknesses from $\frac{1}{25}$ in. (1 mm) to $\frac{1}{2}$ in. (12·5 mm) in colours, and up to

98A Drawer unit with sliders in medium impact polystyrene *By courtesy of Prestige Caterers. Photograph: Council of Industrial Design*

2 in. (50 mm) in the clear sheet. It is also supplied in clear rod and tube up to 1 in. (25 mm) diameter. Although not as hard as fused glass it has the same clarity and appearance and can be cut very easily with circular saw, band-saw or very fine-toothed handsaw, using low speed and light pressure and feed. It is easily drilled with the normal twist-drill lubricated with a trace of thin oil, and can be bent to simple curves at a temperature just short of boiling water (94 °C; 201 °F). For accurate bending a wood former should be used, the perspex sheet heated before an electric fire or similar source of heat, bent over the former, covered with a cloth and held in position for from one to two minutes to cool and set. Cut edges can be stuck together with simple heat, chloroform or ether, or special perspex cement, and frameless showcases are now made almost exclusively by this method, with the meeting edges either butted and polished (wet and dry paper, burnishing pastes, etc.) or mitred together, both methods giving invisible joints if well done. There is a growing tendency also to design carcase furniture in flat sheets and simple chair forms in moulded resin, for it is an excellent structural material with outstanding qualities of clarity, strength, rigidity, stability and durability under quite severe conditions of wear, as witness its use in aircraft-work. It is, however, relatively expensive, although no doubt constant research and development, as with all other plastics, will eventually cheapen costs.

Nylon

Nylon (polyamide) has universal uses as a fibre material for it can be cold drawn to five times its original strength, thus straightening the chain molecules and imparting great strength and excellent wear resistance. It is also invaluable as a sheet material and for castings, mouldings and extruded sections for it is tough, resilient and provides noiseless and frictionless surfaces invaluable for furniture guides, sliders, rollers, etc. It is also used in knock-down fittings, whilst barbed or serrated nylon dowel-pegs can be glued into such loose-textured materials as chipboard to provide secure anchorages for screws. As it is a thermoplastic without the hard brittleness of the thermosetting resins it can be cut, shaped and drilled with normal hand-tools.

For particulars, manipulating data and sources of supply of other plastics readers are referred to the manufacturers concerned, lists of which can be obtained from the various periodic journals devoted to the subject and to the standard text-books available at most libraries.

Decorative plastic laminates

Familiarly known as *Formica*, *Arborite*, *Wareite*, etc., these are composed of layers of kraft paper impregnated with phenolic resins, whilst the surface pattern which can be purely decorative in an infinite range of designs or as an exact simulation of real wood grains is printed on a cover paper, and coated with a scratch-resistant sur-

99 Decorative plastic laminate details

face of melamine resin. Figure 99:1 shows (A) the kraft papers, (B) the cover paper and (C) the melamine coating. Heat pressing of the assembled pack between stainless-steel platens polished to mirror finish induces a chemical change or polymerisation, resulting in a homogeneous sheet possessing outstanding qualities of lightness, toughness, durability and resistance to heat, moisture, acids and alkalies, etc. Standard sheets with the pattern on one face only are usually $\frac{1}{16}$ in. (0·062 in. or 1·58 mm), but a full range of thicknesses is also available, 0·032 in. (0·81 mm) for vertical facings, wall claddings, etc., 0·040 in. (1·01 mm) for light use in horizontal positions, 0·052 in. (1·32 mm) for post forming (heat bending), and 0·10 in. (2·54 mm) to $1\frac{1}{2}$ in. (38 mm) built up of separate laminations or with a sandwich core of other materials (ply, etc.). Thicknesses of $\frac{1}{8}$ in. (3·17 mm) and over are self-supporting (99:2). A cheap-quality backing or balancing veneer composed of kraft papers only with no surface pattern is available for use on the undersides of core material to counteract the pull.

Cutting procedures

Laminated plastic veneers can be cut with circular saws, using square tipped teeth without set, band-saws with hack-saw-shaped teeth, or fine-toothed backed tenon-saws, in all cases cutting with the face uppermost. For machine-saws in production-work tungsten-carbide teeth should be used, for the resin content is very hard on cutting edges; whilst if there is any tendency for the back to chip or 'rag out' with any type of saw the teeth should be resharpened, and the veneer sheet firmly supported with applied top pressure if possible. An alternative hand method which gives no rag is to score the face with a hardened steel scraper or cutting tool—a special blade is available for Stanley trimming-knives—and the sheet will then snap easily with a clean fracture, as in glass cutting. Narrow cross-cuts, corners, etc. can be cut with a fine-toothed hack-saw, whilst for contour cutting portable electric sabre-saws or fret-saws with metal-piercing blades can be used, but support must be adequate with strips of waste material, hardboard, etc. clamped to the face to prevent chipping on the upward stroke.

Trimming edges

Cut edges can be trimmed with a heavy jack-plane, using short, quick strokes and not attempting to follow through; or with steel cabinet-scrapers, or fine-cut saw-files. If the edges require polishing a dead smooth file, or 400 grit wet and dry silicon carbide paper, will ease out the scratches, and a little fine cutting-down paste or metal polish (*Brasso*, etc.). followed up with a wipe of thin oil will restore the lustre. Scratches on the face of the sheet can also be eased out with cutting-down paste, always provided they do not penetrate to the cover paper, and matt black laminates are usually enhanced by rubbing over with finest No. 0000 wire wool, but it must be carefully done. Spilt glue, paint, etc. can be lifted with a razor-blade as in cleaning glass, and oil, greasy thumb-prints, especially on matt black veneers, eradicated by wiping over with french chalk.

Laying techniques

Composite assemblies $\frac{1}{8}$ in. (3 mm) and thicker are self-supporting; but the standard $\frac{1}{16}$ in. (1·5 mm) veneer requires bonding, either to a rigid framework, or to plywood or chipboard sheeting not less than $\frac{3}{4}$ in. (19 mm) thick. Generally speaking, solid timber groundworks are quite unsuitable, as the laminated veneer is virtually inert and cannot move in sympathy. Additionally, the reverse side of the groundwork must also be veneered to counteract the pull as in wood veneering, unless the support is very firmly fixed. A special backing quality laminate composed of kraft papers is available, although ·024 in. (0·6 mm) wood veneers can also be used. Care should be taken to choose groundworks whose faces are smooth, fine grained and without strong figure such as Columbian pine, etc., otherwise the raised grain will telegraph through to the surface in time. Cross-members in made-up frameworks should not be glued together or they will also eventually shadow through.

Treatment of edges

All edges should be eased back to prevent lifting and possible impact damage (99:3). If the edges of the groundwork are also covered they should be laid first, trimmed off flush and the top applied (99:4), the front bevel being formed with a fine-cut file. Mitred edges (99:5) are possible but hardly sensible, as the resultant sharp corners positively invite impact damage, and a more satisfactory treatment is shown in 99:6. Other treatments are shown in 99:7, 8 and 9, and where hardwood lippings are used they can be glued on first and the top cut to exact size and laid afterwards, or the top laid first and then the hardwood lipping. Either method calls for skilful working, for the lippings must be cleaned off flush with the laminate, and the easier way is to glue on the lipping and flush it down to the exact projection to receive the laminate, using a loose waste strip as guide; any fractional adjustment necessary after the top has been laid can then be done by protecting the top with a strip of cellulose tape, and sanding down the high spots. If the top is laid first and the lipping after then a slight bevel (99:9) will keep the cutting tool away from the laminate. Treatment for sinks, washbasins, etc. is shown in 99:10, where a fairly wide lipping (A) is applied in case there is any water seepage which might delaminate the plywood layers, with a proprietary mastic bedding (B) between the lipping and the rim of the sink.

Gluing procedures

Several types of gap-filling rubber-based impact glues are available for hand laying, which only require moderate pressure as they give a powerful and immediate tack. They set by evaporation or absorption of the spirit solvent, and do not attain maximum strength for at least 14 days. An advantage of this type is that they retain a certain measure of elasticity, and will thus withstand fractional movements of the base. They are however only heat resistant to about 60 °C (140 °F) and although damp proof will not stand continuous moist conditions.

In using this type of adhesive over large areas speed is essential. The groundwork must be perfectly level, dust free and free from grease, etc., whilst spreading with gauged metal spreader, wooden squeegee or roller should be reasonably full and even, with both surfaces coated and allowed to air dry until the glue is tacky and no longer moist. The coated sheet must be carefully positioned, dropped into place, rolled or

thumped down with the clenched fist to expel any trapped air, and if pre-cut to exact size then a useful precaution is to tack temporary battens to the groundwork, and use these as locating shoulders. Any spilt glue should be cleaned off with a suitable solvent, petrol, cellulose thinners, etc., or allowed to tack off and rolled up with the finger-tips, whilst rollers should be cleaned immediately. If any edge tends to lift it should be cramped down, and the assembly left for some hours before further manipulation.

Plastic laminates can be laid with casein, Cascamite One Shot or gap-filling synthetic resin glues, and this is the standard production method, although cramping pressures are necessary. One of the best glues for this purpose is *Aerolite* 306 with *GUX* hardener in which a proportion of glycerine has been added to the hardener to impart a measure of flexibility. Application is the same as for wood veneering (Chapter 22), but hot pressing should not exceed 71 °C (160 °F), with pressures only sufficient to bring both surfaces into intimate contact, and not exceeding 40 lb per sq. in. (2·812 Kgf/cm²). This method is preferable to hand laying with impact glues which are more suitable for on-site work, for with cramping pressures the surface will be flatter, and the glue film will be both heat and damp resistant within the limits set by the laminate itself and the groundwork.

Bending

The standard $\frac{1}{16}$ in. (1·5 mm) veneer can be cold bent to simple curves of not less than 8 in. (203 mm) radius, although narrow strips will probably follow a tighter curve without fracturing. The curve should be cut very full in the length with sufficient overhang to follow the sweep, and the waste trimmed off afterwards. For more acute curves either the standard laminate must be heat softened up to but not exceeding 150 °C (302 °F), which is just short of the blistering point, and set between formers, or for very acute curves to a maximum of about 1 in. (25 mm) radius special post-forming grades should be used (99:11). Most manufacturers issue their own data sheets for post-forming operations, and the schedules recommended should be closely followed.

Heat-resistant qualities

Standard quality veneers are proof against surface temperature not exceeding 150 °C (302 °F), but will not resist intense localised heat, such as neglected cigarette ends, etc. Incorporating a metal foil in the laminate will tend to spread such localised heat over a wider area, and a cigarette-proof grade is available which gives reasonable protection. Such heat-resistant grades are not suitable for continuously damp situations (kitchen-sink fitments, etc.), and will not bend so readily as the standard grades.

Real wood laminates

Plastic laminates in which the top sheet is true wood veneer instead of printed paper are available (Belfort, etc.). The sheets have the authentic depth, warmth and natural beauty of wood, although the grain is filled with resin and the natural texture is lost. In all other respects, methods of manufacture, toughness, durability, resistance to heat, moisture, acids, stains, etc., and cutting and laying procedures are identical, whilst the cost compares favourably with that of other laminates.

Plastic coverings, leathercloths, etc.

Besides the innumerable transparent or patterned sheet materials, polyvinyl acetate resins (PVC) are coated on a variety of base materials, wool (*Yana*), cotton twill and jersey fabric (*Lionide*, *Ambla*, *Flexknit*, etc.), to yield light-, medium- and heavy-weight cloths which have all the advantages of true plastics, viz. long flex life without ageing, resistance to spilt acids, stains and greases, water resistance, etc. Some are produced as impregnated woven fabrics for upholstery, etc., similar in all respects to natural woven materials, whilst others are close coated and grained in so exact a simulation of natural leather that it is sometimes difficult to tell the difference unless the edges are examined. These have a rapidly expanding use in wall coverings, sprung and foam-covered seating, etc., with the added advantages of cheapness and continuous widths free from all defects, although they lack the beauty of the natural material, and have not the same recovery value under seating pressure as good leather.

Leathers

Natural cowhides, specially dressed, softened by a crimping action which pushes the fibres over each other so that they can slide easily giving the requisite suppleness, are extensively used in upholstery, and are commonly known as *furniture*-hides. They are slit from the tanned hides to a usual thickness of about $\frac{1}{16}$ in. (1·5 mm) and are invariably grained between rollers, pigmented or dyed, and dressed with a spray coat of synthetic lacquer. The grains can be heavy, medium or light textured, and are done either to accentuate the natural grain texture, or to even out the applied colour and to mask the inevitable defects which occur in every hide, viz. barbed-wire weals and punctures of the 'prick' or warble fly which, it is estimated, cost the tanning industry over a million pounds sterling a year in spoilt hides. The coloration can be an opaque dressing, sealed with a little gum arabic, or straight aniline dyes which penetrate the hide and yield a clearer finish than the heavy pigments which lie on the surface and tend to show as white cracks if the hide is heavily pulled or dressed. The advantage of leather, apart from its intrinsic beauty, is its tolerance of wetting, pulling and stretching over acute compound shapes, whilst it has a natural resilience which will accommodate considerable deflection. A typical cowhide will contain from 50 to 60 sq. ft (4·645 to 5·574 m²) measured out to all edges, and 100 shows the dimensions to be expected from an average hide (the standard allowance for waste in cutting to final dimensions should not be less than 60 per cent). Goat-skins—Cape Levant, Morocco, Niger, etc.—are much smaller and more expensive, and usually reserved for table linings, small seatings, etc. They are either aniline or vegetable dyed, and native skins are invariably untextured. Skivers (sheep-skin), calf-skin, etc. are rarely used in furniture as they are more delicate and wear too easily. Shagreen (shark's skin) is only used in small panels for ornamental boxes, etc.; and occasionally other exotic leathers are used as fashion dictates, but cowhide and goat-skins are the mainstays, with plastic-coated cloths (leathercloths) a fair

100 Cowhide measurement

substitute. A description of table-lining methods is given in Chapter 26, page 265.

Metal furniture

Hitherto metal furniture was largely made of mild steel tube, hence the familiar name 'tubular steel furniture'; moreover, designers tended to think in terms of wood forms and then to translate those forms into metal sections. Modern metal furniture is now designed as such, taking into full account the qualities of stability, flexibility and hardness which allow considerable reduction in sectional dimensions over comparable wood forms. As a viable material for certain kinds of furniture metal commends itself for its consistent quality which is of great importance in large-scale manufacture; it can be worked to precision limits and its hygienic, non-porous, smooth surfaces, toughness and great strength render it eminently suitable for hospital, kitchen, school, office and dismountable furniture. Disadvantages are more aesthetic than practical, and it is no doubt the coldness, hardness and somewhat clinical appearance without texture or variety which mitigates against its universal adoption in domestic furniture, although it will harmonise with wood to good effect if restraint is exercised.

Materials

A range of solid and hollow metal extrusions is available, i.e. flat strip, rod, channel, L- and T-sections, square and round tube, etc. First choice is stainless steel, but it is expensive in first cost and more difficult to fabricate. Mild steel is the norm, either chrome, nickel or aluminium plated, or with baked-on enamel or shrunk-on plastic coverings. Chromium plating gives great brilliance and depth but the surface is porous, hence the rust pitting of chromed steel components in outdoor conditions unless plated over a skin of copper or nickel; whilst nickel-plated surfaces give a softer shine similar in some respects to stainless steel. Anodised light alloys are also used extensively, whilst bright metal finishes can be matted with very fine wire scratching-brushes or No. 0000 wire wool, and this satin matt effect is usually preferred for domestic interiors.

Manipulation

Methods of attachment or jointing are by brazing, torch or arc welding, metal connectors or screw assemblies. Chair posts, table legs, etc. are normally fitted with protective caps of hard rubber, plastic or knock-in wooden caps cut slightly oversize and driven in wedge tight. Connection of wood members, cross-rails, etc. can be done by securing a threaded bolt to the metal section and carrying it through a prebored hole in the wood member. with a captive nut in a small mortise which can be tightened up to take up the slack if the wood shrinks. Alternatively, there are knock-down fittings available. Flat strips can be bent cold round suitable formers in a bending machine, but tubes must be filled with rammed sand, steel balls, pitch, etc. and the ends securely plugged or the bending will kink the inner curve. Metal extrusion L-, T- or U-sections, etc. are filled or packed up with thin metal strips before bending, and stout sections may have to be heated. For methods of fabrication reference should be made to the standard books on metal-working, for it is hardly within the province of a woodworkshop and is usually done by engineers or outside specialists, although there are many patent methods of assembly which are procurable for run of the mill work.

Part 3   Basic techniques
15   Preparation of timber

Preliminaries to any sound construction are (1) a full cutting list of all the pieces required; (2) good timber free from natural defects, accurately sawn and planed up flat, square and out of winding; (3) careful planning of the work ahead, including the choosing of appropriate jointing methods, the order in which they are to be cut, and the order and method in which the various pieces and parts are to be assembled in the completed carcase. This last is important and must be accurately visualised if there are to be no last-minute hitches, with carefully cut joints glued ready for assembly unable to be driven home because the direction of entry conflicts with other parts already in position.

Setting out

The timber must first be cut to approximate length, and it is always better to square off from either a sawn edge or a pencil-line along the length if the planks are waney. If an incorrect line is drawn—and all measurements should always be checked and double checked—then it should be cancelled out and a broad arrow drawn against the corrected measurement (101:1A). The ends of the plank should be carefully examined for hidden splits and the first few inches of any plank which has been stored for any length of time may have to be sacrificed. Due allowance for working must be made, with $\frac{1}{4}$ in. (6 mm) on the width and $\frac{1}{2}$ in. (12 mm) on the length for the first rough sawing to dimension unless the cuts are machine-made and accurate. Customary allowance for planing up (surfacing) sawn thicknesses are usually $\frac{3}{32}$ in. (2·5 mm) for each wrot (finished) face.

Sawing out

The rip-saw is used for long-grain sawing, the large crosscut or crosscut panel-saw for cutting across the grain, and the temptation to use the finer tenon- and dovetail-saws for rough work should be strenuously resisted, for more often than not the plank will be gritty. A usual tendency on the part of the beginner is to saw too fast, and in comparison the skilled worker's pace is almost leisurely, but he will cut more wood in the end and it will be accurate. Every effort should be made to saw not only on the line but also truly vertical, as this will save not only timber but a great deal of unnecessary work at later stages. At the commencement of the cut the heel of the saw should be placed on the mark, steadied in the vertical position with the thumb and the kerf established with a few light upward strokes, not forgetting to withdraw the thumb out of harm's way before the full downward thrust is applied to the saw (102). A few strokes with a candle end along the saw-blade will reduce friction and lighten the work.

Planing up (surfacing)

Either the fore- or jack-plane is used for the first rough levelling, the try-plane for true levelling and the finely set smoothing-plane for final surfacing. Contrary to some writers the cutting edges of the irons should be square and not ground convex, although the jack-plane iron can have the corners dubbed over to prevent digging in. The set of the back iron should be adjusted to the depth of the cut required and the relative hardness or softness of the timber, for its sole function is to support the cutting iron and break up the chip, therefore it can be set back as much as $\frac{1}{16}$ in. (1·5 mm) for mild softwoods, but perhaps only $\frac{1}{64}$ in. (0·5 mm) for hard refractory timbers. The projection of the cutting iron also depends on the nature of the timber; it should be fed down gradually until it gives a clean easy shaving without shuddering or digging in. The sole of the plane can be lubricated with the candle end to cut down friction.

In planing up wide boards the best or face surface should first be levelled off along, across or diagonally according to how the grain works

101 Jointing details

1

A

B

2

3

4
A
STRONG
A
B
NO STRENGTH
NO STRENGTH
C

5

6

7
BATTEN

8
FACE
FACE

(interlocked grain is best planed diagonally to prevent tearing out), and tested with the winding-sticks, placing one at each end and sighting through with the eye level with the nearest stick and about 12 in. (305 mm) away. Any slight tilt to the further stick will then disclose whether the board is in winding, for although all edges may appear straight the diagonals may be curved. If the tilt to the further stick is say $\frac{1}{8}$ in. (3 mm) then it can be assumed that the board winds $\frac{1}{16}$ in. (1·5 mm) in its length, and about half that amount must be taken off the high further corner, and the other half from the near opposite corner by working diagonally across the board. When the board is out of winding then the try-plane should be capable of taking fine shavings the full length of the board over the entire area, to be followed up by the finely set smoothing-plane to ease out any ridges and roughened patches. During all these operations constant watch should be kept on the general levelness along the length and across the width, either with a straight-edge or the sole of the try-plane tilted on its edge. No attempt should be made to scrape or sand the surface at this stage for it is bound to attract small scratches, bruises and dents during subsequent operations, but badly torn grain should be got rid of as much as possible so that little if any thickness will be lost in the final finishing. When the surface is planed perfectly true and out of winding it should be marked with a 'face' mark (101:1B) which should never be omitted from any piece of prepared timber.

Shooting or squaring edges

Immediately the face surface is true the leading or best edge should be trued or shot perfectly straight in its length and at right angles to the face, checking carefully with the try-square all along the length; it is then known as the 'tried' edge and is marked accordingly (1B). This is, perhaps, the most difficult of all planing operations, for whilst it is comparatively easy to plane a straight edge with a long try-plane, always remembering that pressure is applied at the front of the plane at the commencement of the stroke and gradually transferred to the back as the plane moves forward, it is much more difficult to keep the edge truly square to the face. If there is a

tendency to form a bevelled edge no attempt should be made to correct it by tilting the sole of the plane, but the cutting iron should be slid over to the high side with the fingers under the sole to form a guide (103) and the high edge taken down until the final shaving covers the entire width. However, should the tendency to bevel over still persist then the cutting iron should be examined

102 Cross cutting plank with handsaw

103 Correcting bevelled edge

for tilt, the bench top checked for general levelness with the floor, with the vice square to the bench-top and, therefore, truly vertical. The worker's own stance should also be checked, for the ability to shoot a square edge must be mastered for accurate work and every effort made to achieve it.

Edging thin boards

If the edges are too thin to adequately support the sole of the plane then the shooting-board should be used; or if too long for the board then the timber should be cramped to the bench-top with a packing length under to form its own shooting-board, and the plane slid along on its side; but the bench-top itself must be perfectly flat.

Thicknessing, etc.

Immediately the best edge has been shot then the actual thickness of the board must be gauged all round with a marking-gauge, and levelled off exactly to the gauge lines. The exact width of the board is then determined either by ticking off against a rule placed on edge and not laid flat across the board which may tend to give a false reading, or preferably marking in with a pencil-gauge (104), or with a panel-gauge; the edge is then trued up accordingly. If several boards have to be planed up to an exact and similar width then it will pay to cut a thin lath to the exact dimension, carefully squaring the ends on the shooting-board and using it as a trial stick or template. The lath itself should not be less than 1 in. (25 mm) wide, for it is then easier to see that it is laid square across the face of the board and not at a slight angle which again will give a false reading. The length of all boards should, of course, be kept full at this stage to allow for final dimensioning. After several boards for any one carcase have been surfaced they should not be stacked haphazardly until they are needed, but should either be placed one on top of each other on a level bench and weighted down, or stood on edge with a space between so that the air can reach every surface. They should also be protected from direct sunlight and the sooner they are framed together the better, although sufficient time must be given for freshly worked timber

104   Marking width with pencil-gauge

to settle down and adjust itself to the prevailing atmospheric conditions. For this reason timber taken straight from the timber-yard is often roughly skimmed over on both faces and allowed to settle for as long as possible before the general levelling, otherwise too much thickness could be lost if the boards go hollow or crook in length. In machine-planing every board must be flatted on one face on the overhand to take out the wind before it is thicknessed, or the pressure of the rollers will merely bend it flat whilst it is being cut and it will spring back to its original shape immediately it is released.

Squaring ends

The shooting-board is used for squaring ends, but if the timber is too wide or too heavy to be held on the board then the ends will have to be shot in the vice and checked against a long try-square. The practice of nicking off the far corner to prevent the grain splintering out is not to be recommended, and it is advisable to learn how to use the try-plane in both directions, leading with the left hand, reversing the plane and leading with the right. An alternative method is to cramp a block at the far corner to support the grain, and a similar packing piece is sometimes necessary when squaring ends on the shooting-board.

Marking out

Face-marks and edge-marks must be bold and should be done with a thick soft pencil. For the first approximate dimensioning of lengths, etc. a B or HB pencil can be used, but for accurate dimensions at later stages a 2H or 4H is necessary, whilst shoulder-lines should always be cut in with a knife.

Casting of surfaced boards

If a board does cast after it has been levelled only experience will give the knowledge of how much the cast can be corrected when the construction is framed together. As an expedient, boards which go in rounding in their width can sometimes be corrected by the old trick of wetting a level stretch of concrete floor, waiting until the water sheen dries off and then laying the hollow side downwards on the damp surface, weighting it if necessary. Alternatively, stout bearers can be cramped across either side, using packing pieces to force the board over to the other extreme; but there is no guarantee that these measures will prove permanent. Thin sawn boards which are badly rounded and present difficulties in planing up can be panel pinned on the corners to the bench-top, the pins well punched in and the board surfaced, but the boards will resume their original shape once they have been released, and everything depends on whether the stiffness of the supporting frame-work will hold them flat without undue strain. The most satisafactory solution is to reject all timber which shows pronounced movement, but sometimes it is a hard decision to take and therefore worth experimenting.

Jointing techniques

The techniques of jointing sections of wood together to form rigid self-supporting and permanent structures have been evolved through many centuries of trial and experiment to accom-modate the natural movement of timber, and can rarely be improved upon. Only in the case of prefabricated timbers (plywoods, particle-boards, etc.), where the total movement is relatively small, have any worthwhile developments taken place (see *Knock-down fittings*, page 365), but in the main the machine has merely adapted pure hand-techniques, obviously simplifying them wherever possible and making greater use of the immensely strong adhesives now available, but still relying on the same fundamental principles. The best illustration of this is the dovetail joint, one of the most intricate to cut but still the best method of jointing two pieces of wood together at right angles to each other, where the machine, instead of evolving a simple worthwhile substitute—if that were possible—has accepted the joint as such, and only altered it sufficiently to allow for the rotary movements of the cutting-tool.

There are very many different varieties of joints to cover every possible contingency, but before describing them in detail some reference should be made to the function of the joints, what they have to do and how they have to do it. Glue is in itself a wonderful jointing medium, but wood is wood and imposes its own conditions. Thus two pieces of timber can be glued side by side with their grain direction parallel and will then, if properly jointed, be as strong as a single piece (101:4A), but the same two pieces cannot be glued end to end satisfactorily (A–B), for the cut pores of the end grain will merely suck up the glue like a sponge, preventing any permanent bond. It is true of course that end grain can be repeatedly sized with weak glue until the open pores are choked, and this will undoubtedly strengthen the bond, but the joint itself is still not good enough, and will always fail under any sudden impact because the natural elasticity of the long fibres lying side by side (A–A) is not there to cushion the shock; moreover, the interaction of a good glue with a wood surface is more subtle than a mere bonding skin. In the same way two pieces of wood with the grain or fibres opposed to each other (B–C) will shrink across their width in opposite directions, and this natural shrinkage is so powerful nothing can permanently oppose it. Even if the junction is reinforced then the shrinkage will travel until it finds the weakest link which will ultimately

SQUARE CUT

ANGLE CUT

COMPOUND CUT

HALVING

NOTCH

TRENCH

HOUSING

GROOVE (1)

SOCKET

REBATE

GROOVE (2)

105   Basic cuts in jointing

fail (101:5). Jointing methods are, therefore, designed to hold or lock sections of timber together, either in the same plane or in opposing planes, so that the method of attachment is permanent and proof against loading stresses, thrusts, sudden impact, the wear and tear of daily use and the constant movement of the wood fibres themselves ceaselessly moving in sympathy with the atmosphere surrounding them. All these factors must be taken into account, and whereas in heavy constructional work it is possible to calculate almost precisely the moments of compression, tension and shear to which the wood members will be subjected, unfortunately this is not possible with furniture except under controlled conditions, for although it is composed of upright piers or stanchions, bearers, cantilevers and distance-pieces as in any fabricated structure, the wood sections themselves are too delicate, the timber is chosen for beauty rather than strength, the variety of timbers used is considerable, and the amount of use to which the piece of furniture will be put can only be broadly assessed. The cabinet-maker has, therefore, very little scientific data to help him, and he must rely almost entirely on

tradition, instinct and as much practical experience as he can muster.

Jointing methods

Methods of jointing wood together can be classified under four broad headings: (a) butted joints, either edge to edge, side to side or end to end, with or without additional reinforcement; (b) interlocking joints where one piece of wood is cut or shaped to fit a corresponding socket in the other piece; (c) mechanical joints which permit controlled movement; (d) knock-up and knock-down metal or plastic fittings which secure the various wood sections together to form rigid structures. These last fittings are described under the section devoted to metalwork, whilst the remaining headings tend to overlap each other, and it is usually easier to group the joints somewhat arbitrarily under their separate types or classes, i.e. edge joints, etc., mortise and tenon joints, dovetails, mitres, housings, etc., etc., and this is the procedure adopted in the following chapters. The basic cuts on which all jointing methods are founded are illustrated in 105.

16 Edge joints, housings, halved and bridle joints

Edge joints (butt joints)

These are used for jointing up narrow widths, facings, lippings, glued fillets, blocks, etc., and can be either plain glued or reinforced with tongues, dowels or screws.

Plain glued edge joints

Two methods are available: (*a*) straight shot joints coated with hot hide glue and immediately rubbed together, with the natural suck of the glue providing sufficient pull to effect a close joint, and known as *rubbed* joints; (*b*) joints shot fractionally hollow by the thickness of a piece of thin blotting-paper and pulled together with cramping actions. The advantage of the latter method is that the ends of the jointed boards are forced into compression and will not open if there is any subsequent shrinkage. Cold-setting resin glues can be used for these cramped-up joints, giving plenty of time for assembly so that boards warped in the length can be cramped at half pressure, tapped down flush and the cramps then tightened.

Rubbed joints

Assuming that several narrow boards have to be jointed together with hide-type glue the boards should be arranged on the bench, choosing the best face uppermost, matching the grain and colour and wherever possible reversing the heart side so that any subsequent rounding is equalised without losing too much thickness (101:3); the boards are then marked as shown (101:2, 6). The first board is gripped in the vice and the second board placed on it edge to edge and tested with a straight-edge across the total width. Any tilt either way on the top board must be corrected by replaning the edges; but if the boards have been shot on an overhand-planer with incorrectly set fence, or on a shooting-board which is out of true, then reversing the face of each alternative board will correct the tilt

(101:8). The top board should be swivelled slightly and should bind at both ends, whilst finger pressure applied simultaneously at both ends will disclose whether there is any tendency to rock, denoting that the edges are in winding. After establishing that the boards seat along their entire length with their faces in one line, then the other boards should be tried in like manner until the assembly is complete.

Gluing up rubbed joints

Hide glue should be used, thin and hot, and after slightly warming the boards the first is gripped in the vice, the next tilted against it so that the glue-brush covers both edges at one stroke. The second board is then planed in position and rubbed backwards and forwards three or four times to squeeze out the surplus glue, keeping the hands low down and at either end if possible to avoid breaking the joint. Joints over about 3 ft (1·0 m) long should not be attempted single handed, and in any case long lengths should be cramped and not rubbed. If the assembly is composed of several boards they should be glued up in pairs wherever possible, and the glue allowed to harden before any further rubbing; whilst freshly jointed boards should not be laid flat but stood under their own weight against an inclined batten (101:7), leaving them for at least 24 hours before final surfacing.

Cramped joints

Long lengths and boards glued with cold-setting resin glues must be cramped and are first shot fractionally hollow. In theory one sash-cramp should suffice, but in practice it is better to use three, with one at each end underneath and one in the middle on top to counteract any tendency for the cramps to pull the assembly in rounding, checking that the boards seat on the sash-bars, and testing the upper surface with a straight-edge. If resin glues are used there will be plenty of time to adjust the assembly, tapping down any boards which are inclined to spring. In all gluing operations with resin glues containing acid hardeners, scraps of newspaper should be used to isolate glue-covered wood from steel jaws or bars, or iron staining may result. Surplus glue should be wiped clean with damp rags, for resin glues are hard on cutting edges.

Edge jointing thin boards

Thin boards can be rub jointed with hide glue if perfectly flat, but if sash cramped together it may be necessary to use G-cramp bearers across the width to hold the boards flat. Cast or rounded boards can be glued up in this way, always providing the edges have been shot truly square in the first place; but the boards will revert to their former shape when pressure is released.

Tongued and grooved joints

Where there is considerable loading of the surface as in unsupported table flaps, etc., edge joints can be strengthened with tongues which increase the gluing area. Tongues can be worked in the solid (106:1) or both edges grooved and a loose tongue inserted (106:2). These loose tongues were formerly cut from solid timber, either cross grain or diagonal (feather) grain, but plywood is now universally used, matching the ply to the thickness of the cutter. The boards are not shot hollow, whilst the tongue itself, whether loose or worked in the solid, should be a hand-tight fit and no more, and slightly bare of the full depth of the groove to allow for surplus glue, allowing $\frac{3}{16}$ in.(5 mm) thick tongues entering about $\frac{1}{4}$ in. (6 mm) for $\frac{3}{4}$ in. (19 mm) boards, and $\frac{1}{4}$ in. (6 mm) thick for 1 in. (25 mm) boards. Thicker boards require double tongues (106:3). If the grooves are worked with a spindle-moulder or router they can be stopped well clear of the ends and the tongues cut back accordingly (106:5), but if worked with grooving- or combination-plane or circular saw it is more difficult to stop the grooves and they can be allowed to run through, either showing the ends of the tongues—which is not objectionable if well done —or cutting back and filling in with carefully selected end-grain timber (106:6). Twin grooves

and loose tongues (106:2) save timber width; moreover, solid tongues (106:1) worked with matched cutters in a combination-plane are not wholly satisfactory, for the carefully shot edge has to be cut back to form the tongue, and the tightness of the joint may suffer. With machine-cutters, however, solid tongues are so easily formed they are standard practice in production-work and 107 shows the variations possible. A good tongued and grooved joint will help to pull up a cast board, but should not be relied upon to correct a pronounced warp. Faults in tongued joints are shown in 106:4 where in (A) the tongue is too long, preventing the edges meeting; (B) too thick, forcing the grooves open; and (C) too short, weakening the joint. Typical applications are also shown on this page. Figure 106:7 is a tongued and grooved table-top; 106:8, 9 shows two forms of applied lippings to ply or laminboard, etc.; 106:10 is a light framework with ply panel suitable for small doors, provided the panel is also glued into the groove; 106:11 is a carcase cheek tongued into a post or leg in preference to a series of small tenons which have to be cut laboriously by hand; 106:12 is the corner of a tongued carcase, with (A) a stronger variation as the long lap at X is unsupported, and (B) a mitred lip and tongue; 106:13 is a simple box structure; 106:14 is a shaped carcase plinth or cornice; and 106:15 is a method of working tongues on a bevelled edge where the block (A) gives a right-angled seating for the plough-plane. Other applications are shown in succeeding chapters.

Dowelled edge joints

These are no longer used to any great extent (although some examples of cheap continental furniture use short stub dowels extensively in carcase framings), but handworkers may find the process useful, particularly where the jointing methods must be hidden (109:1). The boards are shot slightly hollow and a marking-gauge is run down the centre of each edge (108 shows the correct way of using the gauge); the boards are then cramped together and the dowel positions squared across. Boring must be dead accurate (see *Dowelled joints*, Chapter 18, page 190) with a $\frac{3}{8}$ in. (9·5 mm) dowel at about 5 in. (125 mm) centres for up to 1 in. (25 mm) boards, and

1   2   3   4   A   B   C

5   6   7   8   9

10   11   12   A   B   X

13   14   15   A

$\frac{1}{2}$ in. (12·5 mm) dowels for thicker timbers. It is usually reckoned that dowel-pegs should enter about $1\frac{1}{4}$ in. (32 mm) for maximum efficiency, with a slight gap at the bottom of the socket for surplus glue; with the dowel driven home on one edge and the projection checked with the corresponding socket on the other edge. The dowel ends can be chamfered and the sockets countersunk for easy entry, particularly if there are slight errors in the setting out. A single-application glue should be applied to edges and sockets, for water or spirit hardeners applied to the pegs will swell them up and make entry more difficult. Emulsion (PVA) glues should not be used for dowelling, as this type of glue has little if any penetration and a tight hole will merely wipe the glue off the peg. Where boards have to be end butted to increase the overall length, dowels offer a practical method of strengthening the joint.

Slot-screwed joints

An alternative method to dowelling for strengthening edge joints, in which the projecting head of a countersunk steel screw enters a corresponding hole and socket. The hole is bored to the diameter of the head, and the socket cut to receive the shank so that the head of the screw cuts its own path, whilst the bevel of the countersink pulls the edges together (109:2). For a tight fit the boards are first tried in position, and the top board tapped a little way home as indicated by the arrow to make sure everything lines up. It is then removed, the screw given a half turn, the edges glued, driven home and cramped. This joint is not now used to any extent, but may be useful for edge joints which have to be worked on before the glue is thoroughly set, and for dry jointing and secret fixings for panelling, wall fittings, etc.

107 Examples of machine-jointing

Matched, cleated and battened joints

Traditional custom regards the tongued and grooved joint proper as having loose tongues glued in, and the 'matched' joint with tongues worked in the solid; but the introduction of cheap tongued, grooved and beaded or V-jointed matchings for wall linings usurped the latter term, which is now used solely to describe solid-tongue boards which are dry jointed and secret nailed or screwed to supporting battens or frameworks.

Matched boarding (109:3) has little application in furniture, although cottage-style oak furniture sometimes had doors framed together on this principle. Cleated or battened joints are jointed boards stiffened or supported by screwing ledges or battens to the back (109:4). The screw-holes are slotted as shown in the inset so that the screws can slide either way to accommodate the timber movement, and the principle is sometimes used for drawing boards of softish timber, glued on the edges, deeply saw kerfed on the back to take up any movement and prevented from hollowing or rounding on the face by the slot-screwed battens. An alternative method is to taper dovetail the battens (109:5A) which do not need either screws or glue.

108 Holding marking-gauge

109 Jointing details

1

DOWELLED JOINT

12·5 mm
½"

2

SLOT SCREWED JOINT

3

MATCHED JOINT

4

BATTENED

5

A

DOVETAIL CLEATED

6

7

A

B

8

A

B

HOUSED JOINTS

9

SAW

10

Housing joints

Housings are usually taken to mean wide grooves cut across the grain to receive the full thickness of fixed shelving, drawer runners, etc., although they can be worked with the grain also. Probably the only real difference between a housing and a groove is that the latter is designed to take a shouldered tongue and not the full thickness. Trenches are usually taken to mean seatings or wide housings, but the terms are interchangeable.

Housings for fixed shelves can be worked right through or stopped short of the front edge so that they do not show (109:6), in which case the shelf is notched at the front to allow the remainder to enter. In working housings it is not advisable to rely on measurements exclusively, for the shelf could taper fractionally in the thickness, giving a sloppy fit if the housings were squared across and of constant width throughout. A better plan is to square a pencil-line across the cheek, place the shelf end vertically on the cheek against the pencil-line and scribe the thickness both sides with a sharp knife pressed hard against the shelf. A portable electric router can be used to cut the housings, working against a batten cramped to the cheek; or if cut by hand the correct depth is gauged on the back edge, a hole bored at the front to the correct depth, the hole cut out square, the knife-cuts deepened and a small bevel formed to act as a guide for the tenon-saw, the sides sawn down to depth and the waste chopped out with a chisel or routered away with the hand-router (110). Failing a router or in positions where it cannot be used, a temporary depth-gauge can be made by driving a panel-pin through a block of wood with the point projecting the required depth as shown in 110. Working the block backwards and forwards will scratch the high spots which can then be levelled. If the sawing has been accurate the shelf will fit tightly first time, but if not then the sides of the housing must be eased with an edge-trimming plane or chisel. The same setting of the marking-gauge used for the depth must be used to mark the shoulder cut on the shelf which should be sawn in fractionally bare of the mark so that the shoulder pulls tight against the cheek when assembled. Housing depths can be about $\frac{3}{16}$ in. (5 mm) for normal work, and there is little point in recessing more deeply; whilst the set in from the front edge of the cheek can be about $\frac{1}{4}$ in.

(6 mm). The strength of the joint relies on the overall tightness, and a good joint will probably require knocking home with a mallet. Drawer runners in plywood cheeks need only be recessed about $\frac{1}{8}$ in. (3 mm) for they can be glued and screwed if necessary, and in any case the loading is up against the cheek and there is little strain; but drawer runners in solid timber cheeks will probably require a $\frac{3}{16}$ in. (5 mm) deep housing for they must not be glued across the grain (see *Carcase work*, Chapter 27, page 271). Dovetail housings (109:7) are used where there is any considerable side pull as in tall cupboards, etc., where the sides may tend to bow outwards in the length. They can be bareface, i.e. tapered one side (B), or double (A); with the former more usual as the bareface at the top helps to keep the shelf square. The dovetail housings are usually cut to rather less than half the thickness of the cheek and run right through; although they can be stopped about $\frac{5}{16}$ in. (8 mm) from the front edge, which is simple enough with a portable electric router and dovetail-cutter, but more difficult to cut solely by hand. A shaped block (109:9) can be used as a guide for sawing in, and another (109:10) as a seating for chisel cuts to the shelf. Such joints must be tight enough to be effective, yet free to slide across the width of the cheek; and as the glue always tends to swell up the fibres making assembly more difficult a stopped and tapered (diminished) form (109:8) is sometimes adopted, in which the back portion is an open housing and only the front few inches (100 mm) (B) are taper dovetailed. The taper can run the full length if required (A), but here again the fit is fairly critical, and if too tight the shelf will not travel the full distance. For most normal work there is much to be said for a straight-sided housing, and provided it is really tight infinitely preferable to a badly cut, complicated joint.

Bevelled and coopered joints

Bevelled joints are edge joints at any preset angle other than 45°, at which angle they are termed *mitre* joints; whilst coopered joints are usually taken to mean several bevelled joints assembled together, as in coopered barrels. Both terms are, therefore, in essence synonymous. Their application is in splay corners and in cylindrical falls, bow fronts, pillars, columns, etc. built up from solid sections and rounded to shape. They can be tongued together, but are more often merely glued, butted together, rubbed or cramped and later reinforced with glue blocks, although good joints should not necessarily need them. The usual difficulty is to plane the edges at the required angle. It can be done easily enough on the overhand-planer with the fence set to the required angle, but hand-planing in a vice and using an adjustable bevel instead of a try-square for testing presents some problems, for it is very easy to lose width if both edges have to be bevelled, thus forming a taper section. A good method is to use packing pieces cut at the correct angle temporarily nailed to the shooting-board. If the angle of the splay or bevel required is $67\frac{1}{2}°$ as in building up an octagonal column, then the packing pieces must be $22\frac{1}{2}°$ to make up the required $90°$ at which the plane works (111:3).* In order to obtain the correct

angle of any splay it is first necessary to draw an end view full size (111:1) and set the adjustable bevel, template or protractor accordingly. Having ascertained the correct angle it should then be drawn at each end of the timber section to be bevelled, and the pencil should also be rubbed along the leading or base edge (111:2). Each section must be to exact width and truly parallel, and the last fine shaving taken off should just—but only just—take out the pencil-rubbing on the base edge, leaving only a darkened arris or corner.

Rubbed joints glued with hide glue present little difficulty, and in building up an octagonal column the eight pieces are first glued in pairs and carefully stood on end or otherwise supported, so that there is no strain on the joints whilst the glue sets. The quarter sections are then connected into half sections, and finally the two halves are glued together, first trying them in the dry state, for fractional errors do creep in and some adjustment may be necessary. If the bevels are to be glued with resin glue, supporting

* Six sides will require angles of $60°$ and $30°$, ten sides $72°$ and $18°$ and twelve sides $75°$ and $15°$.

111 Bevel and halving joints

A

2

PENCIL RUB

A

BLOCK

3

$67\frac{1}{2}°$

$22\frac{1}{2}°$

A

B

ELEVATION

4

C

PLAN

5

HALVED JOINTS

6

7

8

9

A

10

11

A

X

12

13

14

cradles may have to be used for cramping up, or the pieces temporarily held with adhesive tape, bound with stout twine and wedges driven under the twine to pull the assembly up. A fairly slow-setting glue should be used, for with all the pieces assembled together at the same time the final adjustment must not be hurried, and the cross-distances between the internal flat should be carefully checked. If the column is to be rounded a cardboard circle to the exact finished shape should be used for marking out the ends.

An alternative method of cramping up splay corners sometimes advocated is to glue temporary wood lugs or blocks to the outer faces at such an angle that the cramp gives a direct pull without slip, but it is a laborious and somewhat uncertain process, and should only be adopted as a last resort. Much can be done with stout blind cord or twine, looped round and twisted with a stick (see *Mitre and scribed joints*, Chapter 20, page 207), for the pull exerted is fairly considerable. Pads of thick rubber or felt will sometimes prevent a metal cramp slipping on an awkward slope, and it is always worth trying an assembly in the dry state to see whether the cramps will bite.

Halved joints

Several different forms of halving joint are used which are easy to cut and usually regarded as first exercises for students, although they have practical applications in skeleton grounds, frame-works, etc. In particular, the cross halving (111:6) gives a stronger connection than either tenons or dowels. Where the two pieces to be joined are of equal thickness, both halves or laps should be approximately equal, the separate pieces clearly marked on the face and leading edge, and all gauging done from these, using the same gauge setting throughout so that the amount left in one piece (A) will equal the amount taken out of the other piece.

In working, the pieces should be positioned, ticked in pencil either side, the cutting-lines squared across with a knife and the depths of the laps gauged in as before described. The shoulders are then sawn in on the waste, the waste chiselled away (111:7) from either side and finished off with a metal shoulder-plane. *Edge cross halvings*, i.e. halvings in the depth are liable to fracture

along the grain under any sudden impact and an improved version is shown in 113:1 which prevents any side give, although some strength is sacrificed. '*L*' or *corner halvings* (111:8) can be cut entirely with the small tenon-saw and if accurate can be assembled without further treatment as the slight ribbing of a fine saw will give a key for the glue. Figure 111:9 shows an *oblique halving* with the required angle set out with the adjustable bevel, and in 111:8, 9 both pieces can be left slightly full in the length and flushed off afterwards. The correct method of holding a try-square or bevel whilst squaring across is shown in (112), with the thumb pressed hard against the stock (A) to hold it tight against the wood.

'*T*' *halvings* are constructed in the same manner as *cross halvings*, etc., and can be straight, or single dovetail taper (111:10) and double taper (111:11) to withstand a direct pull. The dovetail rake is marked out as described under *Dovetailing joints* (Chapter 19), with the slope set in a fraction from the top corner (111:10A) to give a seating for the saw. Figure 111:12 shows an oblique single dovetail taper housing often used in gallows brackets for shelving. Any pull in the direction of the arrows is protected by the shoulder X. A stopped version of the double taper used in connecting rails in table and carcase stands is shown at 111:11A.

Mitre halvings (111:13)

These are relatively weak as the gluing area is halved (111:13), and they are, therefore, confined to light frames where the strain is negligible or where the edges are moulded and must show a mitre. Sash-bar halvings (111:14) are part cross

112 Holding try-square

181

halvings and part mitre halvings. The square recesses are cut first and the mitres after, using a mitre template for final trimming.

All halvings are glued, some can be screwed for additional strength, as shrinkage is bound to occur across the width, with rupturing of the glue-lines if the sections are wide.

Bridle joints, etc. (113)

Angle or *corner bridles* (113:2) are sometimes referred to as 'slot' mortise and tenon joints, and the procedure is virtually the same as for tenoned work. They must be marked out with a mortise-gauge, working always from the face sides, and set to give a slot about one-third the total thickness, with equal substance left on either side. They are stronger than the corner halving as the gluing area is doubled, and the stout shoulders take the strain. 'T' bridles (113:3) form a stronger connection than 'T' halvings, and are the usual method of connecting middle legs to continuous

top rails, where two short tenons would have little strength. If the top rail is thinner than the legs the mortise-gauge must be reset accordingly (113:4) and if the rail is curved then a flat must be formed on the face of the rail so that the gauge works parallel. In cutting the slots it is quicker to saw the shoulders down to the full depth, bore a hole with brace and bit through the waste from either side (113:6) and finish off with a chisel. The slots are usually cut first and the tenon part cut and pared to fit, for it is easier to chisel across the tenon than to pare down vertically in the slot. Skew rails (113:7) cannot be bridled, and must be notched in and glue blocked from behind as shown. The rails can meet square at A if preferred.

Mitre bridles (113:5) are useful in framed-up work, mirrors, etc., and form a strong joint. Any moulding or rebating to the frame must be done first before the tenon and slot are cut. A stopped form is shown at (A) which is more delicate but not so strong.

113   Bridle joints, etc.

BRIDLE JOINTS

17 Mortise and tenon joints

These are probably the best known of all wood-working joints, sometimes very much abused and badly cut but still capable of holding together. The variations are many and only the principles and the main types need be given.

Mortise and tenon joints are usually referred to as *wedged through* (114:1) and *stub* or *blind* (114:2); the former more applicable to joiners' work where the end grain of the tenon shows on the edge of the stile and is painted over, but as it has decorative possibilities it is included. The familiar type for furniture is the *stub tenon* with or without haunching (114:3) whose function it is to keep the unsupported part of the rail from twisting on the face.

All tenoned work follows the same general principles. The width of the mortises is slightly over one-third the thickness of the stile (114:5) but pitched according to the width of the hand- or power-chisel available, whilst the rail width in corner mortising is also divided into three, one-third for the haunch or seating and two-thirds for the tenon, less a bare $\frac{1}{16}$ in. (1·5 mm) shoulder at the bottom edge to cover any slight gap caused by a slack tenon or bruising of the mortise socket end in levering out the waste in hand-methods. The final width of the tenon itself less the haunch becomes the length of the mortise cut to receive it. In all framed-up work it is always better to provide an extra length to the stiles to form a horn (114:1) at top and bottom which helps to prevent the splitting of softish timber whilst deeply mortising, and also to protect the corners from incidental damage. These horns are left on until the door is fitted.

Where the stiles and rails are grooved or rebated for panels the mortises are pitched to coincide with their position; they can be wider but not narrower than any groove or rebate in the rail. The mortise depth should be slightly more than the length of the tenon so that a small gap is left for surplus glue, whilst plenty of wood substance should be left between the bottom of the mortise and the outer edge of the stile, certainly not less than $\frac{3}{16}$ in. (5 mm) even for a small door.

Haunches

Grooved frameworks will require haunches to fill them; if there is no groove a secret haunch (114:4) can be fitted; although light doors may not require haunching and the modern tendency is to omit them if possible.

Setting out, etc.

Cutting lists usually take the gross length of the rails right across the width of the frame irrespective of the type of tenon. Setting out can be done entirely by measurement, but in practice it is better to mark the stiles clearly with top marks 'left' and 'right', and face marks uppermost on the inside or panel edge, and place them on the bench-top in the finished position, allowing an extra $\frac{1}{8}$ in. (3 mm) on the overall width for cleaning off and fitting. The rails are then marked and placed over the stiles also in the correct position, and allowing $\frac{1}{8}$ in. (3 mm) extra on the height. The critical positions of the rail shoulders, i.e. the net panel opening width, are then ticked, also the opening height on the stiles. The stiles are then hand-cramped together and all the measurements, actual height of door frame (plus $\frac{1}{8}$ in. (3 mm) extra), depth of haunch or seating, position of mortise allowing for any groove or rebate in the rails, squared across and the rails similarly treated for shoulder length (width of panel opening) and length of tenon. The actual width of the tenon and the depth of the haunch can be decided later after the mortise has been cut. The mortise-gauge is then set for the width of the mortise and gauged from the face sides on both stiles and rails, after which the mortises can be chopped, first boring out a series of vertical holes to save labour. When completed the tenons can be sawn in with the cuts always on the waste side of the marks. Figures 115 and 116 show the rail canted over first for one cut and then for the other, with the rail uprighted for the final cut. The shoulder-lines are cut in with a knife and sawn through, and the tenons offered against the mortise for their final width and position of haunch. (Figure 117 also shows use of bench-hook for sawing shoulders, small stuff, etc.)

HORN

STILE

RAIL

WEDGED THROUGH

1

STUB OR BLIND

2

HAUNCHED

3

6

7 8

9 10

MORTICE

4

HAUNCH

SHOULDER

CHEEK

SECRET HAUNCH

11

5

⅓ | ⅔

TENON

⅓ MORTICE

12

Types of tenon

Several variations are possible, 114:6 is used only in the cheapest work for thin slats into thicker frameworks such as play-pens, garden seats, etc., and the depth of the mortises must be positive as there are no shoulders on the rails to limit the depth of entry. Figure 114:7 is better as it has one cut shoulder and allows the top of the rail to be rounded over if necessary, whilst 114:8 is better still as it gives a positive square location. Figure 114:9 is edge shouldered on one or both sides if the thickness allows, but no rounding of the rail is possible unless the mortises have round ends also. Figure 114:10 is the orthodox method where the rail lines up with the face of the legs or stile and the tenon must be offset.

Wedged through mortise and tenon

This is shown in 114:1 and 118:1 and is taken through the stile with a little extra length for flushing off, and wedged from the outside. The mortise is cut slightly full in the length on the outside to accommodate the wedges which are glued and driven home as the frame is assembled. These wedges can be at either end which is normal for joiners' work, or darker timber is used and treated as a decoration in any of the positions shown alongside (118:1).

Stub or blind mortise and tenon

The socket or mortise is blind and, therefore, hidden from the outside, and is the usual form for cabinet-work (114:2).

115   Sawing in tenon (first cut)

116 Sawing in tenon (second cut)

117 Using bench-hook

Long and short shoulder mortise and tenon

Figure 114:11 shows the extra shoulder length required to fill the rebate formed to receive a panel which is beaded in from the back. The setting out of this type of tenon is described in *Door-work* (Chapter 31).

Moulded frame mortise and tenon

Here again the frame is rebated for a panel and the moulding must be cut and mitred on the face to receive the rail. If the moulded frame is grooved for the panel (114:12) and not rebated,

186

then either both sides of the groove must be cut away and mitred to receive the rail, or the back shoulder of the rail must be shortened to allow for the extra width of the back stile. The position of grooves, rebates and mouldings are marked during the critical setting out but must not be worked until after the mortises have been chopped out; the offset of the moulding on the face must, of course, be on the same level as the depth of the rebate. Tenon cheeks are sawn in as before or the marks will be lost, but the tenon shoulders are better left uncut until the moulding has been run.

Miscellaneous tenons

Figure 118:2 shows the single stub tenon for connecting drawer rails to carcase sides, but the length of the tenon can only be a bare $\frac{1}{2}$ in. (12·5 mm) in a $\frac{3}{4}$ in. (19 mm) carcase cheek and double tenons are better (118:3). For instance, two $\frac{5}{8}$ in. (16 mm) wide tenons spaced apart $\frac{3}{8}$ in. (9·5 mm) in a $2\frac{1}{4}$ in. (57 mm) wide rail offer nearly twice the gluing surface as compared with a single $1\frac{1}{4}$ in. (32 mm) wide tenon, moreover shrinkage is less. Figure 118:4 is a mitre shoulder tenon useful where a rail meets a leg or post on a curve which would result in a feather edge at the springing-line if the normal type of square shoulder were used (see also *Legs, underframings, stools with stands*, Chapter 30, page 288). The joint is first cut as an orthodox mortise and tenon joint, allowing about $\frac{1}{4}$ in. of shoulder below the tenon for the mitre cut, and the sloping shoulders are then set out and cut. A square shoulder terminating in a mitre cut can be used instead of the sloping shoulder, the only difference being in the appearance. The curve to the rail can be cut beforehand, but sufficiently full to allow final shaping to the exact curve after the rails have been fitted. Figure 118:5 is the tongued shoulder tenon useful where a heavy tenon is set back, leaving a wide shoulder; whilst 118:6 are twin tenons for heavy work which give a more secure fixing without taking out too much strength in a single wide mortise. Figure 118:7 shows pinning used for short uprights or divisions between drawer rails, and for partitions in large carcases; the tenons can be wedged as shown if necessary. In modern work pinning tenons are often dispensed with, and the upright is housed and screwed from above, but where the rail below has to take transmitted weight wedged pinning tenons are better. Figure 118:8 is a false tenon either slotted or mortised into wild grain which has little intrinsic strength; it is also useful in repair work where the original tenon has snapped off, and provided it is tightly fitted there is little difference in the ultimate strength. Figure 118:9 shows the carpenters' draw bore tenon sometimes used in reproduction oak-work. The joint is cut in the usual manner, the tenon withdrawn and a waste piece slipped into the mortise socket; the hole for the pin is then bored through, the waste piece withdrawn and the tenon pushed home. If the same bit is fed through the hole to prick a position-mark on the tenon, and the mark is then moved about $\frac{1}{16}$ in. (1·5 mm) up and in towards the shoulder (A), a hole bored through the tenon will be slightly offset and will pull the parts together when a tapered drive pin is driven through the joint. Draw boring can be used in corner bridles or open slot tenons, and is an excellent way of securing these joints. Figure 118:11 is the fox wedged tenon in which the wedges are placed in position as shown, and driven in as the rail enters. This joint is of academic rather than practical interest; for if the undercutting of the shoulders of the mortise socket is too great the joint will be slack, or if not enough, then the wedges will not fully enter the saw kerfs, and will prevent the tenon from fully entering. Figure 118:12 is the combined bridle and tenon which is useful for long tables with intermediate legs and continuous rails. The position of the joint can be reversed to show either the rail butting against the leg on either side, or passing over the leg in an unbroken line. Figure 118:10 shows double tenons used in wide rails or narrow carcase cheeks into legs or posts, and divided, as shown, to counteract the inevitable shrinkage of a single wide tenon. This type is no longer used to any great extent in modern furniture, in which a continuous tongue in a shallow groove is usually sufficient to hold the joint.

Loose tenons

Loose tenons for demountable structures which are not glued together are shown in 119:1. Figure 119:1 shows the *keyed* tenon in which a

119 Loose tenons

single thick tenon is taken through the post, slotted and then keyed together with a tapered wedge. The slot should pass a little way into the mortise (A) so that the wedge bears against the post. This type is used on stretcher rails in reproduction oak refectory-tables, collapsible forms, etc. Figure 119:2 is the tenon and bolt, with a stub tenon entering the post and secured with a headed bolt passing through from the outside and held with a square nut in a mortise cut to allow it to enter, but not to revolve. Another example of this technique but without tenons is the handrail bolt (119:3), used for jointing two pieces of timber in the same plane,

i.e. fireside kerbs, handrails, etc. A special double-threaded bolt is used with circular nuts (A) slotted to take a screwdriver-blade or stout punch. If only one bolt is used the ends should be prevented from swivelling round by short stub dowels, or more commonly with wire nails either side of the central bolt knocked in and pinched off leaving about $\frac{1}{8}$ in. (3 mm) protruding. The nuts are inserted in the mortises, the bolt fed through and the nuts tightened by tapping them round, after which the mortise holes are plugged. Examples of well-fitted mortises and tenons are illustrated in 120A and drawer dovetails in 120B.

120A Rebated frames showing alternative methods

Joints open   Joints closed

120B Drawer dovetail

Joint open

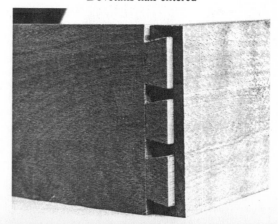

Dovetails half entered

18 Dowelled joints

Spiral, grooved, and fluted or faceted dowel-pegs offer greater holding power than the standard smooth birch dowel-rod, and dowelled constructions are now used extensively in lieu of mortises and tenons. Providing the dowels are a good fit and enter not less than $1\frac{1}{4}$ in. (32 mm) either side of the joint-line there is probably little difference in the ultimate strength. Figure 122:1 shows the standard birch dowel which should be saw-kerfed as shown to provide an escape route for trapped air and also for surplus glue; 122:2 shows the spiral grooved dowel and 122:3 the fluted dowel. Dowel-pegs can be chamfered or rounded with a dowel-rounder as in 122:4, and the seating countersunk at (B) to facilitate entry. A small gap should be left at (A,C) for trapped glue, and all dowels should be checked for diameter. If oversize they can be knocked through a dowel pop or plate (121) which can be purchased or simply made out of a piece of $\frac{1}{4}$ in. (6 mm) mild steel bar, accurately bored and countersunk on the underside. Some workers keep several dowel-bits in each size, for not only do the rods vary but also the critical diameter of the bits. Dowel-rod should be kept in a warm, dry place and bought well in advance of requirements.

Setting out, etc.

The usual diameter of dowels for normal work is $\frac{3}{8}$ in. (9·5 mm) with $\frac{1}{4}$ in. (6·0 mm) for thin stuff and $\frac{1}{2}$ in. (12·5 mm) or more for stout frameworks. At least two dowels should be used to prevent swivelling of the joint; but if a light rail can only accommodate one, then a panel-pin should be driven through the framework from the back either side of the joint-line to grip the dowel. Spacing must be accurately done with a minimum of $\frac{3}{16}$ in. (5 mm) wood substance left either side of the dowel socket, and $\frac{1}{4}$ in. (6 mm) between the bottom of the socket and the outer face, for subsequent shrinkage can shadow through if only a minimum of wood is left. Figure 112:5 shows the spacing for a normal rail $1\frac{7}{8}$ in. (47·5 mm) by $\frac{3}{4}$ in. (19 mm) finish, and

122:6 staggered dowels in larger sections. Actual setting out is simple if the two members can be cramped together in the vice (122:7), with a gauge-line run down the middle of the edge, working always from the face sides, and the positions squared across. Square sections may have to be marked out with a wooden template (122:8), or a dowel-jig of the Woden type (123); whilst an accurate hand-method is to lightly tap veneer pins truly vertical into the correct centres in one piece, nip off the pins leaving $\frac{1}{8}$ in. protruding, offer up the other piece in the correct position, and lightly tap the other end to register the imprint of the pin ends which can then be withdrawn and the sockets bored exactly on the pricked centres. Figure 124 shows the pins cut off ready for marking.

121 Dowel pop

Boring sockets

Any expedient should be adopted to ensure truly vertical boring of the sockets. If done by hand, using a Russell Jennings' pattern dowel-bit in a bit- or arm-brace, help should be enlisted in sighting for the upright. Drilling at an angle always presents problems, for the wings of the bit tend to follow the grain, and an expedient adopted in the writer's own workshops for precision compound angle drilling was to fix the work either horizontally or vertically, thread the spindle of a $\frac{1}{3}$ hp (0·25 kW) electric motor for a $\frac{1}{2}$ in. (12·5 mm) capacity Jacob's chuck (or use a drill-gun), mount the motor or gun on a baseboard running between wood guide rails securely fixed at the correct compound angle, and feed the motorised bit forward to the correct socket depth. Alternatively, the motor can be fixed and the work fed forwards. Methods such as this might appear to be unnecessarily complicated for

122 Dowelling practice

MARKING ——

123 Woden dowelling jig
By courtesy of Woden Tools Limited

a relatively simple operation, but with a dozen or more holes to drill much wasted time and labour can be avoided, and the motor with its threaded shaft is always a useful power source. A home-made horizontal dowel-boring machine is illustrated in 48. This included rise and fall and lateral sliding table, depth stop, etc. assembled by an engineer friend from a scrap-metal milling-machine bought from a local dealer's yard, and using the motor already described.

Assembling dowelled work

One side of the work should be dowelled, the pegs tapped fully home, surplus glue wiped off and the projection of each peg checked with its corresponding socket; it can then be dowelled

124 Setting out dowel positions

dowels in the final gluing up, for if tight dowels are used it may prove impossible to withdraw them without breaking the pegs, owing to the vacuum created in the socket. For assembly single-application glues (hide, Cascamite One Shot, etc. but not PVA emulsion-type glues) should be used and applied to the sockets only, for very liquid glues or separate hardeners applied to the pegs may swell the fibres and prevent entry. Sockets out of line or bored at an angle should be filled with glued pegs and rebored correctly, for any bending or crushing of the dowel-pegs will destroy much of the ultimate strength. Timbers which split easily may have to be nipped with a G-cramp across the thickness if the dowel is tight and the surplus glue cannot readily escape. Sash-cramps across the assembly may be necessary to pull the dowels up, but a good joint should not need them whilst the glue is setting, and this is one of the advantages of this method of assembly.

Applications

Typical applications are shown in 122 where two $\frac{3}{8}$ in. (9·5 mm) dowels are used to each joint instead of mortises and tenons in a simple framework (122:9); long and short shoulder joint (122:10); a stub tenon and dowels for a grooved frame (the position of grooves, rebates, mouldings, etc. must be marked out first but not worked until after the dowel sockets have been drilled) (122:11); a moulded and rebated frame (122:12).

into the other member without waiting for the glue to harden. If a trial assembly is made in the dry (unglued) state spare dowels should be sanded to a loose fit and replaced with tight

19 Dovetail joints

Dovetails

Rapid developments in woodworking-machine techniques have evolved distinctive jointing procedures which are often as good as, and in some instances superior to, the traditional hand-cut joints they have replaced. An outstanding exception, however, is the dovetail, for here the handmade joint still equals and in some respects surpasses the machine-made copy. Nevertheless, even the machine joint with all its compromises dictated by the simple mechanics of power-operated tools is still a very good joint indeed, with ample reserves of strength. In short, the dovetail, whether hand- or machine-cut, is still the best method of jointing two pieces of wood together in their width and at right angles to each other.

Before describing the actual dovetailing joints and their many variations it is necessary to define precisely the various terms used, for the nomenclature as between hand- and machine-work differs radically. Thus in handwork (125:1) where (A) is the drawer front and (B) the drawer side, (C) is the actual dovetail and (D) the pin; but in machine dovetails (125:2) the drawer front (A) becomes the female part and the drawer side (B) the male part, whilst 125:3D in the male part is the pin with its corresponding socket in the female part. Again, the angle or slope of the dovetail which constitutes its holding power against lateral strain is known as the 'rake', 'bevel' or 'pitch' in hand dovetails, and is measured in terms of proportionate rise, i.e. rise of 1 in 5, 1 in 6, 1 in 7, etc., whereas the slope of a machine-cut dovetail is usually standardised at 20°, and the term 'pitch' refers to the spacing of the pins, i.e. $\frac{1}{2}$ in. (12·5 mm), $\frac{3}{4}$ in (19 mm), 1 in. (25 mm), etc. measured from the centre of one pin to the centre of the next (125:3, 4). Other terms with different values are described under the appropriate headings, but the main structural difference between the two types is that hand dovetails can be spaced at random, whereas the spacing of machine dovetails is arbitrarily set by the machine, with the pins (male) and the sockets (female) equal in width, therefore any spacing out to fit a predetermined width of drawer side can only be done by varying the pitch.

Hand-cut dovetails

Three types are used, (a) through dovetails which show on both sides of a corner joint (126:1); (b) lapped dovetails which show on one face but are concealed on the other by a lap or lip (126:2); (c) secret dovetails in which the joint is entirely hidden (127:2). For an understanding of the principles involved—which are intrinsically the same for both hand and machine dovetails with only the procedure differing—it is necessary to describe the setting out and cutting of all three types in some detail.

125 Dovetails

HAND DOVETAILS

MACHINE DOVETAILS

Through dovetails

These show as end-grain wedge-shaped pins on one surface and square or oblong end-grain tails on the other (126:1). The true shape of both tail and pin resemble a dove's tail after which they are named, and in through dovetailing by hand it is usual to make the tails at their widest part about twice that of the pins, but for extra strong work they can be equal and are colloquially known as 'cistern dovetails'. There are, therefore, no hard and fast rules regarding their width, and as with all other types a compromise is usually effected between strength and appearance.

Setting out

The two sides to be joined need not be of equal thickness, but the thickness of each must be constant across the width and the long-grain edges must be parallel. It is advisable to shoot the ends truly square and to the overall length, as this facilitates the setting out which must be accurately done, but a fractional fullness in the length can be left for subsequent cleaning off. Assuming that the ends have been shot square and to the true length then either a sharp marking-gauge or a cutting-gauge is set to the exact thickness of one piece (126:1A) and gauged all round the end of the other piece (B); the thickness of (B) is then similarly gauged round (A). The spacing of the separate dovetails must now be determined, and whilst an experienced worker might trust his eye alone the beginner should adopt the following procedure. Determine first the width of the end-grain pins (B) and assuming that each pin is to be approximately $\frac{1}{2}$ in. (12·5 mm) in width gauge a $\frac{1}{4}$ in. (6 mm) from each parallel edge of 126:6A to accommodate half a pin, and divide the space between into as many divisions as there will be whole pins. If these are, say, four then five divisions are required, and 5 in. (127 mm) (or any number of inches (millimetres) easily divisible by five) is measured off on the rule and measured obliquely across the board as shown; the divisions can then be drawn in to give the exact centre of four equally spaced pins.

Dovetail rakes or bevels

The actual rake of the dovetail must now be decided. For carcase-work where strength is necessary and appearance of little consequence the slope can correspond to a slope of 1 in 5 or 1 in 6; whilst for show-work, drawer sides, etc., 1 in 7, and for very fine decorative dovetailing 1 in 8, can be used, always bearing in mind that the rake must not be too coarse, i.e. much below 1 in 5, or the short grain will be too weak, whilst too fine a pin, i.e. over 1 in 8, will have no real holding power. To set out these rakes it is only necessary to square a line across the bench-top and measure off the distances as in 126:3, setting an adjustable bevel to the rake or making up a simple wooden template (126:7). With proficiency neither bevel nor template will be required, and the eye alone will soon grow accustomed to the required slopes.

Cutting the dovetails

In practice it hardly matters whether the actual pins or the tails are treated first (although in some instances, tall carcase sides and in secret dovetails the pins must be worked first and the tails from them), but as a rule the tail side is set out and the pin side from it. After marking out the tail side in pencil (126:6, 7) the pin sockets or cores are sawn in with the fine dovetail saw, with the tail piece upended in the vice and tilted over to bring the markings vertical (128). This sawing in should be on the pencil-line, square across the edge and down to the gauge-lines, but the pin sockets should not be chopped out at this stage, which is the mistake beginners often make, for the actual pins must be marked out before any chopping away can be done. The pin piece (B) is then upended in the vice (126:10), and the tail piece packed up and placed on it truly square with the edges flush (the drawing shows the positioning for a lap dovetail in which the tail piece is set back for the lap). The point of the saw is then drawn through the cuts, transferring them to the end grain of the pin piece, and once this is done then the pin sockets on the tail piece can be chopped out, working from either side in a series of bevel cuts (126:11), so that the waste is fully supported with the last cuts vertical and exactly on the gauge-line; the end shoulders can then be sawn in with the fine dovetail-saw. Sawing in of the pins in the pin piece can now be done, again upending in the vice and sawing-in as

THROUGH

LAP

1 : 8

1 : 6

1 : 5

BEVEL

126:8 but down to the gauge-line on either side for through dovetails, with a centre cut in each tail socket to clear the waste. It is a useful precaution to mark this waste '0' as in 126:9, and the sawing must always be on the waste side and alongside, but never on the gauge-marks or the pins will be too small. Alternatively, instead of sawing out small wedged-shaped pieces alongside the pins as for lap dovetails (126:8), the pins are sawn in and the waste partially sawn away with a scroll-saw. It hardly matters which, but here again a fast worker will not bother to set up another tool.

Chopping out of the sockets will be done as for the tail piece, and it is customary to incline the vertical cuts through the thickness fractionally inwards towards the centre so that the bed of the socket is undercut, but the cuts must not go over the gauge-lines on the faces. When all the cutting has been finished the dovetails can be tried together, but they should never be knocked fully home until they are glued up, for it is axiomatic that a good dovetail only fits once. Application of through dovetails is in box sides, etc. and in all right-angled framings where it does not matter if the joint shows.

Lapped dovetails

This is the usual type for drawer sides (126:4), carcase-work (126:5), etc. where one face must not show the joint and the dovetails are set back by a small lap or lip. Setting out and working is the same as for through dovetails, but the full thickness of the tail side must be gauged on the inner face of the pin side only, the width of the lap or set-back determined—$\frac{3}{16}$ in. (5 mm) in a $\frac{3}{4}$ in. 19 mm) thickness is usual but not arbitrary— the gauge reset and the lap gauged in from the inner face of the pin side and all round the tail piece. Figure 126:4 shows a typical setting out for a drawer side with two widely spaced whole pins sufficient for an average drawer up to say 6 in. (152 mm) deep, and three pins for larger drawers; whilst 126:5 shows coarser carcase dovetails connecting, for example, a carcase top to a cheek. Small dovetails are provided at front and back to prevent any twisting of the cheek edges, but the main dovetails can be widely spaced with the tails about two and a half times the width of the pins as a fair average. Sawing in the tail

sockets on the pin piece can be done as in 126:8, whilst most of the waste can be cleared with the saw or bored out as in 126:12; the remainder is then chopped out as shown, again bevelling inwards as in the inset. In all setting out so far described for both through and lap dovetails no allowance has been made in lengths and widths for cleaning off, and this must be at the discretion of the worker. If the jointing is good only a thin shaving will be required to flush the surfaces and provide a smoothly running drawer, but if the worker is uncertain and wishes to make allowances then he must set his gauge-marks in accordingly. As with all woodworking activities the only true guide is positive experience, often bitter but nevertheless inevitable. On no account should dovetails be 'bishoped', i.e. hit with a hammer to spread the fibres and tighten up a slack fit. If there are gaps between the tails and pins—and it can happen to anyone—then it is perfectly legitimate to drive in small glued wedges of matching end grain which, if neatly done, will be invisible. Very tall carcase sides which carry the pins cannot be upended in the vice for marking, therefore the pins must be worked first and the tails marked from them with a scriber or knife point, as with secret lap and secret mitre dovetails.

Secret (double lap) dovetails

These are used where open dovetails would be unsightly, but as one lap must show end grain the jointing method could be entirely hidden with secret mitre dovetails which are, not much more trouble to cut. The double lap dovetail does, however, have certain applications, and 127:1 shows two forms, (B) side lap and (C) top lap, according to the use. In working the joint the projecting lap piece is rebated out (A) to the depth of the secret lap (the laps are usually made square in section). The pin piece is then set out and cut in the normal manner, and the tail piece set out from the pin piece as in secret mitre dovetailing (127:3), using an awl point as shown. A variation of this joint is shown in 127:4 where the carcase top is correspondingly thicker by the amount of lap, and rebated and moulded as shown to give the appearance of equal framing edges on top and side with a recessed moulding over.

127 Dovetailing details (2)

DOUBLE LAP

A
B
C

SECRET MITRE

D
E
F
X

4

5

6

7

8

X   X

Secret mitre dovetails

These are reserved for high-class work in flush carcases, boxes, plinths, etc. where strength is essential and appearance of paramount importance. They are most useful joints and still used extensively by handworkers, but they must be accurately done or the joint will show as a gapped mitre.

The first requirement is that both top and side should be exactly equal in thickness or they will not mitre correctly. A gauge is set to this thickness and marked on the inside (2D), the mitre-lines are then cut in with a knife. The width of the lap should then be fixed, the gauge set accordingly and marked in from both inside faces. Where the downward projection of this gauge-line (x) coincides with the accurately cut mitre-line will lie the depth of the rebate, which must be formed in both pieces before the dovetails can be set out. In all cases the pins must be marked and cut first, and as the adjustable bevel or dovetail template cannot be used over the projecting lap a small card template should be cut at the correct bevel to lie in the rebate. Each half pin must be set in with a square cut shoulder to allow the end mitres, and at this stage these mitre cuts can be sawn in on the waste side of the line for final adjustment later. The tails are then marked with an awl (127:3) and the marks squared across the

rebate. In sawing both pins and tails, which must be cut diagonally, it hardly matters if the saw kerf nicks the projecting lap so long as it is kept well clear of the outside edge, for the final mitreing of the laps will clean out the nicks. When all the chopping out has been done the long side mitres are first roughly chiselled away and finally cleaned up with a finely set shoulder-plane. If necessary a piece of wood placed at a true angle of 45° can be G-cramped to the outer face to act as guide and bed for the plane, with a little wax rubbed over the mitre of the bed piece to prevent the plane-iron digging in. When the mitres are true throughout their length the end mitres should be pared down until they fit. A variation of this joint is shown in F where the small end pin at either side helps to prevent the end mitres opening. Plenty of long cramps and stout bearers should be available when gluing up long lengths of dovetailing in case either of the pieces have bowed slightly in the width, but no amount of cramping will close a gapped mitre which has been incorrectly cut, or whose hidden dovetails do not seat properly. This joint should, therefore, not be attempted in long lengths before experience has been gained.

Decorative through dovetails

These are used for show-work where the dovetails provide their own decorative element. In essence they are common through dovetails (127:6), with very wide tails and smaller pins introduced into the tails to hold the centres. They must be accurately set out and very neatly cut or the decorative element will be lost. Marking on the face side must be lightly done, and deepened only where the sockets occur (127:7), whilst after the tails have been marked on the pin piece the sockets (x, x8) are chopped down from the inside to the middle gauge-line. The pin piece is then turned over and the smaller sockets chopped out from the face, with waste pieces inserted in x, x to support the cuts.

Dovetails need not necessarily follow the traditional pattern and the writer has used other forms, of which 127:5 is an example. The dovetail is cut and trimmed and marked round for the socket in the end grain. Holding power is as good if not better than the usual form of dovetail, providing the width of the tail is not too great.

128 Cutting dovetails in drawer-work

Rebated or mitre box corner dovetail joints

Small boxes, trays, etc. are often rebated for a lid (129:1A) and if through dovetailed in the normal way may show a small gap on one piece at the end of the rebate; the half pin is, therefore, set out below the rebate, and the shoulder of the pin piece brought forward to close the gap. Figure 129:2 is an alternative form where the gap is sealed by the tail piece. If the top of the box or frame shows a mitred edge (129:3) the top pin is not cut through at x, and if the sides are rebated then the depth of the mitre should equal that of the rebate.

Canted dovetails (bevelled work)

If one piece is canted as in a drawer front (250:6) the dovetails must not be set out at right angles to the cant (250:8) but equal either side of a line drawn parallel to the long edge (250:7) or there will be weak grain at 250:8 xx. If the front is upright and the side canted then the tails are set out in the usual way, but the shoulders are sawn parallel to the bevel of the long side edge and not at right angles. Whichever piece is canted must be cut full to allow for the bevelling, and the bevel clearly marked or part of the half pin may be lost if the allowance is insufficient. (See also *Double bevel dovetail joints*, and also *Canted fronts*, page 326.)

Double bevel dovetail joints

These joints are sometimes used for bevel-sided hoppers, knife-boxes, etc., and although rarely used are worth describing for the sake of the principles involved in setting out bevelled work. Reference should be made to the bevel joints in 111:4 which illustrate the procedure. A full-size drawing is necessary from which the true length (A) and the true width (B) can be obtained, also the edge bevel in the thickness of each piece shown by the arrowed line (C). All the bevels are marked and worked holding the bevel at right angles to the edges of the sloping ends and not parallel with the sides. A marking-gauge cannot be used for setting out the dovetails and depths, etc. must be marked with pencil and adjustable bevel, whilst the dovetails are cut to slope equally either side of lines drawn parallel with the sides (see *Canted dovetails* above), but the pins are, of course, parallel. In cutting the dovetails above the piece should be canted to bring the cuts vertical as in 111:5 but marking the pins by drawing the saw point through the tail kerfs is difficult owing to the slope, therefore it is better to chop out the dovetails and mark round them on the pin piece with an awl.

Carcase dovetails

Where a side rail is grooved or tenoned into a leg or post as in a framed-up carcase the shoulders

129   Box dovetails

of the two dovetails must be offset, moreover in tenoned work the tenon and haunches must be set down by an amount at least equal to the depth of the larger dovetail. Figure 130:1 shows a typical assembly with front rail dovetailed into post and side rail. The side rail and post are assembled first and flushed off, the thickness of the front rail gauged in the post and pencilled in on the side rail if the gauge cannot reach, the larger dovetail set out, using the same gauging for the smaller dovetail if the shoulders line through, or resetting it if it projects (130:2). Subsequent marking is as for other forms of lap dovetail. Where the carcase cheek is either solid timber or plywood, etc. a front rail (130:3B) and intermediate rails (A) are lap dovetailed in, and the latter either dovetailed as (B) or with a single large tail (A) which can be prevented from lifting by a countersunk screw. Continuous tops should be as 126:5 with a small dovetail at front and back to prevent the cheeks from curling. A suitable rake for carcase dovetails is about 1 in 5, and the spacing can be fairly coarse with the width of the tails about two and a half times that

of the pins (2·5 : 1), but there are no fixed rules, although the narrower the tails the greater the holding power.

Slot (slip) dovetails

These are cut in the width rather than the thickness and are used in stretcher frames, plinths, cornices, etc.; they can be either bare face, i.e. tapered on one side only (130:4A), double tapered (130:4B) or stopped (130:5), with the last more laborious as they cannot be sawn through but must be chopped out, therefore they are only used where the actual joints must be hidden on one face. In practice, bareface dovetails are sufficient for normal work, and they can be further strengthened with a glue block in the bareface corner.

Corner lock joint

Also known as *box lock* or *finger* joint it has considerable decorative possibilities if cleanly cut in good timber (131:1). It is usually regarded

130 Carcase dovetails

as a machine joint but can be cut easily but somewhat laboriously by hand, for the pins must be fine (about $\frac{3}{16}$ in. (5 mm) or $\frac{1}{4}$ in. (6 mm) wide) as there are no bevelled shoulders to hold the joint, which relies entirely on the glue to hold it. Setting out and cutting is the same as for dovetails, but the timber width must be equally divided and very accurately set out. Cutting can be simplified by placing the two ends together in the vice (131:2), and offsetting one by the thickness of the saw-blade, cutting one side of each pin into the waste (w), and then reversing the offset as shown by the arrows. The pins which remain after the sockets have been chopped are shaded in the drawing.

Machine dovetails

Machine dovetails are easily recognisable in finished work, for both pins and sockets are equal in width and the rake is fairly coarse (20 per cent). As already mentioned the hand-cut terms are transposed, and the tail (drawer side) becomes the pin or male piece entering a socket in the female piece (drawer front). In machining lap dovetails both pieces are cut together, the male vertically and the lapped female horizontally, therefore the movement of the finger plates and the rotation of the cutters, one for each pin and corresponding socket, gives a rounded base to both pin and socket. In theory this could detract from the strength of the dovetails, but with a machine of the Brookman type (133), the cutting is so exact that in all probability the total strength is as good as, and in many cases greater than, in the average hand-cut dovetails which often only touch where they show; moreover, it can be argued that equal spacing of the pins equalises the shrinkage across the width. Disadvantages are coarseness of appearance in show dovetails, and the difficulty of fitting an arbitrary grouping of whole pins into an odd width. In handwork and with, for example, a drawer side $4\frac{3}{8}$ in. (111 mm) wide the dovetails would be spaced accordingly, but in machine-work a pitch must be chosen which will best fit without sacrificing part of the shoulder adjoining a pin, a fault often seen in cheap mass-production work. The normal practice is to use 1 in. (25 mm) pitch furniture-style pins, and to limit the drawer width accordingly, with other pitches for special work or where it is necessary to reduce the width and therefore the spacing of the individual pins. The actual length of the pin can be varied plus or minus 25 per cent over the normal, thus the thickness of the female piece (drawer front) and the width of the lap is immaterial.

Figure 132 shows the various types of dovetail possible with the Brookman dovetailing machines (133 and 134), with the 25 spindle automatic version with pneumatic cramps capable of cutting two drawer sides and two fronts simultaneously. These machines can also be used for dovetailing curved drawer fronts, thus their versatility is very great.

131 Corner lock joint

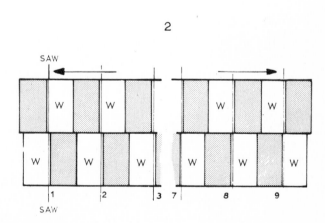

Dovetailing accessories

Where short runs do not warrant the use of a dovetailing machine, accessories can be obtained for most types of spindle moulding machine and router (including portable routers), incorporating suitable jigs or finger plates into which the single cutter is fed. Particulars of these can be obtained from the manufacturers concerned. For the handworker not completely wedded to hand dovetailing, and lacking sufficient practice to cut dovetails as speedily as the hardened professional, a worthwhile accessory is the Arcoy dovetailing unit for use with the standard drill-gun (135). This gives good machine-type dovetails, but as the male pin is square and the socket slightly rounded on the base, slight gaps are visible in through dovetails, and its use is, therefore, confined to lap dovetails for drawer sides, etc. and dovetail housings.

By courtesy of R. S. Brookman Limited

132 Machine dovetails

FURNITURE LAP   SECRET LAP   SECRET MITRE

FURNITURE BOX   BOX TAPER   CORNER LOCK

134 The Brookman 35 spindle automatic dove-tailer with pneumatic cramps
By courtesy of R. S. Brookman Limited

135 Arcoy dovetailing accessory
By courtesy of Arcoy Products Limited

136 Cutting dovetails with Arcoy dovetailing accessory *By courtesy of Arcoy Products Limited*

20 Mitre and scribed joints

If two pieces of wood of equal section are to be joined together without the end grain showing then the mitre cut between them must halve the overall angle. Thus if they meet at 90° then the mitre cut is 45° (137:1); if 120° then 60°, etc. (137:2). If, however, the meeting pieces are of unequal section then a true mitre of 45° will result in a longer cut in the larger section, with the result as shown by the dotted line (137:3), therefore the mitre must be 'faked', i.e. the angle pitched so that the meeting cuts are equal in each piece.

Curved mitres

Halving the angle also applies where a curved moulding meets a straight moulding of equal section, but in order to agree either the profile of one must be altered to coincide or the mitre-line must be curved (137:4). Mouldings of the same curvature but curving the opposite way, or those in which one curvature is quicker than the other, must also have curved mitres, and the only exception is two mouldings of the same curvature and with the same direction which require a straight cut (137:4B). Methods of determining the curve are described under *Workshop geometry and drawing*, Chapter 6, page 87.

Mitre joints

Undoubtedly the strongest mitre joint is the secret mitre dovetail (*see Dovetail joints*, Chapter 19, page 198) but these are not suitable for small sections or flat frames. Various other mitre joints are shown in 137: the tongued mitre (137:5), (the tongue can be either loose or worked in the solid); the tenon and mitre (137:6); the dovetail and mitre (137:7); the keyed mitre (137:8); the dovetail keyed mitre (137:9), with the direction of entry indicated by the arrow; and the through dovetail and mitre (137:10) often used in cheval mirror-frames, etc.

Applications of mitre joints are shown in the mitre and lap (137:11), suitable for plinths, cornices or where the joint can be further strengthened by an inner glued block; and 137:12 which is a tongued version which should not require a block. A method often adopted for small boxes and frameworks, and in fact all light mitre junctions, is the veneer keyed mitre (137:13), in which the sections are butt mitred, glued and assembled, and diagonal saw cuts run through the corners in which pieces of stout veneer matched to the saw kerf for thickness are glued and inserted, and cleaned off flush when dry. If well done, accurately spaced and with a carefully chosen veneer it can be almost invisible. Figure 137:14 is the plain butt mitre with a strengthening glue block which is rubbed in position with either hide or resin glues. The joint is strong enough for most practical purposes. In all butted mitres, and particularly in 137:11, 13 and 14, the end grain should be repeatedly sized with weak glue until the pores are filled, enabling the joint to hold together whilst it is being further strengthened. Tongued, keyed and through mitred edges in which part of the joint is visible should not be veneered over, for the joint will inevitably shadow through the veneer in time. The only exception is the veneer keyed mitre (137:13), which will give no trouble if the slips are fairly thin.

Cutting mitres

The mitre-square or fixed mitre is used for marking true mitres (45°); the adjustable bevel for all other angles. Some jig or guide is necessary for sawing, and the simplest form is the wooden mitre box easily made up either as a permanent tool or as and when required. A precision mitre-saw with hacksaw-type blade adjustable to any angle and extensively used by picture-framers is shown in 138, also the mitre-trimmer (139) which is also adjustable. Both these tools are virtually indispensable where there is much mitring to be done. For occasional use the beechwood mitre shooting-block (137:15) enables mitres in the width to be accurately planed up, with the donkey's ear shooting-board (137:16) for mitres in the thickness. In cutting mitres by hand a fine

139   Hand mitre-trimmer set to trim true mitre

saw should be used, with the cut into the mould-ing wherever possible, and not out of it, so that the rag of the saw is at the back or bed of the

moulding and not in the face. If the tip of the moulding tends to splinter away whilst the mitre is being shot, a packing piece should be inserted at the back to support the fibres, with the plane or trimmer cuts as fine as possible. Very large mouldings may have to be trimmed freehand, upending the timber in the vice and planing off with a smoothing-plane or block-plane, working diagonally and constantly check-ing with the mitre-square. When mitring round a carcase with front and side mouldings, complete the front moulding first and then the two sides, or two mitres will have to be fitted simultane-ously if the front is left to last. If all four corners have to be mitred as with the lippings of a panel or top, simultaneous fitting cannot be avoided, and a waste piece is mitre cut and used as a checking piece at each corner. Two opposite sides are then mitred and sash-cramped in posi-tion, checking for correct length with the waste piece; the contiguous mitres are then fitted. The same procedure can be adopted in gluing up. A simply made mitre-marking tool for sections moulded in the thickness which are difficult to mark with fixed mitre or adjustable bevel is shown in 140. The suggested dimensions can be varied as necessary.

Gluing and cramping mitred work

It is a sad truth that mitres never seem to fit so accurately after they have been glued. In theory they should meet exactly, but in most cases positive pressure has to be applied. In applying mitred lippings or mouldings to a panel the two ends can be temporarily dry cramped in position, the sides glued and sash-cramped across from underneath, the ends then withdrawn, glued and replaced. Where, however, there is no supporting panel as in a mirror-frame, etc., other means must be adopted, for any attempt to sash cramp all four sections together usually ends in frustration, for the glue acts as a lubricant and the mitres slide. Picture-framers' corner cramps are hardly suitable as they are only intended to hold the corners whilst they are being nailed, and there is no positive pressure to the mitres. Flexible band-cramps are suitable and exert considerable pressure, but they are somewhat expensive and an excellent substitute is the old corner cramping device of four shaped wood blocks with a straining wire or cord (see page

45). This can be simply made as needed and will pull the stoutest frame together provided the cord is strong enough. The wood corner blocks should be waxed or otherwise protected from the glue, and the completed frame laid out on a level base and weighted down at the corners to prevent twist, checking the diagonals of the frame for squareness. It is advisable to size the end grain of the mitres before the final assembly.

Mitre cuts for small breaks

Where the moulding to be mitred is wider than the actual break (141:1) then the points of intersection of the true mitres which halve the overall angle will lie inside the width of the moulding, and small wedge-shaped pieces must be inserted. These in turn will create new overall angles which again must be halved as shown at 141:1A.

Masons' mitres

These are a legacy from the stonemason's craft in which simple mouldings or chamfers were worked in the solid, and the mitre return carved as shown in 141:5. A more elaborate form was known as a 'bishop's mitre' (141:6), and both are now only used in reproduction oak-work.

140 Mitre-marker

9" 228 mm

9"

1½" 38 mm

Scribed work

Scribing or shaping one piece to fit over another, as in a moulded and rebated framework (137:17), is an alternative to mitring and gives the same overall appearance; whilst any shrinkage is disguised and will not show as an open gap (x) visible in mitred work. Scribes are, however, more difficult to cut and their application more limited, for external angles (141:2) cannot be scribed, nor can undercut mouldings (141:4). The inner angle (141:2) and the moulding (141:3) can be scribed.

Cutting scribes

The mortised piece is rebated, moulded and cut back in the normal manner (137:17B), but the moulding is not mitre cut. The tenoned piece (137:17A) is also moulded and rebated and the moulding mitred; it is then pared away exactly on the mitre-line with a suitable scribing (incannelled) gouge so that it fits exactly over the other. When assembled the general appearance will be that of an accurately fitted mitre, except for the small offset at the base of the moulding where the cut will be square.

The general term 'Scribe' also means to mark or score in order to indicate the exact outline which must be followed when fitting to an uneven surface or another irregular outline. Methods of scribing are described in *Workshop organisation* Chapter 5, page 68.

21 Miscellaneous joints

Three-way joints

Methods of forming three-way joints are illustrated in 142 which shows the constructions.

142 Three-way joints

4 ONE THIRD LAP JOINT

Scarf joints

Alternatively known as *splicing* these joints are used to extend the length of timbers and are more applicable to carpentry although they have applications in furniture repair-work. Figure 143:1 shows the simple half lap splice, 143:2 the bevel halving splice, 143:3 the tabled joint, and 143:4 the hooked splice. Figure 143:2 and 3 will resist end pull and to some extent a side swivel, whilst in 143:4 less timber is taken away at the root (x) and the joint is correspondingly stronger. Simple scarfing or splicing (143:5) relies on the glue only and provided the joint is long enough, with from 8 to 10 times the thickness in thin plywoods, the union can be as strong as a single length. Solid timbers are usually scarfed at 9 times the thickness, but some timbers will hold at lesser rakes.

Showcase joints

Figure 144:1 shows the simplest form of three-way joint for glass showcase framing, in which the horizontal frame is mitre jointed together and cut away at (x) to receive the mitred vertical member (A); the joint is then strengthened with strips of fine linen canvas (B) glued into the rebates. Constructional details of a combined dovetail and tenon joint are also given. Figures 144:2 and 3 are dovetailed together and 144:5 shows the first setting out. These two members are glued together (144:6) and then mortised for the tenoned member (144:4). Both the development of light metal sections and special cements for gluing glass panels at right angles to each other have largely done away with the necessity for these wood joints, which are now of academic interest only.

Mechanical joints

Finger joint and knuckle joint

Swing legs for card and occasional tables, etc. were hinged to the underframing by either the finger or knuckle joint (see also *Tables*, Chapter 36), and whilst they have been largely superceded by metal fittings there is no doubt that a pivoted wood joint correctly made will give good, if not better, service over a period of years.

Figure 145:1, 2 shows the finger joint which is simpler to cut as all the work can be done with saw and chisel, with (A) as the fixed part screwed to the table framing and (B) the moving part or wing. The notches are cut at an angle of 45°, both parts secured with a central metal pin, the moving part (B) opened out in stages, and the rounding gradually chiselled away. Figure 145:3, 4 is the knuckle joint of more refined appearance, and here again (A) is fixed and (B) free to move through 180° if necessary. The circles and diagonals are set out as in 145:4, saw cuts run in at the necks (x), the shapes worked and the shoulders cut. The knuckles are then set out, usually five or more in number and allowing three projecting knuckles in the fixed piece (A) and two in (B). Sawing-in must be done on the waste side shown unshaded in the inset drawing (145:3), the unwanted knuckles sawn out, and the interiors hollowed with a scribing-gouge to take the swing of the opposing protruding knuckle. When the two parts can be fitted, waste pieces are cramped either side to keep them together and a sash-cramp across the length to pull them tight, after which they can be bored through either end in the exact centre for a suitable metal pin, which can be $\frac{3}{16}$ in. (4·5 mm) steel rod or a large french nail. The joint can be lubricated with candle grease and should be reasonably tight but smooth in action. The stopping angle of the wing can be adjusted by altering the angle of the diagonal shoulders, and a good medium hardwood should be used, preferably not beech which is very prone to worm; with $\frac{7}{8}$ in. (22 mm) finished thickness for light brackets in Pembroke-type tables, etc., and $1\frac{1}{8}$ in. (28·5 mm) for heavier swing legs.

Sculptured joints

The term *sculptured* is applied to jointed parts fitted together and shaped to a continuous curve unbroken at the line of the joint as if the whole structure were carved out of a solid piece (although that is not the object of the technique, for the change in grain direction will always show, and the chief considerations are, or should be, flowing structural lines and smooth, unbroken surfaces with no sharp angles). This type of joint is usually confined to chair-work, although it has applications in table framing, and the final

143 Scarf (spliced) joints

1   HALF LAP SPLICE

2   BEVEL HALVING SPLICE

3   TABLE) JOINT

4   HOOKED SPLICE

5   76mm 3″   9·5mm   3/8″   1 IN 8   LONG SPLICE (PLY ETC)

144 Showcase joints

shaping must be done after the joints have been assembled. Preliminary drawings are necessary setting out full-size plans, elevations and cross-sections, with the latter in great detail if the work is to be executed by a third person. The timber must be thick enough to take the shaping with plenty to spare, and in order to facilitate the final shaping some of the first rough cutting can be done before assembly, but wherever possible square faces should be left for setting out the joints and final cramping up. Figure 146 illustrates the technique, and the drawings 146:1 show a turned taper leg with a square block left for the jointing which is cut away on the dotted lines to give the dowel seating, and also a square face (146:3A) for a direct pull for the cramps. The completed joint is shown in 146:2, whilst 146:4 is a simply made rasp for final finishing

145 Finger and knuckle joints

made out of a two-pronged stick over which abrasive paper of the appropriate grade is wrapped. It should be remembered that the sweetness of the final curves is largely in the hands of the executant no matter how detailed the drawings may be, therefore for very exact work a full-size model in clay or softwood may be necessary.

146 Sculptured joint details

22 Veneering, marquetry and inlay

The art of veneering—and there is or should be considerable art in the selection and matching of veneers—is over 4000 years old; it is not in any sense a method of covering up shoddy workmanship or materials as the strict dictionary definition would imply (to veneer: to gloss over, to cover up). Many rare and costly timbers with wild, distorted or intrinsically weak grain cannot be used in solid form but only in thin sheets mounted on stable backgrounds; moreover, the ever-increasing demand for carcase furniture would very soon deplete if not totally exhaust even the most common decorative hardwoods if they were consistently used in any thickness. Thus the practice of veneering fulfils several very important functions: (a) more balanced methods of construction are possible; (b) the use of available timbers is vastly extended; (c) rare hardwoods often of small dimension can be built up to yield large unbroken surfaces, or matched and jointed to achieve rich repeat patterns and decorative effects. Undoubtedly, veneered surfaces are more delicate than timber in solid form, but the inherent weaknesses associated with traditional methods of veneering, viz. lifting, splitting, blistering, buckling under applied heat or moisture and lack of sparkle due to the choking of the surface pores with glue have been overcome by the use of synthetic resin adhesives which form permanent bonds but do not penetrate to the surface of the veneers and, therefore, do not cloud their beauty. Moreover, such resin-bonded surfaces are tough, heat and water resistant and if carefully laid indistinguishable from solid timber.

Preparation of groundworks, etc.

Either solid or prefabricated timber (plywoods, chipboard, etc.) can be used for veneering provided they are stable, mild mannered, not too coarse in the grain and free from defects, although heated animal glues (hide glues) should not be used for chipboards as they tend to swell up the surface chips. Very absorbent timbers should be sized before laying, defects cut out and filled with plugs cut to follow the grain (147:1); holes and depressions filled with plastic wood, wood-dust and glue, or plaster of Paris and glue (not wax-based stoppers or putty). The usual advice given that the groundwork should be well scoured with a toothing-plane to roughen up the surface as a key for the glue is not strictly accurate. The old toothing-plane is undoubtedly an excellent tool for the general hand-levelling of bumpy surfaces, but glue sticks by molecular attraction, although some degree of mechanical attachment is usually present, therefore keyed surfaces are not really necessary (and might even interfere with the bond). Provided the surface is reasonably absorbent and not glazed with age or dirt, or with a very hard burnished grain, a light scouring with abrasive paper followed up with a thorough dusting is all that is necessary, and this applies to veneers also. These should be laid 'with the grain' on groundworks of solid timber which are liable to shrink across the width, but 'across the grain' of prefabricated timbers if these are already faced with knife-cut veneers, as the innumerable stress cracks caused in the cutting will only augment those in the facing veneers if they are both laid together with grains parallel (see *Veneers*, Chapter 11). End grain should be repeatedly sized with weak glue to lessen the absorption, but even this is a risky procedure and end-grain veneering should be avoided wherever possible. Veneering over surface joints, lap dovetails, tenon shoulders, etc. should also be avoided, for they will eventually show through as definite sinkages or stress-marks in the face veneers (153:1, 2).

Hand-veneering with hide glues

Almost without exception all veneering of new work is now done with modern synthetic resin or casein glues—the latter may be considered a natural plastic—using cramping pressure. However, the traditional hand method of employing hot hide (Scotch) glue and a heated household iron is still extremely useful in the repair of valuable antique furniture and in situations where no

BEARERS   SOFTENING   CAUL

VENEER   GROUND

cramping facilities are available, therefore the process is described in some detail, for in capable hands it can be done quickly and cheaply and its permanence is beyond question. Basic requirements for hand-laying are: freshly made glue, thin and as hot as possible (animal glues must never be boiled), plenty of clean hot water (not taken from the iron glue-pot), clean rag, thin absorbent paper for taping, veneer pins, a fairly stout Warrington pattern hammer, household iron and heating stove, or heavy-weight electric iron, and veneering-hammer. A heated room or workshop is necessary, and in the old workshops veneering by hand methods was never attempted in cold or humid weather or until the workshop had been warmed up after the day's start.

Hand laying veneers

The veneers must be laid one sheet at a time, for built-up patterns taped together cannot be laid by this process as will become evident. A fast worker could no doubt lay a sideboard top without using the heated iron, but the veneer sheet would have to be very amenable, and it is wise not to attempt large areas without the iron until proficiency is achieved. The usual practice is to evenly coat the groundwork with thin glue, swab the outer surface of the veneer sheet with hot water to prevent it curling up once it touches the glue, add a few dabs from the glue-brush to lubricate the heated iron, lay the veneer on the glued surface, smoothing it out from the centre to exclude the air, and heat a section with the iron, lightly swabbing the veneer to prevent the iron sticking. As the glue starts to flow with the heat from the iron the surplus must be squeezed out towards the edges with the veneering-hammer, but the iron must not be too hot or steam will be generated and the veneer will stretch. A good test is to hold the iron an inch or so away from the cheek when it should feel hot but not uncomfortably so. The method of handling the veneering-hammer is not arbitrary, it can be held in one hand or two, pushed or pulled, but the movement should be zigzag (147:3) and wherever possible away from the centre. The amount of pressure applied will, of course, depend on the type of veneer, for thick spiteful veneers may require two-handed pressure and

148A Holding the veneer-hammer with one hand

148B Holding the veneer-hammer with both hands

mild veneers only light pressure with one hand, but the strokes of the hammer must always overlap and must be repeated until each patch or section has chilled off and stuck before moving on to heat and press the next section. It is a good plan to lay a sheet of spent abrasive paper on the bench near by, for the iron will rapidly blacken with burnt glue and should be cleaned on the sheet from time to time. Figures 148A, B show methods of holding the veneering-hammer, and a commonly adopted procedure of laying is depicted in 147:2, starting at A and following in the order shown, 1, 2, 3, 4, etc., working with the grain as much as possible, for hammering across the grain will stretch the wet veneer and subsequent shrinkage across the width will be considerable. Figure 147:3 shows another method favoured by some workers, working from the centre outwards, but here again there are no arbitrary rules and much depends on the nature of the veneer and the speed of the worker. Excessive use of water should be avoided, with sufficient only to keep the veneer supple and the iron from sticking. Small local patches or blisters which refuse to stick can often be persuaded with a weight applied, covering the blister with a scrap of paper to prevent the weight sticking. Persistent blisters can be detected by tapping with the finger-nail; and if the glue has set the blister should be slit with a sharp knife along the grain, fresh glue inserted, covered with a scrap of paper and weighted down. If veneering is done without the aid of a heated iron the groundwork should be warmed, the veneer swabbed with hot water, the groundwork quickly spread with thin glue, the veneer applied and smoothed over with the palms to exude the air, and hammered down as already described. When the panel is dry, and 24 hours should be allowed for this, it should be closely examined for blisters, either tapping with the finger-nail or sweeping the finger-tips over the surface, when the presence of blisters will be indicated by a slight whisper. The pein of a Warrington pattern hammer can be used for narrow widths or small patches which require extra pressure.

Protection of edges

Edges of veneers laid with hide glue have a tendency to lift or splinter out particularly in the long grain, and they are, therefore, protected either by applied mouldings or lippings, or as in traditional work with narrow cross-bandings of veneer. The process is described under the appropriate heading. The shrinkage pull of face veneers as they dry out must be compensated for by a corresponding balancing veneer (page 219) applied to the underside of the panel, and this is also described. Veneer edges laid with resin glues do not need protection (153:3, 4), but balance veneering is also necessary.

Trimming edges

Veneers should be laid with a generous overlap all round in case they slip during laying, and should not be trimmed back until thoroughly dry. Cross-grain edges may have to be knifed across the face before trimming back with chisel and finely set plane, although veneers laid with resin glues have not the same propensity for splintering out. An excellent veneer-trimmer is illustrated on 149 which cuts the overhang tight against the edge even across the grain, and is invaluable if there is much trimming to be done.

Jointing veneers (hide glues)

If the veneer leaf is insufficient to cover the width one leaf is laid as already described and the next with a 1 in. (25 mm) overlap (147:4). The centre-line of the overlap is then cut through with a sharp knife, working against a straight-edge, the edges carefully lifted, fresh glue inserted if necessary, the area reheated and hammered down, and the joint taped with paper to hold the edges together whilst the glue sets. If the joint subsequently opens it is usually a sign that either too much water has been used or too much pressure applied across the grain, stretching the moist veneer. Built-up patterns, matched curls, etc. are laid in the same way, centre- or guide-lines drawn across the groundwork and ticked on the edges, the first sheet laid to overlap the guide-line, the second sheet laid and knifed through (147:5). Diamonds and quarters, etc. can also be treated in this manner, taking care to cut them the same overall size and positioning them with equal laps or the grain matching will be lost, but they are better laid as taped patterns between cauls. Burrs and curls with violently contrasted grain which have buckled badly should also be laid with cauls, but the veneers must be flatted before laying (see *Flatting veneers*, page 219), although here again an experienced worker might prefer to soak the burrs in very hot water, using the thinnest possible glue and repeatedly hammering down until the veneer sticks.

Caul veneering (hide glues)

In this method the veneers are shot square, taped together and laid as a single sheet without preliminary dampening, therefore stretching is eliminated and the method is always used for laying thick saw-cut veneers, complicated patterns and marquetry-work where any swelling of the individual pieces would inevitably ruin the design. The groundwork is glued and allowed to chill off, the veneer assembly laid on the guide-lines and held in the correct position with staples or fine veneer pins tapped in and pinched off level. It is then covered with a heated caul of softwood or thick zinc sheet with an interleaving of newspaper to prevent the caul sticking, and pressure is applied with cross-bearers and cramps (147:6). The bearers should be fractionally rounded in the length to spread the pressure from the centre outwards, and the cramps tightened in the order shown (147:7). Softening, composed of several thicknesses of newspaper, thick felt or rubber sheeting can be used to even out any irregularities, but they must be warmed throughout or the glue will not flow. Modern veneering practice follows the same principles, but cold-setting resin adhesives have eliminated the necessity for heated cauls, although they can be used to greatly accelerate the setting time.

Pressure veneering with resin glues

Resin glues offer very definite advantages, for the glues set at ordinary room temperatures and the application of heat is optional according to the required rapidity of the set. As the veneers do not have to be dampened no water is used except as a solvent for the glue, therefore stretching and

subsequent shrinkage is negligible; moreover, there is or should be little if any penetration to the wood surface, the pores of the wood are not choked with glue, and all the lustre is retained. Edges do not have to be protected as with hide glues, and in fact veneered surfaces can be shaped, moulded and run out to a feather edge without the veneers lifting, whilst the surfaces are harder, with greater wear resistance, and are impervious to moderate heat and moisture. Lastly, veneers can be shot square, assembled in complex patterns, taped together and laid as a single sheet with the certainty that if properly prepared there will be no gapping of joints, with a good joint in straight-grained timber almost invisible to the naked eye.

Pressure is always necessary with synthetic resin glues for they have no natural suck (impact glues suitable for laying formica, etc. are quite unsuitable for permanent veneer-work), but it need only be sufficient to bring both surfaces into intimate contact and to maintain that contact until the glue has set. Various forms of veneer-press are used and 150–2 show representative examples. The principle is the same throughout, i.e. to maintain sufficient positive pressure to bend or flatten the veneer on to its former or groundwork, and excessive pressure over and above the minimum requirements should be avoided or glue-starved joints will result. A thin skin only of glue should be used, and the object, therefore, is not to squeeze out the surplus glue as in hand-veneering but merely to establish the requisite intimate contact. Some form of veneer-press is virtually indispensable for every trade-shop no matter how small, for it will soon pay for its keep, and one of the most suitable for the general run of work is the hand-operated screw veneer-press (150) with open ends. With this type extra long work beyond the capacity of the standard daylight press can be veneered in sections, or the oversail at the ends clamped between bearers and G-cramps. Alternatively, very long panels can be slit into convenient sections in the long-grain direction of the face veneers, grooved for loose tongues and each section veneered and then assembled. The process is simple enough and highly effective, but the grooving must be very accurately set out if the veneered surfaces are to line up. Failing any kind of press large areas can be satisfactorily

150 Quick-acting hand-operated screw veneer-press with open ends *By courtesy of Interwood Limited*

veneered with nothing more elaborate than stout cross-bearers and sash-cramps as in caul veneering, but some local blistering must be expected which, incidentally, is not as difficult to lay as some writers would make out. A simple way of checking that the cross-bearers are exerting full pressure in the centre of the panel is to slip tags of newspaper under the bearers at intervals. A slight pull on the tags will disclose whether the pressure is uniform throughout.

Preparation and laying (resin glues)

The groundwork is prepared in the same way as for hammer veneering, laying the veneers 'with the grain' on solid timber and 'across the grain' of plywoods, etc. The surfaces should not be roughened or keyed except for a light sanding to break through any surface glazing or grime, followed by a thorough dusting to clean the fibres. Any general-purpose single-application

resin glue can be used for cold pressing at room temperatures, but special veneering glues such as *Aerolite KL* (CIBA (ARL) Ltd) with gap-filling powder hardener are preferable. The glue should be mixed exactly in accordance with the maker's instructions and applied to the groundwork in a thin coat, spreading it evenly with spatula, palette-knife or more satisfactorily rolling it out with a photographic rubber roller or trough hand spreader, carefully checking for bald spots, as there will be no surplus glue to level them out in the pressing, and allowing a few minutes air drying according to the make of glue. Cramping pressure in handwork can be as for caul veneering with hide glue, but the bearers need not be rounded always providing that they bite in the centre, and a good test of this is to insert tags of newspaper under the bearers which should be firmly gripped when the cramps are tightened. As there is plenty of time for assembly both face and counter (backing) veneers can be

151 Twin vacuum shapers and veneer-press with mobile dome *By courtesy of Interwood Limited*

152 Shell-forming press
By courtesy of Interwood Limited

laid at the same time with an interleaving of paper, cellophane, or waxed hardboard to prevent the veneers sticking to the cover boards or cauls. Setting time will be according to the type of glue and the working temperature, but work under strain should have more than the minimum before the cramps are released. For more detailed information as to working procedures reference should be made to the printed instructions of the manufacturers concerned.

Veneering with casein glues

Casein glue, prepared from the non-fatty solids in milk, is regarded as a natural thermoplastic (polymer), requiring the addition of water only and setting by the evaporation of that water content, although it can be made thermosetting with the addition of formaldehyde. Subject to the individual manufacturers' recommendations the working procedures can therefore be the same as for other forms of synthetic resin (plastic) glues.

Balancing veneers

Veneers laid with hide glue will pull even the stoutest groundwork hollow as they dry out, and even resin glues with their reduced moisture content will cause slight hollowing. If the groundwork is firmly anchored to a stout supporting frame or locked in a carcase construction it may not call for additional treatment, although solid timber grounds should always be veneered on the heart or rounded side to equalise the

natural pull (153:5, 7); but in all unsupported work the reverse side must be treated with a balancing veneer (153:8). Ideally, this balancing or 'backing' veneer should be of the same thickness and of similar or comparable species as the face veneer, but in practice balancing veneers are usually makore (cherry mahogany), African mahogany, sapelewood, etc. They are laid with the grain direction similar to the face veneers, but the joints need only be knifed and fitted together without matching unless the work is visible. Balance veneering is sometimes referred to as *Counter veneering*, but it should not be confused with the latter which is a distinct process described under its own heading on page 226.

Flatting veneers

Only experience will tell whether a buckled veneer can be laid satisfactorily without preliminary flatting. A good veneer-press, whether screw operated, hydraulic or vacuum, will flatten most stubborn veneers but it may be at the expense of extensive splitting and cracking, therefore badly crumpled or spiteful veneers should always be flatted, using either water alone or a weak solution of glue size (1 part glue to 5 parts water). The veneers should be thoroughly moistened and flatted between warm

boards with light cramping pressure or weighted down. They should be turned occasionally to prevent them sticking, and pressed individually and not in a pack unless interleaved with cellophane or waxed hardboard. Oily woods such as rosewood and satinwood do not require moistening and can be flatted with heat alone. Either hide glue or a very weak mix of resin glue and water can be used for size, for resin glue will take over either, and the flatted veneers must be dried thoroughly before laying, keeping them between weighted boards until ready for use. If the veneers have split open during the flatting—and strong burrs and curls are sometimes prone to this—only actual experience will tell whether the split can be pulled together and strapped in position, but usually it is advisable to accept the split, knife the sheet through and joint together or patch the gap, for if a stubborn sheet is arbitrarily pulled together it may ruck further up during the pressing. If the splits are wide open they can be covered with gummed paper strip on the face and filled on the underneath with Brummer stopping, which will prevent the glue forming a glass-hard filling in the crack. The Brummer can then be scraped out in the final finishing, and the crack patched or filled with suitable stopping.

Laying blisters

Blisters and loose patches can be located by tapping with the finger-nail to disclose a hollow sound, or the fingertips brushed rapidly backwards and forwards which gives a slight whisper over the hollow places. Contrary to the general idea blisters in veneers laid with resin glues are by no means difficult to lay. The veneer should be slit with a razor-blade or sharp knife along the grain, fresh glue inserted, rubbed hard with the pein of a hammer to expel the surplus glue, taped with paper or cellulose tape, covered with a warmed steel scraper or wood block and weighted down for a moment or so. A soldering-iron or electric iron can be used, but all the excess glue must be squeezed out first or the heat will fuse it into a solid lump under the veneer. If blisters occur in very pale or delicate woods a piece of white blackboard chalk rubbed along the edges of the cut will help to disguise the scar, and in fact all joints in pale timbers can be treated in

this way, keeping the chalk to the outer edges of the joints only.*

Veneering chipboard

Chipboard (particle-board) should be veneered with synthetic resin glue, for hide glues may or may not take over the resin impregnated surface and water-based glues tend to swell up the chips. If resin glues are not available the outer skin of the board should be broken through with coarse abrasive paper and a test for adhesion made, or the manufacturer of the board consulted. Synthetic resin glues adhere perfectly and give no trouble. If the boards are supplied already veneered with a common backing quality veneer, usually agba (tola) or African mahogany, the decorative face veneer should be crossed as usual, as this locks the minute cracks always present in knife-cut veneers. Furniture quality chipboards with fine chips in the surface layers should not require counter veneering with backing quality veneers, but if the coarse chipboards (building boards) are used then they should be double veneered (see *Counter veneering*, page 226).

Jointing veneers

The trimming and jointing of narrow veneers to form larger panels is done by special saws or power-operated guillotines in production-work, but knife cutting by hand is rarely satisfactory and the veneers should be shot as in jointing up narrow boards. Single leaves can be planed up on the shooting-board (159:1) if adequately supported as shown, or a pack of veneers can be cramped between two wood straight-edges and either held in the vice (154) or passed over the planer. If the veneer edges tend to splinter out or crumble they can be supported with strips of adhesive tape whilst they are being planed. After shooting, the edges are strapped together with adhesive tape, with a final strip along the entire length of the joint (155), and whilst gummed paper tape is normally used, clear cellulose tape has very definite advantages even though it is

* Hide glue mixed with flake-white and Salisbury glue (rabbit skin glue) were used for delicate inlays in traditional work, and both types are still obtainable from polishers' sundriesmen.

154 Shooting edges of veneers

155 Strapping veneers

156 Hand-operated veneer-guillotine
By courtesy of Interwood Limited

more expensive, for the joints can be examined for tightness against the light and the tape is more easily peeled off after pressing. Tape-splicers in production-work apply mechanical methods to the same principle, and the two leaves of veneer are pushed together by angled rollers whilst a continuous strip of gummed paper tape is wetted and pressed down by a front roller. With tapeless splicers the veneer edges are first coated with a mixture of hide glue and formaldehyde and allowed to dry. A heated roller in the splicer then liquefies and sets the glue as the two edges are fed together, with sufficient strength of bond which enables the veneers to be handled as a single sheet.

Wedge jointing (finger jointing) veneers

Short veneers which are merely butt jointed together end to end to increase the overall length show the joint as a hard line saturated with glue no matter how skilfully they are laid. Whilst this is acceptable in matched curls (163:4) it can be objectionable in long runs of straight-grained timber. Finger or wedge jointing will, however, provide an almost invisible match with the grain of the separate veneers merging into each other.

Setting out finger jointing

The veneers chosen should be reasonably straight grained and not too pronounced in figure. The butt ends of the matched veneers taken in strict order from the bundle should be overlapped by the amount required for the fingering, always remembering that the longer the fingers the more they will approximate to the direction of the long grain and the less evident they will be when laid. A small allowance, say $\frac{3}{8}$ in. (9·5 mm) over and above the length of the fingers, should be made at each end to support the cuts, and two lines should be squared across the top veneer $\frac{3}{8}$ in. (9·5 mm) from the end of the top veneer and $\frac{3}{8}$ in. (9·5 mm) from the position of the end of the under veneer. Within this box parallel lines should be drawn and the position of the fingers marked in with a hard pencil; the fingers are then cut in with a sharp knife, the waste lifted and the two veneers pushed tightly together and strapped in position. Figure 158 illustrates the various

222

stages, and the completed finger joint which was not 'faked' in any way shows the joint as a slight deviation only in the grain direction on the right-hand side of the completed panel. The method can also be used in random lengths of veneers, providing the grain is reasonably uniform throughout the several sheets.

Finger jointing is a traditional hand process, but wedge joint veneer shaping machines working on the principle of a small fly-press are now available with up to 12 right-hand and 12 left-hand knives to cut joints up to 14 in. (355 mm) in width. The principle is also employed in the scarf jointing of heavy constructional timbers, but precision machines are required as the fingering cannot be sawn by hand accurately enough to give the requisite tightness at the tips.

Cross veneering

All veneers laid at right angles to the grain direction of the groundwork are classed as cross

157 Automatic veneer-splicer
By courtesy of Interwood Limited

158 End jointing veneers with finger joint

veneers, but more specifically the term *cross veneering* is applied to narrow widths laid across door-frames, mirror surrounds, etc.; *border crossbanding* to narrow edge borders on panel- and table-tops; *crossbanding (counter veneering)* to an under veneer laid on groundworks and then covered with a face veneer, and *balance* veneering to compensating veneers laid on the underside of groundworks.

Cross veneering of door stiles and rails can be done with hide glue using either hammer or caul techniques, or with cramping pieces or veneer-press using cold-setting resin glues. Assuming that the door-frame shown in 159:2 has to be veneered on the face and back only there is no problem and the operation is straightforward, but if the door edges are veneered also then the framed-up door must first be shot to the opening with due allowance for the veneer thickness plus the necessary clearance all round, for there can be no easing to fit afterwards. Probably the surest method is to trial fit the door, strap small pieces of the actual veneer either side of each corner, hinge with one steel screw in the centre of each plate and then adjust as necessary. If the door is slack in the opening then one stile and one rail can be double veneered on the edges, for the veneer edges will be covered by the face veneers. The edge veneers can run with the grain but the face veneers are cut across the veneer sheet (or from running sheets if matching veneers are required), keeping the same faces uppermost throughout to prevent some strips appearing darker as the light catches them, and cutting the strips rather full in width. If the corners are butted together as in Elizabethan walnut-work the edge to each corner must be shot on a shooting-board and lined up on the inner edge of the frame (159:2x), but for mitred work (159:2A) it is only necessary to pencil in the mitre-line and fit the corners accordingly. It hardly matters if all four corners are done first, working in to the centre in each case, or the strips laid in sequence round the frame, but in practice it is easier to fit two straight ends at the centre rather than one straight end and one mitre simultaneously. With hide glue narrow strips hardly need wetting before laying, and this should be avoided wherever possible, as it only swells up the strips, nor need the strips be laid with an overlap for it is simple enough to cut

each strip exactly square, glue, hammer in position and tape the joint with a temporary weight placed over it to keep it from curling. If cramping techniques are employed it is better to use resin glue, fitting, gluing and cramping each section in sequence, for there will be ample time to fit the joints; whilst for press-work with either hide glue and cauls or resin glue and veneer-press the strips can be assembled, taped and laid as a whole, knocking in fine veneer pins and pinching off the tops to prevent the veneers floating in the press. The glue should be thoroughly hard before the surplus edges are trimmed back, and care should be taken not to dub or round over the faces when cleaning up. In fact, it will always pay to tack waste pieces of the same thickness as the frame to the bench to act as an oversail for the plane, scraper or sanding block.

Cross veneering moulded frames

Wherever practicable frames moulded on the inner edges should be put together dry, flushed off smooth, face veneered and then moulded and assembled. Alternatively, the moulding can be worked in strips and planted on. If the framework must be moulded and assembled before veneering, endeavour to keep the veneer flush with the inside edges of the frame and clear of the moulding which can have a coat of polish to prevent the surplus glue adhering. Whilst it is always risky to veneer the frame sections first and then cut the joints the expert worker might not hesitate to do so.

Border crossbandings

Various treatments are shown in (159:3–6) with (3) against an inlaid boxwood or ebony line, (4, 5) shaped bandings and (6) a shaped panel. In all handwork the central panel is laid first, trimmed back with a cutting-gauge or against a template, the inlaid line or banding fitted, glued and held in position with either cramping blocks or veneer pins knocked in alongside, and the crossband then cut, fitted and laid. If the crossband is fairly narrow the separate pieces cut from the veneer sheet can be rubbed glued in position and then taped, or cellulose tape can be used with resin glues as it has a certain degree of elasticity and can be stretched tight to give sufficient pressure (155). Press-work will either call for dry fitting of the whole surface securely taped together and laid in one operation, or two or more pressings of central veneer, inlay banding and crossbanding. A method often adopted by the writer for this type of work was to press the centre first, trim back, dry fit both banding and crossbanding with cellulose tape, leaving the straight joints unstrapped, and then fold back the bandings with the tapes acting as hinges, glue the groundwork, tape the straight joints and press. This method is, of course, not possible with curved bandings, and the cellulose tape cannot be used with animal glues as it will not stick to wet surfaces. If the bandings are thicker than the central veneers and the panel is pressed between cauls or cover boards, softening material (newspaper, felt, rubber sheeting, etc.) will have to be used to accommodate the differences), but rubber bag (vacuum) presses will automatically do this.

Crossbandings were first used as safe edges for veneered work, for long-grain veneer has a tendency to lift or splinter out at the edges if laid with animal glues. Resin glues seal the edges effectively and require no cross-bands, but the method is still used in reproduction furniture and as a form of surface decoration.

Crossbanding (counter veneering)

Both terms are synonymous and refer to a cross-band underlay laid at right angles to the grain direction of the groundwork (153:9A), and then veneered over with a face veneer with the grain direction again recrossed. Thus in unsupported

work two balancing veneers on the underside of the groundwork will be necessary to counteract the pull of the crossband and face veneer, and the assembly will be in effect a five-ply construction counting the panel as one ply. The process is useful for grounds built up in segments (153:10) or surface joints which might shadow through a single face veneer, and for the coarser grades of chipboard. If solid timber is counter veneered, which was often done in richly veneered traditional furniture, the core panel must be a mild amenable timber, thoroughly seasoned and bone-dry, or shrinkage of the core will buckle or stress the veneers.

Yorkite crossbanding veneer

A recent development is the use of a manu-factured pure wood cellulose fibre sheet in lieu of a natural wood veneer, produced by the NVF Company of Wilmington, Delaware, USA, and marketed in the United Kingdom under the brand name *Yorkite* by J. Burns Limited, Chad-well Heath, Essex. This material resembles a very stiff brown paper (it can also be obtained in white for pale woods), and as it is a tough, dense, resin-free sheet of uniform thickness and obtainable in continuous rolls up to 54 in. (1·371 m) wide it offers definite advantages. It is particularly useful as an underlay for spiteful curls and burrs which otherwise have a tendency to crack and craze over a period of time, and as a preventative against the telegraphing through of coarse chip particle boards, etc. Additionally the grain direction of the face veneers can be in any direction irrespective of the groundwork. A

160   Cross-banding table edge

range of thicknesses is available, of which $\frac{1}{64}$ in. (·39 mm) is the most popular.

Sandbag veneering

If a vacuum-bag press is not available shapes of double curvature can be veneered with the traditional sandbag techniques. Either a canvas bag or sandbox filled with coarse silver sand is used, and an example of the latter is shown in 159:7. Assuming that a *bombé* shape has been constructed either of segments, wood bricks, or in the traditional examples of *bombé* commodes a solid panel tongued to a jointed framework and shaped to the curves with plane, floats (coarse files) and scrapers, the box is filled with sifted sand and the shaped groundwork to be veneered tamped down until it fits exactly. Register-marks should be ticked on the groundwork and also on the edges of the box so that the curves of the shape will be exactly located in the depressions in the sand, for the sand, being inert will not slide under pressure. The groundwork is then carefully withdrawn and the veneers fitted, tailoring them if necessary and taping them firmly together to form a self-supporting shell. If hide glue is used the groundwork is then glued and allowed to chill off, the veneers placed in position and held with staples or pins in the waste edges, the sandbox thoroughly heated and the ground with its covering of veneers exactly located in the box. It is then cramped down with suitably shaped bearers, applying pressure in the centre first and then both edges simultaneously or the shape will rock over.

Resin glues can be used instead of hide glue, and in fact the heat of the box will accelerate the set, although in this case the sand should be warm rather than hot or precuring will result before the cramps are in position. Canvas bags filled with sand (159:8) follow the same principle and are thumped down over the glued assembly and either cramped or weighted.

Rubber bag veneering

A method of veneering curved work and forming laminated shapes which has supplanted the traditional sandbag technique except for occasional work is the rubber envelope which can take the place of the vacuum-bag press if necessary. Some form of vacuum extraction is required, either a suitable vacuum pump, the intake side of a standard compressor, or the slip side of a blower motor. The household vacuum-cleaner is not suitable as a vacuum of 26 in. (660 mm) of mercury must be induced. The envelopes are procurable from 4 ft (1·22 m) by 3 ft (0·91 m) up to 12 ft (3·65 m) by 5 ft (1·52 m) (Harefield Rubber Co. Ltd, Bell Works, Harefield, Middlesex). The work to be veneered is placed on a suitable flat baseboard or support with loose flaring pieces either side to even out the pull on the rubber, and the whole assembly placed in the envelope, the open end of which is sealed with cramped battens. It is advisable to run crossed shallow grooves in the baseboard and flaring pieces with vertical holes at the intersections to allow the air to be withdrawn evenly. The usual precautions must be

161 Rubber bag veneering

taken, i.e. formers, etc. must be waxed to prevent adhesion or the veneers covered with waste paper, with the veneers stapled through the waste to prevent displacement. Figures 161:1 and 161:2 show an enlarged diagram of a section of the assembly. The envelope can be used for flat-work, curved work and compound shapes with equal success, but the bag must be smoothed out and the shapes under held down as the air is withdrawn, to prevent the rubber drawing under the veneers.

Pattern veneering

Considerable artistry is called for in the selection and matching of veneers for pattern-making, for the results can be beautiful or truly horrible according to the skill of the operator. Modern furniture does not make use of patterned effects, although even a plain front does require careful matching of the individual leaves, therefore the techniques as far as it is possible to describe them should be fully understood even if the art is indefinable. One golden rule should always be observed, however, that of restraint, for a richly figured pack of veneers is an open invitation to flamboyance.

The various methods of matching veneers using two or more leaves taken in strict order from the bundle are as follows:

Balanced matched General term meaning consecutive leaves of veneer of uniform size and matched for grain.
Book form (side matched) 163:1 The first leaf of the bundle opened out as in turning the pages of a book, and matched at the sides with its fellow.
Running (163:2) Consecutive leaves laid out side by side as they rise from the bundle.
Random matched (163:3) Assorted leaves not matched for grain and not necessarily of the same width.
End or butt matched (163:4) The top leaf folded down as in book form matching.
Diamond quarter (163:5) Four consecutive leaves cut diagonally and side and butt matched.
Reverse diamond (163:6) As for diamond quarter.
Quartered (163:7) Four consecutive leaves side and butt matched.
Herringbone (163:8) Two consecutive leaves cut diagonally and side matched.
Inverted herringbone (163:9) As for herringbone.

The running pattern (163:2) is usually adopted for contemporary designs as against the traditional book form pattern. Diamond and herringbone patterns are cut from successive leaves and not from a single sheet, for any wander in the grain will give a twisted effect as shown in 164B. Card templates cut to the required shape can be laid on the veneer and each section knifed through to be shot square and matched with its fellow. The first cutting out should be generous to allow for trimming off so that the grain markings register with each other. As it is sometimes difficult to pick out the best section

162 Matching veneers
    1 Single leaf of veneer before trimming and laying

2 Matched veneer panel with sides B to B and ends C to C

3 Matched veneer panel with sides B to B and ends D to D

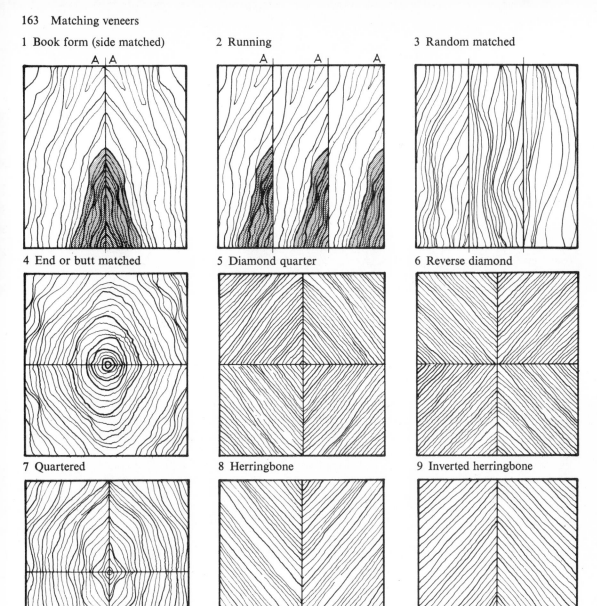

1 Book form (side matched)

2 Running

3 Random matched

4 End or butt matched

5 Diamond quarter

6 Reverse diamond

7 Quartered

8 Herringbone

9 Inverted herringbone

4 Matched veneer panel with sides A to A and ends C to C

5 Matched veneer panel with sides A to A and ends D to D

from a sheet of wild grain a cardboard window the size of the template can be cut, placed over the leaf and the best section chosen and marked in pencil. When the first section has been cut the remainder of the leaf can be used as a window for successive sections. To judge the effect of book form matching of sections which are to be cut from large sheets of veneer a piece of un-framed mirror glass should be placed at right angles to the chosen area and the effect of doubling viewed in the glass, and this will prevent bad errors of choice. A point to watch in all veneer matching is how the pores of the wood run, for if the sheet is cut with the pores diagonal with the thickness, folding the sheet over in book form fashion will reverse the inclination of the pores, and the play of light over the surface may strike correspondingly darker in opposing sections, particularly in such timbers as coarse African mahogany curls. The effect can be pronounced enough to ruin the appearance of side or end matching in vertical surfaces, but it can be observed before laying by opening out the leaves, wetting them on the face surfaces, standing them upright and viewing them from a distance.

Built-up patterns of various shaped sections—and the variety is endless—should be assembled on a ground-plan drawn on stiff cartridge paper and each piece shot to shape, taped to its fellow and pressed. Complicated patterns which cannot be cut with knife and straight-edge will have to be sawn out with a fret-saw as in marquetry cutting. If the veneers are crumpled they should be flatted before cutting, and if boxwood stringings, band-ings and thick inlays are included they can be cut in and the difference in thicknesses compensated for by layers of softening in the final pressing, but usually it is more satisfactory to tape the various veneer sections together, lay them and then incise for the lines or inlays and re-press (see *Inlay lines, bandings,* etc., page 232). For examples of intricate pattern-work the reader is referred to the innumerable encyclopedias of furniture and to museum-work. No matter how complicated the assembly may appear in the finished work it is always basically as already described, although certain precautions may have to be adopted according to the nature of the veneers. If indivi-dual pieces or sections refuse to lie flat on the ground-plan preventing accurate fitting, it may be necessary to paper tape the plan to a support-ing base and glue each section down with dabs of hide glue, Seccotine or Balsa cement weighted in position until set. The whole assembly is then covered with a glued cover paper, and when thoroughly dry split away from the plan with a sharp knife and the back cleaned off, using as little water as possible (Balsa cement will have to be sanded off). Fragile veneers cut to sharp

164A Diamond quartered panel (correct)

164B Diamond quartered panel (incorrect)

points may have to be reinforced with a glued cover paper before they are cut, and time spent on such preparation will be amply repaid. All cover papers and backings should be glued with thin hide glue in preference to resin adhesives, and in no circumstances should impact glues be used as they are extremely difficult to clean off.

Cleaning off patterned work

Complicated assemblies of different kinds of veneer or veneers with wild fluctuations in grain should be left for as long as possible under pressure, and even when released kept between weighted boards whenever they are not being worked on, for it will take some time for veneers and panel to adjust themselves to the varying stresses, particularly with synthetic resin glues which delay but do not finally inhibit the absorption or evaporation of moisture in accordance with the prevailing atmospheric conditions. Thick saw-cut veneers can be levelled off with a finely adjusted smoothing-plane, and the Norris plane is admirable for this, but thin knife-cut veneers will have to be treated very much more gently with sharp scraper and abrasive paper. Resin glue assemblies are more laborious to clean off, for any glue that has penetrated to the surface will be glass hard, but they can be repeatedly swabbed with water which will not only lift the glued cover paper but will ease considerably the scraping of very hard woods if done whilst the surface is still wet, but tests should be made for the colours of some veneers leach out and may discolour paler inlays. Even the final sanding may present difficulties, and in the finishing of the Bombay rosewood petals in the bird's-eye maple pilaster illustrated in 165 no water could be used, and it was found necessary to seal the maple with several coats of thin white polish (french polish) before the panel could be sanded, to keep both colour and dust from the very dark rosewood from spreading into the pale ivory-coloured maple grain. Water also must be used very sparingly on hide glue assemblies; whilst raised or fluffy grain will have to be sealed or 'flashed' with dilute white polish, usually known as a 'wash coat', to raise and set the fibres in an upright position so that they are stiff enough to be cut off by the abrasive paper. Where the grain directions conflict as between the individual pieces of veneer the final sanding with 180 or 240 grit abrasive paper will have to be done with a circular movement, and an orbital pad sander is admirable for this.

Column veneering

A traditional and effective method of veneering small circular columns and half columns which does away with the necessity for shaped cauls is to glue the column with hide glue and allow to chill off, cut the veneer with a generous overlap in the width, pin one long edge (if necessary damping it so that it lies flat), wrap the veneer round the column and bind it with a 2 in. (50 mm) continuous calico strip which has been well wetted so that the whole of the area is covered with the strip. The column is then gently heated over a shaving blaze or other source of heat until the glue runs, the webbing again wetted with warm water and then reheated to shrink it and force out the surplus glue. After the glue has set the webbing is removed, the overlap joint cut through, the edges warmed, fresh glue inserted, hammered down and strapped with tape. Jointed up or fragile veneers which do not bend easily may have to be reinforced with a glued paper cover before wrapping, whilst intricate inlays and built-up patterns of small elements may have to be glued firmly to a supporting base

165 Inlaying rosewood motif in veneered pilaster

of thin fabric* which must be dampened slightly before bending and gluing in position. Large columns of either coopered or laminated construction can be made in convenient sections, each section hammer or caul veneered and then reassembled with either tongued and grooved or rubbed joints, but such work belongs more properly to specialised joinery and advanced techniques are employed for repetition work, although the occasional 'one off' usually has to be made up by traditional methods improvised to suit. One thing is very certain, that no matter what new shape is evolved which would seem to call for revolutionary methods it has usually been done before by primitive but essentially practical methods. To state it fairly, the old cabinet-makers knew every worthwhile trick, and the study of antique furniture is the study of man's mastery over his material. The heavily shaped *bombé* commode with its flashing richness of intricate veneer-work may look almost impossible, but it was done with primitive planes and scrapers, a pot of home-made glue and a lump of heated iron. No doubt the old craftsmen had more time in which to develop their skills and we are in too much of a hurry, but in the end they achieved more than we can usually show. The moral, therefore, must surely be 'make haste slowly'.

Diaper-work

Typical examples of these entrancing patterns of repeat squares, diamonds, lozenges and foliage in contrasting woods are shown in 166 and methods of construction on page 167. The contrasts between the various woods should not be too abrupt except in very small sections, and strong figure markings rather than violent alterations in colour or tone, with a good play of light and shade as the direction changes from vertical to horizontal should be used or the charm will be lost. A full size plan should first be drawn out on cartridge paper and the pieces fitted to it. Figure 167:1 shows the build up of a square pattern in which strips are cut across and along the grain of

* Subsequent cracking, crazing and lifting of highly figured or spiteful veneers (mahogany curls, rosewood, etc.) can often be prevented by the traditional method of backing the veneer with glued muslin prior to laying. (See also *Yorkite crossband underlay*, page 226.)

two separate sheets of veneer, the edges shot and taped together (167:2). Strips across the composite sheet can then be built up on the ground-plan as shown (167:2A). In diamond-work the strips are cut at an angle (167:3) and assembled as in 167:4A. If boxwood lines are incorporated (166:4) they can be glued in between the strips and again across the composite strips, and bandings treated similarly. The first cutting of the strips must be very accurate and the widths identical using a sharp cutting-gauge, but the composite strips can be laid against a straight-edge and corrected if necessary. Transparent cellulose tape is invaluable for building up the strips as the joints can be watched for alignment at every stage. In 166:3 strips are cut the width of the separate diamonds and cut to the diamond shape against a template or in a jig; every square is then assembled with its banding and matched against its fellows. The three-dimensional cube effect (166:5) which was always a great favourite, is cut in a jig or from a template using strips of three contrasting woods of identical width, two strips along the grain and one at an angle of 30°. Figure 167:6 is strictly speaking marquetry-work, with separate sheets of veneer pinned together or interleaved with glued paper, marked with a template and cut with a saw and then fitted to the pattern, and eased with fine files where necessary. It takes much longer to assemble but is remarkably effective if the woods are well chosen. Figure 166:1 shows the chess or chequer-board pattern; 166:2 is a square pattern to give a diamond quarter effect; 166:3 has an inlay banding diagonally across the squares. Woods generally used for diaper-work were Macassar ebony, Rio and Bombay rosewoods, Cuba and Honduras mahoganies, satinwood, kingwood, tulipwood, walnut and box, etc., choosing woods with strong markings or stripes. Boxwood, holly and stained blackwood (pearwood) were used for lines and stringings with insets of bone, ivory, tortoiseshell, mother-of-pearl, brass, pewter, etc.

Inlay lines, bandings, etc.

It is a little sad that inlaid lines and bandings are no longer used in modern furniture, for they add great richness and a touch of welcome colour. Figure 168:1 shows various traditional examples, and 168:2–5 the method of assembly in which

composite blocks are built up of layers of contrasting woods and veneers and then sliced as in 168:3, with a special planer or swage-set circular saw projecting only sufficiently above the saw-table to cut the thickness. Reproduction-work still makes use of these bandings, and those usually available from marquetry and veneer sundriesmen include $\frac{1}{16}$ in. (1·5 mm) boxwood and blackwood strings, $\frac{1}{8}$ in. (3 mm) boxwood, blackwood and rose inlay lines, three-line bandings box/black/box and box/rose/box, and some patterned bandings, viz. dentil, check, rope, domino, feather, herringbone, diamond and chevron in combinations of box, blackwood,

mahogany, rosewood, tulipwood, satinwood and walnut, etc.

Lines and bandings can be incorporated in the veneer pattern at the time of assembly and laid as a single sheet; or the veneers can be taped together, laid and then incised for the lines which are cut in with a cutting-gauge or scratch stock working from the edge, or knifed against a template; or if in circles or circular sweeps a waste block can be cramped or paper glued to the surface, with a stub dowel in the centre working in a hole in a straight bar which has been part saw kerfed and screwed together to form a scratch stock. Various forms of cutters for use in

scratch stocks are shown in 167:11, whilst 167:9 illustrates a simply made double knife from old hack-saw blades for use against a template (167:10). If the veneer has been laid with hide glue the waste can be lifted with the heated tang of a file, and eased out with a narrow chisel; but resin glues will require cutting out with the bevel of the chisel flat against the groundwork. If the grooves are fairly tight the line or banding can be glued with hide glue or Seccotine, pressed into position with the pein of a hammer and weighted down if necessary, or taped in position for cold-setting glues and re-pressed. Complicated assemblies may require several such pressings working from the centre outwards; although it is possible to lay thin strings and bandings with resin glues and a soldering-iron or electric iron which will set the glue instantaneously, but there must be no surplus of glue or it will harden into lumps before it can be pressed out. Where the line is fitted against a central veneer with a cross banding to the edges of the panel, the veneer should be cut and trimmed to shape, the line glued and held in position with veneer pins until set, and the cross banding then fitted and glued, strapping it down with cellulose tape tightly stretched to hold it firmly in position. Figure 160 shows the cross banding of a circular table-top done in this way. Square lines rebated into the edge of a top are also anchored in this fashion and cleaned off flush when dry. It is essential that inlaid lines and bandings should be allowed plenty of time to settle, for the contraction of the glue will pull the inlays below the surface if they are cleaned off level too soon. Work containing inlaid brass lines should be brushed over with dilute polish to protect the grain against fine brass-dust, whilst the lines can be scraped flush with a steel scraper and polished with finest silicon carbide paper.

Inlay-work

The general term *inlaying* covers the practice of inletting any one material into another material of different colour or composition, but more specifically *wood inlaying* is divided into *intarsia* in which relatively thick sections are set into suitable depressions cut in the groundwork, and *marquetry* in which the pattern is built up of veneers or materials in veneer thickness and

applied to the groundwork as an oversheet. Confusion often persists between the two terms, for marquetry pictures which adopt a naturalistic approach are sometimes known as 'Intarsia pictures', but in practice it is better to confine the term *inlay* to intarsia or cut-in work, and marquetry to veneered work.

Intarsia-work

Originally developed in the fourteenth century this process uses separate inlays of wood, ivory, bone, tortoiseshell, mother-of-pearl, brass, silver, etc. cut to shape, laid on the ground, the outlines traced with a fine point and the appropriate recesses cut in with woodcarving tools, slightly bevelling the shoulders of the cuts to give a tight fit. Wood thicknesses are usually from $\frac{1}{8}$ in. (3 mm) to $\frac{1}{4}$ in. (6 mm) thickness and can be levelled off flush after laying, but the more precious materials in thin sheets are laid on a bed of plaster of Paris and hide glue suitably coloured. Metal insets can be laid with hide glue if the surface is first rubbed with a slice of garlic to destroy the grease, or preferably with Araldite epoxy glue. The original intarsia-work employed arabesques and elaborate perspectives.

Marquetry-work

This was a later development of true inlay or intarsia-work, and the rendering was always much freer with scrolls, bunches of flowers, etc. covering the ground. Veneers or materials in veneer thickness are used, the pattern cut out, assembled and laid as a single sheet on a suitable ground. Professional cutters have evolved their own methods for the work is highly specialised, and whilst a good general craftsman could no doubt easily master the techniques of cutting and laying, the art lies in the preparation of the design and the selection, matching and shading of the veneers.

Cutting and laying marquetry-work

A full-size drawing of the design is necessary, done with a continuous fine line and coloured to represent the actual veneers used. Working copies of the drawing can be prepared either by tracing through with carbon paper, or more accurately by the traditional method of closely pricking through the lines with a fine needle. Several copies can be pricked at the same time, or the design can be printed through the perforations with a pounce-bag filled with finely powdered asphaltum which must then be heated to fuse the deposited powder, or rubbed through with a pad soaked with heelball and methylated spirit. If the design allows of it two or more sheets of the materials to be used can be pinned or glued together with a waste sheet of veneer under to take the rag of the saw, and the printed design pasted on the top sheet. The whole of the pattern can then be cut out either on a marquetry-cutter's donkey or with the usual form of fret-saw, working on a V-notched table fixed to the bench. The finest jewellers piercing saws can be used (marquetry-cutters often made their own from finest clock steel), and wherever possible the saw cuts are made outside the line of the insets, and on the line of the background; the sheets are then separated and the complete pattern assembled on the master drawing, covered with a surface paper and laid in the usual manner. If, however, the design contains many separate pieces of different woods and differing grain directions, then each piece of veneer must be treated separately, the outline transferred to it, the piece sandwiched

between waste veneer if there are delicate fibres to be supported, the piece cut, numbered and either taped to the surrounding pieces, or butt jointed with quick-setting Balsa cement or PVA glue. When the pattern is complete all traces of glue must be removed from the under face before laying, and some professional workers fill up slight gaps with a mixture of glue and veneer-dust. Local shading of the individual pieces to give chiaroscuro is achieved by scorching the wood in heated silver sand before they are assembled, but it must be skilfully done to be effective. As the veneers are a $\frac{1}{16}$ in. (1·5 mm) or less in thickness the completed surface must be carefully scraped and sanded with a circular motion, and delicate insets may have to be protected from the coloured dust of other insets by coating with white french polish before sanding.

A superb example of modern marquetry-work which must surely equal the best examples of any previous age is to be seen in the reception hall and main entrance of Gallaher Ltd offices in Granite House, Cannon Street, London, E.C.4. Figures 169A–D kindly lent by Gallaher Ltd can give only an approximation of the wonderful richness of these panels which are 16 ft (4·87 m) long and 3 ft (0·91 m) high and composed of 70

169 A–D Marquetry panels in entrance hall of Gallaher Limited, Granite House, Cannon Street, London E.C.4

169A

native and exotic timber species in 20,000 different pieces. The selection, matching and cutting of the veneers was carried out by Mr A. Dunn to sketch designs prepared by Mr George Ramon and drawn in detail by Mr F. Bellan. No staining of any kind was used, and local shading was done by the traditional hot-sand method (see page 242).

Parquetry

Geometrical patterns, squares, rectangles, lozenges, etc., either inlaid, veneered or overlaid are known as 'parquetry-work', typical examples of which are chessboards and parquet flooring. The treatment is the same as for any other inlay- or marquetry-work.

Boulle-work

Marquetry patterns comprising sheets of brass and tortoiseshell in elaborate scroll-work and foliage are known as Boulle-work (Buhl-work) after the celebrated French marquetry-cutter André-Charles Boulle (1642–1732) who perfected the process. Thin sheets of tortoiseshell and brass or silver, or boxwood and blackwood-veneers, were pinned together with a waste veneer under to take the rag of the saw; the design was then glued to the top sheet and the whole pack cut at one operation with a very fine saw in a marquetry-cutter's donkey.* The sheets were then separated

* A marquetry-cutter's donkey is exhibited in the Bethnel Green Museum, London.

and the components fitted together. As all the cutting was done simultaneously the waste of one sheet would obviously fit the waste of another sheet; thus in a simple assembly of say, boxwood ground- and blackwood scroll-work there will be a complete sheet of boxwood ground and black scroll-work, and another of black ground- and box scroll-work. Antique examples exist in which one cheek of the cabinet is black on white and the other cheek white on black, and this economic use of the waste was known as *Boulle* and *counter Boulle*, although it was never practised in the finest work. In fact, although Boulle carried this composite cutting to perfection, skilled marquetry-cutters considered it greatly inferior to the traditional method of cutting each piece separately whereby the grain direction could be varied at will.

Oyster-shell veneering

Thin slices about $\frac{1}{16}$ in. (1·5 mm) thick cut transversely from the branches of lignum vitae, olive, laburnum, mulberry or walnut to yield an oyster-shell effect were often used in traditional furniture. The oysters can be cut and stacked with wood spacers between and weighted down, or short lengths of branch wood buried in dry sand, but the seasoning must be very gradual and prolonged if splitting and casting are to be avoided. They were either trimmed square or

170 Box veneered laburnum oysters with sycamore edging *Designer and maker: Richard Fyson*

octagonal shape, carefully matched, coated with glue size to stop absorption, with a glued cover paper over to prevent them curling, and laid between cauls. Figure 167:7 shows the usual method of matching up but there is no reason why oysters of different sizes should not be laid in a random build-up (167:8). A modern example of oyster-shell veneering is shown in the photograph of a large cigarette-box in 170 designed and made by Mr Richard Fyson, which shows to advantage the careful selection, matching and patching of inevitable defects necessary in the finest work.

Overlay-work

A material which is laid *on* and not *in* another material or ground is known as *overlay*, and typical examples are the applied frets on solid groundworks in Chippendale cabinets, and the lavishly applied overlays of ebony and ivory in Italian and Dutch period work. In applying these frets the groundwork must not be glued for it would be impossible to clean off the surplus glue between the frets, therefore the glue is rolled out on a flat surface, the fret pressed on the glue, quickly transferred to the ground and pinned and weighted down.

Overlays of timber thicker than a veneer and applied to a ground of common timber to save valuable material are usually referred to as *facing-up* work.

Miscellaneous materials

Mother-of-pearl can be obtained prepared for use in various qualities and colours, blue, pink and green being the most expensive. It can be cut with a jeweller's piercing saw and filed to shape, but should be backed with a temporary veneer or sheet of paper before cutting as some varieties are very brittle. If laid with hide glue it should be roughened with a file and any slight curvature taken up with plaster of Paris mixed in the glue. Very little pressure must be used, sufficient only to press the shell home flush with the surface, and final finishing is done with 10:0 grit abrasive paper from which the fierceness of the cut has been knocked off by rubbing two sheets together, followed up by pumice powder and rottenstone. The pearl can be engraved by brushing over with warm wax, scratching through the wax when cold and pouring nitric acid into the scratches, after which mastic suitably coloured is run into the lines to complete the design. Tortoiseshell can be cut and laid in a similar fashion to pearl, and can be cleaned off by scraping and papering and then polishing with dry whiting or rottenstone. It is usual to colour the ground under the shell, or insert gold-foil underneath to increase the brilliance. Ivory is obtainable in fairly large pieces and can be turned, cut and shaped with normal woodworking tools, laid with normal glues and the surfaces flushed off with scraper and file followed up with fine paper and pumice powder, and polished with whiting on a chamois-leather buff. Bone and horn are fair substitutes in small sections but lack the wonderful depth and ripple of real ivory, whilst white plastics are only poor imitations, although valid materials in their own right if treated as such.

Plastic inlays

A method of inlaying wood, metal and other hard materials in a groundwork of suitably coloured polyester resin first developed by William Mitchell at the Royal College of Art in London is illustrated in the coffee-table shown in 316A. The table which has one of a series designed by the writer especially for this inlay, had the wood top inset $\frac{3}{16}$ in. (5 mm) in the yew framing. Cross-sections of various short ends of timber in the workshop, laburnum, Indian laurel, acacia, yew, grey sycamore, oak, brown oak and rosewood were then sawn $\frac{1}{4}$ in. (6 mm) thick, broken up at random, spaced out on the ground and anchored with a little of the polyester resin used. A mix was then made up of resin, accelerator, hardener, and thrixotropic medium which allows a build up without creep or slide, coloured pale green with polyester pigments and poured over the assembly, working it into the gaps with a pointed stick. After hardening, the surface was levelled off flush with scrapers and belt sander, polished with silicon carbide paper and the whole table then sprayed with a clear catalyst finish. The completed table is successful because it treats the plastic as a material in its own right and not as a substitute for other materials, and although it has seen hard service over many years shows no signs of cracking, lifting or failure of any kind. Very oily woods (rosewood, etc.) should not be used for this type of inlay as the natural oil may inhibit the setting of the polyester resin. A photograph of the table-top with a broken-up laburnum oyster as a central motif is also shown (316B).

Sand shading (marquetry-work)

The delicate shading often seen in traditional marquetry-work is done by scorching the veneer in a tray of hot sand. Each piece of veneer is dipped for a few seconds only, and the sand must be clean, sharp, fine silver sand (obtainable from pet shops), uniformly heated. For island shading within the body of the veneer the sand should be heated in an old spoon and poured on repeatedly from both sides, again for a few seconds each time. After shading the pieces should be moistened on the surfaces and dried under a weight.

Storage of veneers

All veneers should be stored flat in a dry, even atmosphere and protected from the light. Decorative veneers, curls, feathers, etc. intended for pattern-making should be numbered with chalk (not wax crayon) in the exact order of cutting and the ends taped to prevent splitting. Repeated handling of veneers should be avoided as much a possible, for they tend to become brittle with age and the wastage caused by careless storage and handling can be greater than the wastage incurred in laying.

Moisture contents

Moisture content at the time of laying should be the same as the groundwork, ideally in the neighbourhood of 9 per cent, but higher contents are not necessarily harmful provided both ground work and veneer are equal and plenty of time is allowed for the completed surface to settle down.

23 Mouldings and lippings

The decline in the popularity of moulded sections dates from the introduction of plywoods and machine techniques, and is a good example of new materials and their manipulation influencing design. Mouldings are, however, both decorative and utilitarian, for subtle curved surfaces catch and reflect the light giving warmth and feeling, whilst softened angles are less easily damaged and more comfortable to handle. Current architectural styles worship severe functional restraint, but whilst rich mouldings may be temporarily out of fashion they usually survive periodic neglect.

Traditional mouldings are developed from Greek examples based on ellipses and Roman examples on circles, but the classic geometric shapes are better suited to bold architectural features, and small-scale furniture mouldings are happier if drawn freehand, with due regard for the type of timber of which they are composed. For instance, fine-grained woods, mahogany, walnut, etc. call for delicate treatment, whilst coarse Gothic details would look ridiculous in any but strong, open-grained timbers such as oak, chestnut and the like. In designing such elements, therefore, certain rules should be observed: (a) the sections must be in scale, i.e. in proportion to the type, size and overall appearance of the carcase; (b) mouldings above eye level should protrude (171:20A), and below eye level recede, otherwise the effect will be lost, whilst undercut mouldings (171:21) should be boldly profiled; (c) composite mouldings (171:22) should be built up of alternate convex and concave profiles. These arbitrary rules can of course be broken, but only with discretion; and an example of bad profiling is the coarse reeded legs of some Victorian furniture in which the bold convex profiles of the reeds are placed side by side with no relieving flat between.

Types of moulding

Traditional shapes are illustrated in 171 with alternative names inset in the sections where applicable. Certain details regularly occur and an astragal or nosing (171:5) becomes a torus bead with one flat (171:10), and a bead moulding with two flats (171:13), whilst a succession of parallel beads becomes a reeding (171:19), and a large flute (171:15) becomes a hollow (171:16). A flat is the slight member between two opposing curves (171:22), and a quirk (shift or turning) a right-angled projection (171:6, 10, etc.). Additionally, an astragal composed of two ellipses meeting at a point becomes a quirked bead because the two curves do not flow into each other.

Cross-grain mouldings

One of the delights of antique walnut furniture is the rich cross-grained mouldings usually found in the best work. Some 30 years ago the fashion was revived, using cross-grain veneers over a solid core; but these mouldings, known as *waterfall* obviously could have no sharp arrises, and the total effect was invariably third rate. Genuine cross-grain mouldings can be worked by hand and even by spindle-moulder, provided the cutters are sharp and the feed-rate gentle. Well-seasoned richly grained timber should be chosen; strips are then cut across the board, the ends matched up, shot square and hide glued to the edge of a waste board with a layer of thick paper between (171:23). The moulding can then be worked in the usual way, adopting the normal precautions for cross-grained work, the glue-line split in the thickness of the paper, the paper soaked off and the moulded sections butt glued in their permanent positions or if practicable the strips can be glued direct to the groundwork and then moulded. In theory, such mouldings should shrink and split open, but provided thoroughly dry timber is used and the sections not too wide, the cross grain will accommodate a certain measure of shrinkage without parting at the joints.

Composite mouldings

Faced-up mouldings of richly figured wood in antique furniture were usually wide in section and glued to a pine core (171:22), no doubt to save

171 Moulding details

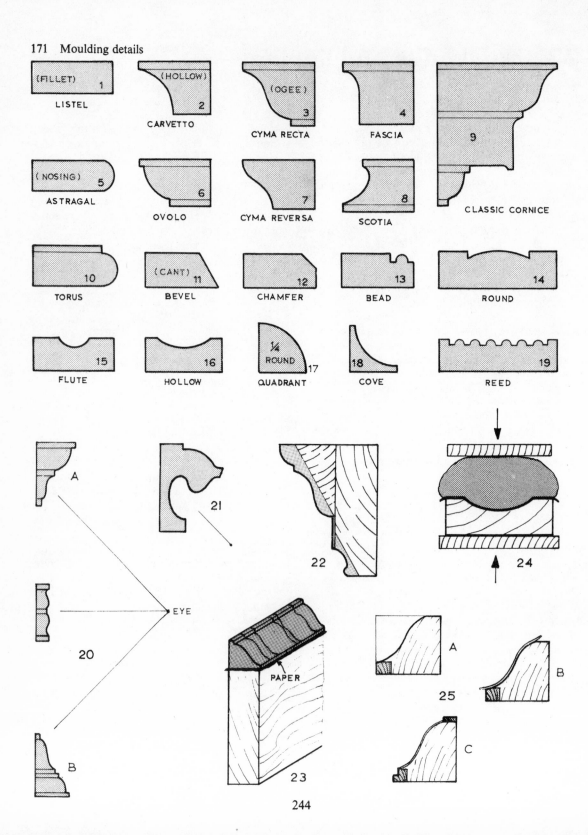

(FILLET) 1
LISTEL

(HOLLOW) 2
CARVETTO

(OGEE) 3
CYMA RECTA

4
FASCIA

9
CLASSIC CORNICE

(NOSING) 5
ASTRAGAL

6
OVOLO

7
CYMA REVERSA

8
SCOTIA

10
TORUS

(CANT) 11
BEVEL

12
CHAMFER

13
BEAD

14
ROUND

15
FLUTE

16
HOLLOW

¼ ROUND 17
QUADRANT

18
COVE

19
REED

A

21

22

24

20

EYE

B

PAPER

23

A

25

B

C

244

valuable timber but also to cut down shrinkage in sections worked cross grain.

Veneered mouldings

Where veneered mouldings have to be veneered and a vacuum-bag press is not available the traditional sandbag method can be employed. The bag should be made up out of twill or coarse linen stout enough to withstand pressure but supple enough to follow the curves, and filled with fine dry silver sand which has been thoroughly sieved. If hide glue is used the bag must be warmed throughout to the melting temperature of the glue, or used cold for synthetic glues, carefully positioned with a generous overhang and thumped down. If there is sufficient volume of sand the weight alone may be sufficient, although resin glues may require a flat board laid along the length and cramped in position (171:24). Hide glue is very suitable for veneered flutings which are stopped at each end, as the heat and moisture will soften the veneer sufficiently to follow the compound curves. If a

moulding to be veneered has sharp quirks or arrises then a composite assembly should be adopted, and 171:25A, B, C show the stages.

Chamfers

Chamfers must be scrupulously set out and cleanly worked if they are to be effective. They should be gauged in pencil, allowing for an equal amount of wood to be removed from both sides of the corner, worked with bullnose rabbet-plane, chamfer or flat-faced spokeshave, scraper, flat file, etc. and checked in the length with a metal straight-edge. The ends are usually stopped and various forms are illustrated in 172:1–5, whilst 172:6 shows a simply constructed hardwood template which will give a constant angle to the slope of the stops. An old-type wooden chamfer-plane is shown in 172:7 which can be made up out of a beech block about 5 in. (127 mm) long and 1 in. (25 mm) thick, or a standard wood rabbet plane can be converted. A square edged iron is used which is set to project to the depth of the chamfer, and the strokes must be gentle or

172 Chamfers

1   2

3   4

the iron will tend to dig in. This type of plane can only work in the middle of the length of a stopped chamfer, but is useful for establishing the cut which can then be extended to the stops with a bullnose rabbet-plane.

Working mouldings

Some form of spindle-moulder or high-speed router is almost indispensable in any trade-workshop, but where such facilities do not exist or the length of moulding required hardly justifies grinding a cutter blank and setting up a machine, then hand methods must be used. Very few craftsmen now own a set of moulding-planes, nor are they freely obtainable, whilst the scratch stock is hardly suitable for deep mouldings. In working the moulding shown in 173:1 much of the rough work can be done by setting in a succession of saw cuts (173:2) and then planing off to the dotted line; or working a series of grooves (173:3) in the order stated, as a firm shoulder must be left for the plough-plane fence. If the capacity of the plane allows it additional grooves can be worked, but the number shown will probably be the limit, and here again the waste is planed off as in 173:2. Final shaping will have to be done with bullnose rabbet- or shoulder-plane, chisel or scraper, and the hollow (173:2A) worked with a gouge or scraper ground to a suitable curve, shown in 174, whilst it will pay to make shaped rubbers out of pine blocks for final sanding (175). If a spindle-moulder is used it will be more usual to form the moulding in two sections (173:4), thus avoiding heavy cuts.

Flutings, reedings, etc.

Flutings can be worked with a scratch stock if small in section (see *Moulded legs*, page 292), but wider flutings must be cut with a gouge or formed with a suitable round moulding-plane if available, and 177 illustrates a typical fluting worked cross grain on a drawer front by the latter method. If necessary, battens can be cramped across the face of the work to form a guide for the plane, but the example shown was worked entirely without guides. The flutes were set out with pencil, the cross-flutes worked first and the half-fluting to the surrounds worked afterwards to take out any chipped edges.

177 Moulding flutes to drawer front

Various moulded details are illustrated in 176. Figure 176:1–2 are carcase or table-top treatments; 176:3–8 show drawer fronts and 176:9–11 carcase edges.

Lippings

Exposed edges of ply, laminboard, chipboard, etc. must be masked or lipped, although in the cheapest work such edges are sometimes filled and stained or painted out with water-based pigments (poster paint, etc.) and then polished. The usual procedure in medium-quality work is to use lippings of veneer (178:1) adopting some form of strip heating to set the glue rapidly, and relying on the face veneers to clip the edges of the edge veneers, but these are not altogether satisfactory for the fractional creep of the alternate grain in ply laminates will tend to throw off the veneer, which will then blister and chip over a period of time. Solid lippings relying only on

178 Lippings

the glue to hold them on ply constructions are also subject to the same defect, for although not so easily damaged they are more liable to split off as they do not have the elasticity of thin veneers. However, solid lippings applied to the long grain of laminboard cores or to chipboard edges are relatively permanent (178:2). Where a thin ply top has to be reinforced a thick solid lipping can be rebated over (178:3), and the increased gluing area will hold it in position. An alternative solid lipping is shown in (178:4), with the inset (A) the method of working, but the advantages are only minimal and admittedly the best methods are tongued lippings worked in the solid (178:5) or with loose ply tongues (178:6). These can be veneered over (178:5) provided the width of the lipping on the face is not more than about $\frac{3}{16}$ in. (5 mm) (for wider lippings will shadow through in time), or left to show as a border (178:6). They can be mitred as in 178:7 which is the neatest finish, or allowed to run through (178:8), in which case the end lippings are planted on first and the side tongues trimmed back to fit.

Lippings which are to be veneered over present no problems in working for they can be fitted and flushed off level with the groundwork when dry, but they should be given plenty of time to settle as the water in the adhesive may cause temporary swelling up of the edges which will sink back

179 Edge lipping cramp

later. On the other hand border lippings will have to be accurately worked fractionally full and with the tongues truly central. The proud edges on the faces will then have to be eased back very carefully with a finely set try-plane working diagonally from the centre of the panel outwards to avoid digging in to the veneered faces, and the last tissue-thin shavings removed with a steel scraper. This method of planing outwards to the edges and not inwards will also prevent any dubbing over of the edges, as the body of the plane will be well supported on the flat panel. A useful cramp for applying solid lippings is the Record edge cramp (179).

24 Wood bending and laminating

Wood bending

Permanent bends of small radii can be achieved in wood either by (1) steam bending, (2) gluing together thin veneers or laminations. In the former method the wood remains a solid section which can be cut, shaped, moulded and jointed in the normal manner, whilst the latter is in effect a multiple veneering technique. Wood can also be bent by prolonged soaking in water which does, however, introduce too much moisture into the wood; and by the old technique of running a series of closely spaced saw cuts into the concave face of the bend to within a bare $\frac{3}{16}$ in. (4 mm) of the convex face, but this latter method is not now practised to any great extent, and either steam-heat bending or laminating is always preferable.

Steam bending

Any piece of wood bent or bowed within the limits of its normal stress range, i.e. where the neutral axis between the stretched convex face and the compressed concave face is roughly equal (180:1) will revert to its normal shape immediately the strain is released, owing to the natural elasticity of its fibres. If the limiting stress according to the timber species is exceeded (180:2) some permanent deformation will occur, but there is always a danger that the fibres will be disrupted (180:3). If, however, the wood is rendered semi-plastic either by heating it with live steam or immersing it in boiling water or heated wet sand its compressibility ratio will be greatly increased, and provided it is locked in position until the fibres have cooled and dried it will set rigid to the desired curve. There will be some recovery as the created internal stresses equalise themselves, but whilst this slight tendency to straighten out cannot be precisely calculated a test-piece in the same species and of the same dimension will usually show the extent of the movement.

In practice prolonged immersion in boiling water or heated wet sand is never as efficient as steam bending, and the latter is to be preferred. The technique is straightforward and all that is required is a sufficient head of steam at atmo-spheric pressure to heat the wood thoroughly to 100 °C (212 °F), and to maintain that temperature for at least 45 minutes for every inch of thickness, i.e. a $1\frac{1}{4}$ in. (32 mm) section will require approximately one hour's steaming. A simple apparatus using a large kettle or oil-drum, a source of heat (Primus stove, coke fire, etc.), a length of rubber hosepipe and a wooden box or metal or earthenware pipe sealed at each end with wooden bungs is shown in 180:4, and is quite sufficient for the occasional bend. Production in quantity would, of course, call for more sophisticated methods if consistent quality with low waste factors are to be achieved.

Bending methods

Immediately the wood is soft enough, i.e. uniformly heated throughout, it is taken from the steam chest and bent by hand, or by mechanical means if of heavy section, round a suitable former. A rough and ready method is to use stout pegs driven into a board, but this is inclined to bruise the wood, the bend may not flow easily between the pegs and the ends are inclined to split as they dry. A more sophisticated method is shown in 180:5 in which a 18 swg spring steel strap slightly wider than the wood section greatly minimises the actual disruption of the fibres in the stretched convex face, permitting bends of much smaller radii. The strap is firmly anchored to stout wood or metal back plates which prevent the ends swivelling, and if oak or other acid timber is to be bent then the strap should have an interleaving of thin aluminium sheet or other protective material. End stops fixed to the back plate are also necessary to keep the strap tight against the bend; they should be spaced to allow a certain fractional creep in the bend length (not exceeding 2 per cent) with the slackness taken up with wooden wedges.

Detachable handles can be clipped or bolted to the back plates, or the plates can be extended to form handles for easy manipulation, and once the bend is completed it can be anchored by a tie-rod and lifted from the former. It should then

180 Solid wood bending

A   1   A   A   2   A   A   3

TUBE

WOOD   VENT

STEAM

DRUM

DRAIN

HEAT

4

STRAP

BEND

6

ROD

BACK PLATE

STOP

5

7

BATTEN

251

be placed in a dry heated atmosphere to set for about 12 hours, after which it can be freed from restraint and allowed to settle naturally for about 2 weeks. With acute bends it is always better to leave the metal strap and tie-rod in position during the actual setting time (180:6), but simple bends may only need a batten nailed across (180:7), thus releasing the strap for further use. Bends of fairly large radii usually tend to straighten out a little after they have dried. The recovery movement is not calculable, and it is usual to bend to a slightly smaller radii to allow for the movement, but bends of small radii may tend to turn inwards, although they should not move once they have set. Very green timber will obviously bend more readily than dry seasoned timber, although hydraulic pressures induced in the moisture-choked cells may cause extensive rupturing; whilst old dry timber is usually too stubborn or too brittle to bend well, therefore the ideal is probably partially seasoned timber with a moisture content of around 25 per cent which the steam heating and subsequent drying will further season to within acceptable limits. Shaped, moulded or round section timber can be steam bent, but some deformation of profiles and slight flattening of rounded faces against the strap must be expected, therefore it is better to bend first and profile after whenever possible. Timbers vary greatly in their bending properties with elm outstanding and home-grown ash, beech and oak fairly equal. Comparative minimum radii of curvature in inches to be expected from (1) supported and (2) unsupported sections 1 in. (25 mm) thick are as follows:

MINIMUM RADII OF CURVATURE

Timber	With supporting metal strap		Without strap	
	in.	mm.	in.	mm.
Home-grown ash	2·5	63	12·0	305
Home-grown beech	1·5	38	13·0	330
Imported birch	3·0	76	17·0	432
Dutch elm	0·4	10	9·5	241
Home-grown oak	2·0	50	13·0	330
Honduras mahogany	12·0	305	28·0	711
Burmah teak	16·0	406	28·0	711
European spruce	30·0	762	—	—

No precise data is available for English walnut but the writer has always found mild, straight-grained walnut roughly comparable to oak or beech, ebony fairly malleable and even oily rosewood capable of simple curvatures if taken in several stages. The quoted figures given in the table are taken from the Forest Products Research Laboratory data.

Laminated bends

Thin strips or laminations of wood glued and bent to a curve will not revert to their former shape because each strip is in effect concentric and of fractionally smaller radii than its immediate neighbour which the adhesive will lock firmly in position. Here again practical application is straightforward and equally applicable to fairly large surfaces, door and drawer fronts, etc., or to square sections as in chair-work. The thickness of the individual laminae must depend on the limiting radius of curvature of the particular timber employed, but as a general rule thicknesses should not exceed $\frac{1}{8}$ in. (3 mm). Thinner laminae of veneer thickness $\frac{1}{32}$ in (0·7 mm) and up will yield stiffer, heavier laminations but will take much longer to build up and require more glue. Gap-filling adhesives should be used, preferably synthetic resin, although animal glues (hide, Casein) are dependable but more troublesome. The laminae are not crossed as in plywood manufacture for maximum strength is required in the long-grain direction, but are laid the same way and in the same strict order as cut from the log (181:1) with the grains exactly matched as far as possible. If the grain directions in the individual sheets are allowed to cross as in 181:2 the glue will inhibit any actual shrinkage movement as indicated by the direction of the arrows, but the latent opposing forces will endeavour to exercise a turning movement, subjecting the assembly to torsion, and twisting or warping may result. In theory and provided the grains are straight and matched throughout it hardly matters whether the number of plies is odd or even, but in practice an odd number of laminae, 9, 11, 13, etc., dependent on the required thickness is generally used, and some slight shrinkage across the width must be allowed for as with solid timber. Curly grain veneer should be avoided for the completed assembly will tend to curve with the curvature of the grain, and spiral grain to twist badly. For this reason a predominantly ductile wood like elm is rarely used because of the wildness of its grain, whilst beech with its straight and even fibres is a firm favour- ite. As with ply and laminboard, etc., sheets and square sections will be stronger and stiffer than solid timbers in the same thickness.

181   Laminated bends

Laminated insets

Where the required wood member is for the most part straight with a curved portion at the end the bend can be achieved by saw kerfing the timber and inserting glue-coated laminae of the exact thickness to fill the gaps. The saw cuts should be staggered in the length and spaced within the capacity of the separate tongues to bend to the desired radius. Figure 181:8 makes the process clear.

Laminating compound shapes

Thin malleable veneers will sometimes conform to very shallow curves in two directions as on the surface of a large sphere, and such double curvature can be assisted by pre-moistening and pressing between heated cauls or formers, but the amount of stretch must be within the elastic limits of the wood plies otherwise the veneers will crease and crumple like a sheet of stiff paper. In traditional compound work soft burr veneers, notably burr walnut, were first soaked in boiling water and laid with the hammer, using very thin hide glue and going over the work repeatedly until complete adhesion was achieved. Stiffer veneer or more acute curves require actual tailoring of the sheets to fit, and in one method the veneers are either cut into strips or 'fashioned' to fit the curve so that the butt edges of the cut-out notches fit exactly. The first sheet is then stapled down to a wooden former, the next sheet glued and applied, drawing out the tacks in the first sheet and restapling through the top sheet. Each tailored sheet is treated similarly, drawing out the tacks and restapling, and leaving the tacks in the last sheet until the glue has set. In another method each sheet is fashioned as before, and the tailored cuts soldered together with hide glue and formaldehyde, using a heated iron to set the glue. Cold glues are used for assembly and the top sheet is strapped with adhesive tape. Templates can be used for cutting the veneers, but several will be required as each sheet will differ fractionally and the tailored cuts should be staggered wherever possible.

Heat setting of bends

A range of slow hardeners is available for synthetic resin glues which will allow plenty of time for complex assemblies in handwork. For production-work low-voltage strip heating is used extensively to accelerate the setting time, and this releases the formers for rapid turnovers.

Continuous strip laminations

The process of forming cylinders, chair bends, etc. by the continuous strip method is fully described in the publications of the Forest Products Research Laboratory (HMSO *Solid and Laminated Wood Bending*, etc.). In quantity production such work is usually undertaken by specialist firms using sophisticated processes and considerable technical know-how. Figure 182 shows a range of production bends.

Bending plywoods, etc.

Fairly stiff resin-bonded plywood to WBP specification can be bent more readily if one side is wetted, or conversely the other side heated. Much depends on the thickness and number of plies, the direction of the bend in relation to the grain direction of the stout hearted core, and to the timber species of which the plywood is composed, therefore actual tests are necessary. If the ply sheet is too stiff to take the curve two or more sheets of thin ply to make up the thickness can be glued and bent between simple formers or merely stapled together as practised in boat hull building, for each sheet becomes concentric and the adhesive will lock the fibres and hold the curve. An admirable ply for this purpose is $\frac{1}{16}$ in. (1·5 mm) birch three-ply readily obtainable, which can be rolled up like a sheet of thin card. Heat softening of wood was well known to traditional craftsmen, who bent their boxwood lines for delicate inlays (purfling) by repeatedly passing them over a heated metal pipe or rod.

Pressing methods

Thin sheets or veneers can be pressed in simple male and female formers (181:3), or over a male former only in a vacuum-bag press (181:7). Square section laminations can be bent and pressed with metal straps terminating in screw bolts over a male former (181:4), or with segmented female formers G-cramped in position as 181:5 which will pull the ends in to the curve.

182 Finishing laminated shapes at the factory of Alesbury Brothers Limited
By courtesy of CIBA (ARL) Limited

183 Bending beech chair backs
By courtesy of Ercol Furniture Limited

Pressure should be applied from the top centre outwards. An inflatable rubber hose can also be used (181:6), but where a straight section meets a curve there is a tendency for the straight to puff out at (x,x) and shaped wood fillers should be used.

One of the best examples of laminated work is the grand piano which must be made to exacting standards, immensely strong, rigid and unaffected by the severest climatic conditions. The craft is highly specialised but in essence the case-work is pure cabinet-making. The heart of the piano is the soundboard of quarter sawn sitka spruce kilned to a moisture content of 6 per cent and then planed to thickness, tongued and grooved, glue jointed, sanded to final dimension and then stored in a kiln at 38 °C (100 °F) for two weeks. It is then cut to shape, shrunk in an oven at 66 °C (150 °F) for up to three hours, which slightly bows the board, before gluing on the ribs which are pressed into position with lance-wood 'go-bars' (186 B). The bridges of quarter sawn beech are then added, and the completed soundboard is then glued to the supporting belt or inner rim composed of eight $\frac{3}{16}$ in. (5 mm)

Parana pine laminations curved in a shaped 'buck' or jig. The separate shaped outer bend or rim, which is the chief external feature of the piano, consists of six $\frac{1}{8}$ in. (3 mm) laminations veneered both sides; whilst cheeks and top are of mahogany core with $\frac{3}{32}$ in. (2 mm) obeche strapping veneers and face veneer over; bottom of three deal laminations $\frac{5}{8}$ in. (16 mm) thick; and panels in veneered chipboard for greater dimensional stability. Keyboard cover or 'fall' is composed of solid mahogany strips spindled to shape and veneered in a vacuum-dome press, whilst the stout legs and head blocks are built up of seven thick laminations double veneered. The wrest plank which receives the tuning pins is made up of three transverse and two longitudinal laminations of quarter sawn beech or Rock Maple kilned to 6 per cent. Resin glues are used throughout, and in the case of the piano illustrated overleaf, Aerolite R with CHW hardener and L48 gap-filling hardener, and Aerolite 301 with GBPX hardener. Prior to the advent of synthetic resin glues pianos for export to tropical countries were composed of solid timber elaborately screwed together.

Saw kerfing

As already mentioned this traditional method is not now used to any great extent, although it has occasional use. In practice a series of saw cuts are run down to within about $\frac{1}{8}$ in. (3 mm) of the outer face (185:1) according to the timber species, and the closer the cuts are the easier the wood will bend, with hard oak requiring a spacing of $\frac{1}{4}$ in. (6 mm) or less. There is a tendency for the bend to form a series of small flats at (A) not discernible in the white but magnified under a gloss polish, therefore highly finished surfaces should not be bent by this method. It is, however, useful for bending sheets of stiff ply or laminboard and 185:2, 3 show its application to lengths of very hard English maple moulding (A) which warped badly after they had been worked. Saw cuts were run in 185:2 down to the dotted line (A), the moulding G-cramped down to a level surface and small glued wedges inserted as 185:3. Plenty of time was allowed for the glue to harden and the straightened moulding gave no further trouble. (See also *Furniture restoration and repairs* Chapter 44 page 474).

185 Saw kerfing

184 Victorian rocking-chair in steam-bent beech

186A Setting ribs to soundboard with lancewood 'go-bars'

186B Gluing up laminated legs

186C Bonding rim to belt

186A–D *by courtesy of Challen (Piano Sales) Limited and CIBA (ARL) Limited*

25   Heat acceleration of glue sets

Whilst all types of glue set faster in warm atmospheres, thermoplastic glues, i.e. heat-melting glues such as hide glue, will soften or liquefy under pronounced heat; but thermosetting glues will cure much more rapidly either by quicker evaporation of the moisture content as in modified animal glues, or by a definite heat reaction in the case of synthetic resin glues. As this rapid acceleration of glue sets is of great importance to furniture-manufacturers seeking quick release of expensive tools, jigs and equipment, considerable research has been directed into the study of the most effective methods of applying heat without scorching the wood or disrupting its fibres, and various processes have been perfected which are now used extensively in industry for edge banding, lipping, laminating, scarfing, veneering and general assembly-work. It should be pointed out, however, that whilst the various processes are simple enough to operate, the more sophisticated methods require the initial services of skilled electricians and expert jig-makers, and as such are only applicable to production in quantity. It is, therefore, proposed to refer to them in broad outline only, and for those who require more detailed information the various pamphlets and technical bulletins issued by Pye Thermal Bonders Ltd of Cambridge, and CIBA (ARL) Ltd of Duxford, Cambridge are invaluable.

Various methods of applying heat to glue-lines are practised: (a) space heating of the surrounding air by any convenient heat source (hot-air blowers, radiant heat sources, etc.) which relies upon the conductivity of the warmed-up wood to transmit sufficient heat to cure the glue; (b) contact heating, also actively heating the wood substance either by hot cauls, steam or electrically heated platens or strip heaters (low voltage heating);* (c) radio-frequency heating, whereby the wood molecules are actively distorted and rotated, thus causing friction and inducing heat

* Low-voltage heating of glue-lines was first perfected by Aero Research Ltd (now (CIBA) ARL Ltd) in 1939, and was used extensively in the production of war-time *Mosquito* aircraft, gliders and assault craft.

according to the electrical resistance of the materials (wood and glue). Of these methods only low-voltage and radio-frequency heating require further explanation.

Low-voltage (LF) heating

This method relies upon the conductivity of the wood to transmit heat from the contact elements to the glue-line. The actual elements can be 26 gauge stainless steel or mild sheet steel tinned against corrosion, and are heated by low-voltage high- amperage currents from a suitable step-down transformer giving a range of tappings usually from 0 to 9 volts for normal work. The heat is generated by the resistance of the metal sheet to the passage of the current, and whilst stainless steel has more resistance and therefore more heat generated for a given power-supply, mild steel is cheaper and more readily obtainable. In practice, therefore, narrow elements up to 6 in. (152 mm) wide used for edge banding, etc. are generally in mild steel, whilst wider elements are made of stainless steel otherwise the amperage required to attain the degree of heat necessary to cure the glue would probably be in excess of the capacity of the transformer.

The metal sheets or 'elements', which can be either flat or curved to conform to whatever shape of jig is used, are laid in contact with the work, and it has been established in practice that various power ratings per square foot are necessary for differently shaped elements. If the length of the element is much greater than the width as in edge banding, etc. then generally speaking a power rating of about 350 W per sq. ft (929 cm²) is required to bring the element to a temperature of 100 °C (212 °F) which is sufficient to ensure a rapid set without scorching the wood. Elements which are nearly square, however, only require a power rating of around 250 W per sq. ft (929 cm²), for more heat is conserved; whilst plastic laminates which need lower pressing temperatures call for about 175 W per sq. ft (929 cm²). The voltage pressure necessary to achieve these ratings is quite low, with a 26 gauge mild steel sheet requiring 0·33 V per ft (304·8 mm) of length to reach a power rating of 250 W per sq. ft (929 cm²), whilst 63 A will be required for every 1 in. (25·4 mm) in width irrespective of the length of the strip. If, therefore, the element is 6 ft (1·828 m) long and 1 in. (25·4 mm) wide it will require 0·33 V × 6 = 1·98 V to cause 63 A of current to flow, but if the element is 6 in. (152·4 mm) wide then 63 A × 6 = 378 A are necessary to achieve the rating, but the voltage will remain the same, viz. 1·98 V. It follows, therefore, that as the amperage increases rapidly with the width of the element some means must be adopted of reducing the amount of current required, and two standard methods are used. As the voltage requirements are low the length of the element can be increased at the expense of the width, either by (a) connecting a series of narrow strips of identical width with brass plates, nuts and bolts (187:1) so that the square element now becomes a continuous ribbon, or (b) cutting slots in a square sheet alternatively from each side to form the continuous ribbon (187:2). If the latter method is adopted the ends of the cuts must be pronged as shown in 187:4 with each prong one-third of the width (w) and at an angle (A) of 90° to each other, or local hot spots will occur and the end of the strip will be much cooler. For all practical purposes method (a) is better, but whichever is used the strips must be identical in width, and cable connections, brass plates, bolts, etc. clean and firmly seated. Measurement of the effective temperature in any part of the continuous strip can be made with a thermo-couple; whilst paints and crayons which change colour when the temperature reaches certain values are obtainable.

Jigs and platens for LF heating

Narrow strip elements can be laid directly against the veneer or laminate in edge banding, etc. but some softening is often necessary to absorb inequalities. If a strip of old bag press rubber is available this can be placed either between the element and the veneer or against the pressure member, with a piece of thin mill-board asbestos to conserve the heat. Figure 187:3 shows a typical disposition. Continuous strip elements (187:1, 2) in panel form cannot be laid directly against the veneer as there are gaps

between the strips, and in order to spread the pressure a sheet of 20 gauge aluminium is often used with an interleaving of $\frac{1}{16}$ in. (1·5 mm) laminated plastic to insulate the strips. The elements can be attached to the wooden pressure former with again a thin layer of asbestos to conserve the heat, and a softening pad if necessary (187:5). Platens or jigs can be made of plywood or blockboard on a rigid softwood foundation, and shaped to fit for curved work. Pressure must be positive and of the order of 50 lb per sq. in. (3·515 Kgf/cm²), for inadequate pressures will allow thick glue-lines to form which will boil under heat, forming an air-filled froth which will eventually collapse. Raising the pressure naturally raises the boiling-point of the glue, and if 50 lb per sq. in. (3·515 Kgf/cm²) cannot be attained then the amount of heat will have to be reduced well below the boiling-point of the glue at the particular pressure applied, with consequent longer pressing times. With the working temperature of the element within the range 100 °C (212 °F) to 110 °C (230 °F), which is well below the scorching temperature of the wood, a normal synthetic resin glue will set in about 30 seconds plus the time taken for the heat to travel from the element to the glue-line. A general rule for this heat transfer is 1 min. per mm of thickness separating the element from the furthest glue-line up to a total of 6 mm and $1\frac{1}{2}$ min. per mm for thicknesses up to 12 mm, therefore a built-up lamination 12 mm thick with core veneers 2 mm thick and face veneer 1 mm thick will take $11 \times 1\frac{1}{2} = 16\frac{1}{2}$ min., plus the actual setting time of the glue. For thicknesses over 12 mm it is better to place elements on either side of the lamination, in which case the time is calculated for only half the thickness. In constructional work where there is a considerable thickness of timber in the joint it may only be necessary to cure the glue part way into the joint before it is removed from the jig or press, and to allow residual heat to set the remainder, always providing no great stresses are involved otherwise the joint will spring. Care must be taken in the choice of glue for all low-voltage heating, for a very fast-working glue may have a tendency to precure before the pressure has built up sufficiently, particularly with hand-operated screw presses or jigs, and in case of doubt the advice of the manufacturers should be sought.

Although low-voltage installations are inexpensive and very economical in power they are, as already mentioned, more applicable to quantity production, for individual elements will have to be made up for each particular platen or jig, calling for the services of both jig-maker and electrician; but a heated platen for a standard single daylight screw-operated veneer-press can easily be made which will give all the advantages of a hot press for flat veneering in a small workshop. Another technique is the incorporation of a length of resistance or *Eureka* wire in a tongued and grooved joint during assembly, which when coupled to a step-down transformer will heat the glue sufficiently for the cramps to be withdrawn within a few minutes; the ends of the wire are

187 Glue-line heating

261

then snipped off with the length embedded in the joint unnoticeable. The voltage requirements will depend upon both the thickness and the length of the wire, and must either be calculated by a competent electrician or arrived at by trial and error. Mention should also be made of flexible heating mats after the style of electric blankets which run from standard voltages and do not require transformers, but as the wiring elements are very thin they will not stand rough usage, nor can the mats themselves be cut to shape.

Radio frequency (RF) heating

In this process a suitable generator of say 3 kW capacity will take 6 kW AC current from the mains, and transform it into very high frequencies which when transmitted to the work via suitable platens or electrodes will excite the molecules of the material which is being glued, distorting them and causing them to rotate, and thereby causing friction and inducing heat. The amount of heat generated depends upon the electrical properties of the material, and the poorer its insulating properties the more heat will be generated. Thus the actual glue itself, which must be of the heat reactive (synthetic resin) type, is purposely made more conductive than the wood (which is a good insulator and, therefore, a poor conductor) and will absorb more energy and, therefore, generate more heat.

Three basic methods of applying RF heating to a glue-line are practised: (a) through or transverse heating; (b) glue-line heating; (c) stray field heating. In 'through' heating metal platens are applied on either side of the work (187:7), and the whole mass of wood is heated in order that the glue-line itself can reach the required temperature for a rapid set. This method is generally adopted for laminated bowed doors, etc. in either plywood or constructional veneers, where pressure can be applied on either side by male and female formers which have been lined with non-ferrous metals (copper, brass, aluminium, etc.) to form platens which act as electrodes for the high-frequency voltages to pass through the total thickness of the laminates, dependent of course on the power of the generator and the rapidity of the set required. As with low-voltage heating pressure must be positive and high enough that the glue-lines will not

foam, otherwise lower temperatures and consequent longer setting times must be tolerated. With 'glue-line' heating (187:8) the electrodes are placed on either side of the glue-line, thus allowing most of the energy to be concentrated in the glue itself and ensuring a faster setting time for the same power, but in practice the glue-line must not be more than about 3 in. wide, therefore the technique is confined to butt joints, lippings, etc. On the other hand 'stray field' heating (187:9) is usually adopted when neither 'through' heating nor 'glue-line' heating are feasible, and in all cases where it is physically impossible to place the electrodes on either side of the glue-line. The main disadvantage of this method is the longer setting time required, for there is no heating directly under the electrodes but only in the field between the electrodes, therefore the heat generated within the field must be given time to penetrate to the glue. The greater the thickness of material and, therefore, the greater the required heat penetration the greater the distance there must be between the electrodes, nevertheless faster sets than most other methods can be obtained, and in complicated assemblies all three techniques can be adopted through the same jig (187:6).

Whilst the operation of RF heating does not call for electronic skill a thorough knowledge of the basic working principles is called for, and as the equipment itself (generator, co-axial cable, etc.) is relatively expensive to install only high outputs in quantity production will justify the cost, moreover the generator must be as close to the jig and, therefore, to the method of pressing as possible. Portable outfits for spot setting of small areas of glue are available but their application is fairly limited, for instance in spot tacking veneers in position before pressing. Where large outputs are called for, however, RF heating is probably the cheapest and most efficient process in the long run.

Figure 188A depicts a 12 kW dielectric RF generator for continuous operation; 188B is a RF carcase press with a small mitred corner open carcase being pressed and cured; 188C is an LV heating unit comprising step-down transformer and leads, mild steel heating strip and asbestos strip for softening; 188D is a stray field platen in which the electrodes are placed at an angle of 45°, thus the RF field extends over the full area of the platen and can be used for sub-assemblies, fixing tops, etc. The platen is covered with silicone bonded glass-cloth to yield a smooth surface, and mounted on a $2\frac{3}{8}$ in. (60 mm) insulating ply base with a plastic shield base for the electrodes.

188A   12 kW dielectric RF generator

188B   RF carcase press

188C   LV heating unit

188D   RF stray field platen

188A–D *by courtesy of Pye Thermal Bonders Limited*

189 Radio-frequency pressing of chair members at the factory of Tecta Furniture Limited

191 Bonding wood blocks to timber laminate in radio-frequency jig to form dining-chair backs for SS *Queen Elizabeth 2*

190 Completed stacking chair designed by Clive Latimer for Tecta Furniture Limited

192 Chair back showing wood blocks bonded in position

189–192 by courtesy of CIBA (ARL) Limited

26 Table lining

Hitherto a separate craft, the lining-in of inset leather or baize surfaces to table- and desk-tops was usually passed over to small specialist firms who also gold blocked the borders. The actual laying of the leather, etc. is now often done by the furniture-maker, with any gold border blocked in by a specialist. It should be pointed out in this connection that most leathers are now heavily dressed with synthetic resin lacquers during finishing which may or may not take the leaf or foil, and this should be established before laying.

Inset leather-tops are laid against a shoulder and flush with the surface (they can be very fractionally below but never above). The shoulder was originally formed by gluing on strips of saw-cut veneer, but as ply tops are now usual a raised lipping is used instead (193:1). Two methods of laying are practised: (*a*) the leather is cut oversize and laid from the centre outwards, using a felt-faced pad to smooth out the air pockets. The shoulders are then scored in with the back of a knife or the thumb-nail and the leather cut against a metal straight-edge. This method is very quick in the hands of an experienced worker who will often only score with the nail and trim off the surplus by eye alone. (*b*) The inset surface is carefully measured, or if not truly square a stiff paper template is fitted and used as a pattern. The actual leather panel is then cut fractionally full in size, say $\frac{1}{8}$ in. (3 mm) over the length and the width of an average desk-top. Actual laying requires two pairs of hands, one to locate one end of the sheet in the exact position, the other to hold the other end of the sheet and gently lower it into place. It is then smoothed out from the centre, the edges tucked in tight against the shoulders and any surplus width gently eased away back towards the centre. This method is slower but has more chance of a neat finish if table lining is only occasionally done. If any edge tends to fly leaving a slight gap it can be pulled back into position, and held with fine steel dressmaking pins until the glue has set.

Gluing the groundwork

Hide glue, shoemakers' paste, dextrin, casein and *Cascamite One Shot* glue can be used for laying leather, leathercloths and baizes, whilst Seccotine is useful for edges. Animal and paste glues call for very quick working, whilst if the surface is a large one it may be necessary to glue and lay half the sheet at a time. If the groundwork is

193 Table lining

aborbent it should be sized with weak hide glue, whilst casein and resin glues should be fairly thin and allowed to air dry until they have begun to tack before laying. Particular care must be taken to dust the work thoroughly with a stiff brush before spreading the glue which must be free from lumps or gritty particles, and to work the glue well into the shoulders of the inset. If air bubbles cannot be smoothed out before the glue finally tacks off prick the bubbles with a needle and cover with a padded weight. Where the leather has to be worked over and round the edges (193:2) glue and lay up to the edges, glue the edges and coax the leather over, stretching it gently and evenly and temporarily securing it with fine pins. Rounded edges tend to puff or belly out, and the edges should be repeatedly smoothed over with the thumb. A flexible leather will probably flow over well-rounded corners, but sharp edges are always difficult and the leather will have to be cut. Figure 193:3 shows the most satisfactory method with the cut at

an angle and not on the edge of the corner; whilst 193:4 illustrates a neat method of finishing off underneath, using a hardwood strip which is glued in after the leather has been fixed and allowed to dry. Leather can be worked round acute bends if it is first dampened, but the grain texture is lost and the colour may be affected, therefore it should be avoided if possible.

PVC leathercloths are laid in exactly the same way, but they must be cut to size if method (b) above is adopted as there is not the same measure of elasticity, whilst rounded corners will have to be tailored. Baize is also laid in similar fashion but certain precautions must be taken; there must be no surplus glue and pressure must be very gentle or the glue will soak through, leaving hard white patches which cannot be eradicated. Cheap quality cloths may also shrink back considerably as they dry, and a preliminary test should be made to determine the extent, if any, of the shrinkage.

Part 4   Basic constructions
27   Carcase constructions

General note

The construction of any large carcase must provide for possible distortion or 'ricking', either under the weight of its own members or by applied forces, pushing, pulling, lifting, upending, etc., or by setting on an uneven foundation such as sloping floors. The effect of any such distortion may not be detectable visually, nevertheless doors will bind, drawers jam and connecting joints may fail, therefore overall stiffness and squareness under all normal conditions are essential. Assuming an open-faced rectangular box with top, bottom, two sides and fixed back, any force applied, no matter from what direction, will endeavour to twist the faces of the box, including the open face which will tend to take on a diamond shape (194:1) with the corner angles greater or less than true right angles. If, however, one side of the box is so anchored that it cannot twist then all the other sides will be prevented from twisting and the opening will remain square (194:2), whilst if the opening itself is so stiffened with cross-bracing that the diagonals are preserved then the sides also will be prevented from twisting (194:3). Obviously, this latter method is not practicable in open carcase-work, therefore other methods must be adopted.

Methods of stiffening carcases

Openings can be stiffened by applied side pilasters (194:4) and central pilasters (194:5), but the top and bottom members must be stiff also and the connecting joints as strong as possible. Other methods include pilaster attached to a stiff apron (194:6), L frame (194:7), U frame (194:8), inverted U (194:9), T frame (194:10), I frame (194:11) and H frame (194:12). Methods of increasing the stiffness of flat panels include increasing the thickness (194:13), sandwich panel (194:14), closed box (194:15), cross-ribs reinforcement (194:16), double cross-rib (194:17), and pyramid bracing (194:18). Carcases can also be stiffened by arbitrary fixed cross-rails or shelves or divisions, which in effect either adopt an 'H' or 'I' formation and break up the carcase into smaller boxes, with increased timber thickness relative to the opening. This method is often adopted in open bookcases with loose shelves, where one or more shelves are housed and glued into the sides to increase the stiffness, but such carcases will still rick fractionally if stood on an uneven surface no matter how robust the timber sections are, for increasing the wood dimensions also increases the overall weight, therefore some form of pilaster, stiff apron rail or box plinth is preferable. The principles of deflection and the appropriate methods of combating them are examined in detail in the *Design Manual for Cabinet Furniture* published by the Furniture Development Council.

Carcase constructions

Carcases built up of solid timber throughout must have the grain directions continuous, with the side grains vertical and the top and bottom grains parallel to the leading edges, so that all the shrinkage across the width of the boards is from back to front as indicated by the arrows (195:1). If the grain of the sides were horizontal, and the top and bottom from front to back as 195:2, then a moment's reflection would show that any pronounced shrinkage across the width of the boards would lower the carcase top, close in the sides and jam the doors or drawers, moreover such cross-grain timber would have little bearing strength. Horizontal- or cross-grain effects can be achieved with plywood constructions where there is little if any shrinkage and approximately equal stiffness in either direction, but such effects should be an integral part of the design or they will appear unnatural from the viewpoint of custom and usage. Solid timber carcases which are to be face veneered will have the groundwork as 195:1 and the veneers laid the same way of the grain, but veneered ply

assemblies must have the grains crossed for a balanced construction. Thus the ply ground must be cut to show its grain horizontal as 195:2; which is a point sometimes overlooked in setting out large carcase cheeks. This crossing of the grain in veneered work will mean that the inner cores of laminboard will be upright, which is usually needed for jointing purposes.

Solid timber and plywoods etc. must not be mixed indiscriminately in carcase-work. For instance, solid cheeks and plywood tops, bottoms and fixed shelves would have different shrinkage values, so also would plywood cheeks and solid tops, bottoms, etc. There is, however, no objection to using relatively narrow bearer rails in solid timber to plywood cheeks or vice versa, as the shrinkage will be negligible. In

planning any carcase construction, therefore, a moment's thought as to the probable direction and effect of the normal shrinkage of each part will usually suggest a satisfactory compromise. Framed-up (panelled) carcase sides can be treated as plywood, for here again shrinkage values are usually too small to cause trouble. Carcase backs which are now usually ply or laminboard can have the grain running in either direction, although if the back is visible it is customary to set the grain upright as this is the direction of growth. Vertical-grain veneers in carcase sides, doors and panels should also preserve this feeling of upward growth, with any heaviness in the figure at the base. The exception is in drawer fronts where the grain runs horizontal, for setting the grain upright can give the illusion of structural weakness.* In all carcase work it should be remembered that whilst a well-fitted carcase back, grooved, screwed or glued in position will help to achieve overall stiffness and squareness, it will not automatically ensure such rigidity.

196 Method of correcting warped carcase top by bowing in opposite direction under cramping pressure (see page 280)

195 Carcase shrinkage

Constructional methods

Methods of constructing orthodox carcases with separate tops planted on after assembly are shown in 197. Figure 197:1 shows the usual form of carcase dovetailing for a solid under top, 197:2 front and back bearer rail, 197:3 single

* This rule can be broken if it suits the design and provided there is no shrinkage in the length of the drawer front.

dovetails screwed for extra strength, and 197:4 a solid top part dovetailed and part screwed. Where the carcase cheeks are connected by rails only the intervening spaces must be filled with *Kickers* shown by the dotted lines in 197:2A, which are pinned and glued to the carcase cheeks to prevent the drawer sides kicking up between the rails as the drawer is withdrawn. Figure 197:5 shows the junction of a bearer rail with square post and grooved-in cheek or panelled frame, 197:6 a drawer rail stub tenoned in, and the drawer runner tongued to the front rail and housed into the cheeks. If the carcase cheeks are solid timber then the runners can be glued to the front rail but must be free to slide in the housing as the shrinkage direction differs, therefore they must be fitted dry and secured at the back with a screw working in an open slot. Figure 197:7 is the usual stopped housing joint for shelves which is usually sufficient if the joint is tight, but dovetail or taper dovetail housings can be used if the carcase cheeks have to be pulled in. Figure 197:8 shows the carcase base dovetailed as in the top (197:1). A simple assembly for framed carcases often employed in production-work is to glue and screw a fillet to the top side framing rail and screw the top frame to this, cutting it round the front post as 197:9, 10. Under tops, fixed shelves, rails and carcase bases must be inset by the thickness of the back, and it is as well to form the groove or rebate for these before setting out the carcase joints. The treatment of carcase backs is described in Chapter 28. In all the above constructions usual timber dimensions are $\frac{3}{4}$ in. (19 mm) finish solid cheeks or (18 mm) or (19 mm) ply veneered both sides, under tops and bases $\frac{5}{8}$ in. (16 mm) or $\frac{3}{4}$ in. (19 mm) thick, bearer rails $\frac{5}{8}$ in. (16 mm) or $\frac{3}{4}$ in (19 mm), dependent on the span and the distributed loading, carcase backs $\frac{1}{4}$ in. (6 mm) or $\frac{3}{8}$ in. (9·5 mm) ply or $\frac{5}{8}$ in. (16 mm) laminboard, according to the required stiffness and size of carcase.

Quantity produced furniture in the medium price range often uses $\frac{5}{8}$ in. (16 mm) or $\frac{3}{4}$ in. (19 mm) chipboard or $\frac{5}{16}$ in. (8 mm) or $\frac{7}{16}$ in. (11 mm) ply suitably stiffened with inside frameworks. The aim should be to use the minimum thickness of material consonant with overall stiffness and rigidity, not only for delicacy of treatment but also to cut down weight. Very large carcases are often split vertically into two separate carcases coupled together after erection, and the maker should always check well in advance that stairways, lifts and door openings are wide enough for the passage of large furniture. There is a growing practice to fit small free-running castors to heavy pieces, wardrobes, etc. and this is a sound move.

Other forms of construction are shown in 198. In 198:1 the panelled wardrobe or cupboard construction has side frames dovetailed to the top and bottom rails, and a front pilaster planted on and either tongued and grooved as shown in the inset, or glue blocked on the inside with a small bead or vee groove at the junction with the side frames. In the chest construction (198:2) the pilasters are dispensed with; there are no middle rails to the side frames and the single ply panel is further stiffened by the drawer runners planted on. Figure 198:3 shows the junction of a top bearer rail with a post and frame construction, whilst in 198:4 the side frames are rebated for a ply sheet to yield a flush surface. This method, together with 198:5 in which the ply is press glued over the whole framework and the edges rounded over, is often used in whitewood furniture for subsequent painting. Figure 199:1 is a pedestal desk construction. The meeting of the drawer rail (199:1A) with cheeks flush with the leg posts on the inside is shown at 199:2A, and with cheeks flush with the outside at 199:3. Figure 199:4 is the junction of the base (B) stub tenoned into the post and rebated and screwed into the cheek, as carcase dovetailing cannot be used owing to the different direction of entry. Top kickers (199:1C) will be necessary, also drawer guides as shown in the dotted lines (199:3) if the cheeks are not flush with the posts on the inside; they are merely cut in and pinned and glued to the drawer runners. Figure 199:5 is a knee-hole type desk with suspended drawer units or pedestals. The drawer bases are stub tenoned into the legs, rebated and screwed to the cheeks (199:4) and carcase dovetailed into the inner cheeks. A front apron rail in lieu of centre drawer (which is an inconvenient place for drawer as the sitter has to move back every time it is fully opened) is either tongued, slot dovetailed or dowelled and glue blocked on the inside. In cheap work this rail is often pocket screwed to the cheeks and then

1

C

2

A

A

3

4

B

5

6

7

8

A

9   10

glue blocked, or if the pedestals are to be detachable, fitted with locating dowels glued into the apron rail and dry fitted to the cheeks with a stout block glued to the apron rail and screwed through. The junction of two pedestals can be further strengthened with a centre bearer rail if necessary, and the top is fixed by screwing up through the top rails, pocket screwing through the apron rail, pocket screwing the back if stout enough or screwing up through blocks glued to the back. Figure 199:6, 7 shows the top in position, moulded or square edged. Figure 199:8 shows a similar type of carcase but with the flush top and sides jointed by any of the methods shown in 200:1–12. The inner cheeks are either dovetail housed to the top (199:9) or plain housed and glue blocked (199:10), with the drawer unit bases lap dovetailed to outer and inner cheeks. The legs are made up as a separate unit with stiffening rail at the back (A) and screwed to the carcase. If the continuous backs shown in the diagrams are thin ply only they should be reinforced with a lower stiffening rail lap dovetailed to the inner cheeks.

Flush-top carcases

Where the tops are an integral part of the carcases and not planted on as separate members some form of interlocking joint must be used. Figure 200:1 shows a secret mitre dovetail top, and 200:2 secret lap dovetail, both suitable for solid timber or laminboard but not for ply or chipboard. Figure 200:3 shows the through dovetail and 200:4 finger or box lock joint suitable for solid timber only, 200:5 mitre and tongue for all forms, 200:6 tongue and lap, and 200:7 tongue and mitre for solid timber or laminboard. Figure 200:8 is the double tongue for all forms except in solid timber where opposing shrinkage directions would break the joint. Oversailing tops in any material can be jointed as in 200:9, dowelled, housed (200:10), and tongued (200:11), whilst 200:12 is suitable for inset tops. In theory, these latter joints might not appear strong enough, but in practice and providing they are a tight fit they are quite sufficient for the usual run of carcase furniture, for glue is a wonderful jointing medium where it is allowed to work properly, i.e. of good quality, correctly applied, thick enough to avoid starvation or excessive penetration, but not so thick that in the inevitable contraction as it sets or cures the glue-line cracks or fractures. Mitre tongued, housed and tongued and grooved joints in solid work can be stopped short of the front edge or allowed to run through and the front edge lipped in the normal manner as for ply, etc. Veneer lippings are not recommended as the joints will shadow through in time. Solid lipping on chipboard or long-grain laminboard edges need not be tongued, but plywood lippings should be tongued and grooved.

Fixing tops, plinths, etc.

Planted tops in solid timber liable to shrink across the width are fixed by gluing and screwing to the front rail (201:13) and slot screwing at the back. The centres can be held down by wood buttons (201:15A), or alternatively the centres can be glue blocked and the front and rear slot screwed, but excessive shrinkage might show at the front if the top oversails the rail to a marginal extent only. Prefabricated timber tops can be glued and screwed direct for the shrinkage is negligible. Loose plinths are pocket screwed as 201:14, and (A) shows the tilt to the fixing screws, or they can be secured with metal shrinkage plates (201:16). Table-tops can be fixed with wood buttons (203) free sliding in grooves (201:15A), with the thickness of the buttons slightly less than the depth below the top and the groove, so that the top is pulled down tight as the buttons are screwed on. Metal shrinkage plates can also be used (201:16), and (A) shows the flat variety which are cut in flush on the rail top, and (B) the angled form planted on. Two slots are usually provided to each plate, and the screws must be placed so that the top is free to slide across the width (201:16).

Plywood web reinforcements

A method of strengthening light framing joints in carcase-work extensively employed in kitchen cabinet and whitewood furniture-making is shown in 202. This consists of $\frac{5}{32}$ in. (4 mm) or $\frac{1}{4}$ in. (6 mm) plywood webs glued and nailed as illustrated. Figure 202:1 is applicable to chairwork also, and is used instead of corner brackets, often with two webs to each corner for greater

200 Flush-top carcases

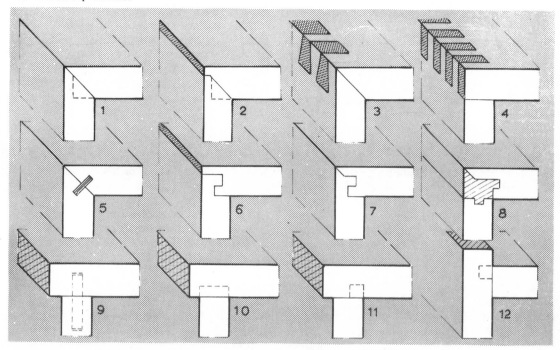

201 Fixing tops, plinths, etc.

holding power, for the webs are only glued in the grooves, but this method is not recommended for quality work. Figures 202:2, 3 are carcase-work examples.

Dust boards

These were a refinement fitted between drawers in carcase-work to protect the drawer contents from falling dust or displaced articles. They are not now fitted to any extent and were only used in the highest quality work. They can be solid, i.e. housed in shelves which act as drawer rails, runners and dust boards, or of panelled construction with the front drawer rail and runners grooved for a thin ply sheet which was pushed in from the back, and held in position by a stiffening back rail tongued into the runner grooves. Alternatively, they can be made up as a complete frame with ply panels and front and back drawer rails stub tenoned and runners housed into the cheeks. Muntins should be provided for wide carcases which can also act as supports for upright divisions between the rails. A cheaper compromise often seen in Victorian furniture was to glue up the carcase with grooved front rails and runners, and push in a thin ply sheet which was left unsupported at the back, but unless the ply is very stout it is bound to sag in time and even foul the lower drawer.

Chipboard carcase construction

Much of quantity produced furniture is now composed of veneered chipboard because of its cheapness, dimensional stability and proved reliability. However, the absence of long-grain fibres does necessitate different jointing procedures, for although tenons and dovetails can be used they are structurally weak, and in any case the random chip structure does ensure that there is no end grain and no excessive glue penetration, therefore plain glued joints with or without tongues or stub dowels for location purposes are effective at whatever angle the boards are cut. Knock-down fittings also provide excellent methods of attachment and have been developed primarily for this material.

Jointing methods

Plain butt joints can be glued straight from the saw if cleanly cut, whilst loose tongues in matched grooves are useful for location to ensure flush surfaces. These tongues add little to the strength of the joint and should be kept relatively small, with a $\frac{5}{32}$ in. (4 mm) thickness by $\frac{3}{4}$ in. (19 mm) in width a fair average. Solid lippings can be glued on direct without tongueing, but if tongues are used they should not be greater than $\frac{1}{4}$ in. (6 mm) wide by $\frac{1}{4}$ in. (6 mm) deep. Veneer lippings are satisfactory and can be double if the chips are coarse and liable to shadow through. The drawings in 204 show the simplest form of construction for a chipboard carcase (204:1), and whilst it is not suggested that it is anything approaching ideal it should be structurally sound enough for small carcases. Joints used are stopped housing joint (204:2), bareface tongue with groove at least $\frac{1}{2}$ in. (12·5 mm) from edge of top (204:3), locating stub dowels with plain glued butt joint (204:4), rebated joint leaving at least $\frac{1}{4}$ in. (6 mm) of substance in the rebated cheek (204:5), plain mitre joint glue blocked on the inside (204:6), veneer lipping (204:7), solid lipping without tongue (204:8), and solid tongued lipping (204:9). Hide glue should only be used for veneering or assembly if approved by the manufacturers of the chipboard concerned, and it is

202 Plywood web reinforcements

more usual to use resin glues throughout, breaking through the glazed surface skin of unveneered boards with a light sanding for increased adhesion.

Carcase assembly with knock-down fittings

KU and KD fittings are described in Chapter 35, page 365, and 205:1–4 shows a typical chipboard wardrobe construction employing these fittings. At the moment of writing only cupboards, wardrobes, simple carcases and chairs are dealt with in this manner, but future developments will no doubt provide for their application in a wide range of carcase-work once customer resistance to the implied (but often mistaken) suggestion of impermanence has been overcome. In practice, these fittings provide rigid fixtures; whilst any looseness which might develop in use can always be corrected with a screwdriver. They can be used for solid timber carcase-work, and

in fact table shrinkage plates, table brace plates and detachable leg fittings are knock-down fittings in the true sense, but the usual run of KD carcase fittings call for dimensionally stable materials.

Carcase assembly

Final assembly of the various component parts is the culmination of many hours patient work and should never be hurried. A preliminary knock up in the dry state can be made but only to establish the direction of entry and the exactness of the fit. Dowelled components can be tried with spare dowel-pegs sanded slack (tight dowels should never be used as the suction in a tight hole can hold them immovable), and there can be no objection to fully seating tenons in order to check the shoulders, but dovetails only fit once and should not be entered beyond the half-way mark. If parts of the carcase can be glued, assembled and set aside to dry well before-hand

205 Knock-down carcase in chipboard

so much the better, but the squareness must be carefully checked, and if rails or fixed shelving are first glued to the carcase cheeks both carcase top and bottom should be partially entered to act as spacers. All joints should be clearly marked and readily distinguishable, tenons in chalk or soft pencil on the face of the rail, mortises also numbered on the face, cheeks marked in bold chalk lettering 'left' and 'right', 'top' and 'base', and other parts according to their location. These precautions might seem needless in straight-forward assemblies, but all tenons look alike when covered with glue, and carcase cheeks have a habit of transposing themselves. A stout hammer and striking-block, mallet, damp rag and pointed stick for cleaning out surplus glue should be ready, also a long rule for checking opening or the spread of legs, long try-square, squaring-rod for the diagonals and a pair of winding-sticks. Before the glue is mixed sufficient cramps should be assembled, tail slides set to the approximate position and G-cramps likewise, with wood cross-bearers and softening pads for the cramps within reach. If hide glue is used then the component parts must be warmed slightly, but resin glues will set at ordinary room temperatures, giving plenty of time for methodical assembly. Dowelled constructions can have the pegs glued into one side, checked for length and the tops chamfered for easy entry.

Most old craftsmen only kissed the joints with glue, a dab on each tenon and perhaps a wipe across the shoulders, a brushful across the end of dovetails which were then smeared across the pin section, a trickle of glue run into the housings. This was deliberate as it saved time applying and time in cleaning up, but the joints did fit and the glue was fairly thick; but with modern glues of low viscosity there is always a danger of starved joints if only a minimum of glue is used and the wood absorbent or the cramping pressure too great. Moreover, there is no comparison between this day and age and 60 years ago, for furniture must now withstand the ravages of central heating, therefore every part should be glued thoroughly and the surplus wiped off with clean damp rags. If the surfaces are delicate then a wash coat of white shellac or cellulose can be applied up to but not over the glue-line to protect the surface, and a stick of chalk rubbed across the extreme edge of meeting joints will prevent a dark glue-line showing on pale timbers, syca-more, holly, cherry, etc. The actual assembly should be done on a firm and level foundation and the work supported so that it does not sag under the weight of the cramps. Immediately assembly is completed it should be checked and rechecked for levelness and squareness. Openings should be checked with wood try-square (206:1A) and set-square (206:1B), carcases with the squaring-rod (206:2). If the diagonals show a difference of say $\frac{1}{8}$ in. (3 mm) (206:3) then the carcase will be $\frac{1}{16}$ in. (1·5 mm) out of square which could be counted as negligible in a medium or large carcase, but greater disparities should be corrected by tilting the cramps (206:4A, 5A). Flat frames, drawers, etc. should be laid on a level foundation and checked for winding, and if the wind cannot be corrected by tilting the cramps then the high corner should be weighted down, packing up the other corner if necessary to force the wind in the opposite direction. If the carcase has to be cramped across the middle of the width, particularly with fixed shelvings in tight housings, stout cross-bearers across the cheeks from front to back should be packed out with a pad of news-paper (206:6) to apply the pressure where it is most needed. If a cheek or top tends to bow inwards it can sometimes be corrected by forcing it to the other extreme as in 206:7 (the distortion shown in 206:4, 6 and 7 is exaggerated for illustration purposes). A close watch should be kept that heavy cramps or cramping pressure do not bow the timber; if so it should be packed up or the pressure eased a little. After checking from every angle the completed work should be left undisturbed until the glue has set, but heavy cramps should not be left in position longer than necessary or the carcase will tend to sag under the weight.

A photograph of a typically shoddy construction is shown in 207. This is a corner of a plan chest extensively supplied to centres of higher education, and whilst the method of construction with $2\frac{1}{2}$ in. (63 mm) by $\frac{13}{16}$ in. (20 mm) stiles, rails and bearers, etc. might be considered reasonable for a chest in the particular price range it is ruined by careless workmanship. Figure 207A is a screwed slot tenon loose in its socket, 207B an open slot tenon screwed from inside which is too big for its groove and has split the stile, 207C is a missing dovetail pin with the corresponding socket filled

with glue, and 207D the groove for the ply bottom running through the pin. No intermediate bearers were fixed across the carcase-tops and bottoms, and the thin ply back is merely pinned and glued to fillets screwed to the framed-up cheeks. The complete chest 4 ft (1·22 m) wide is made up of three separate drawer units of which the one shown is the middle section, and in addition to the faults mentioned none of the screws used throughout the construction were tight in their holes, whilst some could be lifted out with a finger nail. Every chest in the batch of a dozen delivered exhibited identical or equivalent faults and all should have been condemned by a competent factory inspector. Whatever faults the Victorians had (and they could be unbelievably shoddy at times) it was usually the materials and rarely the workmanship which was at fault. Today the materials are uniformly sound and there can be no excuse whatever, even on a cost basis, for such slipshod work as shown in the photograph.

207 Carcase construction showing faulty workmanship

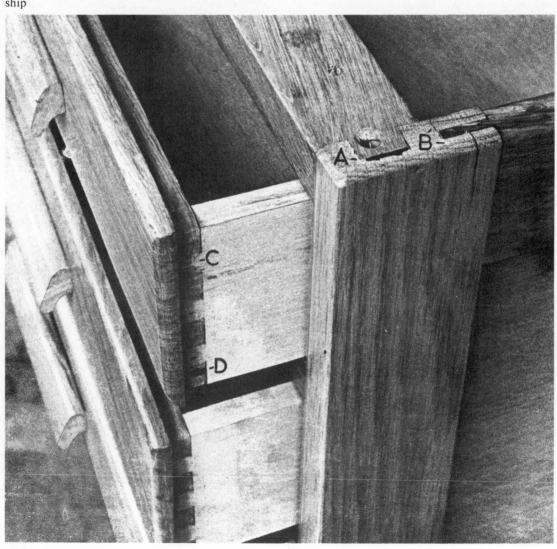

28 Carcase backs

Carcase backs should perform three functions; (1) closing in the opening; (2) adding stiffness and rigidity to the carcase; (3) increasing the back weight, thus reducing any tendency for tall carcases to topple forward when the doors are opened. The thickness of the back and the method of construction will, therefore, depend on the degree of rigidity and the amount of extra weight required, and there is much to be said for the traditional framed-up panelled back, both from the utilitarian and aesthetic standpoints, particularly if solid cedar is used for its permanent moth-repellent properties. Sheet backs of stiff ply or laminboard are normal and satisfactory, but thin ply or hardboard are only used in the cheapest work. An additional advantage of the stout back is its ability to pull a carcase square if for any reason cramping pressure has distorted it.

The usual form of panelled back is shown in 208:1, 2 whilst 208:3 is the flush back of ply or laminboard, etc. Backs for pedestal tables and desks can be in individual units (208:4), or taken across the carcase width in a single sheet (208:6) with a bearer rail dovetailed, dowelled or tenoned between the pedestals to support the lower edge. Figure 208:5 shows the construction of the framed back (208:2) with extra wide top

rail cut to fit the shaped top; the stiles and rails are normally from 2 in. (50 mm) to 3 in. (75 mm) wide and $\frac{5}{8}$ in. (16 mm) finished thickness according to the size of carcase. Panels can be $\frac{3}{16}$ in. (5 mm) or $\frac{1}{4}$ in. (6 mm) ply, or $\frac{5}{16}$ in. (8 mm) or $\frac{3}{8}$ in. (9·5 mm) solid timber mulleted to fit the grooves. Haunching of the tenons is optional, and the framing can be dowelled together instead of the orthodox mortises and tenons. In all cases the carcase base is set back to allow the framing to pass over (208:5A). Backs for planted tops are shown in 208:7, with the top bearer rail set in and the stiles rebated into the cheeks or tongued and grooved as in 208:9. The long edges of the stiles are beaded as shown. Where the top is mitre or double lap dovetailed or tongued and grooved to the cheeks and there is no supporting bearer rail for the top of the framing, the rebate can run through (208:8A), but if the top is not mitred (208:8B) then the rebate must be stopped, or a $\frac{1}{2}$ in. (12·5 mm) by $\frac{3}{4}$ in. (19 mm) fixing fillet screwed to the underside of the top to form the rebate. Tongued and grooved backs (208:9) are usually rebated into the top, and fixing screws into the rebate are not objectionable if mounted in brass sockets, but the back can be pocket screwed from the inside if preferred. As mentioned

208 Carcase backs, details

before the carcase base is setback (208:5A).

Types of solid sheet back are shown in 208:11, 12. Veneered carcases to stand against a wall are not usually lipped on the back edges, but if lippings are provided they must be carefully set out. Figure 208:13A is a bad placing of the opposing grooves in which the small section between the tongues (x) will be lost in the machining unless the lippings are glued on before the side grooves are worked, and even then there will be little strength. Figure 208:13B shows the ideal, but if narrow lippings are essential they can be offset as in 208:13C and the lippings applied before working the side grooves.

29 Plinths and cornices

Plinths

Plinths in traditional work were always project-ing as distinct from recessed, the term itself meaning the lowermost square-shaped projecting part of a base or column from the Greek *phiallos*, a brick. So-called recessed plinths are a com-paratively recent development occasioned no doubt by the necessity of evolving a base which did not require precision fitting in quantity work; moreover, such plinths are not so easily dam-aged and give toe room in tall cupboards and wardrobes. In the best work both types are made separately from the carcase and fixed to the base with buttons, glue blocks, table plates or by pocket screwing. For accurate work the carcase should be made and assembled first, and the carcase base used as a setting-out board for the plinth.

Projecting plinths

The simplest form of projecting plinth is illus-trated in 209:1, 2 in which the front is plain mitred (209:2) or mitre rebated (209:3) and the corners glue blocked, with the back rail flush and lap dovetailed or tongued and grooved, or inset and housed and blocked (209:4). Cross-bearers or stiffeners where necessary are housed and blocked or slip dovetailed, and a plinth moulding or capping is glue blocked to give adequate seating for the main carcase. Corner joints can be more elaborate, i.e. secret mitre or secret lap dovetailed, lap dovetails faced with solid timber (not thin veneer which will shadow the dovetails through in time) or tongued mitres, etc., but complex joints are rarely necessary, for the plinth itself is locked to the carcase and there is no side strain unless the furniture is roughly dragged over uneven surfaces. In assembling, mould the capping piece in one length, set out the positions on the carcase base, bore screw holes for fixing, cut and glue the mitres and screw or cramp temporarily in position with scraps of paper under to prevent the surplus glue adhering. The front, sides and back rail of the actual plinth should then be assembled and glue blocked to the mitred capping mould, making sure that the projection of the latter is equal all round. When dry the temporary screws in the capping mould can be released, the plinth unit cleaned off and set aside for later assembly. If the plinth is to remain detachable then locating blocks which fit inside the capping mould are screwed to the carcase base, and the carcase will then merely rest on the plinth. Traditional bracket plinths are shown in 207:5, 6 and 7, other forms in 209:8, and the construction of shaped plinths in 209:9, 10 and 11. All these plinths can be made up of veneered ply or laminboard, etc., but solid timber is better in case of rough treatment.

Recessed plinths

These can be assembled in the same way or set out by measurement, for the position is not highly critical. Side rails can be set in say $\frac{1}{2}$ in. (12·5 mm) but the front rail $\frac{3}{4}$ in. (19 mm) or more to give adequate toe room, whilst the back rail is usually flush with the carcase. If the car-case is solid timber, fixing will have to allow for the inevitable shrinkage, either with wood buttons or metal shrinkage plates, but plywood carcases can have the plinths pocket screwed (209:13). A fairly common way of constructing these plinths in production-work is to lap dove-tail the sides (209:12), but this is done not for reasons of strength but because it is simpler to mass dovetail a set of parts than it is to mitre saw, shoot and glue block the plinth framing.

A variation often adopted in wardrobes and cupboards is to bring the carcase cheeks down to floor level and tongue an inset rail under the base (209:14). This is a modern rendering of the old method of mitreing in a flush front rail and masking the through housing of the cupboard floor with a planted moulding which was returned along the sides to stimulate an independent plinth. The former method (209:14) is eminently practical and reasonable, but the older method of planted mouldings was merely a sham and never really practicable, for the side mouldings were invariably knocked off in time.

Plinth stools are constructed as described in *Legs, underframings, stools and stands*, Chapter 30, page 297, and are made up as already described.

Cornices

Cornices are now rarely used, but were a feature in traditional work. Strictly speaking, a cornice is the top moulding of the entablature to a column which, in Classic architecture, included frieze mould, frieze (usually ornamented) and cornice mould; but the term *cornice* in furniture is usually taken to include all three.

Cornices can be applied to the carcase (210:2) or treated as a separate unit (210:3), and the latter is the better method. In 210:2 a solid frieze board is applied to the carcase head on the front and glue blocked to the carcase top, with the small part (A) mitred in as a separate piece to hide the end grain of the frieze board on the return. The mouldings are then applied to the frieze board

and returned along the sides, but if a minimum projection only is required they can be trenched into the frieze board as shown. Solid carcase cheeks may, however, present problems as the inevitable shrinkage across the width will tend to cast off the long-grain return mouldings. Doors are usually onset (closing over carcase cheeks) with this type of cornice (210:2). Figure 210:3 shows a built-up cornice framed up in the same manner as a plinth, with the cornice mould, frieze and frieze mould applied as one solid section, or as a series of independent mouldings applied to the cornice frame. Dust boards are fitted in the best work, rebated into the moulding and glued and pinned; whilst the cornice unit is positioned on the carcase top with stub dowels or locating blocks and is left detachable to allow for shrinkage in the carcase. Figure 210:4 shows a solid cornice mould mitred and glue blocked for a dust board which is screwed up or down to the carcase top.

287

30 Legs, underframings, stools and stands

Cabriole legs

Perhaps no single feature in furniture has been so widely used as the cabriole leg (*cabriole*='to bound or leap like a goat'). Present-day application is in reproduction furniture only, but the methods of working are applicable to other shapes.

Figure 211 shows the sequence of operations. The basic shape in profile is drawn on squared paper and a template prepared from hardboard or thick card. The wings of brackets (c) are not cut out of the solid leg but are applied after. If the leg has a club, bun or ball foot much of this can be turned in the lathe (211:2), the outlines then marked out on the block, the cuts (A–A) on the face made first with band- or bow-saw, the waste pieces which show the side shapes clamped or pinned back in position and the cuts (B–B) made. The leg is then shaped with spokeshave,

rasp and scraper, doing as much work to the lower portions as possible before the wings are added unless a chair-maker's vice is available. In cheap work these wings were merely glued, screwed and pelleted, but it is advisable to stagger dowel them (211:3C), and although the bottom dowel contributes little to the strength of the joint it prevents any tendency for the wing to twist. Figure 211:4 shows a leg with carved knee and due allowance must be made for the extra thickness required when cutting out the shape. Between the wars cabriole legs were quantity produced on profile lathes, but all individuality was lost and the hand-carved leg is infinitely superior. If the leg terminates in a ball and claw the rendering should not be too realistic as in many Edwardian examples, for the shape of the claws is not intrinsically beautiful.

211 Marking out cabriole leg

1   2   3   4

Traditional legs

Various other traditional leg shapes are shown in 212. Figure 212:1 is the plain turned Jacobean leg, 212:2 shows the twist, both of which were a feature of oak-work. Part of the twist (212:2) can be done on a slow-running lathe, but the normal procedure in handwork is to turn up a cylinder to contain the twist and whilst it is still in the lathe bind a piece of string tightly round it spiral fashion. A pencil is then drawn along the string and the spiral sawn down just short of its greatest depth with shallow cuts either side. The hollowing is then done with suitable gouges and rasps. A typical inverted cup leg of the Walnut period is shown in 212:3 built up of sections to save timber, with the spigot ends in the thinner sections entering suitable holes in the thicker; or alternatively side pieces can be glued on to a central shaft to form the cup, but the differing grain patterns will show. Figure 212:4 is the Flemish Scroll leg sawn out of the solid and cross veneered and 212:5 the hock leg. Both types are intrinsically weak in the grain and modern practice would prefer a laminated construction, either of three equal sections glued together with grains slightly opposed, or two sections sawn from one thickness to preserve the run of the grain and a thin central veneer with grain opposed. Figure 212:6 is a typical Hepplewhite cabriole leg in the French fashion, 212:7 an eighteenth-century mahogany leg with inlaid

213   Carving mace stand leg   *By courtesy of Eric Coop*

panel of contrasting veneer edged with a boxwood line, 217:8 shows a fluted leg and 212:9 a plain recessed leg in the Adams style. Figures 206:10, 11 are both Sheraton, the former almost contemporary in appearance, and the latter turned and reeded in the cup. These curved reeds must be carved by hand and 213 shows a similar operation to part of a mace stand made some years ago in the writer's workshops. Many of these leg patterns are still used in reproduction-work, but apart from this they can still serve as an inspiration to modern designers, for all have an intrinsic lightness and grace.

214   Tripod and pillar legs

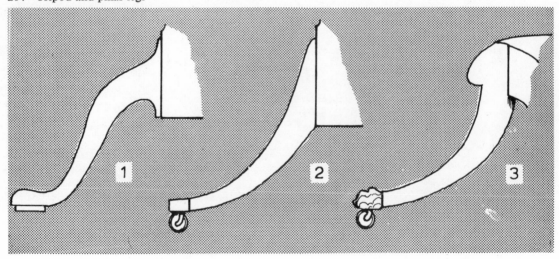

290

215 Pillar leg joints

216 Gluing up tripod leg assembly

Pedestal table or pillar legs

A typical mahogany Chippendale pillar or tripod leg is shown in 214:1; 214:2 shows a Sheraton pillar table leg and 214:3 an early nineteenth-century tripod table leg with brass lion foot castor. All these legs were used in sets of either three of four according to the heaviness and type of table.

Methods of attaching shaped legs to cylindrical pillars or shafts are illustrated in 215. Figure 215:1 is the stopped slot dovetail method with either taper or straight dovetail and shoulders scribed to fit the shaft; 215:2 is a simpler method using dowels, where the shaft is flatted to receive the leg and any chamfer or moulding round the shaft is returned across the top of the leg. The dowels should be $\frac{3}{8}$ in. (9·5 mm) or $\frac{1}{2}$ in. (12·5 mm) spiral cut or fluted to enter not less than $1\frac{1}{4}$ in. (32 mm) and 216 shows the gluing up of such a construction. An alternative method which preserves the shaft moulding intact is shown in 215:3, in which the top of the leg only is scribed to the shaft which is flatted to receive the remainder. This does away with the necessity of scribing the dovetail shoulders. As there is always a tendency for these legs to spread outward in time no matter what jointing method is adopted, all old tables have to be reinforced sooner or later with a brass or steel plate. This is usually very roughly done, for most antique dealers are only concerned to have the job done as cheaply as possible, but a good plate should be let in flush and shaped as shown in 215:4. Figure 323, of a modern version of the pillar table with the legs sculptured into the shaft, was fitted with a $\frac{1}{8}$ in. (3 mm) brass plate at the time of making.

Moulded legs

Moulded legs parallel or tapered with the mouldings stopped or running through can be worked with the spindle-moulder if suitable jigs are made up, or made entirely by hand. In the case of simple flutings these can be worked first, either with a round moulding-plane or scratch stock, and the leg tapered after; although if the fluting is very shallow it will have to be deepened slightly at the tapered end or the form will be lost. It is, therefore, better to taper first and then mould, supporting the leg in a suitable cradle

(217:1), with the leg wedged as in 217:2 so that the sides of the box are parallel to the main axis of the leg. It will also have to be packed up and 217:3 shows the method of arriving at the amount of packing required. The section of the leg top (A) and the bottom (B) are drawn out full size, also the exact shape of the moulding at the top. If lines (x) are then drawn from the extremities of the mouldings to the centre point then the intersection of these lines with the outline of (B) will yield perpendiculars to cut the arc at (C) and (D), and it is only necessary to pack the leg up at its lower end to this level (217:4). The moulding is then worked with a scratch stock as in 217:1, using suitably shaped scrapers to deepen the profile at the lower end if necessary. A typical stopped fluted leg is shown in 217:5, and 217:6–9 illustrate other leg sections with the scratch-stock cutters necessary to work them. These cutters are usually made from old saw- or scraper-blades, and can be square ended and burred over as in the standard scraper, or ground like a plane-iron and then burred which gives a cleaner cutting action. On the other hand the square-ended cutter can be rocked slightly and will cut on both the forward and backward strokes, and may prove to be the better tool with difficult timbers.

Contemporary leg treatments

Contemporary designs are usually devoid of ornamentation and almost exclusively rely on rectangular, circular or ovoid sections either tapered or straight. Figure 218:1 shows a square leg tapered both sides and 218:2 tapered on the inner face only, both with square shoulders (A) for the rails. Figure 218:3 is a curved and tapered leg after the manner of Hepplewhite and 218:4 a turned taper leg. Figure 218:5 is a typical front chair leg of square or rectangular section with rounded outer face and square inner face for the rail (A) tapering off to a circular section at the ends. Figures 218:6–11 show various leg sections commonly used, and 218:10, 11 shaped taper legs.

Rectangular section legs

These present no problems but do rely for their effect on clean, straight-grained timber, scrupulous finishing with the corners very slightly eased,

217 Moulded leg details

218 Contemporary leg designs

especially in chair-work where dead sharp corners may splinter if the grain is spiteful and catch in delicate stockings. If the rounding of the arrises is pronounced then again it should be scrupulously done, not merely dubbed off with an odd piece of abrasive paper, but an exact template of the hollow to fit the rounding made, the corner first eased off with a try-plane so that the correct foundation is laid throughout the length, then finished with any suitable tool and finally sanded, first with a long strip pulled crossways in a circular movement, and then lengthways, using a softwood block moulded to the correct profile.

Turned legs

Round legs are more easily formed in the lathe, but if none is available they can be worked by hand. The block is first planed up to octagonal shape and the arrises so formed planed with a smoothing-plane, creating further arrises which are then taken out with hollow moulding-plane, cooper's spokeshave or curved scraper. The secret of quick and accurate work—and it is only necessary to watch a skilled joiner knocking up stout oak pins for drawbore-work to appreciate how quickly it can be done—is to construct a suitable cradle to hold the wood firmly whilst it

is being shaped, and to take the cuts through from end to end every time, working the leg as a whole and not in sections. This applies equally to round taper legs which are planed square taper and then rounded. Church staves, shafts and poles usually have to be done by hand as they are too long or too whippy in the length for the average lathe, and it is always better to prepare a female template of the rounding rather than trust the eye alone. If the section varies throughout the length, i.e. the taper is a gradual swell, several templates may be necessary, and are simply prepared by arbitrarily fixing several distances along the length and boring holes of the appropriate diameters in a block of hardwood (219:1), which is offered to the work as the rounding proceeds and swivelled round to create a telltale shine on the high spots. If the shaft or leg is oval in section then the templates can be cut out of thick card (219:3) and if the shape of the wood does not permit of the template being slid along from one end then it can be hinged with a paper-fastener as in 220. Adjustable templates can be purchased, composed of thin brass strips free to slide between two rubber-cushioned locking bars (219:2). Whilst this is an admirable tool for many purposes, i.e. complex mouldings, etc. it is usually better to use a totally enclosed template for all-round shaping.

219 Templates for shaped leg, etc.

The time spent in making up these templates is never wasted, for if working by eye alone fractional thickness may be lost which will require easing out the hollow so formed over a considerable distance.

Jointing turned and shaped legs

Mortise or dowel holes in turned legs can be marked out and cut into the square section with the holes plugged with softwood before turning in the lathe, or a simple cradle can be made (222:1) to hold the finished turning. This is an open-sided box with the bottom and sides at true right angles, and the leg held in position by end screwing or nailing and wedging up in the fixed position. All boring out can then be done vertically on one face, the box turned over on its side and the other face also bored vertically to give a right-angled junction. Marking out of mortises can also be done by fixing the work between the lathe centres and using the tool rest as a guide for the pencil; or right-angled marking can be done as shown in 222:2, with a shaped block on which the mortise centres (x, x) are set out G-cramped to the leg. A method of fixing turned taper legs is shown in 221, with a stout spigot turned on the leg. The shoulders of the leg are also sunk for additional strength, and the leg is secured to the block by gluing and wedging from above, after which the block is glued and screwed to the carcase base or framing.

220   Use of card template

221   Fixing block for turned taper leg

222   Marking out joint positions in shaped legs

1

2

Timber for shaped legs

Laminated constructions are always more satis-factory for curved sections, but if solid timber is used it must be carefully chosen if it is to be strong enough to support the load. Taking the hock leg (212:5) as an extreme example, if the curve is gentle and the leg section itself suffici-ently robust there will probably be sufficient sub-stance to accommodate the shearing stresses, but if the curve is carried out too far as in the example, and straight-grained timber with grain parallel to the direction of the thrust or load is used, then the leg will be structurally very weak and liable to snap off under any sudden impact.

If it were possible to find timber with grain direction roughly conforming to the curve then there would be no difficulty, but such timbers only occur in boughwood which is not always available, therefore the grain of normal timber must be pitched to offer maximum strength where the shearing (splitting) stresses are likely to occur. Figure 223 gives three alternative grain directions for the shaped legs of a rosewood Regency-style tripod table. In 223:1 the weak points are (A–A), whilst in 223:2 the run of the grain will not take a dovetail jointing to the pillar base. Admittedly, a dowelled connection could be used but (A) is still very weak. The best

223 Grain direction in shaped leg

296

choice is therefore 223:3 to give the maximum grain length at the weak point (A).

Table and carcase stands and stools

Various forms of leg framing suitable for stands and stools are illustrated in 224. Figure 224:1 shows a typical carcase stand of four straight legs, front framing rail (224:1A), back rail (224:1B) and side rails (224:1C). Jointing up can be with mortises and tenons either mitred as 224:2A, or halved together (224:2B) which gives maximum length over half the width in each tenon. This form of construction with rails inset from the face of the legs allows the tenons to be placed in the best position, but thin flush rails necessitate barefaced tenons (224:3). As, however, there is always a tendency for this type of tenon to pull the framing out of square under cramping pressure it is advisable to provide a small inner shoulder even if it is only $\frac{1}{16}$ in. (2 mm) wide. There should also be a small shoulder at the base of the tenon so that any slackness in the length of the mortise will be hidden by the rail. All these tenons are not shown haunched, and there is no real necessity for this, for corner blocks (224:4) can usually be fitted. Figure 224:5 shows a dowelled construction which is quicker and not necessarily inferior if the dowels are of sufficient length, well fitted and their positions staggered as at (A). A composite joint with one rail tenoned and the other dowelled is shown at 224:5B which is often used in chair-work. The mortise and tenon is cut first, the rail glued in and the dowel holes then bored through the tenon. A point to watch in boring dowel sockets with screw-nose dowel-bits is to keep well clear of the outer face of the leg, and not to allow the long screw of the bit to prick through. If less than about $\frac{3}{16}$ in. (5 mm) substance is left between the bottom of the socket or mortise and the outer face the slight clearance always left for surplus glue has been known to shadow through as a faint depression even in hard oak.

Various other stand layouts are shown in 225:1–4. In 225:1 the long rails are tenoned or dowelled into the legs, and the inset cross-rails slot dovetailed with either double taper or bareface taper (225:5, 6). Figure 225:2 adopts a similar procedure, and if there is any tendency

for the stand to whip the back dovetail slots can be reinforced with stout glue blocks on the inside. Heavy stands (225:3) with one intermediate rail can have the rail double tenoned and wedged (225:7). A stool arrangement is often used for sideboards, where the long rails (225:8) are bridled through and the cross-rails either slot dovetailed or housed and glue blocked on the inside.

A curved stand is shown in 225:9 and various methods of connecting the rails in 225:13. They can be either cut from the solid or laminated, dependent on the sweep. In 225:13A dowels are used to support the weak cross grain in a pronounced sweep in solid timber, and 225:13B a bridled method. If the leg has to follow the curve and lie flush with the rails then the latter must be slightly inset and the leg rounded off after assembly. Figure 225:13C is a dovetail method and 225:13D a bridle and tenon for inset legs, whilst 225:13E shows a tenoned construction halving the tenons as shown by the dotted lines for greater length. A cross-stand for small tables is shown in 225:10, 14 and if the cross is at 90° it can be dowelled together or halved, but if the crossover is at any other angle then it must be halved as in 229:15. In 229:11 the top bearers are dovetailed as 229:16 and the long rails tenoned or dowelled in, whilst in 229:12 the rails are slot dovetailed as 229:17.

Shaped rails in leg framing

If the under edge of a rail is curved it will become a feather edge where it meets the leg if framed up in the usual manner (226:1A). Suggested treatments are shown in 226:1 for flush rails and 226:2 for inset rails. Figure 226:1 in particular has decorative possibilities and is a great favourite with handworkers. Figure 226:3 shows another treatment which is more wasteful of timber but equally effective. A typical example of this sculptured type of leg is shown in 316. Where intermediate legs occur in long rails as in long sideboards they can be bridled as in 226:4. In all cases the final shaping to the curve is eased away after the framework has been assembled. Figure 226:5 is commonly known as the 'Check' joint and 226:6 shows the treatment of a rail with inset bead lining up with the face of the leg. This detail relieves the monotony of a long straight rail joining a square-shaped leg.

226   Shaped rail details

227   Rail and leg joints

LEG

A

1
TOP

2

3

4

5

Canted leg framing

These are shown in 227:1, 2 and only require setting out to the angle as shown by the drawing, but if the legs are canted in both directions (front and side) then the rails will require a compound cut (see *Bevelled and coopered joints*, Chapter 16, page 178), although in practice an angle of a few degrees can be disregarded.

Finger joint for leg framing

Square section chair legs and arms are sometimes jointed with the finger or box lock joint 227:3. The fingers can be cut with band- or tenon-saw as described on page 200, or a series of mortises cut by machine in both members as shown in the inset, and trimmed down to the cuts.

Cabriole leg framings

Figure 227:4 shows a bottom rail tenoned into the upper post of a cabriole leg with applied wing to the leg, and 227:5 a shaped rail in an independent stand arrangement made up of separate elements (A) to save timber. Either a plinth mould (227:5) screwed to the underside of the carcase or a capping mould (A) is fitted, the latter forming a locating rebate for the loose stand.

Round leg framings

The framing up of round section legs is shown in 228:3 either dowelled or tenoned as inset, and the shoulders scribed to fit the rounding; the scribing is easier with a dowelled construction. The dowels should alternate in their length

(228:4), whilst 228:5 shows a tenoned arrangement in which a flat is formed on the leg which does away with the necessity of a scribed rail and gives the same overall appearance. Where the leg is fitted direct to the carcase and not framed up as an independent stand or stool, metal fittings can be used, either screw on or with dovetail slotted plates, and obtainable in a variety of angles for canted legs. Alternatively, a spigot end can be turned on the leg and treated as described on page 295.

Detachable table legs

Figure 228:1 shows the metal brace plate for securing legs to table-tops, etc. The rails must be securely fixed to the tops with screws and glue blocks, truly square and a tight fit against the shoulders of the legs in the fixed position. A stout screw with wood thread for the leg and metal thread for the wing nut is screwed into the leg at the correct angle and elevation (two loose nuts run on the metal screw will lock together enabling it to be turned into the wood with a spanner), and the metal plate is then notched in and screwed to the rails, the leg pushed home (A) and pulled tight with the wing nut. These brace plates can be obtained in pressed sheet steel in heavy-, medium- and light-weight sections for all types of table and stand framings, and are remarkably positive in action. For those purists who insist on handwork throughout (and Exhibition selectors of vast authority and little knowledge have been known to reject such fitting in handwork) a wooden form is shown in 228:2 which works well enough, but the metal form is preferable and can be thoroughly recommended for permanent work of the highest quality.

Stretcher rails in stands, etc.

These are used to brace or stiffen or to act as fixed distance-pieces, and the wood sections are usually kept as light as possible, necessitating skilful jointing. Figure 229:1 shows the stand in 224 with stretcher rails added for additional rigidity, where 229:1A is the front stretcher rail, 229:1B the back stretcher and 229:1C the side stretchers; whilst 229:2 is another layout with rails staggered in the height so that the joints do not clash with each other (229:13). As the wood

sections are slight, barefaced tenons are often necessary (229:8), either shouldered at the top only (229:8A), or at the top and one side (229:8B), dependent on the thickness of the timber. If a dowelled construction is used there must be room for two $\frac{1}{4}$ in. (6 mm) or $\frac{3}{8}$ in. (9 mm) dowels (229:9B), as the joint could swivel on one dowel only; but the rail could be housed or stub tenoned in 229:9A to prevent any movement with one dowel. Very slight stretcher rails can also be tenoned and pinned from underneath (229:10) or taken through and wedged (229:12).

Other arrangements are shown in 229:3–7. In 229:3 the cross-slats are stopped slot dovetailed (229:11), or they can be stub tenoned (229:10) providing there are substantial side rails (229:1C) to prevent the legs casting or splaying outwards and breaking the joints. Magazine racks composed of many slats can be stubbed and pinned into a groove (229:14A), or with dowels taken through and wedged from the outside to form a decorative feature. Diagonal stretchers are shown in 229:4 in which flats are worked on the legs and the stretchers either tenoned in 229:15A or dowelled (229:15B) with a halving joint at the centre cross cover. Figure 229:5 is a double Y in which the long stretcher is either tenoned into the short stretchers (229:16A), or the short stretchers into the long stretcher (229:16B). In 229:6 the curved stretchers can be steam bent and halved together (229:17), or laminated with three or five long strips to each stretcher, building them up to form the crossover. The curved rail in 229:7 can also be bent or laminated, with the back stretcher tenoned in between the back legs and the curved stretcher into the back of the front legs. A small flat is worked on the curved stretcher (229:18) which is glued and screwed from the back. As the two sets of tenons enter from opposing directions a trial assembly of the complete stand should be made in the dry state to determine the sequence.

Solid stands

Solid stands are used in contemporary furniture for table and cabinet stands, divan-type beds and chair sides, etc. They can be of solid core blockboard lipped on all edges with hardwood and face veneered either side (230:1), or built up of light frameworks sheeted with ply, lipped and

229 Carcase stands

303

1   2   3

veneered (230:2). Although the finished appearance would appear to be the same for both types, nevertheless there is a subtle difference, and the former is preferable for high-class work. Solid core blanks can also be built up of ply sheets glued together to make up the thickness, or more economically of flush-door blockwood blanks obtainable up to 2 in. (50 mm) thick. A double tongue and groove for the lippings will be necessary for thicknesses over 1 in. (25 mm) and the lippings can be applied either before or after the face veneering. If applied before and veneered over out to the edges they should not be more than about $\frac{3}{16}$ in. (5 mm) wide, or the junction will shadow through in time. Hollow blanks made up of light softwood framings, tenoned, dowelled or merely spiked together and sheeted with thin ply should have additional rails and muntins for stiffness, and suitably placed uprights for any structural jointing (230:3). The vacant spaces between the framing can be filled with straw-board, glass wool, corrugated or honeycomb paper or metal honeycomb to prevent any shadowing of the framing members through the thin ply due to the trapped air becoming progressively drier with consequent sinkage of the unsupported sheeting material. For cheap work without filling it is customary to bore a series of

holes through the framings as indicated by the dotted lines in 230:3, which allow trapped air to adjust itself to the external atmosphere.

Levelling leg framings, etc.

Some workers cut legs in framed-up work to dead net length before jointing, but the better method is to leave a little waste top and bottom and trim off after assembly. The legs can then be cut to length by measuring down after the tops have been flushed off, or more accurately by standing the framework upside-down on a level surface (sawbench, planer-table), checking that the rails sight through and are not in winding, and then uprighting the stand and packing up the legs until the top is level. A piece of waste wood thicker than the gap between the shortest leg and the level surface is then used as a scribing-block to mark all sides of the four legs, which are then trimmed to the marks. This method is also useful if it is required to increase the back rake or slope of a chair slightly. The front legs are packed up to give the required slope to the back, and then all four legs are scribed and cut; but the alteration must not be too great or the tilt of the front legs will be noticeable, and the backward slope of the seat too much.

31 Door-work

Framed doors

The various parts of a framed-up door, tenoned or dowelled together and with panels of ply or solid timber are shown in 231; the horns (231:1A) are left on whilst the mortises are being cut to prevent the ends splitting and also to protect the heads from damage until the doors are shot to the openings. Solid panels must not be glued in but must be free to slide in the grooves, and the edges of the corners should be lightly waxed for even a little strong resin glue squeezed out of the mortises during assembly has been known to lock a panel and split the timber; but ply panels can be glued all round and will stiffen up light frameworks. Rebated frameworks for panels beaded in from the back require long and short mortise and tenon joints, and if the panels are glass the beads should be pinned only and not glued, whilst heavy-section glass-panelled doors may require wash-leather strips in the rebates to cushion the glass. Rebates for panels can also be formed with raised *bolection* mouldings (231:5), or panel moulds (231:6) and both are glued and pinned to the framework only. Flush panels should be in ply, but *fielded* panels require solid timber, whilst raised panels are usually solid but can be in ply if the edges are lipped and the face veneers carried over the lippings, as in the cocktail cabinet illustrated in 331. Planted panels in solid timber require wood buttons screwed to the back of the panel and sliding in grooves in the framework, but planted plywood panels can be glued direct if the seating is sufficient. The thickness of all panels entering grooves should be checked before assembly with a mullet as shown in 233, worked with the same grooving-cutter as for the stiles and rails.

Setting out framed doors

The stiles are first cut full in height, and the rails the full width including the width of the stiles. Assuming that the door is rebated for a panel then the stiles are first gauged from the face edges with the width of the rebate, and on the backs with the depth of the rebate; they are then cramped together (232:1) and marked in pencil with the actual door height (A), face width of rail (AD), width of haunch (AB), width of tenon (BC) and depth of rebate (CD). They can then be separated, the mortise thickness gauged on, the mortises chopped out and the rebates worked. The haunch socket sides (232:4) can now be cut with a dovetail-saw and chiselled out, using a piece of wood equal to the thickness of the tenon and the length of the haunch as a trial template. In marking out the rails (232:2), gauge in the rebates using the same setting as for the stiles, cramp together, mark the overall door width less the width of the two stiles on the faces, and outside these mark the rebate depth to give the shoulder size on the backs. The rails can now be separated and the marks squared round with a knife, taking care to mark the short shoulder on the face (232:3) and the long shoulder on the back, after which the tenons can be sawn down, the rebates worked and then the tenon shoulders sawn in. Fitting the joint is shown in 232:4. The tenon is marked for width against the mortise, and the length of the haunch from the depth of the haunch socket. The mortise depth is also checked, and the length of the tenon is marked fractionally short to allow for surplus glue, after which the cuts can be made and the tenon tried home. If the tenon shoulders do not line up then they must be checked for squareness, also the squareness of the rail with the stile (232:5), and the overall squareness of the frame opening, using a diagonal squaring-rod or long rule. The old carpenters' trick of dry cramping a frame together and getting rid of any shoulder gaps by running a fine saw through the shoulders on either side is certainly efficacious, but hardly to be recommended in fine cabinet-work. Mortise sides which are out of square with the face (232:6) must be trued up with a chisel, badly sawn tenons corrected with a shoulder-plane and thickened up by gluing on a slip of veneer to the side (232:7). The completed joint should be a smooth, reasonably tight fit not requiring excessive cramping pressure, and should be assembled on a level surface, checking the completed frame with winding-sticks.

231 Door details (1)

A HORN	F BOTTOM RAIL
B STILE (Falling)	G MUNTIN
C STILE (Hingeing)	H TOP PANEL
D TOP RAIL	I BOTTOM PANEL
E MIDDLE RAIL	

1

A
D
B
H   H
G
C
E
I
F

2

GROOVED

REBATED

BOLECTION

FLUSH

FIELDED

RAISED

PLANTED

3

A
6"
15 cm

B
3"
7·5 cm

C
2½"
6·5 cm

D
2"
cm

1.6"
45 cm

2'.9"
83 cm

2"
6 cm

6'.6"
198 cm

5'.6"
167 cm

2½"
6·5 cm

9"
22 cm

3"
7·5 cm

4

5 BOLECTION

6 PANEL

306

Grooved and moulded frameworks

Grooved frameworks present no special features. The width of the rail tenons will be less the depth of the groove and also of the haunch which is essential to fill the groove in the stile, and the joint should be cut first and the groove worked afterwards. A typical example with fielded panels is shown in 234:1. In rebated frameworks with stuck mouldings, i.e. mouldings worked in the solid and not planted on as separate pieces the rebate is worked as before, followed by the moulding which must be to the same depth, whilst the cutting away of the moulding on the stile and the mitre junction on the rail is left to last. The mitre cuts are made with a brass or wood mitre template as in 235. (See also *Mortise and tenon joints*, Chapter 17.)

Dowelled constructions can be used for all framed doors in lieu of mortises and tenons, and

233   Mullet

adequate strength will be attained if the seating of the dowel-pegs is not less than $1\frac{1}{4}$ in. (32 mm) either side of the joint.

Muntins

Vertical divisions between the rails are known as *muntins* (vertical sash-bars in windows which fulfil

the same function are known as *mullions*). Their object when fitted is to stiffen up the panel area by dividing it into smaller sections, and also to increase the overall rigidity of the framing, but they are often used purely for visual effect. As they are distance-pieces, keeping the rails apart rather than pulling them together, they can be stub tenoned and glued into the grooves of the rails with a fine pin through the back of the rail to keep them in position, or if the frame is moulded and rebated, cut in and mitred on the face. Muntins in heavy frameworks may require tenoning in as for the rails, but the tenons should be kept as short as possible, for there is little point in weakening the rails with deep mortises. It is customary to make the width of the muntins the same as, or slightly more than, the width of the rails, but if they are moulded the width should allow for the double moulding and should show the same amount of flat (this also applies to intermediate rails). Examples of muntins occur in framed carcase backs, drawer bottoms and panelling, etc.

Framed bow doors

Framed up bow doors, either dowelled or tenoned together, in which the panels are grooved into the stiles and rails and assembled within the framework at the time of gluing up, present no difficulty; but where loose panels of either wood or glass enter from the back and are secured with loose beads the rebates in the stiles must not be radial to the curve, but parallel to the outer edge of the stile, or the panel will not enter (236:1, 2). In cramping up these doors sash-cramps across the back of the bow (236:3A–B) will pull the joints open on the face, therefore the cramping pull must follow the arc, and a stout bearer should be laid across the face for the cramps to pull on (236:3). If there is any tendency for the face cramps to flatten the bow then a cramp across the back will correct the distortion.

Fitting doors

The bottom edge should be levelled first and offered to the carcase opening, checking that the hingeing stile is square with the carcase side and correcting if necessary. The shutting stile is then offered up, shot to the opening, and lastly the

235   Mitre template

236   Bow doors: setting out and cramping up

head of the frame is levelled to fit the opening, with a final shaving from both head and shutting stile to give the necessary clearance.

Hinge positions

No precise rules can be laid down and appearances must be studied. Joinery pattern doors are usually hinged 6 in. (152 mm) down and 9 in. (228 mm) up from the bottom (231:3A), and wardrobe and cupboard doors as 231:3B, with an additional centre hinge or hinges equally spaced if the door is heavy or bowed in the length. Light cabinet doors are shown in 231:3C, D, whilst framed doors are often hinged to line up with the inner edges of the rails (231:4). It is usual to trial lay the doors in with one central screw to each hinge, and a piece of thin card under the bottom rail to give the necessary clearance; whilst steel screws should be used throughout if the wood is hard and then replaced with brass screws in the final assembly. If brass screws are used from the onset a head may easily twist off, and the whole screw will have to be bored out with a Torus reamer or fine drill. (See also *Hinges and hingeing practice*, Chapter 35, page 344.)

Flush doors

Light pattern flush surface doors for cupboards, wardrobes, etc. are usually made of ply, blockboard, laminboard or chipboard, lipped on the edges (236:2), with the lippings robust enough to support the hinge screws. Heavier doors can be made up of plywood sheets glue pressed to supporting softwood frameworks with cross-rails as 236:3. As the strength of these doors is almost entirely dependent upon the thickness and rigidity of the ply faces and the glue bond to the framework, the frame itself acts as distance-pieces only, and in theory at least can be light in section and jointed together in the simplest possible manner, i.e. tongued into the grooves (236:3), butted (236:4, 6) or stapled together (236:5). If, however, the intermediate rails are widely spaced there is always a danger that the framework will shadow through under a high polish, owing to the suction of the trapped air in the interior; and an expedient sometimes adopted is to bore holes through the bottom and all

interior rails (236:3A) to allow the air to circulate. It is, however, more satisfactory to fill the interior spaces with any convenient material, strawboard slats (236:4), horizontal softwood battens closely spaced (236:5), wood or metal honeycombing (236:6) or even softwood shaving curls placed on edge, but such doors are only economic if produced in quantity, and when the number required is small, solid cores are more practicable for all but the thickest doors. With framed skeleton doors appropriate lock rails and hingeing blocks must be incorporated.

Dustproof doors

Modern practice rarely provides for dustproof doors, although it was common practice in traditional furniture, presumably because sweeping rooms by hand raised dust whereas vacuum-cleaners are now universal. However, the technique is sometimes useful and the illustrations in 234 give representative examples. Figure 234:7 shows a door hung on centre-pin (pivot) hinges, (234:8) a rebated carcase cheek and 234:9 a grooved carcase cheek with allowance for the radius of the curve as the door swings open. Meeting doors must be bevelled slightly to prevent fouling (234:10) which further increases the gap; but the doors can be rebated together (234:11), or a parting bead glued and pinned on 234:12, whilst 234:13 shows a machined joint formerly worked by hand with special moulding-planes. The obvious disadvantage of rebated door stiles is that the right-hand door must be opened first and the left-hand door closed first, and for this reason (234:10) is now common practice.

Shaped flush doors

Curved doors either *bow* (237:1), *serpentine* (237:2), *ox bow* (230:3), etc. can be built up by traditional methods out of solid timber veneered on the face and back. The slats can be coopered (237:4) and then cleaned off to the curve, or offset (237:5), or built in sections (237:6) and shaped with stoup-plane, round Surform tool, shaped scrapers, etc. The slats need not be tongued together in 237:4, 5, and a simple cramping device is shown in 238 composed of sawn bearers with a packing piece (A) and folding

HARDBOARD

RUBBER

wedges (B) which are knocked up to cramp the sections together. Modern methods form shaped doors out of thick constructional veneers or thin sheets of ply pressed between male and female formers (237:7), or over a male former only in a vacuum-bag press (237:8). In constructing matched formers allowance must be made for the thickness of the assembly, as the radius of the curves of inner and outer faces is not identical. The former (237:10) can be constructed of soft-wood bearers accurately band-sawn to the curve and faced with hardboard, well waxed to prevent the veneers sticking. Resin glues should be used for cold pressing, or if hide glue is used then heated cauls of stout sheet zinc or hardwood must be introduced into the assembly. Hand-cramping pressure should be applied to the centre-point, working outwards to each end.

238　Cramping built-up doors

Lipping shaped doors

Solid timber will not require lippings, but veneer assemblies will need the usual form of applied lippings. In very shallow curves it may be possible to bend the lippings to the shape, first saw kerfing the tongues if they are worked in the solid; if not the lippings must be machine-moulded or formed with a portable router or scratch stock on a wide board (237:9), with each length of lipping cut off as it is worked and the sawn edge reshaped for the next. Grooves in the door will have to be worked with a suitable cutting-gauge with rounded or dowel-stubbed stock (see *Hand-tools*, Chapter 2, page 31), or with veneer or plywood assemblies it may be possible to cut and assemble the individual plies so that the groove is formed in the process. The completed assembly should be glue pressed, left under pressure for as long as possible and given time to settle before face

veneering. Any assembly which goes in winding during the settling period should be rejected, for it is never worth the trouble of trying to correct the wind, nor can the lippings, however stiff, be relied upon to pull it back to shape. As the same formers will be used for the face veneering, a centre-line should be drawn on the former (237:10A), and marked on the assembly before it is withdrawn so that it can be accurately repositioned in all subsequent operations.

Barred glass doors

Traditional barred doors are illustrated in 239:1–3 and rely for their appeal on the delicacy of their treatment. Contemporary examples sometimes apply a cut-out pattern or jointed face mouldings to a single sheet of glass with Araldite or Durofix cement, but apart from the sham element the glass cannot be replaced without sacrificing the mouldings, and in the best examples the sash-bars are composed of a face mould and a separate stiffening rib grooved in to form rebates for the glass which is beaded or puttied in (239:4, 5, 6). These face mouldings must be of the same shape and section as the moulded edge of the stiles and rails or the mitres will not meet. Various methods of jointing the ribs are practised: veneer keyed with a dovetail joint for curved sections (239:7); straight mortise and tenon (239:8); angle joint in which the third rib is forked over the other two (239:9); two curved ribs spliced together and slotted into the upright (239:10); and a simple halving joint for crossovers (239:11). The mitred junctions of the face mouldings are shown in 239:12–15.

Sash-bar assembly

Two methods are available. In the simpler the ribs are merely butted together between the framing rebates, and the joints strengthened with glued canvas in the same manner as the strength-ening of a crossover (241). The better method is to joint the ribs as already described, and stub tenon them about $\frac{1}{8}$ in. (3 mm) deep into the framing (240:1, 2). Curved ribs can be simply formed by pressing three or more thick veneers between sawn formers (240:3), and the face mouldings worked on a wide board (240:4). The mitre cuts can be made with the help of a wooden

template (240:5), with a waste piece inserted into the groove as a support. Assembly is made on a board (240:6) on which the setting out is accurately drawn. The ribs are cut, dry jointed and kept in position with blocks nailed to the baseboard, the door-frame is then placed over the assembly, the shoulders of the tenons marked and the position of the mortises in the rebates also gauged. The rib assembly can then be glued together (reinforcing with glued canvas if necessary as shown in 241), for it will spring sufficiently to enter the mortises, the door-frame is replaced on top and the mitre cuts marked, and then sawn in with a small allowance for final trimming. The rib assembly can then be glued in its final position in the frame and the face mouldings trimmed and glued to the ribs. When complete the glass panes are cut with a slight clearance all round and beaded or puttied in.

241 Glued canvas reinforcement

240   Barred door details (2)

If the finished work is to be gloss polished the face mouldings are often polished in the length before they are cut, but this calls for clean and accurate working.

Sliding flush doors (wood)

Sliding actions for light flush doors suitable for sideboards, free-standing cupboards, etc. are shown in 242. The doors are usually composed of laminboard, chipboard, etc. lipped with hardwood all round (the top and bottom lippings can sometimes be omitted in laminboard without detriment) and face veneered in the usual way. Figure 242:1 shows a two-door layout, 242:2, 3 alternative placings for three doors and 242:4 four doors; the arrows give the direction of travel. It will be noticed that in every case the doors overlap by the minimum amount necessary, usually from $\frac{3}{4}$ in. (19 mm) to 1 in. (25 mm), otherwise the openings to the cupboards are restricted; whilst the gap between the doors in the thickness is kept as fine as the type of track and the projection of whatever handles are chosen will allow. Housings about $\frac{3}{16}$ in. (5 mm) deep are also cut in the carcase sides to receive each door in its home position, but these are often omitted in cheaper work. The setting out for this type of door should be done full size, and the open and closed position of the doors carefully studied. In 242:1 the doors are equal in width, but the edge of the front door does not line up with the centre of the carcase. If the width of this door is made equal to the opening beside it then the rear door will be correspondingly larger, which will automatically restrict the cupboard opening. In practice, the unequal appearance of 242:1 in a fairly long carcase is not noticeable with fairly quiet straight-grained face veneers, but might pose problems with very ornamental veneers, and a compromise will have to be struck. Additionally, the position and projection of the handles will have to be watched also. In light free-running doors it hardly matters if the rear door is masked by the front door in the open position, for the rear door can still be moved with light pressure of the finger-tips, but the handle-grips must be unobstructed in heavy doors. Buffer stops may also have to be fitted for very heavy doors otherwise pinched fingers may result (page 318).

Sliding actions

Various sliding actions are illustrated. Figures 242:5, 6 show the standard Chasmood fibre track composed of a strip (A) and a nylon or plastic slider, two of which are mortised up into each door groove. The door tops can be held in position with lengths of fibre track or hardwood strip fed into the grooves. The rear track is fitted first, fed in with the door in position and lightly pinned up, followed by the front door. Figures 242:7, 8, 9 show an improved method (Huwil No. KOF 51) which slides more easily as it is top hung. Two forms of slider 242:7A mortise, and 242:7B face fixing, are shown, also two forms of top channel (242:8). The door bottoms are held in position by nylon studs (242:9) located in the centre of the carcase opening, and leaving a flush floor surface. Other methods are shown in 243. In 243:1 the doors are tongued to slide in grooves with sufficient extra length in the top tongue for it to be lifted up and dropped down into the bottom groove. Figure 243:2 uses hardwood strips in lieu of fibre track, (243:3) plastic or metal plates screwed on at the back of each door; (243:4) the section of another type of plastic plate rounded at the tip for easy travel. Pivot pins which are recessed into the door thickness and also slide in grooves are shown in 243:5, with 243:5A a spring type in which the pin is depressed and clicks into position and is intended as a semi-permanent fixture, and 243:5B with a projecting lug which enables the pin to be depressed, thus releasing the door from its groove. A pivot bolt which works on the same principle is shown at the top of 243:6, together with a plastic slider which rides over the base track without the necessity of mortising in the slider as in 243:6. Other uses for pivot pins and bolts are shown in 243:7 and 7A which illustrate a concertina door with pivots top and bottom sliding in grooves in the carcase, and the separate leaves linked with brass piano hinge; and in 243:8 which shows a lift-up sliding flap. An enlarged detail 243:8A shows the pivot pin mounted on the carcase cheeks, engaging in grooves in the flap. In the inset (243:8B) two pivots either side are used, preventing any side rock as the flap is raised up. The grooves for the pivots must be stopped at the top and the flaps slid in from the back of the carcase.

1

2

3

4

A ⑤

B

⑥

7

7A

8

8A

B

317

Sliding wardrobe doors

Heavy doors, or tall and narrow doors in wardrobes and cupboards are always more satisfactory if they are top hung, and typical sliding actions are illustrated in 244. Figure 244:1 is the Henderson track for doors up to 60lb (27·210 kg) weight, using steel top channel and two nylon pulleys per door screwed to the back, whilst 244:2 is the Coburn *Zip* track for doors up to 25 lb (11·330 kg) weight with nylon sliders (244:2c, D) instead of pulleys. There is no bottom channel with either type, thus preserving a flush surface for easy cleaning, and the doors are held in position by metal or nylon guides (244:1B, 2E) which are screwed to the centre of the carcase base (244:4). As there is a fair gap between the doors a buffer-stop is necessary (244:1A, 4), or pinched fingers will result. The doors can be made dustproof by fitting bevelled strips (244:3) which are glued and pinned to the leading edges, and the necessary clearance is obtained immediately a door is moved.

Sliding glass doors

The general principles are the same as for sliding wood doors. Figure 245:1, 5 show a pair of glass doors which can be either $\frac{3}{16}$ in. (5 mm) or $\frac{1}{4}$ in. (6 mm) plate, dependent on the overall size, and with all edges rounded and polished. These slide in twin channels or grooves at top and bottom of the carcase opening, either worked in the solid or with one wide groove divided by an inset hardwood strip; or various channel sections can be fitted (245:2, 3 and 4). Figure 245:2 is the standard brass channel velvet lined for easy running, as bare metal alone gives a somewhat hard and gritty action; 245:3 is a metal channel with inset plastic strip; and 245:4 a plastic or fibre channel. The last is somewhat clumsy in appearance but offers little friction. All these channels are let in flush, and in every case the top channel is approximately $\frac{3}{8}$ in. (9·5 mm) deep and the base channel $\frac{1}{4}$ in. (6 mm) deep, for assembly is effected by pushing the doors up into the top channel and letting them fall into the base. In

244 Sliding doors: wardrobes, etc.

effect, therefore, the overall height of the doors will be the exact size of the opening plus $\frac{1}{4}$ in. (6 mm) for the bottom channel, and a bare $\frac{1}{8}$ in. (3 mm) for the top. As these measurements are fairly critical it is rarely safe to order by measurement alone, moreover the carcase may not be truly square, therefore it is a wise precaution to cut sheets of ply or hardboard, test that they enter and run freely in the channels and use these as templates for the glass-merchant.

An improved sliding action for glass doors is shown in 245:5, 6 (Huwil No 62.02) which offers definite advantages. Top and bottom metal channels are provided, also a sprung U section for the bottom of the doors and a metal carriage (245:6A) with inset metal or nylon balls. As this carriage is free to travel independently it must be longer than the width of the door or the latter will tip off, and assuming a 3 ft (914 mm) wide carcase opening with two doors then the top and bottom channels will be 3 ft (914 mm) long, the U channel two lengths 18 in. (457 mm) long, and the carriage two lengths 2 ft 2 in. (660 mm) long. Here again the doors are lifted up into the deeper groove of the top channel and allowed to fall into the lower. This fitting is an improvement on the older type of carriage (245:7) in which small vulcanite wheels were used.

Handles for glass doors

Cheaper doors have oblong finger-grips of about $\frac{1}{8}$ in. (3 mm) thickness glass cemented to the plate (246:2), but undoubtedly the better method is a cut finger-grip (246:1) which is run in with a grinding-wheel. Alternatively, thin sections of wood, preferably built up of several sheets of veneer to overcome shrinkage can be glued to

the glass with Araldite cement (246:3, 4), and in the writer's experience have proved satisfactory in use, although obviously they will not stand hard knocks.

Dustproofing glass doors

As with wood doors the carcase sides should be grooved to form a dust seal, whilst the actual gap between the doors can be closed with the bristle fitting (Huwil No. M1A) as shown in 245:8, 8A. The bristle assembly clips over the edge of the glass and requires no other fixing. The impact of a free-running glass door against the sides of a carcase can be fairly considerable, and the grooves should be lined with velvet or small felt, leather or rubber buffers can be fitted to absorb the shock.

It should be stressed that as with all types of flush sliding door, if the carcase is made up of laminboard, chipboard, etc., the hardwood lippings to the edges should be wide enough to accommodate all the groovings, or the ragged core will be visible when the doors are slid open. This hardly matters if the grooves are cased in, but in any case the tongues of the lippings should be placed well away from the grooving, and care in setting out will be amply repaid.

32 Drawer-work

Various types of drawer are shown in 247. Figure 247:1 is a sectional elevation of an orthodox inset drawer sliding on front drawer rail and side runners; (247:2) an onset drawer which fits under the carcase top but over the cheek ends, with the drawer rails set back to give a flush front to the carcase; (247:3) a rebated and moulded drawer front for easy fitting and (247:4) an inset drawer with set-back front rail allowing the bottom (or top) edge of the drawer front to overhang and act as a pull. In 247:2 the front drawer rails can be dispensed with if necessary, and the drawer hung on side runners (page 324); whilst the rebated front in 247:3 requires no very accurate fitting and no drawer stops, therefore it is widely used where cheapness of production is the main consideration, as in kitchen cabinets, whitewood furniture etc. Alternative methods of construction are also given. Figure 247:5 is the orthodox lap dovetailing to the front and (247:9) through dovetailing to the back; (247:6) a slip or slot dovetail for rebated fronts with either single or double taper as shown; (247:7) a tongued front and (247:8) a star tonguing applicable to quantity production, although it could be done on a small sawbench if the setting out were very accurate. An alternative method of jointing the back with a full thickness housing into the sides is shown in 247:10 which is satisfactory if the housing is really tight, for there is no strain across the width of the drawer to pull the joint apart. Figure 247:14 is the old method of attaching the bottom, where a quadrant drawer slip is glued and pinned to the drawer side thereby increasing the wearing surface, and 247:15 a flush slip instead of quadrant which gives a neater appearance, with 247:10A the modern method of grooving into the sides. In old work the bottom was solid timber as 247:14, 15, and the drawer sides kept as fine as possible ($\frac{5}{16}$ in. (8 mm)) but modern sides are up to $\frac{1}{2}$ in. (12·5 mm) in thickness, and unless the bottom happens to be solid cedar as 247:14 for moth-proofing, plywood is invariably used which can be glued all round if necessary. Drawer fronts are usually standardised at $\frac{3}{4}$ in. (19 mm) thick; they can be thicker $\frac{7}{8}$ in. (22 mm); but should not be under $\frac{3}{4}$ in. (19 mm) for good work. In factory production the drawers are made slightly slack in the openings to save labour in fitting, which can be a costly business if individually done. There is, however, nothing to equal a well-made hand fitted drawer, for it will continue to slide like silk, giving continual satisfaction to its owner over many years. A good test is whether the act of shutting one drawer puffs out all the others in the carcase, and although this can be cured very easily by boring a few holes in the back of the carcase to relieve the air pressure, the writer has yet to meet a proud owner who would allow this to be done.

Materials for drawer-work

Drawer fronts can be solid timber which is preferable, or laminboard or ply, for both can be lap dovetailed if care be taken; chipboard is unsuitable. Drawer sides should be in hard good-wearing timber with oak the favourite, but teak and prime quality mahogany are good and agba a fair substitute if a pale timber is necessary. Soft hardwoods such as obeche, etc. should not be used, whilst common pine wears quickly (unless it is very resinous) as old examples show. Backs are usually $\frac{1}{4}$ in. (6 mm) or $\frac{5}{16}$ in. (8 mm) thick and can be in any common timber, although here again oak is used in the best work. Solid bottoms can be in English cedar or oak about $\frac{5}{16}$ in. (8 mm) thick and mulleted into the grooves as 247:14, but $\frac{5}{32}$ in. (4 mm) good-quality ply, preferably limba, oak, gaboon or birch is usual. The grain of solid bottoms must, of course, run from side to side or shrinkage will pull them out of the side grooves; they can be glued to the front groove and should override the back by about $\frac{1}{4}$ in. (6 mm) to which they are open slot screwed. The grain of ply bottoms can run either way, but custom and usage usually dictates from side to side. Wide drawers may need thicker ply, but it is

more usual to support the bottom with a centre muntin about 2 in. (50 mm) wide by $\frac{5}{8}$ in. (16 mm) thick, lap dovetailed at the front and rebated and screwed to the back (247:16).

Setting out and jointing up drawers

The drawer front is first cut roughly to size with the long edges parallel, and shot fractionally bevelled on all four edges so that it fits the opening half-way (247:11). The drawer sides, which must be of constant thickness, are also shot to the opening, fractionally sloping in the length so that they slide in half-way (247:12). This is the ideal to work for in hand-fitted work, and assumes that the worker is prepared to spend the time necessary to secure a perfect fit. The sides are then cut to length, allowing for the front dovetail lap and the necessary clearance at the back of the carcase, and the ends are shot truly square. The back is cut correspondingly narrower to allow for the ply bottom to pass under, with a set down from the top of about $\frac{3}{16}$ in. (5 mm) for clearance; the drawer front is placed on it and the length marked with a knife. The ends are then shot square, leaving the knife-marks on the wood to give just that fractional fullness in the length. All the parts are clearly marked in pencil as they are fitted, the front with face and edge marks and left and right, the back with a triangle on the outside, and each side with a quadrant (247:13). The grooving for the bottom in the front and sides is gauged in before the dovetails are set out, or part of a pin may be lost, showing an unsightly gap. Dovetails are at the discretion of the maker, very fine (1 in 8) as in the best traditional work, or the more robust 1 in 6 for modern work. Purists may insist that they should be as fine as possible, but drawers are not left open for the dovetails to be admired, and the first consideration must surely be the strength of the joint. If the front is slip dovetailed (247:6) or rebated (247:3), setting out for the carcase opening will have to be done by measurement; although with the latter it is possible to through dovetail and apply a false front after to form a rebate, but the practice is not to be recommended if it can be avoided for the false front could be thrown off in time under repeated impacts.

Assembly

Drawer dovetails should never be tried right home before assembly as they only fit once, and the worker should have enough confidence in his jointing to accept that they will fit. Some craftsmen use only a minimum of glue, thickly coating the ends of the sides and wiping them across the pins on the assumption that as the dovetails are mostly end grain there is little point in gluing every socket. However, it is better to have too much glue than too little, providing it is thin enough to be squeezed out; one drawer side is laid flat on the bench, the front and back pushed home, the other side placed in position and tapped down with a mallet using a block of wood to cushion the blows. A sash-cramp should be kept handy in case the drawer needs a nip across the width or from front to back, but it should not need much cramping, and if a cramp does have to be left on whilst the glue sets the drawer should be set on a level surface free from winding. After wiping off the excess glue with a clean wet rag (some workers give the insides a coat of polish before assembly to prevent the glue staining), the drawer is checked for squareness with a rod and left undisturbed until the glue has set and the bottom can be cut and fitted. If the drawer is fractionally out of true the bottom can be cut to pull it square, but it is rarely possible to correct a wind.

Fitting drawers

Any protruding pins are flushed off and the back of the drawer is fitted to the opening. From then on it will be a question of gently easing from back to front until the whole drawer enters sweetly. Chalk-marks along the sides and edges usually disclose high spots, and if the carcase back can be left off a torch can be shone through to show up any tightness. At this stage the bottom is in position to support the drawer, but it is not finally fixed until last, running a little glue into the front groove to hold it, and either screwing or pinning at the back, unless it is a solid bottom in which case it should be open slot screwed so that it is free to move. Drawers which run harshly can be lubricated with a candle end (not soft waxes which quickly pick up dirt), although a well-fitted drawer should run sweetly enough without the need of lubrication.

Drawer stops

Drawers must not hit against the carcase back or they may force the back off in time, quite apart from the noise of the impact. It is, therefore, usual to allow a generous clearance, say $\frac{1}{2}$ in. (12·5 mm) at the back, and fit stops to prevent the drawer entering too far. The drawing (248) gives the usual type, two of which are pinned and glued to the front rail. They can be of hardwood or ply, fractionally thinner than the set-up of the drawer bottom; the thickness of the drawer front is gauged in on the rail, the stops glued and temporarily veneer pinned in position and the drawer pushed home. If the position is not correct the stops can be tapped over, the pins hammered in flush and the glue left to set. Drawer fronts are often fractionally inset (bare $\frac{1}{32}$ in.; 1 mm) as this enhances their appearance, but if flush they should be flush and not slightly proud.

248   Drawer stop

Side-hung drawers

Drawers can be side hung by screwing 1 in. (25 mm) by $\frac{1}{4}$ in. (6 mm) fillets to the carcase cheeks and corresponding $\frac{1}{4}$ in. (6 mm) deep trenches in the sides. The principle is an old one revived; it gives fractional sweeter running for the drawers as the bearing surface is reduced, but wear on the fillets and in the housings may cause the drawers to drop and foul the fronts below. However, the method is often used, for it saves both space and time fitting drawer rails, although the carcase must be stiff enough to stand on its own without cross-ties, and in tall carcases it may be necessary to fit at least one intermediate drawer rail to hold the cheeks in. The screwed fillets should be in a hard-wearing wood and the drawer sides also, and 249:1A shows the usual

form, with a machined trench in the drawer side and the side fillet rounded to fit, which automatically becomes the drawer stop. Figure 249:2 is a hand method with the trench running through the length of the side and stopped by an extra wide pin in the front, but this method should not be used for heavy drawers unless front rail stops are also fitted or the front may be forced off in time. Figure 249:3 shows the application to a plan chest, with 249:3A a cover board screwed to the sides to prevent plans riding up over the drawer back.

Extension drawers

Metal extension slides for filing-drawers are available in a variety of supporting weights (249:4), enabling a heavily loaded drawer to be withdrawn to its full extent easily and without tipping; the larger slides include a quick-release trigger enabling the drawer to be released from the carcase channel. This outer or case channel (249:5, 6) is screwed to the carcase cheek and the inner drawer channel to the drawer side, which must be set in by the amount of clearance necessary according to the track. The slides are bought in pairs, right and left hand, and in a limited range of lengths, whilst some can be cut to suit most carcase depths. Fitting the tracks is fairly critical, for the whole of the weight is taken by the slides and the drawer sides are kept just clear of the front rails (no runners are necessary) so that there is no rub. If the carcase back can be left off it will help the positioning, and if a dummy drawer side is cut from waste wood, the drawer channel screwed to the board, the board run in and planed off on the bottom edge until it is just clear of the rail when it is slid into the case channel, it will serve as an accurate template for the final fixing. Filing-drawers are usually fitted with hanging pocket-type files, and 249:7 shows a $\frac{5}{8}$ in. (16 mm) by $\frac{1}{8}$ in. (3 mm) brass strip runner which is screwed to the front and back (or both sides according to how the files run) with brass screws and distance-collars.

Drawer positioning and depths

There are no arbitrary rules regarding the number, dimensions or positioning of drawers in carcases, although the old custom was to graduate

the depth of the drawers with the deepest drawer at the base to allow for visual foreshortening, whilst deep drawers were never placed at the top as they tend to look somewhat overbalanced. These refinements are often neglected but always worth considering for good proportionment, moreover drawers should never be too deep or they tend to hide their contents and are heavy to pull out, whilst over-wide drawers are inclined to rock as they are pushed home especially if they are a little slack in the openings. Drawers in cabinets and chests can be from 3 in. (76 mm) deep outside measurement up to say 9 in. (228 mm) deep, always remembering that a good $\frac{1}{2}$ in. (12·5 mm) is lost from the inside depth. Filing-drawer dimensions will be governed by the standard size of the file hangers used; planchest drawers should fit the standard paper sizes, allowing 3 ft 6½ in. (1·08 m) by 2 ft 6½ in. (774 mm), 2 ft 11 in. (889 mm) by 2 ft (609 mm), etc. and 3 in. (76 mm) deep, all inside measurements. In old work of very high quality both carcase and drawer backs were made fractionally wider than the fronts so that the drawers automatically tightened up as they were withdrawn, but it is doubtful whether anything is gained by working to such precision limits.

Shaped drawer fronts

Traditional shaped drawer fronts (bow, serpentine, etc.) can be cut out of the solid (250:1), built up in brick formation (250:2), or laminated from thin ply sheets or constructional veneers (250:3). Figure 250:1 is only suitable for very slight curves or the short grain will be too weak and will not support the dovetails, therefore 250:2 is better for pronounced curves, for the separate blocks can be cut, fitted and glued together to contain the shape; but the modern technique of laminating is undoubtedly the best. Figure 250:4 shows a more intricate shape which in old work was built up on a solid base (250:4A), worked with moulding-planes and richly veneered. A softish pine was used for the applied strips, and although any shrinkage across the depth of the drawer front could cast off the strips, furniture was not subjected to central-heating conditions, moreover the face veneers were thicker and any blistering not unduly evident. Here again, therefore, a laminated base is

the only satisfactory solution under modern conditions, and the same principle of applied moulded strips can be used providing the wood is amenable. Face veneering can be done either with a vacuum-bag press or by the traditional method of laying the acute curves with heated sandbags, trimming back and hammer veneering the straight sections. In old examples the veneer was either laid diagonally to counteract the shrinkage of the solid base, or soft, flexible burr veneers were used, immersed in boiling water to soften them, and then laid with very thin hide glue, repeatedly hammered down until the veneer stuck. In setting out shaped-fronts the ends must not be shot square to the bow but to the base or chord of the bow (250:5) and a convenient method is to cramp the shape to a board and use the try-square as shown, whilst a small flat is worked for the drawer sides (250:5 A). Laminated build-ups will have to be lipped on the edges or cock beads applied. With the former, the dovetail lap edges need not be lipped if the constructional veneers are fairly thick, for they will hardly show when polished.

Canted fronts

Slight cants (250:6) can be worked in the solid, but if steep then the whole front must be canted (250:7), and the dovetails set out on lines drawn parallel to the long edges of the drawer sides. Setting out the pins square to the canted front as in 250:8 would result in short grain at the points (x, x).

Cock beads

Any bead which stands proud of the surface as distinct from flush or sunk is known as a 'cock bead', but the term is usually taken to apply to small beads or edgings to drawer fronts and cupboard doors (250:9). The usual form is a raised bead (250:10A), but it can be square (250:10B). Both should be kept as fine as possible, say a bare $\frac{1}{8}$ in. (3 mm) in width for a normal drawer, and fractionally proud of the carcase edge (250:10C). The top bead usually covers the thickness of the drawer top (250:9), with the sides rebated to the pins and the bottom a similar amount, mitring the corners all round. The rebates should be worked after the drawer

COCK BEADS

251   Cock beads to drawer front

has been fitted to the opening, and whilst some workers might set the top edge down for the bead beforehand, the former method of fitting as for a plain front and then gauging in the exact thickness of the cock bead all round and rebating is more accurate (250:11). A point to watch is the provision of a wider half pin at the top (250:12) to accommodate the bead.

Drawer rails, runners, kickers and guides (252)

A typical carcase framing for a chest (2) is shown in 252:1, with (A) the top bearer rails dovetailed into the cheeks, (B) the lower drawer rail twin stub tenoned in, (C) the central division, (D) drawer runners, (E) kickers whose function it is to prevent the drawer sides kicking up as the drawer is withdrawn. In solid work the drawer runners (3D) are stub tenoned and glued into grooves in the front rail and housed to the cheeks, but the housings must not be glued, and the runners are secured by open slot screwing at the back. Ply or laminboard cheeks have the runners housed and glued with a small pin (A) driven in at an angle to hold the runner flush with the front rail. The centre division (C) has a front upright tenoned and wedged to top and bottom rails, and a long-grain division tongued in with a wide double runner (D) screwed up. An alternative method of forming the centre division is shown in 252:5, and is supported by a dovetailed hanger at the back (6F). Figure 252:9 shows another method suitable for flush-top carcases, with the division dowelled or dovetail housed to the top, housed and screwed to front rail, and drawer runner stub tenoned to front rail. Fillets for side-hung drawers are shown in 252:7, whilst in 252:8 where a framed carcase construction (252:10) is used, drawer guides (G) glued to the runners are required to pack out the carcase cheeks.

33 Fall flaps, secretaires, cylinder falls and tambours

Fall flaps

Fall flaps for writing bureaux and cabinets where it is essential to preserve an uninterrupted flush writing surface are hinged with back flap hinges, and can be rebated over the carcase cheeks as in the traditional sloping-front bureau, or inset between the cheeks which is the usual method for modern bureaux, writing fitments, cocktail cabinets in sideboards, etc. If the front is rebated (253:1) and the rebate worked along the front and down both sides (but not at the bottom), then a gap will show at the hingeing point which was usually concealed in older examples by a shaped wing-piece glued to the carcase edges as shown by the dotted line x. A better method is to stop the rebate as illustrated in the main drawing (253:1) and the inset (253:1A). Inset flaps are hinged with a rebated fall flap joint (253:2), and the inset (253:2A) shows the flap in the lowered position. An additional bearer rail is provided under the flap, hollowed to receive the swing of the fall. Alternative methods of hingeing are (253:3) pivot hinges described under *Centre and pivot hinges* (Chapter 35, page 347), with the slight gap at the end of the recessed hinge not visible in either the open or closed position, and the patented stopped pivot hinge in 253:4 which supports the flap in the open position. This is only obtainable in mild steel, and whilst it is strong enough for small flaps would require additional stays for very heavy flaps. Figure 253:5 shows a method sometimes adopted in sideboards and wall fittings, using either butt or piano hinges, but the flap falls below the level of the inner base and is unsuitable for writing surfaces unless the flap is very deep. Chapter 35, *Metal fittings and brasswork* should also be consulted for hingeing methods.

Secretaires

These provide useful writing space and storage for papers in the top drawer of a chest or cabinet (254:1). The drawer front is a simple fall flap rebated as shown (254:2) to give a flush surface, hinged with brass back flaps and supported on brass quadrant stays which are recessed into the thickness of the drawer sides. It is obvious that the design of the chest must allow for the standard writing height of 2 ft 5 in. (736 mm) or 2 ft 6 in. (762 mm). As the hinged drawer front gives no support to the drawer sides a thick bottom must be provided, lap dovetailed into the sides; although the back portion can be of lighter ply to cut down weight, grooved into the thick sides. The drawer front is held in the upright position by link plates at either end which engage in spring-loaded push-button catches recessed into the sides, both of which must be pressed simultaneously to release the front (254:3). As the drawer sides must be relatively thick the stationery divisions or 'pigeon holing' can be grooved in or built up as a separate unit. A wooden stop is fitted to the bottom of the drawer preventing it from being pulled out beyond the half-way mark, which can be , adapted from the old method of secret fixing shown in 255, in which a thin, springy lath was fixed to the drawer bottom and engaged against the front drawer rail. To release the drawer the hand was inserted under the rail and the lath pressed up. Secretaire drawers can be adapted for toilet articles, etc. in a man's dressing-chest, and some examples have a hinged mirror which lifts up and is supported at the correct angle by a simple wooden strut. Brass catches and quadrants for secretaires are still obtainable.

Cylinder falls

These are rigid falls travelling in a circular path and are more wasteful of space than a tambour front, therefore they are rarely if ever used in modern work, nevertheless the construction is worth recording. A typical example is shown in 254:4, and in designing these falls due allowance must be made for the method of assembly. In

253 Fall flap details

254:5, where the fall is approximately half the total depth of the carcase, the top containing the fall must be made up as a separate unit so that the fall can be entered from the bottom, whilst in 254:6 where the fall is less than a true quadrant entry can be from the back. In both cases the thick lock rail, which can have a moulded or recessed handle grip, is tongued to receive the cylinder fall and is glued in position after assembly. The fall itself can be constructed of laminated veneers or two sheets of thin $\frac{1}{8}$ in. (3 mm) ply pressed between sawn formers, or coopered as in 254:8. The latter method is probably more positive although difficult to make, for it will keep its shape, whereas laminated falls tend to spread a little after release from the cramps and the flattening of the curve must be established by trial and error. Face and balancing veneering can be done either between shaped cauls or formers or in a vacuum-press, or more simply by the traditional hand method with hide glue. In the best work the fall is tongued at the sides to engage in a circular groove worked in the carcase cheeks (254:7), with $\frac{3}{16}$ in. (5 mm) or $\frac{1}{4}$ in. (6 mm) falls entering the full thickness, and the lock rail can have shallow tongues or can be cut back as shown. If the fall is not grooved into the sides there is always the danger of the end rubbing and scarring the polish, for it is virtually impossible to prevent a certain amount of side play in the quadrant arms, but a curved cover fillet can be fitted on the outside to cover the rub. Methods of swivelling the fall are shown in 254:5, 6 which will have to be purpose made out of sheet brass or steel, pivoted to a screw plate and either flanged for screwing to the fall, or side screwed to a shaped block glued to the fall. Figure 254:8 shows a slotted bar movement cut from $\frac{3}{16}$ in. (4·5 mm) mild steel which pulls the writing-top forward as the fall is raised. The bar is screwed to the fall but free to rotate and slide on a centre pivot screwed to the carcase cheek and another pivot on the writing-flap, and the length of the slots which control the movement can only be established by making full-size drawings of the closed and open positions. With all these movements the stationery case must either have independent cheeks set in to allow free passage of the metal arms, or distance-pieces (254:8x, x) for the slotted bar movement. A closing fillet (y) can also be fitted to close the gap at the top. The locking rail can be fitted with a box or piano lock. Antique examples of cylinder falls show the falls coopered up out of very thin stuff, reinforced with glued canvas at the back.

Stationery cases

Often called 'pigeon holing' these are designed to hold the usual stationery sizes, and 254:9 shows typical examples. They are best made up as separate units, through dovetailed together (254:11) or rebated, glued and pinned (A), with a slight clearance for easy entry, screwed to the carcase cheeks and the gaps sealed with a cover mould (B). In fine work the main elements are either $\frac{3}{16}$ in. (5 mm) or $\frac{1}{4}$ in. (6 mm) thick, with the divisions no more than $\frac{1}{8}$ in. 3 mm) vee grooved (254:10), glued, and veneer pinned together. The vee groove can be cut with a sharp knife against a bevelled block, and the divisions polished before assembly.

255 Drawer stop

Tambours

Tambours are flexible screens composed of narrow slats of wood mounted on a silk, canvas or leathercloth backing, and running in grooves which control the travel. The system originated in France in the seventeenth century, was introduced into England in the eighteenth century, fell into disuse in the Victorian era, was popularised by the American pattern roll-top desk and has since been firmly re-established, forming as it does an admirable space-saving method of closing carcase openings. Tambours can be vertical, rising or falling (256:1, 2) or horizontal, moving from side to side (256:3, 4), and can be secured with a bird's beak, sliding door or box lock. They can be built up of solid slats, moulded, chamfered or rounded on the edges, or veneered in simulation of a solid sheet.

Vertical tambours

These can open from the top (falling, 256:5) or at the bottom (rising, 256:6) and require careful planning for there are certain pitfalls in this type as distinct from the horizontal form. If the vertical opening is tall (256:1) then a falling tambour could rattle down under its own weight immediately the lock is released, and if the carcase is shallow in depth it could partially return from the fully opened position if most of the weight is transferred to the back. On the other hand, a rising tambour requires more physical strength to lift it from a low position, and if very tall could either rattle down at the back as it opens or down at the front as it is closed. This is assuming a sweet, free-running tambour (as it should be), and methods of restraining the unwanted movement, which can be pronounced in long tambours of heavy timber, include coil springs recessed into the carcase cheeks (Wilkes Berger Engineering Co. Ltd), with the locking rail attached to nylon cords; lazy-tong springs housed at the back of the carcase to absorb the downward movement; and felt restraining pads recessed into the sides of the grooves which grip the tongues of the slats and slow down the movement. These are compromises, however, and it is usually better to avoid large and heavy tambours or to split them into two wherever possible. These objections do not apply to wide but shallow tambours fitted to roll-top desks, or small vertical tambours in writing-cabinets and wall fitments.

Horizontal tambours

These can open from one side or the other (256:7, 8), or two separate tambours can meet in the middle (256:9). They should not be too tall in relation to their width or they are inclined to judder.

Setting out

A full-size drawing must be made, and the requirements of a successful tambour is that it should have a truly square carcase with opposite ends or sides parallel, and accurately positioned grooves of constant depth to take the slats—which are always shouldered in the best work—

sweetly round the curve. Planted fillets (256:11A) to form the running groove can be used, with a tongue worked on the thick locking rail, which simplifies the installation, but it is better to work grooves in the solid (256:10A), and extra wide lippings should be provided in laminboard carcases or the core-work will show in the grooves, and the travel will not be so smooth. From 257 it will be seen that the grooves are radiused at the corners to carry the tambour round and out of sight, and slightly widened at the bends to prevent the slats jamming. This can be accurately detailed in the drawing by using a cardboard template cut to the shouldered section of the slat, and trial worked round the bend; whilst the cover fillet (257:2F) which hides the slats as they commence to open on the bend must be set to give sufficient clearance, for any rub-marks on the face of the tambour must be avoided. If the grooves are formed by planted fillets the completed tambour shutter can be placed in position and the fillets screwed on, but for grooves worked in the solid provision must be made for running the tambour in from the back (257:2, 3), and the groove is run out either as 257:1A or B. If the run out at 257:1A is adopted then it must be filled in with a shaped piece screwed on after the tambour has been installed. The locking rail, of which various forms are shown in 256:13A, B, C, prevents the tambour from passing behind the front cover fillet (257:2F), but as it is of thicker section it cannot be entered from the back and must be sprung in from the front after the tambour has been finally run in, with the flexible backing glued on or taken into the rebate and held with fine screws through a planted bead (256:13B, C). A false top or bottom for vertical tambours, or false sides (257:1D) and back (257:1E) for horizontal tambours, must be provided, not only to hide the movement but also to prevent the contents of the carcase from interfering with the travel. In all detailing it is wise to provide for withdrawal of the tambour at any future date without unduly interfering with the carcase-work, therefore the back should be fully detachable.

Working procedures

The individual slats can be $\frac{1}{4}$ in. (6 mm) wide for small delicate tambours, up to $\frac{3}{4}$ in. (19 mm)

257 Tambour details

1

A   BACK   B

C

E

C   D

$1\frac{1}{8}"$ R
28 mm

2

$1\frac{1}{8}"$ R
28 mm

C

F

3

4

5

6

A

7   A

8

336

wide for large carcases, with $\frac{1}{2}$ in. (12·5 mm) or $\frac{5}{8}$ in. (16 mm) about the usual. Thicknesses of the slats can be from $\frac{3}{16}$ in. (5 mm) for small work, up to $\frac{5}{16}$ in. (8 mm) for average shutters, with a $\frac{3}{16}$ in. (5 mm) tongue on the latter running in a $\frac{1}{8}$ in. (3 mm) or $\frac{3}{16}$ in. (5 mm) deep groove. Total overall length of the slats will be the exact opening plus the depth of the two grooves and minus a bare $\frac{1}{16}$ in. (1·5 mm) clearance, and the net length between the shoulders of the tongues pitched to give a clearance of $\frac{1}{32}$ in. (0·75 mm) either side or top and bottom, so that the slats ride in the grooves on the ends of the tongues and not on the shoulders. These tolerances may prove too tight in practice, but it is better to start with a tight tambour and ease the shoulders, for loose-running tambours are always noisy. Grooves which are sunk and not formed by planted fillets must be accurately worked to a constant depth throughout, either by plough-plane on the straight and chiselling out for the bend, or with hand or portable electric router against a suitable template, with a trial slat run off, shouldered and offered to the grooves to test the travel. This trial slat can then be used as a pattern for all the other slats which must be

accurately sawn and planed to finished dimension, with a generous allowance for rejects. Figure 257:4 shows a method of working chamfered slats by hand from a solid width, and 257:8 levelling off to thickness by cross-planing on a supporting board. When sufficient slats have been prepared they are assembled on a flat surface, sprung slats rejected, the remainder matched for colour and grain, spreading any pronounced differences over the total width and then numbering them in the exact order in which they are to be assembled. The tongued ends can now be spindled, or the slats laid out and firmly held in position with covering battens (257:5) exactly on the shoulder-lines and the shoulders cut with a fine dovetail-saw, and then planed off with a metal shoulder-plane, working to a template pinned alongside to yield a constant thickness of tongue throughout. After checking that the shoulders line up and the net shoulder length is constant throughout, the faces are sanded, the slats turned over and the backs sanded. The slats can also be polished on the face and the edges also sealed, as this will prevent surplus glue from adhering and will make the final finishing much easier. The flexible back can now be glued on,

258 Office drinks sideboard, teak framing, walnut tambour front. Top and sides covered black leather with brass inlay edging strip. *Designed by William Mitchell Des.RCA and Ernest Joyce MSIA. Made in author's workshops*

the slats firmly held by rebated battens (257:6) with folding wedges top and bottom to drive them together. This backing can be silk for delicate slats, fine linen canvas reinforced if necessary with three webbing straps spaced apart and tacked over the glued canvas, or preferably a good quality leathercloth with a closely woven twill backing. It should be long enough to cover the locking rail, and any semi-flexible glue which will not crack at the joints can be used (hide, PVA, etc.), rolling it evenly over the back of the slats and smoothing down the cloth with hand pressure. The flexible backing should be kept back from the edges (257:6A) about $\frac{3}{8}$ in. (9·5 mm) on either side. Very oily timbers, teak, rosewood, etc. may have to be degreased for increased glue adhesion, using cellulose thinners or methylated spirits and not carbon tetrachloride which is often advocated and which can be highly poisonous under certain conditions. When the glue is dry the tambour can be rolled and unrolled a few times to make it flexible, the tongued ends rubbed over with a candle end and fed into the grooves. The locking rail is then sprung in, the flexible backing temporarily fixed and the tambour tried. Only when it is sweetly running should the

backing be anchored with screws and a few dabs of glue. Locking rails can be shaped to form handle grips by running a length of moulding as 257:7A, and then cutting and rounding as shown in the sections, and can be made wide enough to accommodate a suitable lock, or the lock can be mortised into a pilaster or apron rail.

Veneered tambours

Tambours can be veneered over (256:12D), and if the slats fit tightly the effect will be that of a single sheet of veneer. Timber for the slats should be of approximate equal colour to the veneer; they are finished to dimension, cramped together faces uppermost, veneered with a single sheet or matched pattern, and then carefully knifed through from the back on a fractionally curved surface to open the joints sufficiently for the passage of the knife. Refractory veneers may need scoring on the face before cutting and the edge sanding should only take off the whiskers or the cuts will show. Backing veneers are not necessary as the flexible backing will act as balancer. In a well-fitted veneer tambour the joints should not be visible.

34 Trays

Contemporary sideboards and wardrobes (259:1, 2) often include interior trays for storage. These can have shaped fronts (259:3, 4) in which the contents are visible, or 259:5 which is suitable for cutlery, etc. Construction can be lap dovetails (259:3), through dovetails (259:4) or box lock joint (259:5), and in all cases the ply bottoms are grooved in as shown in 259:5. The trays can run on the usual type of drawer rail (259:3A), side hung on fillets screwed to the carcase cheeks (259:4B), or sliding on screwed fillets under the trays (259:4C); the latter is useful for trays which have neither shaped fronts nor handle grips as sufficient space is left between each tray for finger-grip. In all cases the trays are a fairly slack fit and slide easily. Where the carcase doors are inset as in 259:6 and hung on standard butts, a false cheek (E) must be fitted which allows the tray to clear the door as it is withdrawn. Figure 259:5 can also be used as a filing-tray for office purposes, and sizes range from $2\frac{1}{2}$ in. (63 mm) to 3 in. (76 mm) deep by 14 in. (355 mm) to 15 in. (381 mm) long and $10\frac{1}{2}$ in. (266 mm) to 12 in. (304 mm) wide, with the back, sides and front of equal thickness and about $\frac{5}{16}$ in. (8 mm) or $\frac{3}{8}$ in. (9·5 mm) thick. The ply bottoms need only be about $\frac{1}{8}$ in. (3 mm) thick.

Trays for specimens

Specimen cabinets and trays (259:7) fall into two classes; (a) those intended for reference and research purposes where the individual specimens can be removed for first-hand inspection; (b) those intended for viewing only, with airtight, dustproof and/or thief-proof protection in museums and public galleries. The latter are specialist fitments calling for precision manufacture, and 259 refers only to those normally made by furniture-makers for private collectors, or the occasional 'one off' for special display purposes. Whichever type they are, however, the trays should be close fitting as in drawer-work and interchangeable throughout.

Coin trays

These are made up in the usual manner with grooved-in ply bottoms which are velvet lined. Separate recesses for each coin are sunk with a suitable expansion bit, and a smaller hole bored through the centre to allow the finger-tip to be inserted from underneath to tip the coin out of its recess (259:8). If the recess is shallow the velvet will usually stretch sufficiently to fit the depression, with the centre hole trimmed out with a sharp knife after the glue has set. The velvet can be laid with shoemakers' paste or other suitable adhesive as described in *Table lining*, Chapter 26, page 265, taking care to use only a minimum of glue and allowing it to tack off before the velvet is smoothed down. Cabinets for precious coins are normally provided with locking doors or hinged cover fillets at each side which can be locked in position (259:13).

Entomological trays

Trays for insects, etc. should be provided with glazed dustproof covers which are made up as separate frames, veneer keyed at the corners (259:16); the inset shows the section. A rebate is worked on the tray sides (259:9), with a velvet puff or strip to form a dust seal, or both rebate and frame moulded as at 259:10. If the front and sides of the tray are of equal height a stopped rebate will be necessary at the front unless the dovetails are set out as in 259:9, commencing with a half tail instead of a pin; but the tray sides can be lowered, the dovetails set out in the usual manner (259:11), with the frame oversailing the sides as in 259:12. If the glazed frame is sunk all round as in 259:9 finger-nail grips will have to be provided as 259:14. The beds of the trays are covered with a suitable antiseptic material, prepared peat or treated cork, etc. to allow the insects to be pinned through, and the glazed frames screwed down in the rebates if necessary.

Cabinets for specimen trays are not normally fitted with individual drawer rails if the trays are shallow and numerous, and the tray sides can be

trenched for side fillets (259:4B). Tie rails may, however, be necessary at intervals of about 2 ft (609 mm) to prevent movement of the carcase cheeks in tall cabinets. Some method of stopping the individual trays from being fully withdrawn may have to be included, either as a precaution against loss, or to prevent a tray tipping out and spilling its content. If the glazed frames are screwed down in the tray rebates the stopping mechanism will have to be installed from the back, with the carcase back treated either as a hinged door or easily removable, with small bolts screwed to the tray backs working in stopped slots grooved into the running fillets. If the stopping mechanism can be fitted inside the trays then a simple brass pivot and screw plate can pass through the tray side to engage in the stopped slot (259:15). Rubber buffers may also have to be fitted to the back of the cabinet to cushion the shock of free-running trays. As already mentioned the trays should be interchangeable, calling for very careful setting out and assembly, and it is advisable to make up various jigs for cutting to length, jointing, etc. Assembly of both trays and frames can be done on a flat board, with another board screwed to it which is the exact inside dimension of the tray or frame. If the component parts are closely fitted to the inner board and the material has been accurately machined, all units should be identical.

35 Metal fittings and brasswork

Nails, screws, etc.

Apart from panel and veneer pins the furniture-maker has little use for nails except for softwood fixings, etc., but in passing it should be noted that oval wire nails have less tendency to split the wood than the round variety, nevertheless they bend more easily and the lost-head nail which is a larger version of the panel-pin is usually preferred, with the screw nail which has a twisted as distinct from a cut thread greater holding power in chipboard. Special panel-pins or nails with hardened tips are also available for hardboards as it is difficult to break the hard glazed skin of the boards with the ordinary type which often bend. Some workers give either a pushing or pulling action to the hammer-head when driving a nail (260:1), and this certainly reduces any tendency for the nail to bend under the impact of the head. In all probability this slight swing to the hammer keeps the hammer-head flat to the nail-head, whilst a direct vertical swing may tend to offer it at an angle (260:2), but this is guesswork only and may have no scientific basis. The hammer-head must be clean and kept polished on a piece of spent abrasive paper, as a pitted or dirty head will usually bend the nail.

260 Impact of hammer stroke

Wood screws

Conventional wood screws commonly used are the *Countersunk head* (261:2A), *round head* for fixing metal to wood (261:2B), and *raised head* (261:2C), obtainable in brass, steel, japanned (round head), coppered, chrome, BMA finish, etc. according to the type. The length of a screw is taken as all that part of the screw concealed by the wood, thus the length of a countersunk screw will be the overall length (261:1), round head from under the head, and raised head from the junction of the raised head with the countersinking. The diameter of all British screw-heads is twice the diameter of the shank, the angle of the countersink 45° to the central axis, and the length of the actual thread three-fifths (0·6) of the stated length. A useful formula for the determination of the stated gauge number is — diameter of head in $\frac{1}{32}$ in. − 3 = screw gauge number, thus diameter of head $\frac{13}{32}$ in. − 3 = 10 which is the gauge number. The diameter of the shank can be calculated from the gauge number by taking the known diameter of a No. 1 screw as 0·066 in. with an additional 0·014 in. for each subsequent increase in the number of the gauge—thus a No. 8 screw will be 0.066 in. (No. 1 screw) − 7(0·014) or 0·164 in. diameter. This will be the size of the hole required for a No. 8 screw shank, but as drill sizes are in $\frac{1}{64}$ in. the nearest approximate size will have to be used, and the formula commonly adopted is to add 3 to the gauge number to give the size of the drill in $\frac{1}{64}$ in. Thus No. 8 screw plus 3 = $\frac{11}{64}$ in. which is 0·172 in. in diameter. The table page 343 gives the usual British drill sizes for the shank or clearance hole, and for the hole to receive the thread.

Recessed head screws

These are available in countersunk, round head and raised head forms, and have a cross slot in lieu of the single slot which gives less tendency for the screwdriver to ride up axially as torque is applied (cam out), and therefore less danger of marring the work if the driver slips. Special shaped screwdrivers are required and advantages claimed are, more positive engagement of the driver in the slot, easier alignment of the screw and the work, particularly at difficult angles, increased speed of driving and more power. This type of screw has almost universal application in production-work with power screwdrivers for rapid assembly, but the conservative craftsman still clings faithfully to the conventional screw, and on balance the single-slot screw would appear to be more decorative, although this may well be the prejudice of ingrained habit.

As every workshop inevitably collects an assortment of odd screws over the years a useful gauge can be made by inserting a large-diameter screw in a piece of waste wood, nipping two short lengths of brass strip round the shank with

Screw No.	Clearance Hole in.	Drill Hole in.
0	$\frac{1}{16}$	$\frac{3}{64}$
1	$\frac{5}{64}$	$\frac{3}{64}$
2/3	$\frac{3}{32}$	$\frac{1}{16}$
4	$\frac{7}{64}$	$\frac{5}{64}$
5	$\frac{1}{8}$	$\frac{5}{64}$
6	$\frac{9}{64}$	$\frac{5}{64}$
7	$\frac{5}{32}$	$\frac{3}{32}$
8	$\frac{11}{64}$	$\frac{3}{32}$
9	$\frac{3}{16}$	$\frac{1}{8}$
10	$\frac{13}{64}$	$\frac{1}{8}$
11	$\frac{7}{32}$	$\frac{1}{8}$
12	$\frac{15}{64}$	$\frac{1}{8}$
14	$\frac{1}{4}$	$\frac{5}{32}$

Metric values for all the above quoted inch sizes will depend on the units ultimately adopted by the International Standards Organisation, as there are many different units quite unrelated to each other in use throughout the metric world at the present time (see *Metrication*, page 14).

panel-pins either side, and soldering on a brass cross-piece. Screws of known gauge number can then be slid between the strips, the exact position dotted with a centre-punch and the gauge number and drill sizes scratched on the brass. Figure 261:4 shows the gauge with a No. 12 screw so marked.

Screw sockets and cups

Some confusion often exists between the two types, and the writer has sometimes bought gross packets clearly labelled 'screw cups' which were in fact 'screw sockets'. The socket type 261:3A is recessed flush into the wood with a countersink bit, whilst cups (261:3B) lie on the surface and require no sinking. Both types are used for countersunk screws which may have to be withdrawn at any time, and also for neatness of finished appearance. The sockets are preferable but must be accurately fitted, and 285 shows the difference between screws carelessly placed and sunk, and those neatly fixed in sockets which are sanded off flush after the screws have been driven home.

Hinges and hingeing practice

Rapid assembly of furniture components in production-work call for face-fixing hinges, or hinges which can be sunk in circular recesses drilled or routered out instead of a hand-cut oblong recess, and many new types have been developed with this in view. These new hinges do not, however, supersede the traditional types but implement them, and for the handworker the familiar types of square or oblong, cast or extruded brass hinges remain viable.

261 Screw types, etc.

Butt hinges

Steel hinges are used in joinery and brass in furniture. The standard brass butt is shown in 262:1, with 262:1A the section of the solid drawn type, and 262:1B the cheaper pressed or folded pattern. Plastic hinges are also available, suitable for light work. The width across the plates (leaves or flaps) is governed by the overall length which is the listed size, and four ranges are usually available—*narrow suite*, *broad suite*, *strong suite* and *extra-wide broad suite*, with lengths rising in $\frac{1}{4}$ in. (6 mm) for 1 in. (24 mm) to 2 in. (50 mm) long, and in $\frac{1}{2}$ in. (12 mm) increases after. Variations of this type of hinge are, *lift-off butt* (262:4) for doors which have to be removed from time to time without disturbing the setting; *strap hinge* (262:3) for narrow sections; *loose pin hinge* also known as *ball-tipped hinge* (262:5), where it is required to throw the door clear of the carcase frame with the whole of the hinge knuckle protruding. Figure 262:6 is the *stopped hinge* opening through 90° only for box lids, etc., 262:2 is the *back flap hinge* with wide plates for table leaves and rebated fall flaps; 262:8 is the *clock case hinge* with one plate wider to allow for a projecting door (262:17), and 262:7 the *piano hinge* in continuous strip form for supporting long lengths, supplied in either drilled and countersunk or undrilled blanks. Figure 263:1 is the *rule joint* or *table hinge* with an extra wide plate to clear the hollow in a moulded rule joint, and with the knuckle on the reverse side to allow a full 90° drop (263:2).

Hingeing butts

So long as the hinges amply support the door or flap the actual positions are not critical, although appearance must be studied and reference should be made to *Door-work*, Chapter 31, page 306. The plates can be let in equally (262:9), or the total thickness of the hinge cut into either the door or the carcase (262:10), for it is the position of the knuckle which governs the throw of the hinge. If cut in as 262:9 a well-fitted door flush with the carcase edge might tend to bind on the corners, whilst with an inset door the knuckle would cut across the projection, therefore on balance the method shown in 262:10 is usually adopted, as this gives a neat finish and allows the stile to clear the carcase end immediately it begins to open. It is, however, necessary to take the strain off the screws by recessing both carcase cheek and stile, tapering the housings as shown, and a marking-gauge is first set to the total thickness at the knuckle and gauged on the face of the stile. The width of the hinge to the exact centre of the pin is then gauged on the edge of the stile and the recess cut from the full thickness at the front to the thickness of one plate at the back. The hinge is then screwed to the stile using one centre screw only, placed in position in the opening, a piece of thin card placed under the door to provide the necessary clearance, the position of the hinge marked on the carcase cheek, the gauge reset to the width of the hinge and marked accordingly, and the recess cut from nothing at the face to the thickness of one plate at the back. The door can now be tried in with another centre screw and the setting adjusted if necessary. The full complement of screws should only be used when the setting is correct, and steel screws should be used for testing, eventually replacing with brass. In very hard woods, oak, etc. it is advisable to run in steel screws throughout and then replace with brass in the final assembly, for it is very easy to scar a slot or twist off the head of a small brass screw in difficult woods. If a screw hole has to be moved fractionally a piece of match-stick inserted in the hole will usually provide sufficient bite, whilst empty cigarette-cartons are useful for packing up hinges.

As already mentioned it is the position of the knuckle which determines the throw of a hinge, and a preliminary test can be made by drawing a plan of the fixed section on cartridge paper and the moving part on tracing paper; a pin driven through the position of the hinge-pin centre will then allow the tracing to be rotated, showing the extent of the throw. Figures 262:11–15 give various knuckle positions and the angle of opening to be expected (the hinge proportions are exaggerated for illustration purposes), and 262:16 shows the various stages in cutting in and marking out. The positioning of clock-case hinges is illustrated in 262:17, where the centre of the pin must lie on the extreme edge of the moulding with the knuckle clear of the latter.

Rule joint hinge

Figure 263:2 gives the setting out for the rule

262   Hinges (1)

1

A

B

2

3

4

5

6

7

8

9

10

11

12

180°

13

120°

14
90°

15
90°

16

17

joint hinge used for fall flaps on gate-leg tables, etc. in which the countersinking is on the reverse side of the knuckle, with the pin centre placed in the centre of the quadrant describing the moulding. In practice, the pin is moved very fractionally to the right to give a slight clearance, or the mouldings will grind against each other.

Counter flap and card-table hinges

Counter flaps which lift up and over need hinges without projecting knuckles, and 263:5 shows a common type with double pin and connecting link let in flush. The same principle is applied to card-table hinges, either top face fixing (263:3) or edge fixing (263:4), both of which allow the table-leaf to move through 180°. As the hinges are handmade and vary slightly in dimension each hinge must be separately gauged for.

Centre and pivot hinges

Centre hinges either straight (262:9) or necked (262:10) have one loose plate with steel pivot pin and raised seating for clearance, and the other with socket hole for the pin. Figure 262:11 shows the necked pivot hinge in light steel strip. The name *centre hinge* is usually reserved for the original hand-wrought cast brass hinge still obtainable, but all too often of appalling quality and finish as compared with pre-war examples; whilst machine-stamped hinges with either fixed or loose plates and generally of good quality are commonly referred to as *pivot hinges*. As the action is the same throughout subsequent descriptions will refer to both types as *pivot hinges*.

264   Finding hinge position

Fixing pivot hinges

Straight pivot hinges are used where the centres lie within the wood thickness (265:1), necked or cranked hinges where it is necessary to throw the door clear of the carcase (265:5), or through an angle of 270° as in the fold-back doors for television cabinets, etc. Various applications are also shown which are self-explanatory. In fitting these hinges a working drawing should be made to determine the exact position of the pivot (265:2). It is a matter of choice which part of the hinge, pin or socket, is fitted to the door, but in practice it is easier to fix a pivot plate to the bottom of the carcase and the other pivot plate to the top of the door. All the recesses are first cut, the bottom pivot plate and socket plate screwed in position, the top socket plate screwed to the carcase, the door tipped on the bottom plate, the top pivot plate placed on its socket plate and the door head slid on and fixed. It is evident that the recess for the top door plate must be carried out to the edge of the stile to allow the hinge to be slid on (265:1). *Recesses* for *necked hinges* are cut round the hinge (265:5), whose shape usually permits a swivel entry, but it is advisable to check this before assembly, and if the hinge plate will not slide easily into the cranked recess then part of the plate should be filed away rather than cutting out the recess and leaving too little wood substance. If the gap left for the passage of a straight plate would be visible—although it is normally hidden—then the fixing procedure can be reversed or the gap filled in with a glued strip (265:1). These hinges are sold in pairs, right and left hand, and are not suitable for tall wardrobe doors which usually require a third centrally placed hinge to keep them from bowing. They can be used for fall flaps (Chapter 33, page 330) in which case the socket plates are screwed to the carcase cheeks, the pin plates placed in the sockets and the flap slid on in the horizontal position.

Miscellaneous hinges

Figure 263:8 shows a secretaire combined hinge and stay for light flaps, and 263:6 the *reversible screen hinge* which allows the separate wings of a screen to fold either way. With these the screen thickness must not be more than the distance between the knuckle centres, whilst if it is less the movement will not be affected but the wings will show a gap. An invisible hinge of the *Soss* type is shown in 263:7 and fixing positions in 266. In 266:1, 2 the hinge is centrally placed, whilst 266:3, 4 show an inset door with hinge off centre, and 263:5, 6 an onset door. These hinges are made in a range of sizes for different door thicknesses and are usually placed centrally in the door thickness, although there is some latitude as shown in 266:3, 4 and a trial assembly in waste wood may be necessary, for mortises once cut cannot be shifted as with the screw holes of a butt hinge.

New hinges

The necessity for rapid assemblies in production-work has brought about a minor revolution in hingeing techniques, and new types of hinge are continually appearing, mostly from continental sources. Some show boldly and can be featured, for the finish is usually excellent, whilst others are partially or wholly hidden. It should be borne in mind, however, that imported hinges which call for machine-drilled or routered recesses are made in metric sizes only, therefore standard inch bits and drills will not fit exactly, and the recesses will have to be enlarged by hand.

Figure 267:1 shows the *cylindrical door hinge* for secret fixing which gives a full 180° opening and only requires the boring of two holes. The main body is split and tightening the set screws exerts a tightening action within the hole. This type is not suitable for anything but light pattern doors or flaps, as any strain on the hinge can pull it bodily from the hole unless it is anchored by a

FLAP

side screw passing through the thickness of the wood. Figure 267:2 is the *Sepa invisible hinge* with seven steel pins and full 180° opening, very positive in action and an improvement on the Soss-type hinge for heavy doors, as the latter can exhibit a fractional drop when first fitted which is difficult to correct. A single-door high-quality decorative *cranked hinge* (S. Greeman & Co., No. SG 307/04) is shown in 267:3 which gives an opening of 270°, and 267:4 a decorative *lift-off hinge* (No. SG 1999/23), whilst 267:5 is a *door*

and flap hinge No. SG 3412). A pivot hinge for lay-on (onset) doors (No. SG 846) is shown in 267:6 in which a $\frac{1}{4}$ in. (6 mm) groove is cut to receive the knuckle which is flush with the face and edge of the door. This type is suitable for tall wardrobe or cupboard doors which require an additional central hinge. Figure 267:7 is the *Oni semi-mortice hinge* with either two or three leaves (267:7A, B) for single or double doors hingeing from one central division, and 267:8 the *Onyx concealed hinge*. This type can be positioned

267   New-type hinges

1

— 2 —

— 3 —

— 4 —

— 5 —

— 6 —

A

B

7

— 8 —

A

B

— 9 —

as shown at 267:8A or 267:8B, but a dummy run should be made for the position of the hinge can be varied within narrow limits, and final adjustment after assembly is made with the set screw provided. Figure 267:9 is the *Oni semi-invisible hinge* with concealed pivot point. All three types (267:7, 8 and 9) can be obtained from N. F. Ramsey & Co. Ltd, 59/61 Theobald's Road, London W.C.1., together with fixing instructions. An improved table-flap hinge is shown in 266:7 and 266:8 shows a semi-secret pivot hinge for fall flaps. Both are obtainable from Wilkes Berger Engineering Co. Ltd, 141–9 Curtain Road, London E.C.2.

Certain types of hinge require very narrow slots (268) and these can be worked by hand with the hinge-slotting tool shown in 7.

268   Hinge slots

Locks and locking actions

The Victorians fitted locks to everything, even their whisky (hence the whisky tantalus), but the modern tendency is to dispense with them wherever possible, whilst the cheap pattern single-lever pressed-steel locks often fitted to mass-produced furniture can only be regarded as catches or securing devices, for they offer little or no protection. Thus if locks must be fitted for protection they should be the best of their respective kind.

Locks are made to differ, i.e. to require different keys, by increasing the number or the position of the levers or gates which must be lifted by the key before it will shoot the dead bolt; by enlarging the diameter of the pin; and by shortening the pin socket in the key. Thus four good four-lever brass locks taken from the same dozen box and requiring different keys can often be adapted to accept one master key by rearranging the order of the levers, or by drilling out the socket in the

key to fit the different pins; and as delivery of special 'differs' or master keying can often take up to 12 months for delivery some adaption (including taking out one or more levers if they do not fit) is sometimes necessary, although not to be recommended if it can possibly be avoided. Purpose-made individual locks of beautiful workmanship can still be obtained from Bramahs Ltd, 30/1 Oldbury Place, London W.1 and although obviously much more expensive than the one- two- or four-lever brass lock with cast riveted cap are not out of proportion to the total making cost of a good piece of furniture. If maximum protection is required *Yale*-type locks with projecting cylinder nozzles can be obtained from stock which will give an infinite number of differs, with master keying up to 200 differs if required.

Types of lock

Figure 269:1 shows the *straight cupboard lock* screwed to the inner face of the door, and with a through bolt shooting right or left as required; 269:2 shows the *cut cupboard lock* which must be bought right or left hand as the case is cut into the door and the bolt can only shoot one way; 269:3 is the *mortise cupboard lock* again in right and left hand versions. The standard *cut till* or *drawer lock* is shown in 269:4, also obtainable in mortise form, whilst two- or three- way keyholes as 269:6, 8 are often obtainable in both cupboard and till locks which gives a measure of changeability. Striking plates as 269:6, 7 are standard throughout and usually bought separately, but the *box lock* (269:5) requires its own striking plate as the twin bolts shoot up and sideways to lock the lid. Figure 269:6 is the usual form of mortise-type *sliding door* or *hook lock*, again right or left handed, and also obtainable as a cut lock, whilst 269:7 is another type in which the hook dead bolt is at the back of the case and can be used in the centre edge of the outer sliding door instead of separate locks to each door. A cheap alternative often fitted to production furniture with sliding doors is the cylinder type (269:9), in which the key and barrel shown at the back of the lock are inserted into the cylinder to engage in a socket in the rear door, and turning the key releases the barrel which remains in the body of the lock. A combined *latch* and *dead bolt*

1

2

3

4

5

6

7

lock suitable for roll-top desks and known as such is shown in 269:8, whilst 270:1 is the brass *piano mortise lock*, and 270:2 the *link plate lock* for doors closing over the cupboard cheeks (A). A typical *slam* or *spring lock* and striking plate are shown in 270:4, 5 which can be closed without a key but requires unlocking to open it, whilst 270:3 is the *Bramah till lock* with projecting nozzle which forms its own escutcheon plate. The fitting of the latter requires very careful setting out, as a suitable hole for the nozzle must be bored through the face of the work exactly of the right size and in the correct position, and the setting out should be done from a cardboard template. The traditional *bird's-beak lock* beloved of the old school of craft examiners, which was used for roll-top desks, has lately been reintroduced in a streamlined form for television and radio cabinets. With this type (270:6) twin bolts shoot out either side to engage in the striking plate. Figure 270:7 shows the usual form of lock chisel for cutting in bolts, etc.

Fitting locks

The cutting in of a typical till or drawer lock is shown in 271. The dimensions of the face plate are first lightly set out and gauged on the drawer top as 271:1 and the recess cut, keeping well inside the lines in case the face plate is slightly out of square. The position of the case is then marked and sawn as 271:2, and then cut out slightly full so the body of the lock can be placed in position and the face plate checked against the setting out marks on the top edge. These are then corrected, recessed out, the lock offered up as 271:3 and the back plate scribed round to be recessed as 271:4. A slight tap on the lock will then register the position of the projecting pin, a hole is bored through to the face, and the keyhole cut from the face side with a small block in the cap recess to support the wood; the lock can then be screwed

in position as 271:5. To mark the position of the striking plate rub a little lampblack or dirty grease over the lock bolt, turn the key smartly to register the bolt position on the underside of the lock rail and then cut away for the plate. If there are many locks with striking plates to be fitted (the plate is often omitted in cheaper work) it will be worth acquiring a lock chisel (270:7). Striking plates for box locks have projecting nibs (269:5), and the plate is placed in position over the bolt, the lid shut and the marks transferred with gentle pressure. As already mentioned *Bramah* locks with their own integral escutcheon plate must be precision fitted, but the pin is dead central with the back plate whereas it is offset in most other types of lock, and this does simplify the setting out which should be done with a cardboard template.

271   Fitting till locks

Sliding door locks

Fitting is as for till locks and 272:1, 2 shows the hook lock for inset sliding doors, 272:3, 4 the back hook lock for onset doors, and 272:5, 6 a cylinder lock primarily intended for glass doors which can be adapted for use provided the cylinder is long enough for the door thickness.

Fall flap locks

Fall flaps which are inset, i.e. closing within the carcase framing can be secured with standard till or drawer locks, but lay-on or onset flaps closing over the carcase framing require either purpose-made locks (Bramah Ltd), link plate locks or special flap locks of which the *Huwil No.* 0351 shown in 273 is a typical example. This lock can be used with striking plate 273:1, 2A for both

inset or lay-on flaps, and with threaded bush and collared pin (273:3B) for lay-on flaps only. Figure 273:4 is the *Huwil No.* 0348 for inset flaps in which the bolt shoots up into a standard striking plate.

Sliding glass door locks

Methods of locking sliding glass doors are shown in 273:5, 6. Figure 273:5 is the *Huwil ratchet-bar lock No.* 06.80 for glass thickness from $\frac{5}{32}$ in. (4 mm) to $\frac{5}{16}$ in. (8 mm), and requires no drilling as the ratchet-bar assembly is thumb screwed to the leading edge of the rear glass in any convenient position. The detachable lock is slid on to this bar and prevents either door being moved. Figure 273:6 is a plan drawing of a *Huwil No.* 0087 cylinder type which passes through a hole

272 Sliding-door locks

Pedestal locking actions

drilled in the front glass and is secured with a nut and set screw; the projecting circular bolt shoots out to bear against the edge of the rear glass, thus preventing any movement of either.

Pedestal locking actions

Locking actions for pedestal drawers in which the locking of one drawer—usually at the top—automatically secures all the other drawers in the pedestal were usually effected by incorporating a spring-loaded vertical sliding bar at the rear of the carcase. Arms or pegs were fixed to the bar which engaged in slots cut in the drawer sides, and a sloping ramp cut into the top drawer side automatically raised all the pegs and thus released all the other drawers as the top drawer was partially withdrawn, whilst if the drawer was pushed fully home then a back spring attached to the bar pulled the pegs down into the

slots. The disadvantages of this older method are obvious, and improved types are shown in 274 in which the throw of the desk lock itself actuates the pegs. Both types are *Huwil* pedestal locking actions. 274:1 shows lock *No.* 0906 in which the throw of the lock rotates a cog which engages in a metal rack so that the slider with its pegs (274:3A) is forced downwards, releasing the drawers. The cylinder of the lock is mortised into the edge of the carcase side (274:2) and held in position with a pronged plate (274:1B) mortised in from the side, whilst the metal slider moves freely behind two or more metal strips (274:1A) which are recessed in and screwed to the inner carcase face. Slots are cut into the bottom of the drawer sides (274:3) and corresponding slots in the drawer rails (x) in the elevation (267:5) to accommodate the travel. The exact position and number of the pegs must be clearly detailed when ordering as there are no standard dimensions. For the small user not ordering in quantity lock *No.* 0912 (274:4) is more suitable, as the pegs are freely adjustable and can be fixed at the required distances by turning the slotted heads. This particular type of lock is mortised into the knee-hole side of the pedestal at a convenient distance under the top (274:6). Both these locks must be ordered right or left hand, and in both also the metal slider (274:1A, 4) can be recessed in flush as 274:2, or face screwed as 274:5 in which case drawer guides (Y, Y) must be fitted to fill the gap. As with all fittings of a specialist nature the unit should be designed round the fitting rather than the fitting laboriously altered to fit an arbitrary design. Other types of these locks are available, and the designer should consult the *Huwil Werk* catalogue or his usual supplier for further details.

Escutcheons (key-plates)

Constant use of a key in a lock can scar the wood surface and escutcheons are, therefore, both decorative and utilitarian. Figure 275:1 shows the usual pattern thread escutcheon split at the base and pressed into an appropriate hole in the drawer front; the slight spring offered by the split grips the wood, and the shape of the hole can be marked out by placing the escutcheon in position and smartly tapping with a hammer. Figure 275:2 is a heavier type (*Huwil No.* 9221) with a fine hole in the base for a fixing pin, 275:3 the disc plate for surface fixing with brass escutcheon pins, 275:4 the disc plate with screw-in thread, and 275:5 an oblong plate. The cheaper varieties are stamped out of sheet brass, sunk flush and glued with Araldite epoxy glue but the Huwil patterns have either pin fixings, screw-in threads or small metal tongues (275:5) which are knocked into the wood thickness. Plates can also be formed from ebony, rosewood, box, bone or ivory, etc. (275:6) cut to outline, recessed and glued, the keyhole cut and sanded off flush.

Stays

Wardrobe, flap and fall stays are shown in 276. Figure 276:1 shows the *wardrobe stay* used to limit the swing of a door or to support a fall flap, 276:2 is the *quadrant stay* and 276:3 is the *rule joint stay* also for flaps and supplied right and left handed. The latter has been almost entirely superseded by the improved *fall flap stay* (276:4) with silent nylon glide (276:4A) which can be used in either the vertical or horizontal position. A combined *pivot hinge and stay* for flaps is shown in 276:5, and a slotted version in 276:6 which lifts the flap clear of the framing rail. Both types are made in mild steel electro-brassed for greater strength. Figure 276:7 is the *radiogram lid stay* with adjustable friction movement, and 276:8 one type of *cocktail cabinet stay* which automatically lowers the flap as the lid is raised. The fixing position for this type of stay must be found by trial and error with a bradawl driven through one of the screw holes into the carcase

275 Escutcheon

cheek, and the centre plate is large enough to cover several trial holes which may be necessary before the critical centre is located. Fixing positions for quadrant, rule joint and improved fall flap stays are shown in 277:1, 2, 3. In 277:2 the flap plate is fixed at a distance from the hinge knuckle equal to half the length of the stay measured from pin to pin. The carcase plate must then be fixed on a line drawn parallel to the base as shown.

As with most other hardware items the traditional types have remained unchanged for many years, but modern production methods and the increasing use of chipboard with its reduced holding power for screws, etc. call for constant innovations. Figure 277:5 shows the *Huwil No. 3635 varioscope fall flap stay* with adjustable brake which retards the downward movement, thus there is no danger of a heavy chipboard flap tearing out the fixing screws if allowed to fall. A stay for upward flaps (277:6) is also shown (*Huwil No.* 3618), with stopping device which holds the flap either side of the horizontal according to the adjustment. A slight upward lift beyond the automatic stop releases the catch and allows the flap to be lowered. Figure 277:4 shows the *improved fall flap stay* (276:4) mounted in a horizontal position.

276 Stays

Catches

Magnetic catches with *ferrite* or *ticonal* nickel alloy magnets (the latter have greater holding power in small diameters) have a practically unlimited life with a probable strength loss of not more than 1 per cent over ten years. Figure 278:1 is the smallest type for gluing in with a pull of about $2\frac{1}{2}$ lb (1·134 kg) and suitable for very light doors and flaps, 278:2 is a stronger type with ribbed brass or nylon case and about $4\frac{1}{2}$ lb (2·041 kg) pull, and 278·3 is a face fixing type in a range of pulls from $4\frac{1}{2}$ lbs. (2·041 kg) to over 40 lb (18·143 kg) according to the size. A mortise version suitable for light doors, etc. is shown in 278:4. All these catches require intimate contact with the metal striking plate, and therefore are not suitable for bowed or warped doors which require a more positive catch to pull them in. In fitting, the magnet catch is fixed first with the striking plate placed in position on the magnet. The back of the plate is then rubbed over with chalk and the door pressed against it to register the position. To check that both magnet and plate are in perfect contact throughout a trace of oil is smeared over the magnet face, and if the oil fails to register exactly to the ends and sides of the plate it should be packed out accordingly.

Ball, bale and double ball catches are shown in 278:5, 5A and 6; the double ball type is useful for the heavier type of door or one which has bowed slightly, for the compression on each spring-loaded ball can be adjusted by the retaining screws. Single ball catches, either barrel (278:5) or plated (bales, 278:5A) can be fitted at top or

277 Flap stays fixing positions

278 Catches, bookcase fittings, etc.

1

2

3

4

5 BALL

5A BALE'S

6 DOUBLE

7

8

9

10

A

B

C

A

361

bottom or on the side, and either to the door or to the carcase framing, although with striking plate (278:5) and ball on the door the edge of the carcase will be crushed with the passage of the ball, but the lip striking plate (278:5A) can be cut off flush with the outer edge and gently tapped down to lead the ball in to the socket. Alternatively, the ball can be located in the carcase framing, but here again a slight depression must be gouged out under the striking plate to receive the ball and this will be noticeable on the door edge if below eye level. In effect, therefore, the position of ball and plate should be chosen to give the neatest appearance. As to whether one or two ball catches are necessary per door (at top and bottom) depends entirely on the size and power of the ball ($\frac{3}{8}$ in. (9·5 mm) is a good average), the size of the door and whether it requires pulling in; although doors in slight winding are usually corrected by throwing out either the top or bottom hinge, and generally speaking a perfectly flat small or medium-sized door will only require one catch. In fixing ball catches the barrel should be a reasonably tight fit in its prebored hole and tapped home with a hammer on a wood block to protect the ball. Normally, the projecting rim is hammered flush, but some woods tend to crush badly and it is advisable to score the exact diameter of the rim with the wing tip of a sharp bit before the hole is bored for the barrel.

Bookcase fittings

Loose shelves in cupboards and bookcases can be adjusted at various heights by several methods. Studs and sockets (278:7, 8) require holes to take the sockets drilled at regular intervals in the carcase sides back and front. Positions can be squared across the matched carcase cheeks and drilled before assembly, and if they are very numerous it will be convenient to prepare a wood or metal template bar bored out at the correct intervals—1 in. (25 mm), 1½ in. (38 mm) or 2 in. (50 mm) etc. according to the estimated use— which can be G-cramped to the carcase cheeks and the holes rapidly bored with a drill-gun and bit, limiting the depth with a small block of hardwood a tight fit on the drill. Figure 278:9 is the bookcase strip which requires housings worked at two levels (278:9A), whilst 278:10 is the *magic shelf wire* which is completely invisible

when assembled. Holes $\frac{1}{8}$ in. (3 mm) diameter are bored to take the wires at distance apart (front to back) fractionally less than the overall length of the wire (278:10A) which is sprung in position with a corresponding stopped groove (278:10C) worked at each end of the shelf. The wires are obtainable in various lengths or in short sections (278:10B), two of which will be needed per shelf end. The system is very positive in action, and the wires cannot be displaced with the shelf in position as there is only sufficient play in the groove depth to ensure an easy sliding fit.

Bolts

Cabinet bolts can be flush sunk or the open type screwed to the face, with the latter either necked or straight. Necked bolts (279:1) are used where the door fits against the shoulder of a rebate (279:1A), but the flush type or the extruded open-face fixing type (279:2) are usual for light cabinet-work. Various forms of automatic self-closing or self-aligning bolts are available and manufacturers' catalogues should be consulted.

279   Cupboard bolts

Castors and gliders

Castors and wheels are available in great variety from light pattern swivel castors for tea-trolleys, etc. to heavy duty ball-bearing castors for mounting machinery. Figure 280:1 shows a fixed wheel castor, (280:2) the orbit swivel castor, both with plate fixings either square, oblong, round or shaped for corners, whilst 280:3 illustrates the grip-neck method of fixing in which the socket with its pronged base is hammered into the leg and the peg pushed home, and 280:4 the wood screw type. Metal thread screws for fixing to metal are also available. Before choosing the type, usage and working conditions must be allowed for, and if maximum manœuvrability is required then four swivel castors should be used, but for heavy loads and long runs two fixed and two swivel are better, with the trolley pushed from the swivel end. Cast-iron wheels are suitable for concrete and rough gritty surfaces, whilst indoor use calls for hard- or soft-tyred rubber or plastic, or cast brass or electro-brassed steel for the smallest types. The castors can be hidden behind a curtain rail (280:7), but the trolley must be wide enough to permit the full swing of the castor within the curtain without sacrificing overall stability.

Gliders or floor protectors are suitable for furniture which is not often moved. With their greater bearing surface there is less indentation or wear on floors and coverings; moreover, it is not advisable to fit very free-running castors to chairs or divan beds, particularly if used by old people or invalids. Types vary from the simple knock in nickel-plated furniture glide, to the more sophisticated pattern (280:6) which shows the *Armstrong quad glider*.

Height adjusters

These are often essential for four-point contact on uneven surfaces (three-point contact will automatically adjust itself). Figure 280:5 shows the *Plastiglide* which is screwed into a tapped socket mounted in the leg, but for heavy desks and tables, etc. either the stem should have a hexagonal nut or a small hole bored through for a tommy bar so the adjuster can be raised or lowered under load.

Handles, knobs and pulls

It is axiomatic that handles can make or mar a piece of furniture. The first essential is that they should provide the necessary grip, robust enough for a direct pull on heavy drawers or doors, discreet enough not to usurp more than their fair share of visual interest. There are no golden

280 Castors and gliders

1   2   3   4

5   6   7

281 Wood handles

rules and good taste alone must decide their selection and placing. A flamboyant piece of furniture might require flamboyant handles, or handles so unobtrusive that they are hardly noticeable; plain, utilitarian furniture, utilitarian handles or some added richness to relieve stark surfaces. One thing only is certain; the designer must visualise the handles as part of his total conception; they must grow out of and not be added to his design merely as an afterthought.

Number and placing of handles

Here again there are no rules. If one handle will open a drawer without having to rock it from side to side so much the better. If two handles are necessary they can be placed in the usual positions, viz. on the quarter and three-quarter division marks in the drawer width and central in the depth, but this is not arbitrary and the placings can be symmetrical on the quarter lines or asymmetrical if the design composition calls for it, always providing the handles perform their proper function.

Wood handles

Hitherto bought wooden handles were invariably clumsy and in stained common woods, but ornamental knobs and pulls in palisander, teak, walnut, mahogany, etc. are now obtainable, or they can be very easily turned up on a suitable lathe. Kingwood is beautiful for turned knobs if it can be obtained, but ebony, rosewood, satinwood, Indian laurel, walnut and box are excellent. Sycamore can also be used, but care must be taken and the knobs gloss polished on the lathe immediately after the final sanding or the end grain (all knobs are turned out of long-grain stuff) will take on a grubby appearance.

Representative examples are illustrated in 281:1, 2 and 3, whilst 281:4, 5 are hand turned. Methods of fixing are shown in 281:6 where a pilot hole is drilled for the screw, and the short stub dowel inset into the drawer front prevents the knob splitting as the screw is driven home, whilst in 281:7 the dowel-pin is taken through the thickness of the drawer front, saw kerfed and wedged from the back. Large wooden knobs can have the dowel or spigot threaded with tap and die as in much Victorian furniture, but the

methods already described can be as effective. Figure 281:8, 9 are wood pulls worked in the length and cut off as required; they are screwed from the back. Figures 281:10, 11 are typical sliding flush door pulls, the former routered out, but the latter can be turned in a lathe, whilst 281:12 is an oblong routered version. Recessed cabinet handles for door and drawer fronts are shown in 281:13–16, whilst a simple method of forming a grip recess to a drawer front is shown in 281:17, 18. Overlapping holes are bored at an angle, cleaned up with file and abrasive paper and backed with a piece of thin veneered ply glued and screwed on (281:18).

Metal handles

Reproduction brass handles of good quality are obtainable at most architectural ironmongers and in profusion from R. D. Beardmore & Co. Ltd, Percy Street, London W.1. The back plates of these are usually pressed, as distinct from cast in the best antique examples, but the similitude is fair enough. Modern handles in brass, alloy, electro-plated plastic, clear perspex, etc, are available in bewildering variety and some manufacturers' lists contain many hundreds of varieties. In selecting these handles for hand-made furniture it is advisable to exercise restraint, for the more elaborate examples can advertise the fact that they are production-made by the very excellence of their finish, thus destroying the subtle appeal of an individually made piece of furniture. Representative examples are shown in 282. Figure 282:1 and 2 are extruded metal alloy pulls, 282:3 a spun-metal pull for sliding doors, 282:4–20 various types in brass, alloy and plated plastic. Figure 282:21 is a flush pull in two parts recessed into the door or drawer and screwed together from the back. Types of finishes for all these handles varies with the pattern, and the *Huwil Werk* catalogue from which some of these examples have been taken lists no less than 95 distinct finishes, from 'polished continental silver anodised' to 'matt black coated plastic'.

Knock-up (KU) and Knock-down (KD) fittings

Both are mechanical means of assembly employing a variety of metal or nylon fittings which

282   Metal handles

1

2

3

4

5

6

7

8

9

10

11

12

13

15

14

16

17

18

19

20

21

1

7

A

2

B

C

D

3

4

5

8

6

285   Spacing of screws (see page 343)

replace standard jointing procedures. Knock-up fittings are those designed for the speedy erection of structures providing permanent fixtures which will not be dismantled; knock-down fittings speed erection plus the ability to dismantle, i.e. knock down at any time and for any number of times. In theory, at least, manufacturers can produce with these fittings standardised components which can be stored and transported in the flat for erection later by the retailer or customer in his own home. In practice, many retailers are reluctant to undertake the erection (which is simple enough in all conscience and usually requires only a screwdriver or spanner); they often insist upon delivery in the assembled state and the main advantage is lost, for full knock-down assemblies often cost more to manufacture unless full advantage is taken of systematised production on a large scale. However, many manufacturers do use one or other forms of KU or KD assembly for very cogent reasons; (a) a large proportion of present-day furniture is composed of veneered chipboard which does not lend itself to traditional jointing methods; (b) machining processes can be simplified with less handling of components; (c) the spray coating and surfacing of flat components is easier and cheaper than handling bulky items of furniture.

The basic requirements of good KU or KD fittings are that they should (a) positively locate the joint; (b) ensure a tight joint when correctly assembled and tightened; (c) distribute the load evenly throughout the structure. Many different types are available which satisfy these requirements and which can be divided into three categories: (1) threaded fittings in which a suitable bush or receiver is onset or inset on one component and the other component locked to it with a barbed dowel or metal screw; (2) interlocking fittings in which both components have a screwed-on part which lock together either with screws or by knocking together; (3) cam action fittings onset or inset, in which a hook fixed to one component engages in a cam-operated fitting in the other and is tightened by operating the cam with a screwdriver. The most usual form in the cheaper ranges of furniture, particularly with the use of chipboard, is the threaded fitting, but the fixing is usually visible on the face of the work either as a screw head or a metal or plastic cover plate. Interlocking fittings are usually surface mounted, therefore they are confined to hidden interiors, and whilst very easy to fix, for there is no machining to be done, they are not so strong or so positive as the cam action fitting which is the method usually adopted for better class work. Representative examples are shown in 283. Figure 283:1 is the barbed dowel and glued-in nylon bush (S. Spegelman & Co. Ltd), (283:3) a shorter version with twin bushes suitable for knock-up assemblies, and 283:2 a KU and KD form using a shake-proof screw in lieu

of dowel which is, however, visible on the face of the work, although detachable brass cover caps are available. Figure 283:4 is the slotted plate for connecting flat panels, 283:5 a corner version, 283:6 the Flott plastic dovetail fitting, 283:7 a bush and screw, easy to fix and with brass cover plate for screw, 283:8 the mortise type, very neat in appearance and with adequate strength for all normal carcases. Applications for these fittings are shown in (283:9–17). A typical cam operated fitting (Huwil Fix) is illustrated in 284. This is composed of a plastic cover (284:7A), metal socket (284:7B), connecting screw (284:7C) and eccentric wheel (284:7D). Figure 284:1 shows a corner connection with two wheels, 284:2 a side connection with fluted metal socket and cover screw, 284:3 a slim fitting for carcase thicknesses down to $\frac{1}{2}$ in. (12·5 mm), 284:4 a double way with two connecting screws and fluted screw socket,

286 Cranked pivot or centre hinges fixed to upper and lower cabinet doors (see page 265).

287 Huwil Fix knock-down fitting

369

284:5 the standard version of 284:3 for thicknesses down to $\frac{5}{8}$ in. (16 mm) especially in chipboard, and 284:6 a double way with two wheels and double-ended connecting screw. Applications are shown in a typical large wall unit composed of upper and lower units (284:8), and assembly is effected by insetting and gluing in the metal socket, screwing in the connecting screw to the correct projection to allow the collared head to engage in the eccentric (cam operated) wheel, and turning the wheel clockwise with a screwdriver to engage the cam, after which the plastic cover can be pressed in position over the wheel. Figure 287 shows a two-way fitting in chipboard, and all the fittings are remarkably strong and positive in action, but as with all other mortise types of KD fittings the holes and recesses must be accurately positioned and machined to a constant depth.

Part 5 Furniture examples
36 Tables

The general term 'furniture' has wide meanings, but from the standpoint of the cabinet-maker he will limit its range to four main types or classes as follows:

Supporting units	Tables, trolleys, desks, writing fitments, working tops, etc.
Seating units	Chairs, stools, settees, etc.
Reclining units	Beds, Divans, Daybeds, etc.
Storage units	Cabinets, chests, sideboards, wardrobes, bookcases, wall fitments, etc.

Additionally there will be miscellaneous items including mirrors, occasional furniture, some kinds of wall panelling and small articles of woodware commonly known as *treen* which do not fit readily into any of the above categories. Obviously, only a fraction of all these can be included, nor is it necessary to describe in detail a great number of variety of furniture examples, for the underlying principles of construction remain the same throughout, and all that is needed is the application of basic techniques already described under the various chapter headings in Parts 3 and 4. In all probability the only real difference between a good cabinet-maker and an indifferent one will be the former's ability to think for himself and to apply his knowledge.

Tables

General note

The normal height for any working-top in the seated position is now accepted as between $28\frac{1}{2}$ in. (72 cm) to 29 in. (73·5 cm) with chair seats $10\frac{1}{2}$ in. (27 cm) to $11\frac{1}{2}$ in. (29 cm) lower. Elbow-room, i.e. width around the perimeter of the table for each sitter, should be not less than 23 in. (58 cm). Normal width of table-tops is taken as 30 in. (76 cm), but if there are flower-bowls, candles, etc. then 34 in. (86 cm) will be required. A square table for four people should be 40 in. (101 cm) by 40 in. (101 cm), whilst six can be accommodated at a rectangular top 60 in. (152 cm) by 30 in. (76 cm). Circular tops 44 in. (112 cm) in diameter will seat four, and 48 in. (122 cm) six. Table legs should not interfere with sitters, and 20 in. (51 cm) clear space between legs is required for each.

Types of table

Refectory-tables; long narrow trestle-type tables with fixed tops, so called after the monks' refectory or dining-room in the Middle Ages. *Extending tables*; incorporating some form of lengthening the top for additional sitters, of which the oldest type is the *draw leaf* extension table dating from the fifteenth century and still one of the most popular forms. *Board-room and conference tables*: very large tables usually composed of smaller units linked together. *Drop-leaf tables*, in which the side leaves hang vertically in the closed position and are supported by brackets, sliders, or in the case of the *gate-leg* table by a hinged leg or leg frame. *Double top tables*, in which the top leaf or leaves fold over and are supported by brackets or by pivoting the top. *Pedestal tables*: usually circular or D end and supported by a central podium or pillar terminating in three (tripod) or four legs. *Pembroke tables*: small rectangular tables with drop leaves on the long sides supported by brackets, and an end drawer or drawers. *Sofa-tables*: rectangular tables with drawers on the long side and small flaps at the end supported by brackets. *Side-tables*: generic term usually referring to all types of occasional table placed against a wall, writing-tables, hall-tables, etc. *Console-tables*; strictly a bracketed table-top without legs fixed to a wall and supporting a pier-mirror, but now usually applied to all side-tables placed against a wall. *Coffee-tables*: originally small circular tables with tray-type tops, but now embracing a wide range of low occasional tables. *Sewing-tables* with drawers or lift-up lid and sewing

288 Boardroom-table and chairs in Cuban mahogany for Imperial Chemical Industries Limited *Designed by R. D. Russell RDI. Table made by author's workshops, chairs made by Gordon Russell Limited*

289 Detail of table and chairs

290 Rosewood boardroom-table and chairs NEDDY boardroom   *By courtesy of Ministry of Public Building and Works*

291 Directors' dining-room furniture in rosewood for Courtauld Limited   *Designed by Edward Barnsley CBE, made at Barnsley workshops*

292   Table and sideboard in Rio rosewood
Designed by David Powell Des.RCA. David Powell workshops

compartment. *Nest of tables*: usually three small tea- or occasional tables diminishing in size and nesting together.

Refectory-tables

This old type is still popular and large numbers of reproduction refectory oak tables with solid tops are made. Figure 293:1 shows a representative example and 293:2 the method of construction, with 293:3 another form with square column and shaped brackets tenoned or dowelled to the column, and tenoned, dowelled or screwed to the foot. Figure 293:4 shows various table-tops: solid timber rub jointed or tongued and grooved (293:4A); solid planks with end clamps (293:4B); flush panelled (293:4C); plywood or laminboard, etc. veneered and lipped (293:4D) with a double-tongued lipping for thick tops (293:4F); and thin ply, etc. with wide rebated lipping in which the increased gluing area will hold without the necessity of tongueing (293:4E, G). Other examples of this type appear in 294. In 294:1, carried out in English cherry with 1 in. (25 mm) finished thickness jointed top, the 3 in. (76 mm) legs are formed of two thick laminations (the

3 in. (76 mm) plank cut through the centre) and glued together with a veneer thickness between to hold the short grain (294:2), and the centre block dowelled in on either side. A top stretcher rail is dovetailed and screwed to the ledges or top bearers, and a lower stretcher rail diamond tenoned through the leg blocks and wedged as 294:1. The jointed boards of the top are tongued together, with the ends of the tongues cut back and decorative insets of contrasting wood inset as 294:2A. Figure 294:3 shows a table end with turned twin columns, and figure 292 a contemporary version with a veneered and lipped laminboard top and a stand in solid Rio rosewood.

Fixing tops

Solid tops must be fixed with slot screws, wood buttons or metal shrinkage plates (see also *Flush-top carcases*, page 274) to allow for shrinkage; the centre is permanently fixed and the outer edges free to slide. Ply and laminboard tops can be fixed with metal shrinkage plates, or screwed through the stretcher rail and top bearers without fear of movement.

1

2

3

4

A

B

C

D

E

F

G

Extending tables

These are of two types: *telescopic* in which dove-tailed or keyed sliding frames fit within each other, and are pulled out as with a telescope to receive extra leaves which must be stored else-where; and *extending leaf* tables in which the stands are fixed and only the leaves slide open, with the extra leaf or leaves stored within the framework of the table. Figure 295:2 shows the principle of the telescopic tables with frames extended; 295:1 the table closed, 295:3 the separate frames sliding on stout tongues with cross-rails dovetailed on, and 295:4 dovetail keys which do not require connecting rails across the frames if the keys are stout enough. Tables of this description were often actuated by a long quick-thread screw working in a tapped barrel, and actuated by a detachable handle at one end; but as there was always a tendency for the separate frames to sag in the open position a middle leg was often fitted, and the frames themselves were planed in rounding on the top edges by as much as $\frac{3}{8}$ in. (9·5 mm) over the length of a long table. This extending system was a great favourite in large Victorian and Edwardian households, but has now been superseded by the smaller types of sliding-leaf extending table, whilst large board-room- and conference-tables are now usually made up of smaller units coupled together as required.

Fixed stand extending table

Figure 295:5 shows the simplest type with loose centre leaf stored within the framework of the legs. Rebated sliders or lopers are secured to the underside of the outer leaves, and engage in corresponding rebates worked in the side rails screwed to the table rails (295:6), with 295:7 the detail of the rebates and the end table rails notched out to allow the sliders to pass through as the outer leaves are pulled apart. Locating pins or keys and matching sockets must be provided in the leaf edges for location (see also page 379); also stub dowels let into the underside of the sliders to limit the travel, and centre stops to prevent the leaves passing over the halfway mark. The loose centre leaf can be stored under-neath, with a $\frac{1}{4}$ in. (6 mm) ply tray bottom screwed to bearers dovetailed to the end rails, one of which has an opening cut to receive the leaf (295:6A). A half-moon hand hole should be cut out of the ply bottom, and a slight scoop cut in the underside of the leaf sufficient for the tips of the fingers. Another version of the sliding action is shown in 295:8, where the sliders are rebated as 295:8A and screwed to the outer leaves with a moulded bar-handle grip 295:8B. This type of slider is also used with drop-leaf tables where the centre leaf is fixed to the table framing, and the sliders are made up as complete frames which are pulled out to support the drop leaves in the raised position.

Draw-leaf tables

This is the most popular of all extending table movements, and details are given in 296. Figure 296:1 shows the elevation divided on the centre-line (CL) to show the closed and open positions

1

2

3

4

5

6

A

7

TOP

SLIDER

RAIL

8

A

B

296 Draw-leaf extending table

1

CLOSED   OPEN

C L

4

A

SLOT

B

RAIL

5

RAIL   A

2

A

B

3

A   B

X

378

of the leaves which should be of identical thickness as the main top. Figure 296:2 is the underview plan with the bearer rail (296:2A) of the same thickness as the leaves, and firmly screwed to the table framing. Cross-guides are screwed to the bearer rail, and the diminishing sliders (296:2B) whose width should be twice the thickness of the tops, are firmly screwed to the two leaves and free to slide between the cross-guides, with a dowel-peg (296:3x) to limit the travel. Slots equal in depth to half the width of the sliders are cut in the end framing, and the angle at which the sliders are cut to diminish is shown by the dotted line at 296:4B. The main top is not fixed, for it has to be raised slightly to allow the leaves to be pulled out and slid back, and it is held in position by shaped blocks (296:5) glued and screwed to the underside, with small locating blocks screwed to the main block to guide the top into the correct position over the notched bearer rail (296:2A). As a refinement card-table pivots or coach bolts welded to a fixing plate are screwed to the underside of the main top, passed through the bearer rail and set to allow the required upward movement, but these are hardly necessary unless the table is frequently upended. Baize strips stuck to the top edges of the end rails provide a sweet sliding action to the leaves as they are withdrawn.

Flip-top (up and over) extending table

With this type the centre leaf is in two halves hinged together with Soss-type invisible hinges (297:1, 2), and pivoted at the sides to cross rails so that the complete hinged leaf can be folded up and swung down within the table framing (296:3); the outer leaves are then slid back to close the gap. These outer leaves have sliders attached, with worked tongues sliding in grooves in the sides of the table, and the cross rails must be notched out to allow their passage. The sliders can be kept short, in which case the leg shoulders will act as stops limiting the travel (297:6, 8), but the tops will be unsupported at 297:8x and careless handling could place too much strain on the short lengths of tongueing. If on the other hand they are extended out almost to the edges of the leaves (297:5), then either the side rails must be flush with the legs on the insides or packing pieces must be inserted (297:7) to take the grooves. The grooves must also be worked across the inner faces of the legs, and the end rails notched out as for the cross rails. Short stub dowels must be let into the grooves on the halfway mark, and also on the under edge of the sliders to limit the travel in either direction. Locating pins or keys must be fitted to the leaves; either short dowels entering corresponding sockets on the opposing edges or inset oblong keys of hardwood tapered in all directions (297:5), with appropriate mortises cut to receive them. If the sockets are placed either side of the centre leaf and keys on the outer leaves the positions must be offset, and each outer leaf must have both keys and sockets; but if they are fitted in sequence, i.e. key on outer leaf, socket on centre leaf, key on centre leaf, socket on outer leaf, then the keyed edge of the centre leaf must be set back from the cross rail by moving the pivot plate over to allow the key to clear the cross rail as the leaf is swung down. The position of the hinged centre leaf in the closed (under) position is not critical provided it does not foul the table sides, and the approximate position can be found on the drawing by placing the folded leaf in a central position, and placing the pivot point (297:9x) on the centre of an arc swung from the edge of the folded leaf to the outer edge of the table. The placing of the pivot point itself is, however, highly critical, and it can best be done by holding the folded leaf between the cross rails of the stand in the approximate position as indicated by the drawing. The pivot point will lie on a vertical line drawn halfway between the exact centre of the table framing (A) and the hinged side edge (B) of the leaf; and it is then only necessary to lay the centre leaf face downwards on a flat surface, register the stand in the correct position with the centre of the stand corresponding with the hinged joint of the centre leaf, place the pin of the pivot plate on the vertical line, prick through for the exact centre, bore and fit the socket, insert the pivot pin and screw the plate down to the leaf; it will then swing on the arc (A–B). The illustrations show a table 6 ft (183 cm) long in the extended position, with outer leaves 2 ft 3 in. (68·5 cm) and centre leaf 1 ft 6 in. (46 cm), closing up to 4 ft 6 in. (137 cm) overall. Table widths can be 2 ft 6 in. (76 cm) to 2 ft 10 in. (86 cm) or wider if necessary, and the tops can be solid

298　Triple flip-top dining-table veneered teak with beech legs　*Designed by Neil Morris MSIA By courtesy of H. Morris Co. Limited Photograph: Council of Industrial Design*

299　Swing leg, fall-flap table in solid English walnut with walnut platters and bowl　*Designed by Ernest Joyce MSIA. Silverwork by Leslie Durbin MVO. Author's workshops*

timber if very carefully chosen, although veneered laminboard is better. The grain of the tops should run across the width, and it will be necessary to fit either a cross-bar or screwed brackets to the cross rails, set at an angle to support the centre leaf and to direct the movement upwards (297:9). Pivot plates can be bought as cranked pivot hinges or as a special pivot-plate assembly for this type of table (297:4).

Gate-leg tables

These superseded the draw-leaf type in the sixteenth century, but their popularity has greatly declined in recent years. They are a useful form for small rooms, and a wide range of tops can be fitted, square, rectangular, circular, elliptical, D ended, serpentine, etc. but the additional legs of the gates are somewhat inconvenient for sitters. The principles of construction are simple; the tops can be double and folded over, or fall leaf and lifted up, to be supported by a swing gate or gates pivoted to the main framing. These gates can be single (300:1, 2), double which is more usual (300:3), twin for large leaves (300:4), whilst a semicircular side-table with double top and single gate is shown in 300:5. Figure 300:6 shows the basic framework with gate open, (300:7) elevation of a typical elliptical top table with turned legs, and a top and bottom plan in 300:8. From these drawings it will be seen that the side framing rails must be wide or locally increased in width to receive the pivots of the gate framing (300:6, 8), and also where the gate leg is notched over (300:13). The rails of the gates can be relieved slightly (300:7A) to prevent them grinding on the table rails as they are pushed home. The actual pivots can be stout hardwood dowels, $\frac{3}{8}$ in. (9·5 mm) iron rod or brass tube, etc. with the bottom pivot kept short and tipped on, and the upper pivot taken through the top rail and tapped home after assembly (300:12). A little candle grease rubbed over the dowels or rods will prevent squeaking and the sockets should be an easy but not slack fit. Figure 300:10 shows the bottom end rail set in for knee-room, and 300:9 the small stops screwed to the underside of the tops to limit the travel of the gates, whilst 300:14 is an end-fixing card-table hinge for square-edge double tops, 300:15 is a back-flap hinge for square-edge fall-leaf tops, and 300:16 the moulded

rule joint often used. The top ovolo moulding can be carried round the perimeter of the table, and this was usually done in typical examples (300:7). The legs of the gates can be shortened fractionally to accommodate metal gliders (300:11) for easier sliding over hard floor-coverings.

Concertina-action double-top table

Figure 301 shows the side elevation with double top and end-fixing card-table hinges. In 301:2 the back legs (hinged side of top) are not connected to the table frame, but to hinged rails extending as 301:2 and closing up as 301:3. Figure 301:2A shows a special top-fixing hinge often used in old examples, but back flap or piano hinges can be used. The frame when opened is kept rigid by a sliding shelf pulled along the grooves worked in the rails (301:4), and the top is then folded over. Figure 301:5 shows an improved version more rigid in performance, in which stub rails (301:5A) are barefaced tenoned into the legs and a show rail (301:5B) tenoned and glued to the front leg and glued to the adjoining stub rail, and tenoned but not glued to the other leg. The stub rails are knuckle jointed to the hinged rails, which are also knuckle jointed at 301:5C with extra long shoulder bevels to allow the joint to close at the acute angle (301:5D). A cabin hook and eye can be fitted to keep the frame rigid in the open position, as a groove for a slide (301:4) cannot be worked across the knuckle without seriously weakening the joint. The method usually adopted for keeping the back legs in the closed position was to recess a $\frac{3}{16}$ in. (5 mm) wood spring into the underside of the top, with a projecting knob which clipped over the rail as shown in the drawing (303).

Envelope-top card-table

In this variation of the double-top table the upper top which must be square is divided into four triangular sections (301:6) hinged to the under top with centre card-table hinges. The under top is pivoted with a card-table pivot, known as a 'table swivel plate' and still obtainable as such, and a stop (301:8) which allows a movement through 45° in a clockwise direction (301:7).

As the top flaps are flush some method of raising them must be provided, and in traditional examples a wood or metal dowel was inserted in a socket hole bored through the under top about 2 in. (50 mm) in from one corner (301:7x). A $\frac{3}{16}$ in. (5 mm) wood or thin metal spring was fitted over the dowel-peg (301:9A) pressing it up as the top pivoted over the table rail, thus raising the flap by a fractional amount which tipped the point of the flap clear so that it could be raised with the finger-tips. The method was crude enough, nevertheless it worked extremely well in practice, and more sophisticated methods sometimes adopted in modern examples of this type of table are not necessarily more efficient.

302 Antique envelope-flap card-table under repair showing one flap slightly raised

303 Wood spring catch

Swivel-top table

This method is more practicable than either the concertina or envelope-top card-table and is used in contemporary designs. Figure 304:1 is a pedestal type with double top hinged with counter-flap hinge or the more decorative mangle-top hinge (305), whilst 304:4 gives details of the framework and 304:5 the pillar fixing to the cross rails and the feet (304:3). The lower top is pivoted with a card-table pivot or table swivel plate (304:2) taken through a cross-bearer in the framing, and is free to move through 90°. The exact position of the pivot is fairly critical, and is found by drawing a plan of the table in the closed position (304:4A), and an outline of the open position (304:4B). A line at 45° is then drawn through the centre point, and the centre between the points where this line intersects the outer edges of the pivoted top in the closed and open position will be the pivot point (x). The extent of the travel is shown by the dotted lines swung from this centre, and a small stop is screwed to the top to limit the movement. Baize insets glued to the top edges of the framework will ensure an easy sliding movement. The most satisfactory format for a table of this type is square as shown in 304:4, but rectangular shapes are feasible within certain limits, always provided that the width of each leaf is more than half the length of the rectangular framework, or the opened leaves will not cover. A scale drawing will show the permissible variations, and the extent of the overhang which should not be too great in either length or width or the table will be unsteady. Framed-up table stands can be used instead of the pedestal stand shown.

SCALE ▮▮▮▮ INS ▭▭▭▭ CMs

Pembroke tables

Figure 306:1 is an isometric sketch of a Pembroke table with fall flaps on the long sides, and 306:2 the support brackets (either one long one or two short ones according to the size of the flap) knuckle or finger jointed as described under *Mechanical joints*, Chapter 21, page 210. One or two end drawers were provided in old examples, and if only one long drawer was fitted then the other end was treated as a dummy drawer front complete with ring or knob handle. The flaps were either square edge on butt-type hinges, or with table hinges and rule joints as for the sofa-table (309). Average sizes of traditional examples were about 39 in. (99 cm) long, 19 in. (48 cm) wide, with 10 in. (25 mm) flaps either side, and a 2½ in. (6·5 cm) deep drawer, but the measurements can be varied within wide limits.

305 Mangle-top hinge

306 Pembroke table showing bracket

1

2

307 *Left* Rule-joint table top

308 Underneath view of draw-leaf table with panelled top showing one leaf fully opened

Sunderland tables

These worked on the same principle as the Pembroke table, but the tops were narrow and the flaps much deeper, with the result that the tables were not as stable as the Pembroke and, therefore, not so popular. A compromise between the two was sometimes made with large flaps supported by swing legs on the gate-leg table principle.

Sofa tables

Traditional forms have side drawers and end flaps, but without flaps this type of table can easily be adapted for use as dressing or occasional tables, etc. Figure 309:1 shows a table without flaps, 309:2 the sectional elevation and 309:3 an isometric projection of the overall appearance. Figure 309:4 is the usual table with end flaps supported by swing knuckle-jointed brackets as in Pembroke tables, etc., and 309:5 an under plan showing the flap in the raised position. Constructional details are given in 310 with 310:1 the carcase framing, 310:2 leg details from which it will be seen that the side rail is bridled over the upright or standard, with the outer cheek of the latter cut back at 310:2A to allow the bracket to fold back. If flaps are not fitted as 310:1 then the outer cheek can be carried up to the top of the rail, or more neatly finished by setting the rail flush with the legs on the outer face and housing and screwing the standard 310:2B. The shaped legs are set out full size as shown in 310:7, with the shaded portion left on to facilitate cramping up and then cut off after assembly, butt jointed and glued together and mortised for the triangular-shaped tenon of the standard (310:2) which is glued and screwed from the inside. Figure 310:3 is the sectional elevation of a typical drawer front with cock beads, also a reeded edge to the table-top and a small base moulding rebated in, whilst 310:4 is the rule-joint assembly for the flap, and (310:5) the moulded section of the stretcher rail between the two leg frames. The standard is usually rebated out for an inset capping mould mitred all round (310:6), whilst 310:9 shows an alternative method of framing the legs which are tenoned into a block, with a separate moulded capping piece planted on and the standard dowelled in.

Side table

This typical side-table (312:1) was originally made up as a teak display-table for a very valuable and heavy Tang dynasty pottery horse, but is equally suitable as a serving- or library-table, etc. Figure 312:2 gives the detail of leg, tenoned-in rail and planted top, showing the chamfers worked to relieve the otherwise plain design. The original top was $1\frac{1}{2}$ in. (38 mm) blockboard (obtainable as flush door blanks) veneered and lipped, but 312:3 shows an alternative construction with $\frac{5}{8}$ in. (16 mm) ply and wide lipping, and middle stiffening rail glued on. On practical grounds it can be argued that there is little intrinsic difference between a solid and a thick-nessed-up top provided the ply is stout enough, and the outward appearance must be the same, nevertheless there is a very subtle difference which the expert eye will be able to detect.

Coffee-tables

Sizes vary greatly, with tables 4 ft (122 cm) in length and over usually known as *Long Johns*. Figure 314:1, 3 is mortised and tenoned or dowelled together, with a centre bearer rail slip dovetailed or housed and glue blocked, and a solid or veneered and lipped top $\frac{3}{4}$ in. (19 mm) in thickness. Veneered tops can be pocket screwed from underneath, but solid tops will require sliding wood buttons (314:2 and 201), or metal shrinkage plates. Figure 314:4, 7 is another type with skid framing to slide easily over deep carpeting. The top is laminboard veneered with a 1 in. (25 mm) deep lipping (295:6) eased off on the under edge in a gentle curve (314:4A) to meet the $\frac{3}{4}$ in. (19 mm) ends, and is fixed by pocket screwing or screwing up through the rails. The side rails or runners (314:4B) are finger jointed to the legs (314:5), and the cross rails (314:7) mortised and tenoned in. Figure 314:8 is the mosaic-top table illustrated in 316:A. The chipboard top (314:9) is set in $\frac{1}{4}$ in. (6 mm) for the plastic mosaic, with a small inset stringing in plumwood, whilst the legs are shaped from the solid as shown in 314:10, 11 and 12, with the rails dowelled in to support the short grain on the curves. The mosaic is formed with $\frac{1}{4}$ in. (6 mm) end-grain sections of various woods sawn off, assembled on the chipboard top and anchored

311 Occasional table in teak showing sculptured joints *Designed by William Mitchell Des.RCA. Author's workshops*

313 Side-table in red lacquer with gold enrichments. Brass caps to legs and red lacquer coffee-table covered with Cape Levant goat-skin
Designed by Ernest Joyce MSIA, Author's workshops

312 Side-table

1

2

$1\frac{1}{2}''$ 38 mm

$2\frac{7}{8}''$ 73 mm

2″ 50 mm

L 48 IN   122 cm
W 20 IN   50 cm
H 30 IN   76 cm

3

SCALE [▮▮▮▮▮▮] INS [▯▯▯▯▯▯▯▯▯▯▯▯] CMs

315 Table in solid oak *Designed by Desmond Ryan. By courtesy of the Royal College of Art*

316A Coffee-table in English yew with mosaic top
designed by William Mitchell Des. RCA
Table designed by Ernest Joyce MSIA

316B Detail of mosaic top

SCALE

INs

CMs

1

2

3

A

4

5

6

A

B

7

8

9

10

with a little of the polyester resin used. The bulk
of the resin, accelerator and thrixotropic medium
were then mixed, suitably coloured with polyester
paste stainers and poured over the assembly,
working it into the spaces with a pointed stick.
After allowing 24 hours to harden thoroughly it
was then cleaned flush with scraper and belt
sander, allowed to settle for several days and
finally surfaced with fine abrasive paper. After
working the chamfer round the edges the table
was then spray polished in the usual manner.

Circular tables are shown in 317. Figure 317:1
has a veneered and lipped laminboard or chipboard top with cross rails tenoned or slot dovetailed to the legs (317:2), and glued and screwed
to the top. The inset circular rail is formed by
routering a groove round the perimeter and at
the junction with the legs (317:3), with sections
of veneered ply bent to the curve and glued in.
Figure 317:4 is a turned lacquered or painted
table in softwood or medium hardwood built
up in sections as 317:5, with the spigot ends
formed on the centre section to save timber
thickness in the larger dimensions; the top is
plywood screwed in position from underneath.
Figure 317:6 is a shaped ply table, with top,
centre and bottom cross rails jointed as 317:8,
dovetailed and dowelled to the uprights (317:7).
Ply of $\frac{1}{16}$ in. (1·5 mm) or $\frac{3}{32}$ in. (2 mm) thickness
is then bent by hand to the curves, glued and
pinned. The ply can run out and be sanded off
flush as shown in 317:7, or the shoulders
(317:7A) inset, with interior glued fillets to
support the long edges of the ply between the
cross rails.

Other types of small table are shown in 318.
Figure 318:1, 2 is a knock-down tiled top table
with $\frac{3}{8}$ in. (9·5 mm) inset ply top rebated into
the side and end rails, and firmly glue blocked
(318:3). The rails are cut away for the detachable
legs, which are attached with angle plates, screws
and wing nuts (318:5) (see page 301), and a small
v-groove is worked round the rails with a corresponding chamfer across the top face edges of
the legs. This type of table is set out to accommodate the standard 4 in. (101 mm) by 4 in. (101 mm)
or 6 in. (152 mm) by 6 in. (152 mm) ceramic tile,
and a $\frac{1}{16}$ in. (1·5 mm) gap must be left around each
tile, each of which is bedded on the ply top with
a suitable plaster or mastic base trowelled on to
a depth of about $\frac{1}{8}$ in. (3 mm), combed into

319   Coffee-table with glass top

ridges and the tiles pressed down flush with the raised rail edges. A piece of $\frac{1}{16}$ in. (1·5 mm) card (318:3A) can be used as a temporary spacer for each tile, and when the mastic has set the gaps are filled with plaster or proprietary filler and wiped smooth. If necessary, the filler can be coloured with water-paints to match the tiles, but the natural white lines are often highly decorative, and they can be protected with white french polish or cellulose lacquer. Figures 318:6, 7 show a sculptured leg Long John table which can have a flush or raised lipping (318:9). The supports for the top are stitched to the legs and side rails with finger jointing cut from the solid (318:8), or as separate insets of coloured hardwood (318:10). The veneered top is dowelled and glued on 318:8, and solid tops are not suitable for this type owing to the possibility of shrinkage across

the width, breaking the method of attachment.

A table with interior illumination (319) is included to show the principles involved. Figure 319:1 is a ply box jointed by any suitable method and lipped on the top edges with wider timber (319:4). The sides of the box are cut away at the base as 319:1 to provide ventilation, and an obscured glass inner top is held in position by wood spacers (319:3, 4) to allow for free circulation of air, for most light fittings emit some degree of heat. The 12 in. (300 mm) strip light is fixed to a cross-bearer fixed across the centre of the box (319:2, 5), and hidden by the obscured glass inner top. The main top is 6 mm or 9 mm plate glass with four shallow recesses drilled out to provide seatings for the stub metal locating dowels (319:4). The light can be coloured by using any stained glass for the inner top.

320 Nest of tables in moulded laminated beech *Designed by Marcel Breuer. Photograph: Council of Industrial Design*

321   Dowelled and tenoned coffee-table framing ready for gluing up

322   Simple coffee-table in teak   *Author's workshops*

323 Pillar table in English walnut with brass ferrules to feet *Designed by R. D. Russell RDI. Made in author's workshops*

324 Furniture for Herbarium, Scotland *By courtesy of Ministry of Public Building and Works*

37 Chests, cabinets, sideboards

Chests of drawers

Chests can be 2 ft (61 cm) to 3 ft 9 in. (114 cm) wide and up to 4 ft 6 in. (137 cm) high with a fairly standard depth of around 18 in. (45 cm). Tall narrow chests or those composed of two separate carcases are usually known as *tallboys*. Chests can be placed on plinths or stump legs 4 in. (10 cm.) to 5 in. (12 cm) high, or on stools up to about 10 in. (25 cm) to 12 in. (30 cm) high; the latter is more convenient for drawers in constant use. All these measurements are the generally accepted standard and in no sense arbitrary.

Mahogany chest of drawers

The chest illustrated (325) was constructed of solid Honduras mahogany throughout, with secret mitre dovetailed carcase and the long drawers veneered with richly figured Honduras mahogany also. The small top drawers and their inset surround were cut from a single board, and as it would have been impossible to saw out the drawer openings from the board without an appreciable gap showing round each drawer, the board was cut full in length, split into three widths with the middle section cut to form the openings, and then carefully matched and butt glued together again with the joints invisible. The long drawers were of solid Honduras mahogany also, veneered both sides and the edges slightly chamfered. Top drawers had orthodox runners, guides and central division, but the lower drawers were grooved for side runners screwed to the carcase cheeks. An inset base rail was fixed above the solid bottom to receive the dowel ends of the turned legs which were carried through both thicknesses, levelled off and wedged from above. The shaped bar handles were formed of five thicknesses of plain mahogany veneer glued and G-cramped between shaped softwood blocks, with bareface tenons cut on the ends of the handles, taken through the drawer fronts and wedged from the inside. The top drawers were provided with small turned mahogany knob handles.

325 Chest of drawers in solid and veneered Honduras mahogany. Laminated bar handles *Designed by R. D. Russell RDI. Author's workshops*

326 Traditional type chest of drawers with flush fronts. Veneered matched sheets of African mahogany *Designed by Ernest Joyce MSIA. Author's workshops*

327 Bow-fronted chest of drawers in makoré with inlays of ebony and sycamore *Designed by Edward Barnsley CBE. Barnsley workshops*

328 Detail of chest in makoré with sycamore inlays *Designed by Edward Barnsley CBE. Barnsley workshops*

330 Serpentine-fronted tallboy in African mahogany with drawers veneered sapelewood and kingwood handles *Designed by Ernest Joyce MSIA. Author's workshops*

(19 mm) finish serpentine drawer fronts were made up from nine $\frac{3}{32}$ in. (2 mm) gaboon constructional veneers pressed between male and female formers in a screw-press and veneered with striped sapelewood. Drawer sides are $\frac{5}{16}$ in. (8 mm) English oak, flush drawer bottoms and backs $\frac{5}{16}$ in. (8 mm) English cedar, also the panelled backs with 2 in. (50 mm) by $\frac{5}{8}$ in. (16 mm) stiles, rails and muntins, and $\frac{5}{16}$ in. (8 mm) panels mulletted in. The panelled backs are rebated into the carcases with a flush bead at the meeting edges, and all the drawers have a $\frac{1}{16}$ in. (1·5 mm) mahogany cock head. Carcase tops and bottoms are carcase dovetailed, drawer divisions stopped housed into the cheeks, upright centre division housed and screwed top and bottom. The plinth stool is built up of the same mahogany, with 2 in. (50 mm) stump feet and serpentine-shaped rails out of 2½ in. (63·5 mm) square stuff tenoned in. Plinth capping mould and lower carcase mould are $\frac{7}{8}$ in. (22 mm) and $\frac{3}{4}$ in. (19 mm) thickness respectively by 2½ in. (63·5 mm) wide stuff, mitred and screwed in position, and all the mouldings were handworked throughout with small hollow and round planes shaped in the length to fit the curves. The serpentine shape is shown in outline in 329:4, whilst 329:5 is the top moulding, (329:6) the lower carcase capping mould, and 329:8 the plinth mould. The drawer knobs are turned from kingwood, dowelled in and wedged from the back. It is interesting to note that a second chest made to this design in 1952 and in daily use by the writer is still completely mothproof, as the solid cedar linings have not lost their pungent, aromatic scent.

Serpentine-fronted tallboy

This tallboy (329) was primarily designed as a contemporary interpretation of a traditional form and has been on permanent exhibition since first made in 1951. Figure 329:1 shows the elevation and 329:2, 3 the side sectional elevation. As will be seen the tallboy is composed of two separate carcase units with planted top and plinth stool. Carcase top and sides are $\frac{3}{4}$ in. (19 mm) finish first-quality solid African mahogany cut from flat planks over 4 ft (121 cm) wide; sub tops, bases and solid divisions between drawers $\frac{5}{8}$ in. (16 mm) selected western hemlock lipped with mahogany; whilst the $\frac{3}{4}$ in.

Cocktail cabinet

Figure 331A illustrates a cocktail cabinet in English walnut, composed of carcase and separate stand with built-in shelf. Figure 331:1 shows the elevation and 331:2 the side sectional elevation. The carcase is in $\frac{3}{4}$ in. (19 mm) laminboard with exterior veneered walnut from one wide leaf of sufficient length to yield continuous grain throughout, and interior in Nigerian pearwood, with the carcase mitre tongued and grooved at the top, and lap tongued and grooved at the bottom. Alternative methods of jointing are shown in 331:3, with 331:3A tongued and

SCALES

INs   FIGs 1.2   5
CMs   FIG 4   1 2   5
   FIGs 3.5.6.7   1   2   5

331A Cocktail cabinet in English walnut with fluted drawer front *Designed by Ernest Joyce MSIA. Author's workshops*

332 Detail of similar cabinet in sapelewood showing fluted drawer front

as shown by the dotted lines in 331:5, with the raised ply panels lipped, tongued into the framing, moulded on the face edges and veneered over the lippings with matching veneers. Figure 331:6 is the detail of the taper legs with curve formed in the leg and not out of the rail which would result in a feather edge at the junction, whilst 331:7 shows the handworked fluting to the drawer front, and the turned knob handles which were also used for the doors. Figure 332 shows a similar fluted front being worked with round moulding-plane, guided only by carefully set-out pencil-lines. This measure of accuracy is only possible with a plane-iron whose profile has not been distorted by careless sharpening.

333 Working drawer front by hand

grooved for solid timber, 331:3B tongued and grooved with lap set back and an edging strip inserted for laminboard, etc. and 331:3C secret mitre dovetailed for solid timber or laminboard, etc. In both 331:3A and B the front edges are lipped with the corners mitred, as this enables the tongueing to run through for ease in working. Figure 331:4A shows the plan of the leg stand with the veneered and lipped plywood tray grooved into the side rails, and 331:4B the plan of the carcase with the lower shelf cut away to accommodate tall bottles. The upper shelves are fully adjustable on shelf pegs or *magic* wires, and the lower shelf which forms the top of the drawer division is housed into the cheeks. The doors are framed up out of solid walnut mitred and tongued

334 Cabinet in Rio rosewood with painted doors and drawer fronts *Designed by Clive Bacon Des.RCA. By courtesy of Royal College of Art*

336 Single storage cabinet in solid afromosia *Designed by George R. Ingham Des.RCA. By courtesy of Pedley Woodwork Limited. Photograph: Council of Industrial Design*

335 Cupboard unit with knock-down construction in natural beech *Designed by Roland Gibbard Des.RCA. By courtesy of Design Furnishing Contracts Limited. Photograph: Council of Industrial Design*

337 Coin-collector's cabinet in Bombay rosewood and mahogany *Designed by H. S. Slan. Photograph: Council of Industrial Design*

338 Shaped bureau with filing-cabinets veneered English walnut *Designed by Timothy Rendle ARIBA. Author's workshops*

339 Interior of shaped bureau showing centre ·hung upper doors

340 Cabinet in ebony and holly—closed

341 Cabinet in ebony and holly—open *Designed by Jane Young M.Des.RCA. By courtesy of Royal College of Art*

342 Wall storage unit in chipboard veneered mahogany *Designed by Herbert Berry FSIA. By courtesy of Lucas of London Limited. Photograph: Council of Industrial Design*

Sideboards

Sideboards can be tall and fairly narrow or long and low, dependent on the size of the room. Most types provide storage space for bottles, glasses, china and napery, etc. with orthodox drawers or interior trays, adjustable shelves, fall flaps or tambours or side-hung doors. Fixed legs or independent stools or stands are favoured, as there are obvious disadvantages in taking cupboards down to or a little above floor level on a shallow plinth. Reference should be made to the chapters on *Basic Constructions*, which detail stands and stools, carcase constructions, tambours, fall flaps, etc.

A sideboard in Rio rosewood is illustrated in 344, and 345. Dimensions are 5 ft 6½ in. (169 cm) long overall, with separate carcase unit 2 ft 1 in. (63·5 cm) in height and 18 in. (46 cm) deep, and stool 11¼ in. (28·5 cm) high. The sideboard is divided into three compartments, with double tambours to the middle section, and inset doors on butt hinges to the outer sections. Figure 344:1 shows the elevation, 344:2 the sectional side elevation through the tambour section, and 344:3 a plan section of the tambour and shutting edge of

343 Bureau bookcase in English oak *Designed by Ernest Joyce MSIA. Author's workshops*

408

ins
cm
SCALES

3 6 9 12   1 & 2
5 15 25 35 45 55

1

2

3

4

5

6

7

345 Sideboard in Rio rosewood with centre tambours *Designed by Ernest Joyce MSIA. Author's workshops*

the right-hand door with shaped handle grip. Carcase construction is in $\frac{3}{4}$ in. (19 mm) veneered laminboard, doors 1 in. (25 mm) laminboard lipped all round, tambours, show rails, lippings and stool assembly, etc. in solid rosewood. The top is secret mitre dovetailed, and the long rails which take the tambour grooves top and bottom are inset $\frac{3}{16}$ in. (5 mm), with the doors rebated over 344:4 and the door corners slightly rounded. Figure 344:5 shows the leg assembly, 344:6 sections through the handle grips moulded in a continuous length and then shaped, and 344:7 the moulding to the carcase edges. The interior is fitted with trays in the right-hand division and adjustable shelves to the remainder, whilst the tambour division has false cheeks and back to hide and protect the travel. As the rosewood was exceptionally richly marked, varying from purple-black to light tan, and as the photograph had to be taken with only normal workshop lighting much of the detailing has been lost and the handle grips barely discernible, but both tambours and both doors have grips running the full height of each.

346 Dining-room furniture in Australian black-bean with sycamore inlays *Designed by Edward Barnsley CBE. Barnsley workshops*

410

347 Sideboard with cocktail compartment and two drawers, African mahogany veneered courbaril *Designed by Ernest Joyce MSIA. Author's workshops*

348 Sideboard interior showing fall flap stay, adjustable shelf and sliding tray on runners with false check fitted to clear door

Writing-desk

The writing-desk in English walnut (351) was designed on a series of golden sections for a special client. The canted pedestals are fixed by screwing through the bearer rails into the $1\frac{1}{4}$ in. (32 mm) blockboard top, and therefore no stiffening rail is required. The main construction is in $\frac{3}{4}$ in. (19 mm) veneered laminboard, with agba framing rails etc. and walnut lippings mitred at the corners and chamfered all round (349:6). Figure 349:1 shows the elevation, 349:2 the side sectional elevation with the small pen-drawer on orthodox runners, and the other drawers with grooved sides and side runners. A deep filing-drawer is provided for foolscap hangers (see *Drawer-work* Chapter 32, page 324). Figure 349:3 shows the cant of the pedestals, 349:4 the constructional details, 349:5 a section of the legs which are shaped to a round at the base and tenoned up through a double rail thickness as shown, whilst 349:7 gives details of the purpose-made brass handles with turned stems and brazed-on plates out of $\frac{3}{16}$ in. (5 mm) brass, with the facets filed away and machine buffed. Two steel pins are drilled in either side of the fixing screw tapped into the stem to prevent the handle turning. The final polish to the desk shown was one coat of hard cellulose, wire-wooled and matt waxed.

Office desks

With the exception of senior executives' desks which are purposely more ornate for prestige purposes, office desks are simply constructed and to a fairly standard pattern. Figure 350:1 gives a representative example with the flat side frames of 2 in. (50 mm) by $1\frac{1}{8}$ in. (28·5 mm) or $1\frac{1}{4}$ in. (32 mm) stuff, mortised and tenoned or dowelled together, with a $\frac{3}{4}$ in. (19 mm) stretcher rail stub tenoned in. The stout top of $1\frac{1}{8}$ in. (28·5 mm) solid blockboard, or $\frac{5}{8}$ in. (16 mm) ply thicknessed up on the outer edges, is secured to the frames by gluing and screwing; whilst the separate pedestal unit with $\frac{3}{4}$ in. (19 mm) cheeks, recessed top, bottom and drawer rails, etc. and onset drawers, firmly screwed to the side frame and the top is usually sufficient to ensure overall rigidity. A small vee or double chamfer can be worked round the top lower edge and edge framing as 350:2. Standard sizes for this type

1

SCALE

IN
0 3 6   12   24

0 5   15   25   35   45   55
CMs

2

TOP

3

4

5

6

7

of desk are usually 4 ft (122 cm) by 2 ft 6 in. (76 cm). wide and 2 ft 5 in. (74 cm) high, whilst 350:3, 4 and 5 show 5 ft (152 cm) long variations. As these latter have double pedestals the lower stretcher rail can be dispensed with provided the top is stout enough to prevent any sagging action.

Executive desks standing isolated usually have an apron front to hide the knees (350:4), which is merely a sheet of veneered blockboard, etc. either oversailing the frames or inset between them (350:6, 7), and screwed in position through the back of the pedestals.

413

351 Walnut writing-desk with canted front *Designed by Ernest Joyce MSIA. Author's workshops*

352 Print chest with adjustable top covered black leather. Chest in Rio rosewood with two drawers. (HRH Duke of Edinburgh's Prize for elegant design 1962.) *Designed by R. D. Russell RDI. Author's workshops*

353 Office furniture for Permanent Secretary, Board of Trade
By courtesy of Ministry of Public Building and Works

354 Office desk for Ministry of Public Building and Works
By courtesy of Ministry of Public Building and Works

355 Office desk and cabinet in Rio rosewood
Designed by David Powell Des.RCA. David Powell workshops

356 Office furniture for NEDDY private office.
By courtesy of Ministry of Public Building and Works

357 Bow-fronted glazed china cabinet in English walnut *Designed by Edward Barnsley CBE. Barnsley workshops*

Corner cabinets and cupboards

Corner cabinets are useful for display purposes, also for conversion into cocktail cabinets, but are unsuitable as general cupboards, bookcases, etc. owing to the wasted space. Figure 358:1 shows a typical example of a glazed door corner cabinet, and 358:2 a single-door corner cupboard. If tall cabinets are built-in it is usual to set the side pilasters proud of the cheeks and scribe to fit the walls, whilst the angle of the cupboard plan should be slightly more than a right angle as it is never wise to assume that plastered walls will be plumb or the corners at true right angles to each other. Such precautions hardly matter with free-standing cabinets (358:1) as the skirting boards will throw the carcase clear of the walls, but may be necessary with the wall cupboard (358:2).

Construction of corner cabinets, etc.

Tall cabinets can have separate top and bottom carcases, with the cheeks made up of top and bottom framing rails and grooved-in ply panel grooved into the front pilaster and back post (358:3), or solid laminboard cheeks grooved together (358:4). In 358:3 the back post will continue down to floor level, but 358:4 will require a stump leg added. Tops and upper carcase bottom can be framed in as 358:5, dovetailed to the pilasters and either rebated into the cheek rails or screwed to fixing fillets, or tenoned (358:6) and screwed from the outside; whilst the lower carcase bottom will have to be trenched in as 358:10 or treated as the tops (358:11). The pilasters are usually set at right angles to the cheeks, but this is not arbitrary and the angle or splay can be flattened slightly if necessary, but the doors should enter as 358:9 with the appropriate angles taken from a full-size setting out. Drawer arrangements are shown in 358:7, where in 358:7A the length and width are greatly restricted if orthodox runners are used, whereas in 358:7B a larger drawer is possible if a centre muntin is provided dovetailed as shown in 358:8A to fit in sliders (358:8B) screwed to the carcase bottom. This was the method adopted in the cocktail corner cabinet illustrated in 359. A typical base carcase assembly is shown in 358:10 in which the cheeks are carried down to floor level, and 358:11 where an independent plinth or leg framing is added.

In setting out the dovetails (358:9) reference should be made to *Dovetailing Practice, Canted Work*, page 199.

416

359 Corner cocktail cabinet in English burr walnut, interior lined with bleached sapelewood and mahogany curls, three drawers *Designed by Ernest Joyce MSIA. Author's workshops*

360 Showing cabinet doors open

Wall fitments

Figure 361:1 is an example of a backless wall fitment incorporating writing-top, stationery case, cupboard with sliding doors and adjustable shelving for china, books, etc. Construction can be with knock-down fittings (see Chapter 35), or lap dovetailed if the top is above eye level, and the base housed into the ends with a stout bearer rail tenoned through and wedged. Methods of supporting the adjustable shelving are described in Chapter 35, page 362, but it is always advisable to include one or more dovetailed or plain housed fixed shelves for overall rigidity, and to hold the ends in case they are inclined to bow out under central-heating conditions. Fitments can be built up on site to fit alcoves or arbitrary spaces (361:4) or constructed on a modular basis, i.e. multiples of a constant measurement, 4 in. (10 cm), 6 in. (15 cm), etc., or constant width, 21 in. (53 cm), 24 in. (61 cm), etc. with the separate

units brought to the site fully assembled and coupled together by screwing through the cheeks (361:5). The interior fitments, writing compartment, drinks cabinet, etc. can also be built in as part of the structure, or as separate boxes which can be adjusted to any height by screwing through the cheeks into the main divisions. In 361:1 the base shelving is raised up to allow for easy cleaning, but if toe-room only is provided (361:2), then the bearer rail should be brought forward to seal off the gap. Suggested measurements are shown in 361:3, with space above about 63 in. (160 cm), which is the eye level and maximum reach height for the average housewife, treated as 'dead storage' area for occasional access only. If the fitments are taken up to ceiling height any slight gap should be covered with a scribing fillet cut to the ceiling-line, and either planted on as 361:6 or set in and pinned from the back (361:7). The latter also shows an inset side

HEIGHTS

DEAD STORAGE

63 IN.
160cm — EYE LEVEL

6½-10½ IN — BOOKS
16·5 – 26·5 cm

86cm
34 IN — WORKING

29 IN — WRITING
73·5cm

15 IN — BOTTLES
38cm

3 IN — TOE ROOM
7·5cm

14-16 IN WIDE
35-40 cm

2 IN
6 cm
3 IN
7·5 cm

├─ 12 IN ─┤
30 cm

1
2
3
4
5
6
7

A

scribing fillet, as plaster walls are rarely plumb. Tall fitments can be anchored with glass mirror plates, or with battens screwed to the underside of the top shelf and plugged and screwed to the wall.

Wall cabinets

These can be incorporated in the wall fitment already described, or fixed direct to the wall, for they have obvious advantages in small rooms as there is no wasted leg space. Figure 362:1 shows a writing fitment, 362:2 a cupboard with shelf with either glass or laminboard doors, and 362:3 an open bookcase on similar lines. Acceptable dimensions could be $8\frac{1}{2}$ in. (21·5 cm) deep and 20 in. (51 cm) high for the bookshelves,

and $14\frac{1}{2}$ in. (37 cm) deep, 15 in. (38 cm) high and 32 in. (81 cm) wide for the cabinets. Larger sizes are possible providing the fixings are adequate, and the writer has hung a 6 ft (183 cm) long sideboard with $1\frac{1}{4}$ in. (32 mm) thick marble top, by making up a $1\frac{1}{2}$ in. (38 mm) angle-iron framework with projecting ends which were cemented into a 9 in. (228 mm) brick partition wall, with the carcase slid on after the framework had been fixed, but this was a fitting of a permanent nature. Construction of the small cabinets shown can be with any orthodox jointing method, mitre dovetails, through dovetails, etc. or tongued as shown in 362:4, whilst fall flaps can be hung on pivots (362:5), or merely pivoted through the sides with brass screws and sockets (362:6). Figure 362:7 shows a method of wall fixing in which the

362   Wall cupboards and shelving

cabinet is hung from a bevelled rail (362:7A) securely plugged and screwed to the wall, with a corresponding bevelled rail tongued 362:7B or screwed to the plywood back, with the completed assembly as 362:8. This top hanging method will support considerable weights if the wall rail is securely fixed, but if there is any tendency for the carcase bottom to sag it should be stiffened with an inner rail, or an under batten should be screwed to the wall. Small cabinets, bookshelves, etc. can also be fixed with glass mirror plates. The slotted variety 362:9 are easier to fix as the wall screws can be aligned and driven home, and the carcase with its plates attached dropped in position, whereas with 362:10 the carcase must be held in the exact position whilst the wall screws are inserted.

363 Library fitting for magazines, etc. Mahogany frame with perspex supports

364 Library fittings, Herbarium, Scotland
By courtesy of Ministry of Public Building and Works

365–70 Series of interchangeable modular units in ash and painted board *Designed by David Crump M.Des.RCA. By courtesy of Royal College of Art*

38 Bedroom furniture

Wardrobes

Wardrobe sizes are determined by fashions in clothes, and modern designs are usually 5 ft 10 in. (178 cm) overall height, 20 in (51 cm) to 22 in. (56 cm) deep for clothes hung sideways, and with widths of 5 ft (152 cm), 4 ft (122 cm) or 3 ft (91 cm) according to the type. Hanging wardrobes are shown in 371:1, 2, 3, whilst 371:4 is a fitted wardrobe with shelves or trays, and 371:5 a combination robe. Figure 371:6 gives a larger view of the latter, with half the width allocated to full-length hanging space, and the other half divided into short-length hanging space or shelving and four drawers under. Figure 371:9 is a different arrangement with full-length doors, hat shelf and interior trays. Large wardrobes are often known as 'double', and provide a full-length mirror either on the centre pilaster between the doors, or fixed to the interior of one door.

Construction of all types of wardrobe are as for typical box structures already described under *Carcase constructions*, Chapter 27, page 269, but in planning such large carcases without fixed centre divisions or cross shelves due regard must be paid to the overall rigidity, and some method of stiffening must be incorporated with either reinforced head, plinth or central pilaster, and stout well-fitted back. Such reinforcements to prevent 'diamonding' are discussed under *Carcase-work*, page 267, but even with these there is always a tendency for large carcases to rick slightly on uneven flooring, therefore they should be packed up level or inset doors will bind. Partially for this reason manufacturers favour onset doors closing over the carcase cheeks, as any slight rick to the carcase does not upset the hanging to the same degree. If inset doors are fitted (371:7), then false cheeks (371:7A) will be necessary to prevent the trays fouling the doors in the open position, but with onset doors (371:8) there is no difficulty as the drawing shows. Trays (371:9, 10) are usually cut away boldly at the front so that the contents, shirts, underclothing, etc. can be plainly seen. They can be grooved for side runners or with bottom runners (371:10), and this latter method

is preferable as it gives about ¾ in. (19 mm) clearance between the trays which is usually necessary for soft, fluffy articles. Hanging rods for coat-hangers are ⅝ in. (16 mm) or ¾ in. (19 mm) brass-cased steel tube mounted in screw sockets fixed to the cheeks for clothes hung sideways (371:9, 11). For shallow wardrobes which will not accept the full width of the coat-hanger, short rods from front to back are held by socket hangers screwed to the underside of the shelf or top, or pull-out rods or sliders (371:12) can be fitted which enable the hanger to be pulled forward clear of the carcase.

Dressing-tables

Dressing-tables vary from around 27 in. (68·5 cm) to 29 in. (73·5 cm) high exclusive of mirror, or around 48 in. (122 cm) high including mirror, with carcase lengths from 36 in. (91 cm) to 60 in. (152 cm) and an average depth of 18 in. (46 cm). Low dressing-tables about 21 in. (53 cm) to 24 in. (61 cm) high without knee room, and therefore needing low stools to match, are also popular. No hard and fast rules apply to sizes for designs change frequently. Various types are shown in 373. Figure 373:1 shows a chest type 4 ft 10½ in. (148·5 cm) long and 4 ft (122 cm) high overall with single mirror; 373:2 a 4 ft 6 in. (137 cm) kneehole pedestal type with wing mirrors; 373:3 kneehole with centre drawer and single mirror; 373:4 a low type with three-quarter-length cheval mirror; and 373:5 a 3 ft (91 cm) dressing-chest. A dressing-desk with lift-up flap and interior mirror is illustrated in 373:6. The pedestal containing three drawers is made up separately, with legs attached either by tenoning into blocks screwed to the base or tenoned through the carcase base and wedged from the inside. The dressing-box and leg frame is a separate structure with the lower rails tenoned in, and the problem here is to form a strong joint between the box front and back and the pedestal cheek. They cannot be slot dovetailed in, and whilst stub tenons might be strong enough a more practical way is to fit an inside cheek to the

371 Wardrobe details

TRAY

A

7

TRAY

8

1

2

3

4

5

6

9

10

11

12

424

372 Combination wardrobe, eight-drawer chest and dressing-chest with mirror in chipboard veneered afromosia *Designed by A. R. B. Cox. By courtesy of Alfred Cox (Furniture) Limited. Photograph: Council of Industrial Design*

box (373:7), lap dovetailed to the front and back and screwed to the pedestal cheek. This also serves as a support for the lid, which is hinged to the back and closes over the framework. Another type is shown in 373:10 where the two units rest on a separate framework and are screwed together as in 373:7. A ply box for tall scent-bottles is incorporated in the dressing-box (373:11), and in both examples the brass mirror stay is fixed so that the mirror is stopped at the angle most convenient to the user in the seated position. Figure 373:8 is a pedestal type table with planted top and onset drawers closing over the carcase ends, with the drawer rails inset accordingly. If preferred, a front or apron piece can be substituted for the centre drawer which is not altogether convenient, for the user must lean back every time the drawer is opened to its fullest extent. This apron piece can be dovetail housed, tongued in, or dowelled and glue blocked from the inside, and gives a strong junction between

the two pedestals. The frameless mirrors can be treated in various ways. In 373:9A the wing mirrors are permanently fixed to hidden pillars, and the centre mirror pivoted to the wings with friction plates packed out to the required angle. Figure 373:9B shows each mirror pivoted on independent hidden pillars, and 373:9C hidden pillars so placed that the wing mirrors can be butt hinged to the pillars. The various types of mirror fixing are shown in 378–9. Figure 373:12 shows a man's dressing-chest of the military-chest type with or without brass corner plates and flush brass handles, in which a bearer rail is screwed to the top drawer sides and the mirror fixed to this with a length of piano hinge. The drawer sides must be set down by the thickness of the mirror frame plus the protruding knuckle of the hinge, and the drawer is stopped so that the mirror inclines slightly off the vertical, and is supported by the edge of the carcase top in the fully open position.

374 Dressing-table in Indian laurel with wing mirrors closing over centre mirror case *Designed by R. D. Russell RDI. Author's workshops*

375 Wing mirrors in closed position

376 Dressing-table for officers married quarters, War Department *By courtesy of Ministry of Public Building and Works*

377 Dressing-table with writing-tablet, Queen Mary's Hospital *By courtesy of Ministry of Public Building and Works*

Mirrors

Mirrors are usually $\frac{1}{4}$ in. (6 mm) first-quality polished plate glass silvered and protected. Frameless mirrors should have all edges ground and polished, but framed mirrors need only ground edges. Rough cut edges should not be used even in framing, for the sharp edges of the fractures will be clearly visible from the sides, and even with ground edges it is usual to matt black the frame rebates to cut down unwanted reflections.

Framed mirrors

Frames need be of light section only, for the glass itself will keep the framework square and rigid, and the ply back will strengthen the jointing. A typical cheval mirror glass with stand is shown in 378:1, 2 with 1 in. (25 mm) by 1 in. (25 mm) frame jointed as 378:9. The stand (378:1) has a bearer rail tenoned into the tapered standards, and the legs are dowelled on 378:2. Small blocks are screwed to the standards (378:2A), and a thin lath fixed across the width to tie the standards in, whilst the mirror frame is mounted with drop or ring handles screwed through, with a wood button spacer as shown in 378:7. The friction created by giving the drop handles half a turn is usually sufficient to keep the heaviest mirror in the desired position. The mirror glass itself is cut about $\frac{1}{16}$ in. (1·5 mm) bare all round, and held in position with small softwood wedges glued and pinned (378:10, 11), whilst the ply back can be planted on (378:10) or let into a rebate (378:11). It should not be glued in case the glass has to be renewed at any time, but should be brass screwed at frequent intervals. Figure 378:11 also shows a method of forming the frame rebate by gluing on a $\frac{1}{8}$ in. (3 mm) facing piece, often cross-grain saw-cut veneer in old work. Figure 378:3, 4 show a small toilet mirror with stand, with the standards sloping fractionally, and the mirror frame also attached by small drop handles. If wings are added to these toilet mirrors (378:5) the bearer rail shown in 378:3 can be omitted, and the spread of the feet reduced (378:6), as the angle of the wings will support the complete mirror. The framing need only be jointed as 378:8, with a facing thickness to form the rebate, and the wings attached to the standards with brass butts or back-flap hinges. Drop handles cannot be used for this type as they would foul the wings, and a friction-plate assembly is used of which 378:12 is an example of the many types available. The feet of the stands should be tipped with felt or baize to prevent scratching polished surfaces when the mirror is moved.

Shaped mirrors

Figure 379:1, 2 shows a wall mirror with shaped head. The frame can be band-sawn out of solid stuff, jointed together as in old examples, but a better method is to laminate as in 379:3, tenoning the various sections together as 379:4, and facing up with $\frac{1}{8}$ in. (3 mm) stuff to cover the laminations and form the rebate. An alternative method for small mirrors is to build up a laminated block with the double curve cut out in one piece as 379:5. The cross-grain tenons might appear weak, for the grain directions forming the lamination are not crossed as in plywood, but in practice the glue-lines hold the fibres together and the strength is adequate. Straight members jointed to curved members can be cut out of solid stuff, but in principle it is better to use laminations throughout so that the shrinkage values are identical. Circular mirrors 379:6 can be spindle moulded or turned on the end-face plate of a woodturning lathe, building up blocks to form the ring as 379:8, mounting on a plywood disc with a sheet of thick paper glued between, and centring the disc on the metal face plate (379:8A). The individual blocks should be cut and jointed to give as long scarfing joints as possible, and well sized before gluing together; but large mirrors may require the segments jointed together with veneer tongues as in mitre-work, or the face and back of the frame veneered to hold the joints. If the face of the frame is moulded then the back of the frame will have to be glued to the ply disc and the glass rebate formed with a hook turning tool. After turning and sanding in the lathe the frame is separated from the paper interleaving in the usual way, and the back (or face) cleaned off. A standard tilting pillar fitment for mounting circular mirrors on dressing-tables is shown in 379:7, which is taken through the top and secured.

SCALES

IN   CM

A

379   Shaped mirrors

Frameless mirrors

Frameless mirrors with all edges polished 380:1 are supported by a stout ply back, and held in position with chrome-plated clips as inset. Figure 380:2, 3 are bevel shaped all round, whilst 380:4 is mounted on a veneered board and held by special fixing screws with heads tapped for chrome-plated domes (380:5). The screws should be an easy fit in the glass holes, and must not be screwed down tight; moreover if there is the slightest suggestion of bumpiness in the ground, rubber washers (w) should be used to isolate the glass, which could crack if any local strain is imposed.

Hidden pillar mirrors

Small mirrors fixed to dressing-tables will only require one pillar (380:6) screwed to the carcase back, with the mirror supported by a friction stay. The mirror can be released by pressing the forked arms (380:6A) together, and lifting the top plates off their pivots. Larger cheval-type mirrors will require two pillars (380:7), with a more robust stay (380:8) in which the wing arm is secured with a wing nut. The edges of the ply backs used for mounting these mirrors can be masked with thick poster paint, coloured to match the wood finish and then polished in the usual manner.

Bedsteads and divans, etc.

Beds take different forms of which the most popular are: (1) legless sprung-base supports with either steel channel or timber framing for connection to orthodox bedsteads (bedhead and foot), and with spring or foam over-mattresses; (2) divan beds in which a timber-box framework on stump legs is sprung with metal mesh or coil springing covered with fabric, on which a sprung or foam over-mattress is laid, and with a headboard screwed to the box framework. Both forms are specialist made, and the furniture-maker is only concerned with the provision of bedheads and feet or divan headboards.

Bed sizes

Ideally single beds should be as wide as the outstretched elbows of the sleeper and certainly not less than 2 ft 6 in. (76 cm) wide, with 3 ft (91 cm) more convenient. Double beds should be not less than 4 ft (122 cm) wide, with 4 ft 6 in. (137 cm) or 5 ft (152 cm) preferable. Mattress lengths are usually standard at 6 ft 3 in. (190 cm) for people up to 6 ft (183 cm) tall, but can be supplied up to 7 ft (213 cm) long. For easy making heights should be about 20 in. (508 mm) to the top of the over-mattress, but the modern tendency is to place divan beds either on or about 6 in. (152 mm) from floor level, which is not so hygienic and more difficult for the housewife.

Bedsteads

A typical sprung-base support bedstead with detachable bedhead and foot is shown in 381:1. Figure 381:2 shows a corner of the framework mitred and tenoned, and with glued-in plywood panel. This panel can be covered with material (grass matting, etc.) in which case the covering is pasted on with a suitable adhesive (wallpaper paste, shoemakers' paste) and glued and pinned through the weave of the material to a suitable rebate worked in the framework (381:3). The framework can also be caned if it is stout enough to support the pull of the caning, which is fairly considerable over a large area. A shallow rebate is worked on the face, $\frac{1}{2}$ in. (12·5 mm) wide and sufficiently deep to take the thickness of about three layers of cane, with $\frac{1}{8}$ in. (3 mm) holes bored at $\frac{5}{8}$ in. (16 mm) centres. The inner face of the bed foot framework can be sheeted in with a ply panel set in a corresponding rebate to hide the rough back of the caning. It is usual to make bedheads about 6 in. (150 mm) to 8 in. (200 mm) higher than the foot to allow for the pillow, etc. Patent screw fastenings or locking plates are used to connect the wood side rails with the head and foot, and 381:4, 5 show a typical assembly (Huwil No. 25.16) in which the corner plate is screwed to the side rail, and slotted over special screws or nylon bushes let into the head and foot.

Divan headboards

As the divan base is equipped with its own stump legs a headboard only is necessary (381:6), either screwed direct to the box frame of the divan or anchored with special screw-plate assemblies (381:8) through screwed-on supports (381:7),

1

2

3

4

5

6

7

8

9

10

C L

A   B

11

382   Divan bed with under drawers in natural pine
By courtesy of Price Brothers Co. Limited
Photograph: Council of Industrial Design

which can be slotted to allow the headboard to be adjusted to the correct height. Continental-type headboards for double divan beds (381:10) are usually about 7 ft 9 in. (236 cm) long overall, and carry drawer fitments on either side so placed that there is sufficient space between the fitment and the divan bed to allow the bed linen to be tucked in during making. These fitments are made up as independent backless boxes firmly screwed in position from the back of the headboard; they can have central leg supports 381:9, 10A), or if the headboard is fixed to the wall with mirror plates both they and the central supporting struts (381:10B) can be dispensed with. Ideally the top of the fitment should be about 4 in.

(10 cm) higher than the top of the mattress, and this also applies to separate bedside cabinets or tables. The actual headboard is usually a single sheet of $\frac{5}{8}$ in. (16 mm) or $\frac{3}{4}$ in (19 mm) veneered ply, laminboard or chipboard, lipped on the show edges, but it can be framed up, or caned or upholstered. A secret castor fitting for beds, divans, etc. is shown in 381:11, in which case long divan headboards with drawer fitments should be fixed to the wall and not to the divan. The castors should have hard polished tyred wheels for carpets, but soft rubber for slippery tiles and linoleum or the divan will move too easily and could be dangerous for invalids or the elderly.

39 Chair-work

General note

Chairs of compound curvature and subtle shaping require the application of specialist skills, and in many richly ornamented traditional examples the designer prepared his sketches, leaving it to the actual maker to choose the timber and methods of jointing. As it is difficult if not at times impossible to plot all the curves of an elaborate chair in two-dimensional drawings only, the final result was dependent in great measure on the skill and sensitivity of the individual craftsman, and such chairs were highly expensive to manufacture, requiring the wasteful use of heavy timber sections which were rough shaped, jointed and assembled and then sculptured and carved, using special chair-makers' tools. Modern designs employ straight sectioned timber wherever possible, and steam bending or laminating for curved work, thereby effecting considerable economies in both time and materials. Such chairs are relatively simple to make, and do not require the same measure of specialist skill.

Chair sizes

Much research has been done into the principles of restful sitting, but whilst it should be possible to construct the perfect seating medium for any particular user the average chair is designed for unseen customers, male or female, tall or short, fat or thin. Thus carefully calculated moduli based on the law of averages should be approached with caution. For instance, the standard height of a table-top now usually accepted as 29 in. (735 mm) calls for a chair seat height of 17 in. (430 mm) to $17\frac{1}{2}$ in. (440 mm), but this is still too high for many people, and too low for some. What is badly needed, and will no doubt be evolved at some future date, are tables and chairs which can be adjusted at a touch to any individual requirement. In the meantime the measurements given below must be regarded as guide-lines only.

Generally speaking the backward slope of the seat should not produce a knee angle of less than 90° with the feet flat to the floor, whilst the elbow angle at rest on the side arms should not force the shoulders up. If the back is curved then the arch of the curve should be a bare 8 in. (200 mm) above the seat, and the seat should be as deep as possible but not greater than the length of the thigh measured from the fold of the knee to the back. Easy chairs should not be so low or the backward slope of the seat so great that it requires physical leverage against the arms to lift the body from the seated position, and due allowance must be made for the extent of the compression or 'bottoming' of thick foam cushions under load.

Chair construction

Traditional chairs were normally framed together with mortise and tenon joints, for dowel-pegs had to be hand-shaped and boring-bits were primitive. Modern chairs rely more on dowelling techniques, and there can be no valid objection to this providing the pegs are of sufficient length to hold the joint. The usual procedure is to make up the front and back frames first, and then connect with the side rails unless a knock-down assembly (394:1) is used. All chair-work requires accurate full-size drawings from which the correct angles and bevels can be taken, and more elaborate chairs really need a full-size working model or prototype in softwood which can be tested and altered as required.

Chair joints

Top back rail joints are illustrated in 383. Figure 383:1 is a tenon on the rail, 383:2 shows a tenon on the post, and 383:5 a dovetail bridle joint. Where the timber sections are very slight (383:6) the joint can be reinforced by forming a step to support the back thrust and increase the gluing area. Figure 383:3 shows a shaped post and top rail mortised and tenoned together and rounded after assembly. In 383:4 the top dowel has no real holding power but does prevent the top twisting out of line, whilst dowels are also

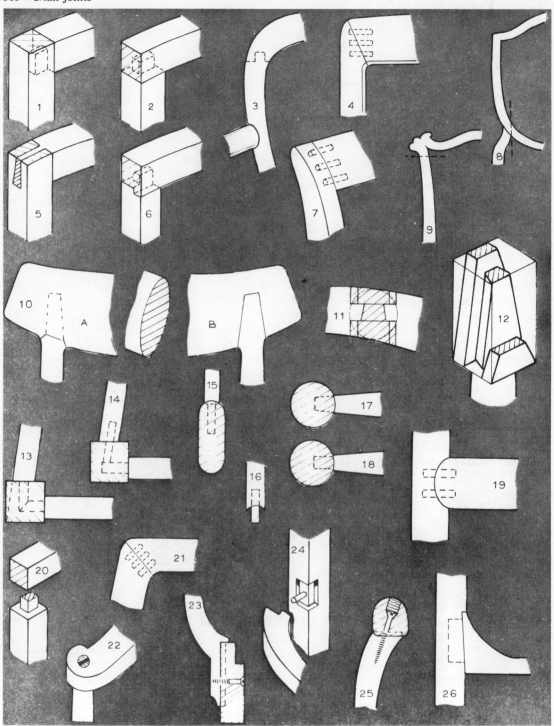

used in 383:7 where it might be difficult to accommodate a tenon in the curve of the back post. The shield back chair in 383:8 and Chippendale carved chair in 383:9 are shown as a matter of interest only, for the heavy carving usually disguises the line of the joint as shown by the dotted lines. A modern treatment in which a bowed, tilted and rounded back rail meets turned back posts is shown in 383:10–12, with 383:10A the front view and 383:10B the back view. Figure 383:11, 12 show the actual joint and the amount of material left on to accommodate the dovetail. The joint must be carefully set out and worked with the final rounding and shaping done when the rail is fully assembled, therefore this type of construction is very expensive and confined to the best handwork only. Figure 383:13 shows a mortise and tenon joint at the junction of front and side seat rails with the front leg. Either a canted tenon or a canted mortise is necessary for the latter, therefore it is more usual to tenon the front rail and dowel the side rail (383:14), in which it is comparatively simple to bore the leg at the correct angle obtained from the full-size drawing. The outer face of the leg is usually planed off after assembly to the line of the rail as indicated by the dotted lines in 383:13. Back seat rails are normally tenoned in to the back posts. Where a rail meets a rounded leg (383:15) a small flat can be worked for square-cut tenon shoulders, but if the rail is also rounded then the leg recess must be scribed to fit. Here again it is simpler to use dowels, cutting the rail end square, marking and boring for the dowels and scribing the rail shoulders to fit the leg before the dowels are glued in 383:16. Figure 383:17 shows a turned spindle entering a round leg, and if a bung borer (taper bit) is available then the spindle is turned to fit the taper, taking care to ensure that the socket depth is correct, for there will be no shoulder to limit the entry. Parallel-sided sockets bored with standard bits will require a turned shoulder on the spindle and a small flat formed on the leg, but in cheap work the taper spindle is merely driven into the parallel hole, with the result that it only bites at the neck. In 383:19, where a pronounced hollow is formed in the leg, it will be easier to use dowels, marking, boring and then fitting the rail to the leg before the dowels are inserted. An improved method of jointing side rails to back posts sometimes adopted in Scandinavian furniture is shown in 384 but it is essentially a machine operation.

The junction of arm rests with leg posts is shown in 383:20 where a small stub tenon can be used, although a single dowel is often effective, for the strain is upwards and not sidewards. Traditional chairs with turned legs and flat arm rests employed a spigot end to the leg taken through and wedged from the top as 383:22, whilst 383:21 is the jointing of a typical modern framework where the overall angle is halved and dowelled together. Figure 383:23 is the junction of arm post with side rails in conventional armchairs, with the arm post housed in and screwed from the inside, and 383:24 the connection with the back post with a stub dowel to take the pull. Older examples were often housed in and screwed and pelleted from the back (383:25), whilst 383:26 is the junction of a downward curved arm rest tenoned in and housed at the top to avoid a feather edge in the final shaping after assembly.

384 Chair rail joint

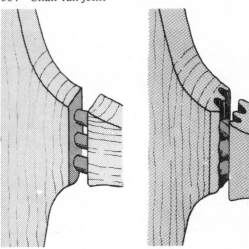

Simple dining-chair

The illustrations in 385 show the construction of this type of chair. Figure 385:1 is the side elevation, 385:2 the seat plan, 385:3 the angle of the rail joints taken from the full-size drawing, 385:4 the stout corner blocks which are glued and screwed into each corner of the seat frame to increase the overall rigidity of the chair. Figure 385:5 is an exploded diagram of the construction,

1

2

3

4

5

6

7

0   3   6   IN

0   5   10 15 CM

FRAME

PLY

FOAM

COVER

A

with the front rail kept down flush with the rebates in the side rails, with a supporting fillet screwed to the back rail for the ply base of the seat. This ply base should be bored to allow the air to escape from the foam-rubber seating, especially if impervious top coverings (leather, plastic cloth, etc.) are used. Figure 385:6, 7 are alternative mortise and tenon joints for front and back posts. The padded back is screwed to the back posts from the inside, and the top cover carried over to hide the framing, or alternatively 6 in. (152 mm) taper dovetail slide connectors can be obtained in which the female part is screwed to the back post, and the male part screwed to the back rest slid down into position after the upholstery is completed. Chairs of this description can have webbed and upholstered drop in seats as shown in *Upholstery*, Chapter 43, page 471 in which case the front rail is flush with the side rails and the $\frac{5}{8}$ in. (16 mm) rebate continued round to receive the seat frame. Figure 401 shows a typical seat frame (401:4) for webbing which can be either dowelled (401:5) or half lapped and screwed (401:6). Suitable dimensions for average seat frames can be 2 in. (51 mm) or $2\frac{1}{2}$ in. (63·5 mm) wide stuff, $\frac{5}{8}$ in. (16 mm) or $\frac{3}{4}$ in. (19 mm) thick, and are usually made of beech which will take closely spaced tacks without splitting, although it is somewhat prone to worm. Figure 401:7 shows the rebate in the chair rails, allowing about $\frac{1}{8}$ in. (3 mm) clearance all round for the thickness of the covering materials.

386 Dining-chair with fluted back in African mahogany *Designed by Ernest Joyce MSIA. Author's workshops*

387 Round chair in beech with cane seat *Designed by Hans J. Wegner. By courtesy of Johannes Hansen, Copenhagen*

389 Detail of chair back and seat with external facings of preformed white formica
By courtesy of CIBA (ARL) Limited

Turned rush-seated chair

Traditional examples of this type of chair often used coppice ash for the back posts, which merely required soaking in hot water to enable the bend to be formed. It is usual to turn first and then bend, although there is always some danger of crushing the rounded surface of the wood if the bend is acute. Modern examples of these chairs are often stained with clear penetrating dyes which do not choke or disguise the grain of the wood, but to avoid uneven coloration the whole chair should be dipped.

Memorial chair

Figure 392 shows a fairly typical oak memorial, chairman's or church chair or orthodox construction with foam-padded seat and hair-stuffed buttoned back. The back panel is solid timber jointed up and fielded. It should be quartered stuff if possible, well dried before insertion in the panel grooves, or shrinkage across the width could be sufficient to pull it out of the grooves. Care must be taken to ensure that no surplus glue squeezes out of the joints to grip the panel in the grooves, as this has been known to split the panel. A more modern version of a bishop's chair with hand-stitched cowhide upholstery is shown in 427.

Easy or lounge chairs

Figure 394:1 shows a lounge chair of knock-down construction, using tenoned or dowelled side frames and separate back frame and front apron rail connected with suitable slot-headed screws engaging in sunk nuts. There is no seat frame as such, and resilient rubber webbing is used for the suspension, anchored with metal clips as shown at 394:1A, A, top rail 394:2A, A, and front rail 394:2B, B. The front rail (394:2B) should have locating stub dowels either side of the central screw to prevent it twisting. Figure 394:3, 4 is another framed-up chair with finger-jointed arm rests and tenoned or dowelled front, side and back rails, with the back frame screwed from the inside into the arm and lower rails. Here again suspension is with resilient webbing.

Swivel chair

A typical swivel-chair action is shown in 400:1, together with 400:2 swivel metal chair action, and 400:3 matching metal settee support. This type of chair should have a fairly firm seat, and the foam padding can be placed on a ply base. Stout cross-bearers are fixed under the seat to take the swivel arms.

1

2

3

SCALE   INCHES
0 1 2 3 4 5 6 7 8 9 10

CMs
0   5   10   15   20   25

391 Shaping the arm of a Wegner chair.
By courtesy of Johannes Hansen, Copenhagen

392 Memorial chair

FIELDED

HAIR STUFFED

FOAM

393 Chancellor's chair Keele University in English oak with upholstery in red Niger goat-skins *Designed and carved by Professor D. W. Pye ARIBA, FSIA. Author's workshops*

395 Lounge chair in American black walnut *Designed by T. A. Marsh, Brighton College of Art*

396 Easy chair in afromosia *Designed and made at Brighton College of Art*

397 Bastiano chair, frame of solid padouk *Designed by Tobia Scarpa. By courtesy of Gavina, Milan*

399 Prototype chair of acrylic sheet made by Imperial Chemical Industries Limited *Designed by Jane Young M.Des.RCA. By courtesy of Royal College of Art*

398 Chair of thrust moulded acrylic sheet supported on high-tensile steel frame *Designed by David Colwell M.Des.RCA. By courtesy of Royal College of Art*

400   Swivel chair and metal actions

401   Stool and seat frame details

SCALE   INS
Cms

446

Stools

Figure 401:1, 2, 3 shows a low fireside- or dressing-stool, with foam upholstery on a ply base pocket screwed to the framework which can be tenoned or dowelled together.

In 402, one of a set of twelve stools, the solid seats out of 3 in. (76 mm) African walnut were dished by hand using spokeshaves and improvised wooden planes with curved soles. The foam padding was stuck to the seat and the leather to the foam padding with rubber cement (upholsterers rubber glue), with the leather eased and stretched round the sharp corners with a minimum of tailoring.

402   Bar stool in Rio rosewood, solid seat dished and shaped, covered foam pad and leather   *Designed by R. D. Russell RDI. Author's workshops*

403   Stools   *Designed by Alva Aalto.   By courtesy of Artek, Helsinki*

404   Stool legs of laminated birch.   *By courtesy of Artek, Helsinki*

447

40 Tea-trays, trolleys, library steps

Tea-tray

A simple tray which illustrates the technique of preforming is illustrated in 405 to 408. This was originally designed some 12 years ago, but is still in demand owing to its exceptional lightness (1 lb 2 oz (510 g)) combined with the overall rigidity, absence of whip under load and great strength which the curved bottom imparts to it. It is made up of a sheet of $\frac{1}{16}$ in. (1·5 mm) birch ply veneered both sides and cold pressed with resin glue be-

tween two formers, either in a press or between G-cramps. Grooves are worked in the $\frac{7}{8}$ in. (22 mm) by $\frac{5}{16}$ in. (8 mm) sides cut from the solid, and in the moulded end-grips into which the shaped bottom is glued. The glue joint between the sides and end-grips is further reinforced with brass screws in neat brass sockets sanded off flush. A convenient size is 20 in. (508 mm) long by $12\frac{1}{2}$ in. (318 mm) wide overall.

405 Preformed tray details

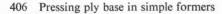

406 Pressing ply base in simple formers

407 Five veneers pressed together to form ply base

Preformed tray with bent ply base and solid sides and ends *Designed by Ernest Joyce MSIA*

Butler's tray

This old form of carrying tray was usually made in two forms; a tall variety on X legs with a turned centre spindle connecting the legs, and the low stool variety illustrated in 409. The former were about 29 in. (737 mm) high and the latter 18 in. (457 mm) high, with elliptical top about 39 in. (981 mm) by 30 in. (762 mm) when fully opened. The fixed top was usually panelled to prevent casting, but modern versions are veneered ply, etc. with the wings in carefully matched solid timber. The ellipse should be set out as described under *Workshop geometry and drawing*, Chapter 6, page 78, and the wings are connected with ordinary back flap hinges. If the hinges work too easily, allowing the wings to fall from the upright carrying position, they can be set very fractionally askew to stiffen the movement. The stool is framed up in the orthodox manner and the top secured with shrinkage plates. Figure 411:1 shows the tray in the carrying position and 411:2 with the wings down.

Tea-trolleys

Tea-trolleys usually vary from about 28 in. (71 cm) to 30 in. (76 cm) high, 22 in. (56 cm) to 27 in. (68 cm) long and 14 in. (36 cm.) to 18 in. (46 cm) wide, with timber sections as light as possible consonant with overall rigidity. If the corner posts are square section (411:3) then the rails can be tenoned in as 411:5, with the $\frac{1}{4}$ in. (6 mm) veneered ply trays grooved into the rails and posts. Thinner posts (411:6) may require the end rails tenoned through and wedged, and the long rails dowelled in. The trolley ends should be glued up first, the grooves extended into the posts, the tray bottoms cut and a trial assembly

made to see that everything fits. In the final assembly a little glue run into the grooves will increase the overall rigidity of the completed framework. Trolleys can have a top and bottom shelf as in 411:3, or an intermediate shelf as 411:4, and one end rail can be flush with the top shelf (411:7) for easier cleaning.

409 Tea-trolley in Australian walnut *Author's workshops*

410 Telephone trolley in teak, handles covered stitched cowhide *Designed by William Mitchell Des.RCA. Author's workshops*

1

2

3

H   26 IN   66 cm
L   30 IN   76 cm
W   18 IN   45 cm

4

H   28 IN   71 cm
L   28 IN   71 cm
W   18 IN   45 cm

5

6

7

Library steps

The library steps shown in 412:1 are 18 in. (46 cm) wide, 18 in. (46 cm) deep and 30 in. (76 cm) high, which is sufficient for normal requirements. Figure 412:2 shows the setting out and a mortised and tenoned construction is used, with the treads not less than a full inch in thickness for a stiff hardwood such as oak. The curved rails are band-sawn out of solid stuff, whilst the posts can be continuous and housed, screwed and pelleted if flush with the edge of the treads (412:3), or built up of sections, housed, mortised and tenoned together if slightly inset (412:4). Castors can be fitted, but are dangerous if very free running, and it is probably safer to tip the posts with hard rubber insets or dome gliders.

412   Library steps

41 Church work

General note

Fixed church work, pews, pulpits, stalls, chancel screens, etc. are usually regarded as a form of highly specialised joinery-work, and as such are beyond the scope of the average furniture-maker who will only be called upon to provide the occasional piece of movable furniture, litany desks, lecterns, altar-tables, bishop's chairs, etc. All too often the work has to match in with existing furnishings, Victorian Gothic, etc. heavily carved and moulded, and opportunities for imaginative work are confined to the very few new churches and church halls which are built from time to time. Where such opportunities exist church authorities will usually consider veneered work and other timbers besides the traditional oak in the contemporary idiom, but in the main the accent will be on the traditional approach, for the study of which the student has only to visit his local church. The illustrations following are, therefore, intended more as guidelines for average sizes than any detailed treatment of the subject. Constructions are usually orthodox and the accent on sturdiness, with moulded members boldly pronounced, for the setting is so much vaster and the viewing distances considerable. For ease in manufacture heavy timber sections are built up as shown in 413, and whilst oak is still a prime favourite there is a growing tendency to use African mahogany, sapelewood and afromosia, etc. Problems of over-heating and consequent shrinkage do not usually arise, except in church halls which are used for other purposes, therefore moisture contents need not be so critical as with domestic furniture, although thoroughly seasoned timber must of course be used. Particular attention should be paid to hard edges which should be well rounded or eased back, especially in the more splintery timbers, and polishes should be hard, avoiding sticky waxes or soft varnishes.

Altar-tables

These can be simple tables draped with richly embroidered side curtains, austere constructions of rectangular uprights in brick, stone or concrete with planted tops, or box forms either framed up with stout corner posts, thick ply panels and bold bolection mouldings (414:8), or flush blockboard front and sides over a stout inner framework, and with mouldings planted on (414:6, 7, 8).

Choir-stall fronts

Construction of these is similar as 414:1, 2, with sloping top and inside shelf 414:3.

Clergyman's desk

Figure 414:4, 5 gives details on similar lines, with well-supported seat in hardwood shown by the dotted lines in 414:5; whilst 415:1, 2 gives a similar desk in greater detail. A boarded floor 415:3 on softwood joists is provided, whilst 415:4 shows the moulding detail to the top, and 415:5 the pilaster mould covering the posts (415:1).

413 Moulding detail in church work

CHOIR STALL FRONT

C L

1

2

3

CLERGYMAN'S DESK

SCALE
ins cms

3
6
9
12
15
18
21
24
27

5
15
25
35
45
55
65

4

5

ALTAR TABLE

C L

6

7

8

SCALE

INS

CMs

1
2
3
4
5

Lecterns

Two forms of lectern are shown in 416, whilst 419 gives details of adjustable lecterns where both the height and the angle of the top can be varied. Figure 419:1 shows a variable height top with a boxed-up standard and a $1\frac{1}{4}$ in. (32 mm) central shaft a sliding fit. The movement is controlled by a brass spring plunger engaging in a series of brass sockets let into the central shaft at $1\frac{1}{2}$ in. (38 mm) intervals. In 419:2 the counter-weight principle as applied to sliding sash-

windows is employed for larger lecterns. The central shaft is slotted to pass freely over a small $\frac{1}{2}$ in. (12·5 mm) pulley fixed to a spindle which rides in brass socket bearings let into the sides or the standard. A length of piano wire is attached to the base of the shaft, looped round the pulley and secured to a suitable weight below. These cast-iron cylindrical sash weights are obtainable from ironmongers in a range of poundages (kilogrammes) but a more exact method is to weigh the complete top and shaft and cast an

SCALE

0	6	12	18	24

INS

0	5	15	25	35	45	55

CMs

EX 6"×2"

15×5 cm

EX 4"×2½"

10×6·3cm

417 Adjustable table lectern with centre pillar *Author's workshops*

418 Lectern in English brown oak for **Liberian** Senate House, Monrovia (1952) *Designed by Ernest Joyce MSIA. Author's workshops*

equivalent amount of scrap lead in a suitable container, embedding a metal hasp for the piano wire at the time of casting. This gives finger-tip control, but the movement must be capable of being locked in any position by inserting a length of metal strip in the side of the shaft, with a brass thumb-screw passing through the side of the standard. A series of holes can be drilled in the metal strip to form locations for the screw. Figure 419:3 shows an adjustable hinged top with the angle of tilt controlled with two brass stays and locking wing nuts.

419 Adjustable lectern

1¼ in
32 mm

1

2

WING NUT

HINGE

3

Altar-rails

These are wide in section and assembled on site, using handrail screws (416:8) to connect the lengths. Figure 416:5 gives the elevation, 416:6 the plan, 416:7 a cross-section of the uprights tenoned in, and 416:8 the handrail and base rail. Sweeps are cut from the solid as the sections are usually stout enough to support the short grain on the curve.

Litany desk

A litany desk with fixed kneeler is shown in 421:1, 2 whilst 422 gives a side elevation of the desk illustrated in 420, with a collapsible kneeler upholstered with foam rubber on a ply base and covered with cowhide. This memorial desk 2 ft 6 in. (76 cm) wide, 1 ft 5½ in. (44 cm) deep and 3 ft (91 cm) high was made at the request of a client who asked for a primrose and ivy carved decoration to be incorporated for remembrance. Details of the St Marks lion and of the form of lettering used are also shown in 422. As the central aisle of the church was fairly narrow the lectern was fitted with hidden ball-type castors so that it could be wheeled to a side aisle when not in use. Construction was in natural brown oak of outstanding coloration, polished with hard (carnauba) wax polish to preserve the great beauty of the wood.

420 Litany desk in brown oak with hinged kneeler
Designed by Ernest Joyce MSIA. Author's workshops

TO THE GLORY OF GOD

21·7·1914   3·2·1956

THIS MEMORIAL IS DEDICATED BY HER PARENTS TO THE DEAR MEMORY OF JOAN ELIZABETH BERRAGE-MOULTON BELOVED DAUGHTER OF SIDNEY & FLORENCE COCKSEDGE.

421 Litany desk with fixed kneeler

SCALE INS

0   3   6   9   12

0   5   10   CMS

SHELF

1

2

ADEWIQ

423A, B Platform lectern in rosewood and Honduras mahogany, plastic inlay front *Designed by William Mitchell Des.RCA. Author's workshops*

A

B

424 Simple litany desk (Bullwood Borstal Institute Church) *By courtesy of Ministry of Public Building and Works*

425 Oak litany desk with pull-out kneeler *Designed by Ernest Joyce MSIA. Author's workshops*

426 Font cover in African mahogany *Author's workshops*

460

427 Bishop's chair in English oak covered hand-stitched leather *Designed by William Mitchell Des.RCA.   Author's workshops*

Part 6 Miscellaneous techniques
42 Wood finishing

The craft of staining, matching, hand and spray finishing is highly specialised and forms a separate trade, therefore the following notes are for general guidance only, and the reader is referred to the standard textbooks on the subject.

General note

Furniture in general use must be polished to seal the pores of the wood, protect the surfaces, accentuate and enhance the beauty of the figure, create highlights and provide as much resistance against heat or spilt liquids as possible. Earliest polishing materials dating back to the time of the Pharaohs were probably nut, poppy and linseed oils, gums, resins, etc., and it was not until 1820 that the familiar french polish was introduced into this country from France. Prior to that Evelyn's Diary refers to the practice of 'Joyners'* laying walnut boards in an oven or warm stable, and when the furniture was completed polishing it over 'with its own oyl, very hot, which makes it look sleek and black', whilst Sheraton advocated using a mixture of soft wax and turpentine. Favourite materials for cabinetmakers of that period were linseed oil for furniture, stained with alkanet root (which yields a permanent red dye) and mixed with brick-dust to produce a polishing putty under the polishing cloth; and hard wax (beeswax, turpentine, copal varnish and yellow ochre) for chairs. Modern practice uses a plethora of materials, natural and synthetic, whose aim it is to hasten, cheapen and give added protection, all of which is achieved to a very marked degree.

It is very doubtful, however, whether any modern method can match the old processes for sheer beauty, for the secret lay in the patient hand-rubbing over long periods whereby the polish was forced into the pores of the wood, and not applied merely as a surface coating.

Polishing materials and processes
Wax polish

One of the oldest and probably the most beautiful of all finishes, as the softened wax penetrates the wood surface and enhances the figure, giving it great depth and warmth. A semi-matt surface with distinctive patina is cheaply and easily achieved, but several applications are required over a period of time for good results. Pure waxes have good moisture resistance, but are very easily marked, with little or no heat resistance dependent on the particular melting-point of the wax. Proprietary polishes with or without silicone additives for greater protection are usually composed of soft waxes (paraffin, etc.), and are not suitable for first coats on bare-wood, although excellent as revivers in finished work. The best mixture for first coats is the old tried formula of pure beeswax and turpentine (1 lb (0·450 kg) wax to $\frac{1}{2}$ pint (280 ml) turps) digested in a water-jacketed pot, and thinned with additional turpentine as necessary. A teaspoonful of pure copal varnish can be added for increased toughness and wear, also carnauba wax (Brazilian palm wax) for hardness and shine. Application should be made with a fairly sloppy paste, rubbed in and stroked off along the grain as in painting with No. 0000 wire wool, and then set aside to harden before burnishing with soft dry cloths. Matt waxes suitable for finishing over thin base coats of cellulose or synthetic lacquer, etc. are composed of soft paraffin-wax and synthetic micro-wax, and do not buff to a gloss finish. A fairly recent development is teak paste reinforced with ethyl cellulose for increased resistance. One of the chief virtues of all wax finishes is their easy renewal.

---

* Furniture was originally made by carpenters and later by joiners who were given exclusive entitlement in 1632 to 'make all kinds of furniture, mortice, tenoned, dowelled and pinned, glued but not nailed together . . .'. Later specialisation produced the cabinet-maker exclusively concerned with furniture.

Oil polish

Linseed oil alone will give moderate heat and water resistance with high gloss if applied sparingly over a period of several months. Each separate application must harden by oxidisation, and 5 per cent white spirits and 5 per cent terebene can be added for easier working but at least 12 coats will be necessary. This method was often used for dining-table tops but it is much too slow for modern requirements, and sophisticated penetrating oils, teak oil etc., have been developed, incorporating rapid oxidising agents capable of achieving a sufficient build-up in two coats only. These new oils are used extensively in modern teak and afromosia furniture, but the resultant finish hardly compares with the older process. As with wax, oil finishes are easily renewed, which is one of the chief advantages.

French polish

This is a specialist craft and should not be attempted without proper training, for the whole secret lies in the minimum and not the maximum amount of polish applied for a full gloss, and thick coats unskilfully applied are no better than cheap varnish. It is often said that a good french-polisher is born and not made, and that not only can he equalise the colours of mixed woods but can actually make some pieces appear lighter by regulating the thickness of polish and therefore the refractive index. Proprietary brands of polish incorporate various gums and synthetics for quick drying and build up, also increased heat and water resistance which is usually poor with straight french polish, but the most beautiful finishes are still obtained with the older method, using flake-orange or garnet shellac disolved in industrial alcohol (methylated spirits, methylated finish, etc.). The best results are only obtained over long periods and 12 months was considered usual for the German vitriol finish on grand pianos. The polish as such is now little used in production work for it is essentially a hand process, but modified polishes are available for spray finishing.

428   Applying rubber in french polishing table-top

Nitro-cellulose lacquers

These are composed of nitro cellulose, alkyd resin and castor oil or glycerine plasticisers, etc. dissolved in various aromatic hydrocarbon solvents according to the type. Originally developed some 40 years ago to replace french polish they have good heat-, water- and spirit-resistant properties, and in spite of fierce competition from harder and more resistant synthetic lacquers still account for about 70 per cent of the total output, presumably because they are familiar, can be used straight from the can and have an unlimited shelf and pot life. Obvious advantages are very quick drying rate giving dustproof coats in a matter of minutes, high transparency, an exceptional even flow and good gloss together with satisfactory amalgamation of successive layers as with french polish. This last is of considerable importance, for each coat applied partially redissolves the underlying coat, therefore any subsequent damage is more easily reparable than with synthetic lacquers which set by polymerisation so that the separate layers do not amalgamate and any renewal usually necessitates stripping down to the bare wood.

Normally, all cellulose lacquers are compounded for spray application and have a solids content of around 34 per cent with low viscosity and a flash point of 32 °C (90 °F), therefore they are subject to the requirements of the Cellulose Regulations 1934 for tradeshops. However, full gloss lacquers can be obtained with a flash point of over 32 °C (90 °F) which are outside the regulations, but owing to the slower solvent evaporation-rate they do not have the rapid set-up of normal lacquers. They can, however, be brush coated, which is satisfactory for thin coats but rather more difficult for a filled grain full gloss over large areas. Cellulose lacquer can be 'pulled over' as in french polishing with a chamois-leather pad soaked in pull-over solutions composed of high-boiling retarder thinners, and recent developments include straight cellulose lacquers for pad polishing, high solids content lacquers for quick build-up, and scratch-resistant lacquers with resistance to bruising without fracture which was one of the disabilities of the older, more brittle formulas.

For those who do not have spraying facilities and prefer soft shine with reasonably good protection a proved specification is as follows:

One coat or more well-thinned clear cellulose lacquer, brushed on, allowed to harden thoroughly, and then wire wooled (grade No. 0000) and waxed, preferably with the lacquer-maker's own matt wax formula.

This treatment yields an acceptable finish for the general run of handmade furniture, but will not give full protection on dining- and coffee-table tops. Either white french polish or polyurethane lacquer can be used for the base coats in lieu of cellulose; but whichever lacquer is used some judgment is needed, for if the coat is too thin rubbing down will strike through to the bare wood in places and show as bald patches under the wax, whilst too thick coats will merely lie on the surface and show the brush-marks.

Synthetic lacquers

These include cold acid catalyst, polyurethane and polyester lacquers, all of which have greatly increased heat, water and spirit resistance, tough films and high gloss, particularly the latter which is extensively used for wireless and television cabinets as there is little if any sinkage, and the gloss is comparable with a vitriol (German) piano finish. Polyester lacquers are, however, unsuitable for small turnovers, for they require dual-feed sprays for intimate dispersal of the catalyst hardener throughout the lacquer, and the resin-dust in surfacing can be an industrial hazard if suitable precautions are not taken.

Acid catalyst lacquers

Originally phenolic resins were used, but modern formulas include urea formaldehyde, melamine and epoxy resins with alkyd plasticisers for increased resistance to wet heat, etc. A two-pack lacquer is the norm, composed of lacquer, syrup and separate acid catalyst, often hydrochloric acid, which must be mixed with the lacquer in the stated proportions. Setting is by polymerisation, but the mixed lacquer has a pot life of several hours and enough can be mixed for the day's work. A one-solution pre-catalysed form is now available with a shelf life of about six months, but the pre-catalysation is obtained by lowering the solids content, therefore the build-up is less rapid.

Polyurethane lacquer

The isocyanate cured polyurethanes were at one time toxic but are now controlled and are outstanding for adhesion, flexibility, gloss, water and chemical resistance. Originally in two-can form with separate hardener they are now obtainable in one-can pre-catalysed solutions. The usual application is by spraying apparatus, but they can be brushed more easily than cellulose lacquers, and pad-application french polish type polyurethane lacquers are available for pure hand methods.

Both acid catalyst and polyurethane lacquers are very suitable for dining-table tops, etc. and a full gloss polish is possible with the use of appropriate grain fillers, sealers and base coats, etc. flatted with wet and dry silicon carbide paper moistened with either white spirit or water (the latter gives a fiercer cut, and the surface should be lubricated with a little common soap), followed up by cutting-down pastes and burnishing creams. They can also be used for thin finishes showing the grain, with the dust nibs cut off with 7/0 abrasive paper, or wire wooled and waxed. The secret of applying these lacquers is to complete the required number of coatings as quickly as possible, for if each coat is allowed to set glass hard then any build-up will lie as separate layers, and any chance cutting through of the top layer in sanding will show up as a blue blaze. With rapid coating (three in one day) each layer tends to soften up the under layer, and some degree of amalgamation is achieved.

Dulling methods

Contemporary finishes usually call for an eggshell, matt or semi-matt surface in preference to a choked-grain full gloss. Most lacquers are available either as full gloss (burnishing lacquers), matt or semi-matt finishes, the matt appearance being obtained by incorporating silex powder or other additives to scatter the light. These matt finishes do, of course, cloud the wood to some degree, and in fact all dulled surfaces cannot be expected to show the clarity of a high gloss which acts as both mirror and magnifying glass. The after dulling of gloss surfaces for an egg-shell gloss effect can also be done with finest grade wire wool which must be skilfully applied to be effective, or with french-polishers' pumice and petrol.

A handful of water-floated pumice powder (or fine silex powder) is stirred into a cupful of petrol and swabbed over the surface, keeping the mixture constantly agitated. Any degree of dulling can be achieved by using a special soft dulling brush kept exclusively for the purpose, and sweeping the brush backwards and forwards as in painting until the petrol has evaporated and only the dust remains. Silex powder need not be graded, but all powdered pumice should be water floated by stirring it into a large bowl of water, allowing a little time for the larger grains to settle, and then decanting the liquid, letting it stand overnight and pouring off the clear water. The degree of fineness of the floated powder will depend on how long the coarser grains have been allowed to settle before decanting, and the process can be repeated several times if necessary.

Satisfactory egg-shell gloss surfaces can only be achieved by carrying out to a full gloss polish and then dulling, and there are no short cuts. The dulling of thin finishes with unfilled grain should not be attempted with the above method or the surface will show white deposits.

Spraying equipment

Production-work uses air or airless sprays in vacuum exhaust or water wash booths, etc. but small portable spray outfits are obtainable which will support one gun with pressures up to 60 lb per sq. in. 4.218 kg/km^2, and sufficient for all but the heaviest materials. These can be the compressor type or fully portable rotary vane type (429), relatively inexpensive and efficient in use. Light pattern spray outfits for the handyman are hardly suitable for serious work, as there must be sufficient pressure and feet cube (m^3) air delivery per minute to fully atomise the spray or extensive spitting, blobbing, tear runs and orange-peel effect will result, and rubbing down will be as difficult and as tedious as with brush-work. Some form of moisture extractor should also be incorporated in the compressor, or as a separate unit installed in the pipeline, or 'blooming' will result. Even with fully efficient moisture extraction—and the very act of compressing air squeezes out the moisture always present—some blooming must be expected on humid days. This can be controlled by adding anti-chill thinners to the lacquer, which retard the evaporation and thus allows the suspended moisture to escape before it is trapped by the setting film, or by over-spraying the lacquered surface with thinners, but the gun must be good for this and the application skilful. Regulations regarding the storage and use of inflammatory materials are fairly stringent, but non-regulation materials are available which are not subject to the legal requirements. Small outfits in which the air is delivered direct from the compressor unit to the gun do not need periodic testing, but air receivers, i.e. storage tanks for air under compression require safety checks at regular intervals. In estimating for spray work it should not be forgotten that on average one-third of the material is lost.

Wood finishing production methods

Present-day techniques include spraying, hot lacquer spraying, airless spraying, dual-feed spraying for polyesters, electrostatic deposition, roller coating and reverse roller coating for sanders and sealers, curtain spraying for gloss finishes and roller printing of wood patterns on chipboard and hardboard. Methods are geared to flow-line production to yield printproof surfaces in the shortest possible time, and call for sophisticated techniques and equipment which become obsolescent almost before they are installed. The small tradeshop cannot hope to keep pace with this mounting tide of new ideas, new approaches and new materials, and it will continue to use traditional methods, hand-polishing and simple spraying, and taking advantage where it may of worthwhile developments. In the meantime, the perfect finish has yet to be evolved.

In conclusion it should be stressed that no matter what method and what material is used the final polish will only be as good as the ground it is laid upon, for no amount of after finishing can ever disguise poor workmanship and shoddy materials. The thick, heavy gloss of cheap furniture is there for a purpose, it masks the imperfections which a clear finish would only magnify. An illustration of this is the superlative finish achieved by the professional gun-stock maker. The completed walnut stock is sponged with clean water to which a little oxalic acid has been added, dried rapidly with a blow-torch or over a gas-ring and sanded immediately. This process is repeated several times with an occasional rubbing over with very fine pumice powder to burnish the wood and seal the grain, and the wood surfaces can be further burnished by 'boning' i.e. rubbing with a block of the same wood. The resultant surface is dead smooth and velvet to the touch, moreover any subsequent exposure to damp conditions will not raise the grain.

Wood stains

These rightly require a complete textbook devoted to their manipulation, therefore only general observations are possible. Of the three categories, water, spirit and oil, the water stains are most troublesome to apply but penetrate fairly deeply and yield the clearest finishes, therefore they are firm favourites with the hand-worker. The old tried recipes are still viable, i.e. vandyke brown crystals disolved in hot water with a little 0·880 ammonia to bite into the wood and a teaspoonful of household detergent to break down surface tensions; mahogany crystals for red staining, water black aniline dye and potassium bichromate. As all photographers will know the last is light sensitive, and an aqueous solution of the orange crystals obtainable at most chemists will yield any shade from fierce red-brown to light tan on certain timbers after exposure to light. The concentrated solution should be stored in brown or covered bottles, diluted and tested on scrap wood for the results are never predictable. Both oak and mahogany are affected (some African mahoganies do not respond), and the results are fairly permanent although inclined to fade somewhat in strong light as will most other stains. Other shades of brown are easily obtainable with mixtures of red, yellow and black anilines with the addition of a little blue for coldness. Modern anilines are reasonably fast to light and some pronouncedly so, and can be obtained from Brodie and Middleton Ltd, 79 Long Acre, London W.C.2 or retail factors.

Before applying water stains the work should be flashed off with clean water, dried, sanded and the dust cleared from the fibres with a stiff brush. Even staining without streakiness is facilitated if the surfaces are first lightly swabbed with water, moreover this dilutes the stain and gives more

429   Portable rotary vane air compressor   *By courtesy of A. Bullows and Co. Limited*

430   Spraying-booth   *By courtesy of the Aerograph de Vilbiss Co. Limited*

time for levelling off. Two coats are always better than one, for one strong coat may strike too dark in places, moreover first coating gives another opportunity to ease off upraised fibres. The stained surface can be coated or finished with all types of polishes.

Painted work

So-called painted work, bedroom and living-room furniture, kitchen furniture, etc. are spray coated with pigmented nitrocellulose, acid catalyst or polyurethane finishes available in gloss and semi-matt formulas. The build up is the same as for clear lacquer finishes, with appropriate pigmented grain fillers, sealers and base coats, etc. and the final surfaces flatted with wet and dry silicon carbide paper, cutting down pastes and burnishing creams. Brush coating can be attempted but is likely to fail on large surfaces, for it is the dead smoothness of this type of finish which constitutes much of its charm.

Compatibility in wood finishes

As so many types of wood finish are now used it is useful to know which finishes will take over each other and which will not. The list below gives the average behaviour:

Oil finish will accept french polish, polyurethane or wax.
French polish will accept cellulose, polyurethane, oil and wax.
Cellulose will accept polyurethane and wax.
Polyurethane will accept oil and wax only.
Polyester will accept oil, polyurethane and wax.
Wax will accept none.

Discretion must be exercised, for whereas the solvent used in cellulose finishes will soften if not actually dissolve french polish and permit the partial fusion of the two coats, the methylated spirit solvent in french polish will not dissolve cellulose and both coats will remain separate, moreover any oil used with the french polish will be prevented from soaking down into the wood and will inhibit final hardening. It should be noted that wax is inimicable to all other finishes, and must be completely removed by stripping, scraping, sanding and degreasing before attempting any other form of finishing.

43 Upholstery

This again is a specialist craft, for a good upholsterer capable of stuffover-work, shaped work and deep buttoning in a full range of materials including leather must be part tailor, dressmaker and leather-worker. However, the introduction of foam pads and resilient rubber webbings has vastly simplified the usual run of upholstery in dining and easy chairs, which is now well within the scope of the average workshop.

Resilient webbings

Invented in 1953 by Pirelli Ltd of Italy these consist of resilient rubber tensioned strips of attractive appearance, and have almost entirely superseded the jute webbings of traditional upholstery. The advantage of Pirelli webbing is that it can be used without sub-frames or springing, and need not be hidden for it is obtainable in various colours and in four qualities for different seating requirements. The webbing is composed of a rayon fabric bonded in rubber and has proved extremely tough, durable and elastic, with negligible loss of recovery over long periods. It is secured by tacks or staples as with jute webbings, or with special patented metal clips with serrated edges (431:1) clenched to the ends of the strips and slipped into a sawn groove (431) in the framework (another form of wire clip is available for metal framing), and it must be tensioned by stretching to a fixed percentage of its original length (plus 5 to 10 per cent) in accordance with the makers' recommendations. The strips can be placed 2 in. (50 mm) to 3 in. (76 mm) apart and need only run one way, with cross-weaving as with jute webbings unnecessary except over large areas. Full details, fixing instructions and samples can be obtained from Progress Mercantile Co. Ltd, 246 Brixton Hill, London S.W.2, or from all upholstery stockists.

Four-point platforms

A fairly recent development of the Pirelli Company is the resilient rubber diaphragm with triangular steel loops (431:4) engaged in metal bosses screwed to the framework of the chair (431:3). They are used instead of webbing for loose cushioning, and the four-point diagonal anchorage eliminates distortion of the side rails, hammocking and localised areas of wear in the cushions (431:5). The diaphragms must be tensioned from 8 to 15 per cent maximum, and the Progress Mercantile Co. Ltd issue instructions for a simply made metal stretching device

431 Upholstery details, resilient rubber springing, etc.

469

432 Detail of chair seat for loose cushion with resilient webbing straps secured by metal fasteners in grooves sawn into rails

433 Rubber diaphragm seat for loose cushion, showing method of fixing

for quick assembly-work. They are available in a range of seat sizes from $15\frac{1}{4}$ in. (387 mm) to $22\frac{1}{2}$ in. (571 mm), therefore the chair must be designed accordingly, but the square format can be stretched to fit square, rectangular or tapered seat frames within the maximum permissible tensioning.

In designing chairs and settees, etc. with resilient webbing or platform suspension in mind both initial and depressional tension must be considered, with timber sections sufficient for the loading. The position of the webbing strips is also important whether from side to side or back to front, and here again there must be specific understanding of the tensions involved. Booklets are available from the suppliers giving the relevant details.

Foam padding

The original and familiar latex rubber foam was first developed by the Dunlop Rubber Company in the early 1930s and completely revolutionised upholstery techniques, to be followed later by polyester and polyether synthetic foams. Apart from differences in performance, latex rubber sponge is foamed by chemical additives (originally soap solutions), therefore the cushions can be shaped or moulded at the time of manufacture, whilst synthetic sponges generate their own carbon dioxide which blows the liquid, and self-foaming is generally too rapid for satisfactory moulding techniques, although recent developments have overcome this disability to some extent. In practice latex foam is more expensive but more efficient, and does not lose its sponginess unless exposed to damp conditions or direct sunlight. On the other hand synthetic foams are tougher but yield (bottom) more rapidly under pressure and the recovery is slower, therefore the effect is a little dead in comparison. Of the two forms of synthetic foam, polyether is more rubber-like and is the form usually adopted for normal work.

Both latex and synthetic foams can be obtained in sheet form (solid foam) and with cavities which cut down weight and give increased softness, and in a range of thicknesses up to 12 in. (305 mm) according to the type. They are also obtainable in a range of densities corresponding to soft, medium, and hard for traffic seating (railway, bus seating, etc.). Pad thicknesses can be built up with rubber adhesives (Bostik, etc.) and can be cut with shears, corrugated kitchen scissors, sharp knives or on the band-saw. They can be glued direct to solid ply bases or placed direct over resilient webbings. Adequate ventilation must be provided, and if covered with impermeable materials, leather, leathercloth and PVC-coated fabrics, solid bases must be pierced with $\frac{1}{4}$ in. (6 mm) holes at 3 in. (76 mm) centres, and loose cushions provided with brass eyelet holes sewn in or potential users will suffer serious embarrassment, as the effect is that of a joke cushion. It is usual to cover foam padding with under-covers of coarse calico if the top covering is leather or PVC, etc. owing to the difference in the recovery rates, but these are unnecessary under open-weave materials except as an added refinement protecting the inner pad from wear. Full particulars can be obtained from the British Latex Foam Manufacturers' Association, Royal Exchange, Cross Street, Manchester who supply an inexpensive instruction book, and also the Progress Mercantile Co. Ltd. who market synthetic foams.

Figures 434–7 show the various stages in the upholstery of a drop-in seat for a dining-chair, using resilient webbing, latex foam padding and top leather cover. Figure 434 shows the fixing of the webbing with each strap stretched to the pencil-mark and secured with three $\frac{5}{8}$ in. (16 mm) improved tacks, whilst in 435 the under-cover of jute sacking hessian is folded to allow for deflection of the webbing and secured with $\frac{3}{8}$ in. (9·5 mm) or $\frac{1}{2}$ in. (12·5 mm) improved tacks. In 436 the foam padding has been cut to shape, the edges roughly chamfered with a $\frac{1}{4}$ in. (6 mm) overhang all round and secured in position with upholsterers' adhesive tape firmly tacked to the framework. The final covers are then stretched evenly over the pad, working from the centres of each side out to the corners and temporarily tacking with $\frac{3}{8}$ in (9·5 mm) or $\frac{1}{2}$ in. (12·5 mm) fine tacks which are not driven home until the stretching and shaping is correct. A little horsehair stuffing can be worked in to the under top cover to raise the dome and increase the firmness of dining-chair seats. Figure 437 shows the leather cover cut to fit.

434 Fixing Pirelli webbing

435   Hessian cover tacked in position

436   Fixing foam pad

44   Furniture restoration and repairs

The repair of modern everyday furniture usually calls for cutting out and replacing broken parts, fixing false tenons or dowels to fractured joints, strengthening joints with metal straps, insets or angle pieces, renewing whole members where necessary, and in general applying normal cabinet-making skills. Valuable antique furniture repairs require expert know-how with carefully matched old timber, scraps of old saw-cut veneer, and a keen appreciation of period, colour and patina, together with considerable skills in carving, veneering, inlaying, marquetry cutting, staining, polishing and lacquering, etc. Any such antique repairs should not be undertaken without considerable experience of the particular type of work, for repairs inexpertly done or out of period can detract from, or even destroy, the market value. Readers who are interested in this type of work should apply to the Rural Industries Bureau, 35 Camp Road, Wimbledon, London, S.W. 19, who have from time to time held courses of instruction in antique repair-work to the highest standards.

Surface damage

Slight bruising of surfaces where the actual fibres are not fractured can often be lifted by the repeated application of a heated iron tip through a wet cloth, creating sufficient steam to swell the fibres up. Bruises in bare wood can also be lifted by flooding the bruise with methylated spirit and setting fire to it, but the wood must not be scorched. There is no guarantee that the bruises will be eradicated entirely, for much depends on the elasticity of the wood fibres and their ability to recover, but it is always worth a trial. Deeper scratches, dents and bad bruising will have to be cut out and plugged with wood or filled with hard stoppers, plastic wood, etc. coloured to match the finished work. If wood plugs are used they should be cut to an elongated diamond shape with the grain direction carefully matched, placed on the damaged surface, scribed round and the recess cut; the plugs should be slightly bevelled in the thickness for a close fit. All possible help

should be given to the polisher by choosing wood of the same species and grain configuration, preferably from old sources in the case of antique furniture, for whilst he will be able to match colours he cannot change or disguise the texture of a wood. Before gluing in the diamonds a piece of white chalk rubbed round the edges will often hold back a dark glue-line in light-coloured timbers. Slight depressions in work polished with nitrocellulose or synthetic finishes can sometimes be filled by pouring a little of the mixed lacquer into a tin lid and leaving it to set until it gels; it can then be worked into the depressions like putty, allowed to harden thoroughly and then cut off. Figure 438:1 shows various surface repairs to a veneered chest with all cuts tapered as mentioned above.

Blisters, etc.

Blisters in modern work can usually be pricked or cut with a knife along the grain and relaid (see *Veneering, marquetry and inlays*, Chapter 22, page 221), but large blisters in old thick saw-cut veneers may not readily respond to treatment. If the whole of the veneered surface has to be lifted off and replaced on a fresh groundwork it may be possible to lift the veneers by steaming or repeatedly swabbing with hot water, but some veneers may be too tough or too brittle for this treatment, and the whole of the ground may have to be planed off down to a level at which the water will soak through the back and loosen the glue. This latter method is only worth the very considerable labour involved if the top surface is especially valuable, and the patina of age must be preserved.

Warped tops

Badly warped tops can often be corrected by saw kerfing, provided the under surface is not visible in the fixed position. A series of parallel cuts are run in with the circular saw, $\frac{1}{4}$ in. (6 mm) apart and to within a full $\frac{1}{8}$ in. (3 mm) of the upper

439 Seventeenth-century French marquetry cabinet under restoration at Victoria and Albert Museum, London, using Araldite epoxy cement *By courtesy of CIBA (ARL) Limited*, and the *Trustees of the Victoria and Albert Museum*

surface. The board is then cramped down to a level surface, and softwood wedge strips or strips of veneer glued into the cuts. The wedges must not be too tight or they will force the warp over in the opposite direction, and plenty of time should be allowed for the work to settle before the cramps are released. Badly warped table-tops in which both surfaces show, as in double-top tables, are almost impossible to correct by any known method to give permanent results, and the only alternatives are to renew the top or slit the existing top into two or more pieces, reversing the strips and re-thicknessing, neither of which would be acceptable in antique-work. In other words the craftsman must resist the invitation to accomplish the impossible by those who do not appreciate what wood really is and how it behaves.

Drawer repairs

Wear is inevitable in all moving parts, and drawers and drawer runners may require exten-

sive renovation, especially if the drawer sides and runners are of soft pine. Figure 438:2 shows a typical old drawer with missing cock beads, dovetails loose, drawer sides worn and solid bottom split and shrunk out of its groove. The sides will have to be cut back (438:3, 4) and fresh pieces glued on. Solid bottoms which have split can be shot and reglued, with the joint taped with glued coarse canvas if necessary, and the width extended with a new piece to take the slotted screws. Loose dovetails will have to be knocked apart and reglued. If the drawer rail and runner are badly worn (438:5) and the existing runner cannot be removed and replaced, then it may be necessary to work a trench in the old runner and glue in a fresh slip of hardwood, covering it with a neat patch on the rail. The trench will have to be chiselled out or worked with a bullnose rabbet-plane, and as a preliminary step a small spur-cutter from a metal plough-plane or a piece of scraper steel can be screwed to a suitable block (438:6) and worked backwards and forwards to cut the side of the trench. In all old work strict watch should be kept for nails and rusty screws from previous repairs which will wreck a cutting edge. Carcase backs which have shrunk may require glued canvas over the splits, and side pieces glued on to make up the width.

Structural repairs

Generally speaking, where structural joints have failed part or all of the construction will have to be taken apart, for there is little point in squeezing glue into the shoulders of a loose tenon and expecting it to hold. Most old work can be knocked apart fairly easily, although a firm but not necessarily a heavy hand may be needed. However, modern adhesives may resist parting, and discretion is, therefore, necessary. Joints filled with old hide glue, usually in thick layers, will have to be cleaned out with repeated applications of hot water; they can then be packed up with veneer slips to make up the slackness, and reglued with either hide or synthetics. If the furniture is antique and valuable great care must be taken to disturb as little of the existing surfaces as possible, and to incorporate only the minimum of new wood, for extensive renovations will always detract from the value. Worm-eaten timbers must be treated if the worm is still active, crumbling parts cut away or built up as described later. If the joints are broken altogether, either dowels or false tenons can be fitted, or new sections scarfed in (see *Scarf joints*, Chapter 21 page 210). Figure 438:8 shows a false tenon fitted; 438:9 a new section of rail inserted and strengthened with a pad or web if it is load bearing, whilst 438:7 is a long scarf joint to a broken chair leg which will need gluing only if the scarf is long enough.

A recent development in the repair of valuable antique furniture has been the use of Araldite epoxy resin adhesive (CIBA (ARL) Ltd) with suitable reactive diluents, fillers and colorants. This type of glue has excellent adhesion to wood, high moisture resistance and most importantly negligible shrinkage in curing, so that it can be built up into solid sections without the usual cracking, crazing and disruption of normal adhesives which will only permit thin lines of glue. In particular, worm-eaten timbers can be repaired, restored and strengthened by surface

application or penetration, and 439 shows a French marquetry cabinet richly veneered with marquetry patterns of kingwood, ebony, tortoise-pewter and staghorn which was recently restored in the Department of Conservation of the Victoria and Albert Museum in London. In this case parts of the stand seriously ravaged by woodworm were cleared away and then made good with a liquid Araldite formulation. Plastic wood formulations can also be used with Araldite to build up missing parts, and the techniques are applicable to a wide range of materials, metal, wood, plastic, terracotta, etc. The CIBA (ARL) Ltd technical bulletin *Araldite in the Restoration of Antiquities* gives specific examples.

440   Renovating Regency-type chairs

Figures 440–2 show the extensive renovation and repair of a set of six Regency-style chairs* carried out by Mr C. M. Lacey of Brighton, England. The chairs in question were beech framed stained in imitation of rosewood, with a beautifully executed Boulle inlay of brass and rosewood veneer on the curved back rails, and as there was no point in using old beech even if it could be obtained (beech is highly susceptible to woodworm), new wood was used throughout. As some of the Boulle inlays were damaged and others altogether missing, rubbings of a complete inlay were made, a clear tracing made and glued to sheet brass of equivalent thickness and colour (brass is obtainable in several tones and colours according to the composition), and the brass sheet then glued to a thick rosewood veneer. The pattern was then cut out with a fine jewellers' piercing saw, the parts assembled and glued to the rails with shaped cauls and G-

* The appellations 'Genuine Antique', 'Genuine Regency' etc., etc., cannot be applied to any furniture made after 1830, which is the fixed datum line. As it would be impossible to distinguish between furniture of the same type or style made in, say, 1820 and 1840, any claim to genuineness must be supported by an original bill of sale or other trustworthy documentary evidence. The terms 'Antique Style', 'Regency Style', etc. therefore mean exactly what they say, i.e. 'in the style of . . .'. They could be genuine antique but are not claimed as such.

cramps. All new work was then stained, the rosewood markings drawn in with indian ink which was the usual practice of the time, and french polished. It was then distressed by the usual methods, viz. beating with rubber or hide hammers, hammer-heads covered in sacking, barbed-wire wrapped round a stick, round pebbles, etc., and scratched with the milled edge of a new coin, with parts which would be expected to show wear, rasped or sanded away. No attempt was made to fake or deliberately deceive with the inclusion of worm-eaten timber or simulated worm holes, and the distressing was only carried out sufficiently to fade in the new work with the old. The completed chairs were then sold in good faith and to a reputable dealer as 'Regency Style, extensively renovated.'

441 Brass inlay part cut

442 Brass inlay completed

45 Timber species and terms

Timber species

In all, some 43,000 different species of wood-forming plants have so been identified, or which some 30,000 could be regarded as timber producers in some form or other and about 10,000 commercially exploitable. Many of these are of local interest only owing to unsuitability, high cost of extraction, non-availability in commercial quantities, etc., but many hundreds remain which are of sufficient importance to merit serious consideration. Certain timber species continually recur, i.e. oak types, walnut types, mahogany types, beech types, etc. whose names are familiar, but in any tropical forest there may be only about 18 timber trees to the acre (0·40 ha) and of these only 2 or 3 will be varieties with known names, and the exploiter must therefore strive to find markets for the remainder in order to make extraction a commercial proposition. For this reason new species are constantly being introduced into world markets, but as large-scale furniture-manufacturers cannot afford to experiment, relying chiefly upon oak, makoré, utile, beech, ramin, idigbo, etc., which are always in uninterrupted and plentiful supply, the newcomers tend to be much cheaper in comparison, although not necessarily inferior in any way. For particulars of these new timbers the reader should refer to the bulletins of the United Africa Company, Shelley House, Noble Street, London E.C.2, one of the largest exploiters of tropical timbers, and to the booklets and leaflets issued by HMSO and the Timber Research and Development Association. Actual performance under test for many of these new varieties can be obtained from the Forest Products Research Laboratory, Princes Risborough, Buckinghamshire, who will always advise potential users.

Timber classification

In the classification of plants including timber the taxonomic (classificatory) headings determined by microscopic inspection of the structure are written in Latin which is the international language adopted, with the genus first which is class or kind of things contained in the particular plant family, then the species which includes the subordinate kinds within the genus, and lastly the family. Thus European oak will be *Quercus* (genus), *robur* (species), family Fagaceae. Within the same family grouping will also be beech, hornbeam, sweet chestnut, etc. but true oaks will always be *Quercus* although the species will differ, i.e. *alba* for American white, *borealis* for American red and *mongolica* for Japanese. However, as timber species are usually discovered and put to use long before the botanist arrives to identify them, they will have been given common names arrived at either by adoption of the local or native nickname, the district of source, the port of shipment or some peculiarity of the timber itself.

The precise botanical classification is not of pressing importance to the cabinet-maker (and half an ounce of practical experience with the timber in question is worth a pound of academic knowledge, at least from the craftsman's point of view), but it will at least warn him what to expect. Thus Australian silky oak belongs to the family Proteaceae, and has nothing in common with true oaks (Fagaceae) except a fancied resemblance in the medullary ray structure, whilst on the other hand both Honduras mahogany (*Swietenia macrophylla* Meliaceae) and Cuban (Spanish) mahogany (*Swietenia mahogani* Meliaceae) will have more in common than African mahogany (*Khaya grandifolia* Meliaceae), sapelewood (*Entandrophragma septentrionale* Meliaceae) and guarea (*Guarea thompsonii* Meliaceae) because the genus differs. If, however, the designer or craftsman wishes to pursue his scientific enquiries further he will usually find that there are classes of instruction in timber technology freely available, and increased knowledge of his material will never be wasted, bearing in mind that for all practical purposes the study of timber does begin at the bench and under the impact of the cutting-tool.

List of timbers

The list following gives descriptions of some of the more widely known timbers suitable for furniture-making. In each case, colour, texture, figure, working properties and behaviour can only be an approximation or general average, for individual trees within each species may differ very considerably. There is, for instance, an appreciable difference between oak grown in the north and in the south of England, which is a matter of a few hundred miles only; there will be considerable differences between trees of the same species and accorded the same commercial gradings grown some 2000 miles apart. Movement or dimensional change is arrived at by adding together the tangential and radial movement values occasioned by a change in environmental humidity of 90 per cent (equivalent to a moisture content in timber of approximately 20 per cent according to the species), down to a humidity of 60 per cent (12 per cent moisture content), with a total movement of 3 per cent denoting a stable timber; 3 to 4·5 per cent a medium, and over 4·5 per cent a relatively unstable timber. Thus idigbo will shrink approximately $\frac{3}{32}$ in. (2·4 mm) tangentially and $\frac{1}{16}$ in. (1·5 mm) radially for every 12 in. (305 mm) in width within the range 18 per cent moisture content (90 per cent air humidity) down to 12 per cent (60 per cent humidity), and can be classed as a small movement or stable timber, whereas beech will shrink $\frac{3}{8}$ in. (9·5 mm) tangentially and about $\frac{3}{16}$ in. (5 mm) radially under the same conditions, and must, therefore, be regarded as a large movement or relatively unstable timber. In practice, actual stability under normal working conditions will depend on the sum of the dimensional changes as given above, and also on the difference between the tangential and radial shrinkage value, with large differences giving greater tendency to warp and twist.

Foreign hardwoods

Timber origin	Colour, texture, figure	Working properties, behaviour, etc.
Abura West Africa	Light brown with pinkish tinge. Fine even texture. No figure.	Medium hard, clean working with some interlocked grain. Fairly stable.
Afromosia West Africa	Resembling teak but paler and finer textured.	Moderately hard, easy working. Non-greasy substitute for Burmah teak. Very stable.
Agba West Africa	Light cream. Close even texture. No figure.	Medium hard, clean, easy working. Excellent construction timber. Stable.
Beech European	White to brownish red when steamed. Fine even texture. Plain figure.	Medium hard, clean working. Good bending wood. Not very stable.
Berlinia West Africa	Reddish brown with dark streaks. Coarse texture.	Moderately hard, heavy and tough. Reasonably stable.
Gedu Nohor (Edinam) West Africa	Characteristic mahogany appearance and cousin to sapelewood.	Medium hard, easy to work but grain interlocked. Stable.
Guarea (Nigerian pearwood) West Africa	Pinkish brown. Fine texture. Straight grain occasionally curled.	Medium hard, easy working with some interlocked grain. Reasonably stable.
Niangon (Nyankom) West Africa	Greyish red-brown. Resembling African mahogany but coarser texture.	Moderately hard, clean working, greasy wood. Stable.
Oak European	Pale cream to light brown. Coarse texture. Good figure. Large flash.	Hard, clean working. Fairly stable.
Oak U.S.A.	White or red according to species. Coarse even texture closer than European oak. Very little figure.	Hard, heavy, clean working. Moderately stable.
Oak Japanese	Pale cream to light brown. Coarse even texture. Little figure. Small flash.	Medium hard, milder working than other oaks. Stable.
Obeche West Africa	White to pale straw. Soft, open but firm texture. No figure.	Softish, easy working and suitable for core work only. Stable.
Ramin Malaya	White to pale straw. Medium texture. Little figure.	Medium hard, clean working. Fairly stable

Timber origin	Colour, texture, figure	Working properties, behaviour, etc.
Sapelewood West Africa	Reddish brown. Coarse even grain. Lustrous stripe.	Fairly hard, easy working but with interlocked grain. Fairly stable when quarter sawn.
Idigbo West Africa	Pale yellow. Even texture. No figure. Good oak substitute.	Medium hard, easy working. Very stable.
Mahogany, Honduras South America	Yellowish brown. Close even texture. Plain lustrous figure.	Medium hard, excellent working properties. Very stable.
Mahogany, African (Dry land)	Deep red brown. Coarse texture. Stripy figure.	Fairly hard, dense, easy working but grain interlocked. Not stable.
Mahogany, African (Lagos, Nigerian, Grand Bassam, etc.)	Light pink brown to red brown. Fairly coarse texture. Stripy figure.	Medium hard, easy working but with interlocked grain. Fairly stable to stable.
Makoré (Cherry mahogany) West Africa	Reddish brown. Fine even texture. Lustrous, stripy figure. Peppery scent.	Medium hard, clean working. Stable.
Mansonia West Africa	Dark greyish brown, resembling walnut. Fine even texture. No figure.	Medium hard, clean working. Very Stable.
Muninga Africa	Handsome gold to red-brown with darker markings.	Moderately hard, clean working. Stable.
Teak (Moulmein) Burmah	Golden brown with occasional black streaks. Lustrous plain figure sometimes rippled.	Medium hard, very easy working but severe on cutting edges. A greasy wood but remarkably stable. The best all-round timber.
Utile West Africa	Greyish pink to red, resembling sapelewood but coarser texture and without pronounced stripe.	Moderately hard, clean working. Stable.
Walnut European	Pale cream to dark brown. Fine even texture, sometimes boldly marked.	Moderately hard, very easy working. Stable.
Walnut U.S.A.	Purplish black-brown, fine even texture, often boldly marked.	Strong, elastic, hard, clean working. Stable.

Timber origin	Colour, texture, figure	Working properties, behaviour, etc.
Walnut (African) West Africa	Bronzy yellow and lustrous with dark streaks. Coarse even texture with ribbon stripes.	Moderately hard, clean working but grain interlocked. Not a true walnut. Reasonably stable.

The dust of both makoré and mansonia is non-poisonous but highly irritant to mucous membranes and occasionally to the skin in susceptible cases, and for this reason they are little used in production runs where large quantities of dust are raised. Hand-creams and light pattern face-masks will give protection to those not unduly allergic to the dust.

Home-grown hardwoods

Ash	White to pinky cream or brown. Coarse textured. Plain figure sometimes with large flash or ripple.	Tough, strong but easy working, ideal bending wood. Stable.
Beech	Whitish yellow. Fine even texture. Plain speckled grain. Quality variable.	Medium hard, strong, clean and easy working. A universal timber. Fairly stable.
Cedar (Atlas, Lebanon, Deodar)	Light brown, strongly aromatic, with clearly marked annual rings. Prone to large dead knots.	Hard, tough working, very durable and capable of fine finish. Stable.
Cherry	Pale yellow to light reddish brown. Fine even texture with silky sheen resembling pale yew.	Medium hard, tough, clean working. Fine finish. Excellent cabinet wood. Stable.
Chestnut, Sweet (Spanish)	Resembling oak in appearance but not so dense. Flash or silver ray similar to oak.	Softer than oak. Clean working. Stable.
Elm (English or common)	Pale dull brown to medium brown. Coarse texture. Bold attractive figure.	Hard, tough, clean working. Warps badly if not bone-dry. Fine finish. Bends extremely well. Stable.
Elm, Dutch	Straighter grain than common elm.	As English elm but not so liable to warp.
Elm, Wych	Very pale brown. Straight grain.	Very clean working. Stable.
Holly	Greenish white to grey. No distinct heartwood. Dense even texture. Some timber can be pure white if correctly seasoned.	Medium hard, very clean working, very fine finish. Suitable for inlays, and for staining as blackwood. Fairly stable.

Timber origin	Colour, texture, figure	Working properties, behaviour, etc.
Lime	Even white to pale brown. Fine uniform texture. Little figure.	Softish, close grained and very clean working. Ideal for carving. Fairly stable.
Maple	Not so white as sycamore. Fine texture with natural lustre. Plain figure.	Medium hard to very hard. Fine finish. Reasonably stable.
Oak	Cream to light yellow-brown. Coarse even texture. Attractive figure with quartered wood showing bold flash.	Medium hard to hard, tough, clean working, good finish. Bends well. Fairly stable.
Pear	Pinkish brown with fine even texture and no apparent figure.	Medium hard, clean working, fine lustrous finish. Stable.
Plane	Resembling beech in appearance but with broader rays. Quartered timber is known as 'lace wood'.	Medium hard, fine finish. Stable.
Sycamore	White to yellow-white. Fine texture, natural silky lustre, sometimes with outstanding 'fiddle' figure when quartered. Known as 'Harewood' when stained silver-grey with iron salt.	Medium hard to hard, fine finish. Stable.
Walnut	Greyish yellow to brown with brown-black markings, often finely figured. Fine grain, but some open texture in coarser varieties. One of the most beautiful of all timbers.	Medium hard, very clean and easy working. Bends well if straight grained. Stable.
Yew	Yellow to brown with red and purple streaks. Fine close grain. Prone to knots, splits, shakes and rind galls.	Tough, hard, but relatively easy working. Fine finish. Bends extremely well and is outstanding for chair-work. Stable.

Exotic hardwoods

Silky oak (She oak) Australia East Africa	Pinky red-brown with characteristic dark eye or ray. Straight even grain, coarse texture. Not a true oak.	Fairly soft but remarkably strong and tough. Easy working but difficult to finish. Fairly stable.
Black Bean Australia	Chocolate-brown with grey-brown streaks somewhat resembling a coarse walnut. Straight-grained even texture.	Hard, strong, somewhat difficult to work but capable of fine finish. Fairly stable.

Timber origin	Colour, texture, figure	Working properties, behaviour, etc.
Laurel Indian	Light brown to brown-black. Superficially resembling walnut but with coarse though even texture.	Hard, heavy, tough working and very strong. Capable of fine finish. Fairly stable.
Rosewood, Rio South America	Tan to violet-brown or purple-black with ink-black streaks and patches. Medium coarse texture. Oily with characteristic scent when freshly worked.	Hard, fairly easy to work, but hard on tools. Capable of fine finish. Stable.
Rosewood, Bombay Indian	Dark brown to purple-black. Straight grain without violent colour fluctuations of Rio Rosewood. Medium, coarse, oily texture.	Rather harder than Rio Rosewood, but fairly easy to work and capable of fine finish. Stable.
Satinwood, East Indian India	Light straw to golden yellow, sometimes exceptionally figured. Fine even texture with remarkable lustre. An outstanding timber.	Hard, very dense and difficult to work, but capable of fine finish. Stable.

Other exotic timbers occasionally available

Blackwood (African)
Exceptionally hard, heavy, brown-black, giving the appearance of almost total blackness as it has no visible grain. An oily, extremely stable and valuable timber reserved for musical instruments, chessmen, knife handles, brush backs, etc.

Cocobolo (Nicaraguan rosewood)
Similar to Rio rosewood but with a pronounced reddish tinge and coarse, visible grain. Not so common as other rosewoods and principally used for brush backs, knife handles, door knobs, etc.

Ebony (Macassar ebony, Andaman marble wood, coromandel, calamander wood, etc.)
All are extremely hard and heavy, very finely textured and somewhat cold to the touch with a marble-like quality. The colours are showy, ranging from dark grey streaked with saffron-green, brown, red and purple to pure black. The trees do not grow much beyond 8 in. (203 mm) to 10 in. (254 mm) in girth and uses are, therefore, confined to small articles.

Kingwood (Violet†a—Brazil)
The veritable king of all woods, violet-brown with black or violet-black streaks. Very hard, heavy and most finely textured. Diameters are never more than about 8 in. (203 mm) and uses are confined to inlays and small articles owing to scarcity and high cost. A near cousin is Pernambuco wood, the most expensive of all timbers and used exclusively in the best violin bows.

Purplewood (aramanth, violetwood)
Colour intense purple or violet. Very hard, heavy, medium coarse to fine texture. Chief uses for ornamental wood are turning, inlays and billiard-cue butts.

Snakewood (Leopardwood, letterwood)
Brown or reddish brown striped with black. Very hard and heavy, fine uniform texture. Small heartwood and only suitable for inlays, door handles, walking-sticks, etc.

It is regrettable that Cuban (Spanish) mahogany, the most universally known of all timbers is no longer available owing to over-exploitation, but small parcels of veneer are occasionally on offer. The familiar Honduras mahogany is still fairly common but is rapidly becoming almost too expensive for cabinet-work, moreover the gradings now accept timber from widely different latitudes and the quality has deteriorated, with occasional boards no better than certain African Dry Lands mahogany of evil repute.

Certain American timbers extensively used in pre-war cabinet-making have also largely disappeared from English markets owing to the high cost of dollar imports. Notable examples are American basswood which is the equivalent of a good English lime, Canary whitewood (American whitewood, tulip tree, yellow poplar, etc.), satin walnut and hazel pine which are the heartwood and sapwood respectively of American sweet gum, and yellow and white pine (*Pinus strobus*). The latter are still available but only in inferior gradings, and owing to the high cost are usually reserved for pattern making. Reliable substitutes for these are Parana pine and western hemlock, both of which have a bad reputation in the timber-trade but only because they shrink and move excessively during seasoning. If, however, they have been correctly treated and are thoroughly dry they can be considered reliable, mild working, resin-free and stable timbers for hidden constructional work.

Timber terms

The following terms are used in the timber trade, but although some are more applicable to softwood gradings they are also used in American hardwood gradings and are therefore included.

Terms denoting quality

Butt Butt length	Main trunk. Specifically lowest part of trunk next to stump.
Boule	French term for superior timber, but specifically imported logs sawn through and through and reassembled in order of cutting.
Prime	The best available in the particular species at any particular time. First quality.
Selects	Selected timber.
Clean	Free from knots.
Clear	Free from visible defects.
C and S	Common and Selects.
Mercantable	Free from defects impairing strength, i.e. sound constructional timber.
FAS	Firsts and Seconds.
FAQ	Fair Average Quality.
U/S	Unsorted.
Av spec	Average specification, i.e. dimensions according to the species.
Broken spec	Denoting withdrawal of certain dimensions from original specification.
Rising in the pile	As stacked without grading or selection.
Crown plank, Pith plank	Centre plank containing pith and heart shakes.
Boxed heart	Timber converted so that the whole of the heart including pith and centre shakes is contained in one piece.
Crook, Knee	Short length of naturally curved timber.
Slabbing	Outside slices of the log containing bark and sap.
Brashy	Short-grained or old, dead or carroty timber.
Brittleheart	Brashy heart caused by compression failures in fibres during growth.
Blackheart	Abnormal black or dark brown discoloration in heartwood not necessarily decayed as in blackhearted ash, etc.
Shipping dry	Sufficiently dry to prevent deterioration (fungoid growths, mould, etc.) during shipment only. (Average moisture content 25 per cent).
Bone-dry	Meaningless term suggesting thoroughly dry timber.

Terms denoting dimension

Quarter girth   Quarter of the girth taken as one side of the equivalent square in measuring timber in the round.

Hoppus measure   System used in timber measurement of round logs which allows about 27 per cent for waste in conversion (bark and wane, etc.).

afb   Allowance for bark.

Billet   Short round log. Short timber split or hewn. Log centre cut and squared or dressed.

Blank   Timber cut to specified dimension and left full to allow for subsequent treatment.

Lumber   Square-edged hardwoods of random widths.

Plank   Sawn timber over 2 in. (50 mm) thick and of varying widths (British Standard 565:1963).*

Board   Sawn timber up to 2 in. (50 mm) thick.*

Batten   Wood of small cross-section. Specifically square sawn softwood $1\frac{7}{8}$ in. (48 mm) to 4 in. (102 mm) thick and 4 in. (102 mm) to 8 in. (204 mm) wide.

Lath   Strip wood of small section. Specifically $\frac{3}{16}$ in. (5 mm) to $\frac{3}{8}$ in. (9·5 mm) thick and 1 in. (25 mm) to $1\frac{1}{4}$ in. (32 mm) wide.

Strip   Square sawn timber 2 in. (50 mm) and under thick and 2 in. (50 mm) to $5\frac{1}{2}$ in. (140 mm) wide.

Squares   Square sawn timber 2 ft (0·60 m) and 2 ft 6 in. (0·76 m) long by $1\frac{1}{2}$ in. (38 mm) by $1\frac{1}{2}$ in. (38 mm) and up.

Scantlings   Square edges dimensions not conforming to other standard terms.

Dimension stock   Timber sawn to specified sizes.

Shorts   Short lengths 3 ft (0·91 m) to 5 ft 9 in. (1·75 m) long and widths 6 in. (152 mm) and up.

SN   Short narrows less than 6 in. (152 mm) wide.

Cube foot, cf   Cubic foot 12 in. (304·8 mm) by 12 in. (304·8 mm) by 12 in. (304·8 mm). i.e. 0·02832 m³

Foot super, fs   Square foot (0·09290 m²) superficial or face measure†

bd ft, fbm, bm   Board foot, board measure, denoting 1 sq. ft (0·09290 m²) (25 mm) thick.

Foot run, ft, run   Running foot (25 mm) length measurement in the particular width.

Av L   Average lengths.

A W   All widths.

Nom   Nominal or sawn size before machining.

Scant   Converted timber of less than specified dimension.

Sawn size   Sawn size before machining, i.e. planing.

Finish, Finished   Net measurement after machining.

Dead, Dead length   Exact length.

Tolerance   The maximum permissible variation for a specified dimension in the sawn size.

---

* Many home-grown timber-merchants prefer to regard Boards as up to $1\frac{1}{4}$ in. (32 mm) thick and Planks as over $1\frac{1}{4}$ in. (32 mm) thick.

† Quotations 'per foot super' are usually taken to mean square foot (0·09290 m²) superficial measure 1 in. (25 mm) thick is the standard measurement, but 'per foot board measure' is strictly speaking more correct. With the introduction of the Metric System into the United Kingdom no doubt the terms 'cube', 'square foot', 'foot run', etc., etc., will eventually disappear.

Terms denoting treatment

Converted timber	Timber sawn from log.
t and t	Sawn through and through. Waney edge timber.
W/E	Waney edge timber following the shape of the log.
S/E	Square edge timber, i.e. waney edge timber trimmed up with edges parallel.
U/E	Unedged timber.
1 W/E, 1 S/E	One waney edge, one square edge from logs squared one side before conversion.
Quartered, Quarter sawn, Rift sawn	Radial cut timber following path of medullary rays.
Plain cut, Slash cut, Flat cut	Tangentially cut timber through and through the log (the middle planks will be quarter cut).
Cleft	Split or riven along the natural cleavage-lines following the medullary rays.
Surfaced	Planed on faces but not to final thickness.
Thicknessed	Planed to exact thickness.
Prepared	Planed to final width and thickness.
par	Planed all round, i.e. prepared.
pe	Planed edge, or plain edge not tongued as in floor-boards.
t & g	Tongued and grooved.
t g & b	Tongued, grooved and beaded.
t g & v	Tongued, grooved and vee-jointed.
Deeping	Resawing through the thickness, i.e. parallel to the wide faces.
Flat Cutting	Resawing through the width, i.e. parallel to the edges.
ad	Air dried.
kd	Kiln dried.

For other terms refer to appropriate chapters.

Metric conversions: Imperial to Metric units

Length
1 inch=25·4 mm (millimetres)
1 foot= 0·3048 m (metres)

Area
1 square inch (1 in.²)=6·4516 cm². (square centimetres)
1 square foot (1 ft²)=0·092 903 04 m² (square metres)

Volume
1 cubic inch (1 in.³)=16·387 064 cm³ (cubic centimetres)
1 cubic foot (1 ft³)=0·028 32 m³ (cubic metres)
1 UK fluid ounce=28·41 ml (millilitres)
1 UK fluid gallon=4·545 96 1 (litres)
(160 fl. oz)

Mass
1 ounce (avoirdupois)=28·350 g (grammes)
1 pound (avoirdupois)=0·453 592 37 kg (kilogrammes)

Density
lbs per cu. ft to kilogrammes per cu. metre
1 lb/cf=16·018 kg/m³

Pressure
lbs force per sq. in. to kilogrammes per sq. cm
1 lbf/in²=0·070 31 kgf/cm²

Temperature
Degrees Fahrenheit to degrees Celsius (Centigrade)

$$\frac{5 \text{ (degrees F}-32)}{9}=\text{degrees Celsius}$$

Degrees Celsius to degrees Fahrenheit

$$\frac{9 \text{ (degrees C)}}{5}+32=\text{degrees Fahrenheit}$$

Conversion factors

To convert	multiply by
inches into millimetres	25·4
millimetres into inches	0·039 37
square inches into square centimetres	6·4516
square centimetres into square inches	0·155

Metric conversions: inches to millimetres

in.	mm	in.	mm
$\frac{1}{32}$	0·793	$\frac{13}{16}$	20·637
$\frac{1}{16}$	1·587	$\frac{7}{8}$	22·225
$\frac{3}{32}$	2·381	$\frac{15}{16}$	23·812
$\frac{1}{8}$	3·175		
$\frac{5}{32}$	3·969		cm
$\frac{3}{16}$	4·762	1	2·54
$\frac{7}{32}$	5·556	2	5·08
$\frac{1}{4}$	6·350	3	7·62
$\frac{9}{32}$	7·144	4	10·16
$\frac{5}{16}$	7·937	5	12·70
$\frac{11}{32}$	8·731	6	15·24
$\frac{3}{8}$	9·525	7	17·78
$\frac{13}{32}$	10·319	8	20·32
$\frac{7}{16}$	11·112	9	22·86
$\frac{15}{32}$	11·906	10	25·4
$\frac{1}{2}$	12·700	20	50·8
$\frac{9}{16}$	14·288	30	76·2
$\frac{5}{8}$	15·875	40	101·6
$\frac{11}{16}$	17·462	50	127·0
$\frac{3}{4}$	19·050	100	254·0

Veneer thicknesses

Veneer Gauge no.	in. thickness	Approx. no. to inch (25·4 mm)	mm thickness
8	0·160	$6\frac{1}{4}$	4·064
11	0·116	$8\frac{1}{2}$	2·946
12	0·104	$9\frac{3}{4}$	2·642
14	0·080	$12\frac{1}{2}$	2·032
17	0·056	18	1·422
19	0·040	25	1·016
20	0·036	28	0·914
21	0·032	$31\frac{1}{4}$	0·813
22	0·028	$35\frac{3}{4}$	0·711
25	0·020	50	0·508
27	0·016	$62\frac{1}{2}$	0·406
35	0·008	125	0·203

Face veneers are usually cut to 22 gauge or approximately 35 to the inch (25 mm) and colloquially known as 'seven mil'.

Bibliography

Some of the publications listed below are now out of print but copies may be consulted at local reference libraries..

Encyclopaedia of World Timbers   F. H. Titmus   Technical Press   1948
Handbook of Hardwoods   H M Stationery Office
Handbook of Home-grown Timbers   (Great Britain)   H M Stationery Office
World Timbers
African Timbers
American Timbers   } Timber Research and Development Association
Timbers of East Asia
Timber Structure and Properties   H. E. Desch   Macmillan   1938
Introduction to Seasoning of Timber   W. H. Brown   Pergamon Press   1965
Synthetic Resins and Plastics   H. M. Langton and R. S. Morrell   Oxford University Press   1951
Plastics in the Furniture Industry   Douglas Norton Buttrey   Macdonald   1964
Glass Fibre Reinforced Plastics   A. de Dani   Newnes   1960
Concise Guide to Plastics   Herbert R. Simonds and J. M. Church   Reinhold   1957
Adhesives   H M Stationery Office
Practical Manual of Industrial Finishes   Albin Letsky   Chapman and Hall   1960
Solid and Laminated Wood Bending   Turner and Stevens   H M Stationery Office
Principles of Machine Woodworking   A. H. Haycock   Technical Press   1948–55
Cost Accounts   Walter William Bigg   Macdonald and Evans   1932
Development and Structure of the Furniture Industry   J. L. Oliver   Pergamon Press   1965
Design Manual of Cabinet Furniture   Furniture Design Council   Pergamon Press   1959
Cabinet Making for Beginners   Charles Hayward   Evans Bros   1947
Tools for Woodwork   Charles Hayward   Evans Bros   1946
Woodwork Joints   Charles Hayward   Evans Bros   1949
Wood Furniture   Helen Hayward   Paul Hamlyn   1965
Encyclopaedia of Furniture   Joseph Aronson   Batsford   1938
Built-in Fitments for Modern Homes   Hans Stolper   Crosby Lockwood   1963
Metal Furniture   E. E. Pfannschmidt Julius Hoffmann Stutgart   1962
Nature and Art of Workmanship   David Pye   Cambridge University Press   1968

Index